Protest Song in East and West Germany since the 1960s

Studies in German Literature, Linguistics, and Culture

Protest Song in East and West Germany since the 1960s

Edited by David Robb

CAMDEN HOUSE
Rochester, New York

First published 2007
by Camden House

Camden House is an imprint of Boydell & Brewer Inc.
668 Mt. Hope Avenue, Rochester, NY 14620, USA
www.camden-house.com
and of Boydell & Brewer Limited
PO Box 9, Woodbridge, Suffolk IP12 3DF, UK
www.boydellandbrewer.com

ISBN-13: 978–1–57113–281–9
ISBN-10: 1–57113–281–3

Library of Congress Cataloging-in-Publication Data

Protest song in East and West Germany since the 1960s / edited by David
    Robb.
        p. cm. — (Studies in German literature, linguistics, and culture)
    Includes bibliographical references (p.   ) and index.
    ISBN-13: 978–1–57113–281–9 (hardcover: alk. paper)
    ISBN-10: 1–57113–281–3 (hardcover: alk. paper)
        1. Protest Songs—Germany—20th century—History and criticism.
    2. Music—Political aspects—Germany—20th century.   I. Robb, David,
    1962– II. Title.   III. Series.

    ML3917.G3P76 2007
    782.42'15990943—dc22

                                                                    2007013056

A catalogue record for this title is available from the British Library.

This publication is printed on acid-free paper.
Printed in the United States of America.

Contents

Acknowledgments

WITHOUT THE SUPPORT OF A NUMBER OF instutions and individuals this book would not have been possible. I would like to thank the British Academy for its award, which enabled me to travel to Germany several times for research purposes, and the School of Languages, Literatures and Performing Arts at the Queen's University of Belfast for granting me a sabbatical to do the research. I am also indebted to Barbara Boock at the Deutsches Volksliedarchiv in Freiburg for her general help and expertise, and to Karin Wolf for introducing me to the video archives of the former Liedzentrum of the Akademie der Künste der DDR. I would also like to thank Karin McPherson for having aquainted me with the life and culture of the GDR.

Lastly, immense thanks are due to the collaborators on this volume, Eckard Holler, Peter Thompson, and Annette Blühdorn, and I am especially grateful to Jim Walker at Camden House for his attention to detail and his tireless encouragement.

D. R.
Belfast, March 2007

Introduction

David Robb

FROM THE 1960s THROUGH THE 1980s the German political song enjoyed substantial popularity in both the Federal Republic and the German Democratic Republic. In West Germany in the early 1960s the influence of the new American and British folk and protest song movement inspired members of the *Jugendbewegung* to rediscover a democratic German folk-song tradition that had been stamped out under Nazi jackboots ("Stiefel in den Dreck gestampft"), as Franz Josef Degenhardt expressed it in the song "Die alten Lieder." This tradition had been documented in Wolfgang Steinitz's two-volume song collection, *Deutsche Volkslieder demokratischen Charakters aus sechs Jahrhunderten,* which had appeared in the GDR in 1954 and 1962. Steinitz was concerned with the *Volkslieder* of the "werktätiges Volk" as opposed to "das Volk" of romantic folklore as propagated in the songs of the Nazis.[1] In addition to these rediscovered folk songs, singers such as Degenhardt and Dieter Süverkrüp began writing their own socially critical songs. German folk and protest songs flourished over the next three decades, functioning as an artistic medium for the political protest of the 1968 students movement and the *neue soziale Bewegungen* of the 1970s and 1980s as well as being a popular commercial commodity for a left-wing intellectual public. In the 1970s and early 1980s acts such as Degenhardt, Wolf Biermann, Hannes Wader, and Konstantin Wecker performed to large audiences that one would normally only associate with rock or pop acts. Degenhardt even had a number one hit single in 1972 with the song "Sacco und Vanzetti."

In the German Democratic Republic the political song was not the commercial industry it was in the West, but nonetheless enjoyed a similar popularity due to its ambiguous position as either treasured revolutionary heritage or forbidden fruit in a climate of censorship. Indeed it was such a controversial force that the expatriation of the singer-songwriter Wolf Biermann in 1976 caused a political scandal that many deem to have heralded the beginning of the end of the GDR. On the official side, political song was a nurtured *Erbe,* and the state-controlled *FDJ-Singebewegung* had a substantial presence within GDR youth culture. The annual highlight of this movement, Das Festival des politischen Liedes in East Berlin, was from 1970 until 1990 a showcase for East and West German as well as international political singers, while also providing a forum for artistic innovation within the genre. In this respect, the *Singebewegung*, although for the most part loyal to the state, was also a training ground for the new critically minded *Liedermacher* of the post-Biermann era, which included Gerhard Gundermann and Hans-Eckardt Wenzel.

In musical and literary terms the modern German political song is a hybrid of high and low culture. On one hand, with roots in the era of the birth of mass culture in the 1920s it displays communicative strategies of the popular song. Yet with its philosophical and poetic aspirations and tendency at times toward musical sophistication the genre also has intellectual ambitions. This hybrid aspect, which contributes greatly to the uniqueness of the German political song, is examined in this volume with reference to the work of political singer-songwriters since the 1960s, and is revealed through the analysis of lyrics, musical approaches, and performance techniques. For example, Wolf Biermann embraced and reinterpreted the profane lyrical tradition of Villon and Brecht while simultaneously incorporating the sophisticated musical techniques of Eisler's revolutionary song. Franz Josef Degenhardt's balladry entailed a parodic reappropriation of the literary *Rollengedicht,* and Konstantin Wecker drew musically on rock and cabaret as well as operatic musical traditions. In the GDR Wenzel and Mensching's group Karls Enkel developed a montage aesthetic by setting "high" texts of revered icons of the GDR literary and philosophical *Erbe* such as Goethe and Marx to popular musical forms including folk, klezmer, rock, and operetta. This had the effect of presenting such well-known texts in an unfamiliar light and, further aided by theatrical techniques, allowed the group to perform these original texts as if they were parodying the GDR.

A major reference point of the book in this respect is the legacy of the revolutionary song tradition in the work of East and West German *Liedermacher.* Chapter 1 deals with the *Vormärz* and 1848 song tradition, which exerted such a powerful influence on the folk-song revival, first in the Federal Republic in the 1960s and then, over a decade later, in the GDR. The *Vormärz* and 1848 song tradition itself embodied the aforementioned duality of high and low art, encompassing the sophisticated poetry of Hoffmann von Fallersleben, Freiligrath, and Herwegh on one hand and the bawdy street balladry of anonymous traveling craftsmen on the other. This book finds that East and West German *Liedermacher* appropriated the 1848 revolutionary heritage differently corresponding to their different political realities and the conditions under which they worked. For example, West German *Liedermacher* of the early 1960s emphasized the *Spottlieder,* which mocked the princes and rulers, reflecting the intellectual youths' rejection of the conservativism of the Adenauer era and the perceived lack of a genuine democracy. On the other hand, Inge Lammel's 1950s collection of 1848 songs, published in the GDR — corresponding to the socialist euphoria of the *Aufbau* years — stressed the militant utopian songs of the 1848 campaign. And decades later the GDR folk groups of the 1970s and 1980s — reacting to the country's socialist stagnation and the desire of many to leave — chose songs dealing with the post-1848 revolutionary reality, that is, defeat and emigration. Another prominent category of *Vormärz* songs that was popularly sung and performed in the GDR folk scene were those that addressed the problem of censorship. These songs, too, were most often sung in a way that passed comment, in a more or less thinly veiled way, on the present.

Chapter 2 deals with the revolutionary song *Erbe* of the twentieth century. This heritage is traced back to the *Kampflieder* of Erich Mühsam in the early years of the century and to the Spartakus uprising of 1919. The chapter then documents the influence of songs of Brecht, Eisler, and Ernst Busch in the workers' and anti-fascist campaigns of the 1920s and early 1930s. It culminates with an assessment of the legacy in song of the Spanish Civil War as embodied in the work of Ernst Busch.

This revolutionary tradition of the twentieth century is highly present in the work of East and West German *Liedermacher* in terms of lyrical motifs, themes, musical styles, and compositional techniques. It, too, like the 1848 tradition, reflects the aforementioned hybridity of high and low art forms. For example, in the early twentieth century Erich Mühsam wrote both trivial, satirical cabaret lyrics and serious, militant *Gebrauchslyrik* intended for use in the class struggle. The political song of the 1920s — in the bourgeois literary cabaret milieu as well as in the proletarian agitprop movement — also reflected the duality of the high and the low. Writers and composers such as Brecht, Eisler, Kurt Tucholsky, Walter Mehring, and Kurt Weill used avant-garde techniques such as montage as a means to create songs for popular use. In the context of the trend toward *Neue Sachlichkeit*, Weill, in his new *Zeitoper*, attempted to make the elitist opera form more widely accessible to the masses using modern technology and elements of popular music. Eisler, too, in his *Kampflieder*, picked compositional elements from both serious and popular music to find the most effective way of communicating Brecht's revolutionary lyrics. In this respect his compositions reflected and developed the montage aesthetic so prevalent in poetry, art, drama, and music of the 1920s and 1930s. In particular the idea of the dialectical relationship between music, text, and delivery in Eisler's political song theory was to have a major influence on political song for the whole of the twentieth century. This will be analyzed in this volume in regard to the work of Wolf Biermann, Konstantin Wecker, and the group Karls Enkel.

The very coexistence of high and low elements within German political song has led to conflicts in various revolutionary periods since the *Vormärz* between advocates of the art song and those of the more simplistic, overtly agitative song as to what constitutes effective political songwriting. This was reflected in Heine's debate with the emotive *Tendenzlyrik* of poets of the 1840s, Benjamin's rejection of the ironic literary cabaret song in the late 1920s in his championing of the militant *Kampflied,* and in Degenhardt's distancing from his earlier, more subtly critical songs by embracing the slogan "Zwischentöne sind bloß Krampf im Klassenkampf" at the height of the student revolts of 1968.

All of these revolutionary movements have been marked in song by the expression of utopianism on one hand and by dashed aspirations on the other. This dichotomy — often described as the *deutsche Misere* — is a recurring theme in the history of German political song. In the GDR, after the euphoria of the *Aufbau* years, it is clear — at the latest from the 1970s onwards — that the theme of the stagnation and the betrayal of the revolutionary tradition takes precedence. This is continually stressed in the work of critical *Liedermacher* such as Biermann and Karls Enkel. Both of these take the theme of the Spanish Civil War — an event that had inspired the most utopian of political songs — to express their preoccupations with the GDR's failure to progress toward utopia.

In my third chapter on narrative role-play I analyze — with reference to the traditional *Gebrauchslyrik* and *Gebrauchsmusik* function of the political song — how singers from Ernst Busch through Degenhardt and Biermann up to Wecker, Wenzel, and Gerhard Gundermann use lyrics, music, and techniques of vocal delivery to create an identifiable narrative with which they play to a targeted audience. A basic model of this was given by Ernst Busch in his rendition of Brecht and Eisler's *Kampflieder,* from the late-1920s onwards, whose narrative was that of the exemplary proletarian hero engaged in the class struggle. Another popularly used narrative since the Weimar Republic is that of outsiders or underdogs who undermine social structures and conventions by virtue of their mere alternative existence. In the 1920s Brecht and Mehring were but two examples of poets who carried forth the tradition of the French Rennaissance vagabond poet François Villon, expressing their disregard for bourgeois convention. Examples of such outsider figures since the 1960s include Degenhardt's role play of Rumpelstilzchen and his invocation of the *Schmuddelkinder* motif, Biermann's Villonesque incarnations of himself, Wecker's identification with social outcasts, and Wenzel and Mensching's exploitation of the figure of the clown. Here, with their costumes, masks, and antics, Wenzel and Mensching, like Biermann's Villonesque persona, play frequently on the image of the profane, grotesque body, which forms a counterpart to the sanctity of dominant ideology and mocks the hollowness of high-blown rhetoric. In a further variation, Franz Josef Degenhardt's parodic *Rollengedichte* reveal the mask of power by exposing the role play of others, often alternating between the first- and third-person perspectives to create an ironic distancing effect.

This volume also provides an insider perspective on the countercultural scenes and structures in both the Federal Republic and the GDR, examining the conditions in which political songs were written and performed. A highly detailed account of the history of the West German folk and *Liedermacher* movement is provided by Eckard Holler, who himself was a young foot soldier on the organizational team of the legendary Burg Waldeck festivals of the 1960s and was later manager of the Tübingen Club Voltaire and co-organizer of the Tübingen Festival in the 1970s and 1980s. Holler traces the development of the political song movement from Peter Rohland's championing of a new German chanson in the *Jugendbewegung* of the early 1960s to the radicalization of the political song scene at the later Burg Waldeck festivals from 1967 through 1969. His conclusions are illustrated with references to the songs of the *Liedermacher* themselves such as Dieter Süverkrüp and Rolf Schwendter. In the case of Franz Josef Degenhardt the songs document his transformation from a critical chanson singer inspired by George Brassens in 1964 to agitprop activist in 1968. Holler's account of his own controversial role in the political hijacking of the 1968 Waldeck Festival by militant members within the festival organization is particularly revealing of the intensity of the bitter ideological conflict of the time of the student movement, and, from the distance of almost forty years, provides a stark contrast with depoliticized public life today.

In this chapter Holler also highlights the important part played by new left-leaning youth associations from the *bündische Jugendbewegung* in the reinvigoration of the German democratic folk-singing culture. Additionally he gives an account of the antagonism that developed between separate political strands of the *Jugendbewegung* represented by two associations who were both resident on the grounds of Burg Waldeck: the Nerother Wandervögel (NWV) and the Arbeitsgemeinschaft Burg Waldeck (ABW). This conflict gives an indication of different attitudes toward the reappraisal of the Nazi past, and shows the conservatism within the *Jugendewegung* that the new wave of left-leaning associations had to overcome. The trend away from communal toward individual singing, and the selection of "democratic" folk songs as opposed to those with nationalistic connotations was an expression of this difference.

In Holler's second chapter he examines the important role of *Liedermacher* in civil solidarity campaigns of the 1970s and early 1980s, in particular the anti-nuclear movement, where singer-songwriter Walter Mossmann was active. Holler also explores the commercialization of the folk scene in the 1970s and 1980s and the increasing government sponsorship of festivals and sociocultural centers. He reveals that the Brandt and Scheel administration effectively took the steam out of the protest movement by diverting it into institutional channels. However, as Holler makes clear, in terms of the rejuvenation of town life and the relaxation of the public atmosphere in the Federal Republic since the 1960s, the folk and political song festivals — in tandem with political liberalization — played a substantial role. The cultural landscape had completely changed.

Similarly, my first-hand experience performing semi-professionally in the GDR folk scene in the 1980s enables me to provide an insider's view of the contradictions political singers encountered in the GDR. While my chapter on the GDR examines literary and musical developments from the late 1970s onwards, it also describes the dilemma of many singers having to conform with a system in order to attain a public platform from which to criticize it. In particular this chapter functions as a case study of the group Karls Enkel and its struggle to maintain artistic and political autonomy in the face of pressure from the FDJ and the Stasi secret police. It also documents the climate of artistic experimentation that evolved as a direct response to censorship in the post-Biermann era: how Karls Enkel, led by *Liedermacher* Wenzel and poet Mensching, branched off into *Liedertheater,* adopting theatrical distancing techniques that enabled them to confront political themes that most other GDR *Liedermacher* did not dare address. Although they are winners of several literary, cabaret, and album awards, Wenzel and Mensching's pioneering (and mostly unpublished) stage work of the 1980s is still mostly unknown in the West. In the last decade, however, Wenzel has gained increasing recognition as a solo artist in the West German *Liedermacher* scene, particularly for his Woody Guthrie interpretations with which he has also toured in the USA.

The main *Liedermacher* dealt with in this volume — Wolf Biermann, Franz Josef Degenhardt, Peter Rohland, Konstantin Wecker, and the duo Hans-Eckardt Wenzel and Steffen Mensching — have been chosen because their work serves as an excellent illustration of a major theme of this book: the creative appropriation of revolutionary song heritage in German political song since the 1960s. At the same time there are individual chapters dedicated to Biermann and Wecker, who, with their strong cults of personality, have the highest present-day media profiles. Peter Thompson examines Biermann's continual search, as a German, a communist, and a Jew, for *Heimat* in a utopian Blochian sense. This journey — from his imprisoned *Heimat* in the GDR where he was banned from performing in public for eleven years through his period of exile from the GDR in the West up to his rejection of the communist utopia in united Germany — has constantly been marked by a "Zerrissenheit" that lies at the basis of his dialectical approach. This is expressed in the songs, according to

Thompson, through the recurring theme of alienation, which is in turn supported by a performance distantiation technique whereby music, lyrics, and delivery continually strain against each other. Thompson argues that Biermann's life journey — which has taken him from defending communism to defending the state of Israel — has constantly been characterized by a dialectical approach that provokes all dogmas and assumptions, thus leading him to intermittently offend even his most fervent supporters. His erstwhile Marxist beliefs mutate by the early 1990s into a left-liberal pragmatism as expressed in the song "Nur wer sich ändert, bleibt sich treu." Thompson, referring to Biermann's latest collection, *Heimat: Neue Gedichte* (2006), concludes that the singer, while as innerly divided ("zerrissen") as he ever was, has now made his peace with communism. But while he no longer believes in revolutionary utopias, judging that these serve the cause of totalitarianism, the dialectic between ideal and reality in Biermann's work is still alive, in Blochian if not in orthodox communist form.

Konstantin Wecker on the other hand, as Annette Blühdorn writes in her chapter, was never bound to Marxist philosophy in the first place. Blühdorn places the singer-songwriter in a position between the idealism of the 1968 movement and the pluralism of postmodernism. Like the Burg Waldeck singers, Wecker believes in progress and sees songs as a means of enlightenment, but not in an ideological, pedagogical sense. Wecker is skeptical of theories and of the ability of songs to lead to concrete changes in society. Rather he advocates a general form of resistance against ideological control and social conformity. This is evident in songs dealing with witch hunts against *Andersdenkenden* and songs that promote the perspectives of social outsiders. Wecker champions the self-determination of the individual and believes that the solving of inner conflicts is a precondition for any meaningful social change. In the last two decades he has supported the anti-globalization and the peace movement, his song "Sage Nein!" voicing his opposition to American military involvement in Iraq. With reference to Wecker's songs Blühdorn echoes a recurring theme in this book, namely the debate between the art song and the overtly agitative song, and places him firmly in the former category.

My final chapter looks at the activities of remnants of the former, closely-knit GDR political song scene that survived unification. It is clear that the creativity with which the *Liedermacher* deconstructed and revamped the revolutionary tradition contributed to the German political song's popular survival through the 1980s. However, the fact that the revolutionary tradition remained a constant point of reference for political song has had implications for the status of the genre in recent years. Artistically this tradition is inextricably linked with a past time; it is musically, lyrically, and ideologically orientated toward a cultural tradition or heritage of a bygone era. Moreover, to echo Michael Brocken's concerns about problems facing perceptions of traditional folk music in the UK,[2] German political song is similarly viewed by some as elitist in its fixation with canon (for example, precisely the Brecht, Eisler, and Weill canon which this volume explores). And after 1990, as Marxism gave way to postmodernism, as utopian visions (and the *Gestus* of political song) were increasingly perceived by youth as irrelevant, no new hybrid interpretation of this canon, be it of an 1848 *Spottlied,* an Eislerian montage, an agit-prop revue, or a 1920s literary chanson was going to reinvigorate the genre of German political song for a mass audience. This does not, however, mean that this tradition will not someday be reincarnated in new forms and again capture the imagination of a larger critically minded public. But political song may no longer be located exclusively in the territory of chanson, folk song, militant song, or street ballad.

The future of the genre is unclear. But this does not detract from the cultural and historical importance of the German political song in its various manifestations throughout the nineteenth and twentieth centuries. In the 1970s and 1980s, during the heyday of the political song, several books by academics such as as Karl Riha,[3] Thomas Rothschild,[4] and Heinz-Ludwig Arnold[5] appeared on the subject in West Germany. These explored *Liedermacher* — particularly Biermann and Degenhardt — from an artistic and formal as well as from a political (mostly left-wing) perspective, but always within terms that were set by the continuing ideological conflict between capitalism and communism. In the GDR there were many newspaper and magazine articles and even Ph.D. dissertations devoted to the state-controlled *Singebewegung,* but due to censorshop there were no serious journalistic or scholarly articles or books published on the work of dissident *Liedermacher* such as Biermann, Bettina Wegner, or Stephan Krawczyk. In the 1980s several newspaper and literary journal articles appeared on the subject of Karls Enkel and Wenzel and Mensching, but always couched in wording that avoided directly addressing the political contradictions that inspired their various songs, poems, and productions. After the fall of the Berlin Wall there was until recently, barring a few exceptions such as Lutz Kirchenwitz's *Folk, Chanson und Liedermacher in der DDR,*[6] published in 1993, a significant silence on this subject, which seemed somehow to belong to a previous era. Indeed when I began my own Ph.D. research into GDR *Liedermacher* in 1991, I encountered a deep uncertainty among singers, promoters, and enthusiasts regarding political song in general, a genre whose survival and importance they had never previously doubted. It was as if the demise of Marxism had caused them to question their whole *raison d'être* — past, present, and future. This malaise was reflected in the cessation of the annual Berlin Festival des politischen Liedes as well as in the closing of the Liedzentrum of the Akademie der Künste in East Berlin in the early 1990s. For many of the people involved, the subsequent decade has entailed a rigorous reassessment of their relationship to the utopias they once believed in and of their expectations of what political song can achieve.

Nonetheless, during this period a few insider organizations such as Das Deutsche Volksliedarchiv in Freiburg and initiatives such as Lied und soziale Bewegung in Berlin and Die Arbeitsgemeinschaft Burg Waldeck have continued their promotion of German folk and political song at an academic and performance level. Since German unification, links have been consolidating between the respective scenes of East and West. The magazine *Folker*, the annual Festival Musik und Politik in Berlin (the successor to the Festival des politischen Liedes, begun in 2000) and the hugely successful Tanz- und Folklore-Festival Rudolstadt are evidence of such collaboration. Now, a decade and a half after the fall of communism, it appears that scholars have had time enough to reassess the significance of the political song phenomenon between 1960 and 1990. A conference entitled *Die Entdeckung des sozialkritischen Liedes* dedicated to Wolfgang Steinitz and held at the Rudolstadt Folk Festival in July 2005 was an indication of academic interest in the reassessment of the postwar political song of East and West Germany. The conference volume, edited by Eckhard John,[7] is one of several recent publications dedicated to this general field of study, which include books by Holger Böning[8] and Annette Blühdorn.[9]

In the final chapter, this author, after two decades in which the political song has become culturally marginalized, widens the search for expressions of the political in popular music. Studies of the essentially apolitical techno youth culture of the 1990s offer interpretations of how techno music and fashion reflects the social and cultural relationships and concerns of young people. But within German avant-garde techno (as opposed to the mainstream variety represented by the Berlin Love Parade) examples of genuine musical attempts to challenge conventional cultural perceptions and attitudes can be found. Echoing the theory of Hanns Eisler, but with little in common with its underlying Marxist principles, the Frankfurt underground label Mille Plateaux, inspired by the philosophy of Deleuze and Guattari, has endeavored to promote sounds that defamiliarize the listener and disrupt a uniformity in music that encourages passivity and conformity. "Intelligent techno," as Simon Reynolds calls it, is neither a popular movement nor does it involve lyrical poetry, two expectations that stalwarts of the pre-1989 political song scene have of their genre. But it does present one of many possible musical directions open to future politically engaged music. In the meantime this volume, in its reassessment of the main artistic and political developments within East and West political song since the 1960s, hopes to convey the richness as well as the political importance of the most recent flowering of this German cultural tradition.

Notes

¹ See Eckhard John, "Die Entdeckung des sozialkritischen Liedes. Wolfgang Steinitz als Wegbereiter eines neuen 'Volkslied'-Verständnisses," in Eckhard John, ed., *Die Entdeckung des sozialkritischen Liedes: Zum 100. Geburtstag von Wolfgang Steinitz*. Volksliedstudien vol. 7 (Münster, New York, Munich, and Berlin: Waxmann, 2006), 15.

² Michael Brocken, *The British Folk Revival 1944–2002* (Aldershot: Ashgate, 2003), 138–41.

³ Karl Riha, *Moritat, Bänkelsong, Protestballade: Zur Geschichte des engagierten Liedes in Deutschland* (Frankfurt am Main: Fischer Taschenbuch, 1975).

⁴ Thomas Rothschild, ed., *Wolf Biermann: Liedermacher und Sozialist* (Reinbeck bei Hamburg, Rowohlt, 1976) and Rothschild, *Liedermacher* (Frankfurt am Main: Fischer Taschenbuch, 1980).

⁵ Heinz-Ludwig Arnold, ed., *Franz Josef Degenhardt: Politische Lieder 1964–1972*, Edition Text und Kritik (Munich: Boorberg Verlag, 1972) and *Wolf Biermann*, Edition Text und Kritik (Munich: Boorberg Verlag, 1980).

⁶ Lutz Kirchenwitz, *Folk, Chanson und Liedermacher in der DDR* (Berlin: Dietz Verlag, 1993).

⁷ John, ed., *Die Entdeckung des sozialkritischen Liedes: Zum 100. Geburtstag von Wolfgang Steinitz*.

⁸ Holger Bönning, *Der Traum von einer Sache: Aufstieg und Fall der Utopien im politischen Lied der Bundesrepublik und der DDR* (Bremen: Edition Lumière, 2004).

⁹ Annette Blühdorn, *Pop and Poetry — Pleasure and Protest: Udo Lindenberg, Konstantin Wecker and the Tradition of German Cabaret* (Oxford, Bern, Berlin, Bruxelles, Frankfurt/Main, New York, Vienna: Peter Lang, 2003).

1: The Reception of *Vormärz* and 1848 Revolutionary Song in West Germany and the GDR

David Robb

FOR THE FOLK AND PROTEST SONG MOVEMENTS of both East and West Germany, the song heritage of the *Vormärz* and the revolution of 1848 was a point of cultural and historical identification. Two clear narratives emerge in these songs: first, that of rebellion linked to utopian idealism, and second, that of defeat and retreat. Within these two general narratives are several sub-categories of songs, for example, parodies of authority, songs of poverty and unemployment, soldiers' songs, songs demanding German unification, and songs of emigration. Almost 120 years after they were first composed, played, and sung, the *Vormärz* and 1848 songs were revived in the West German folk scene; a decade later they were revived once more in the GDR. This chapter will examine the significance of those narratives as focused on by singers at different periods in the development of the two postwar German states.

To commemorate the 150th anniversary of the 1848 revolution in 1998, The German Volkslied Archive in Freiburg compiled a CD of 1848 songs entitled *1848 . . . weil jetzt die Freiheit blüht*.[1] It was performed by some of the most prominent *Liedermacher* and folk artists of the east and west German folk scenes. A sentence from the CD booklet sums up the thematic range of the songs: "Zustände zwischen Euphorie und Resignation teilen sich mit, sarkastische Bemerkungen über Polizeigewalt wechseln mit trotzigem Aufbegehren." This illustrates a relationship that marks German political song from the *Vormärz* through to its revival in the Federal Republic and in the GDR, whereby vibrant utopianism exists side by side with the melancholy of the *deutsche Misere*. The hope of revolutionary change is always dashed by failure: the recurring inability in German history to change the status quo, to have a successful revolution from inside that brings about lasting democratic change.

The songs on *1848 . . . weil jetzt die Freiheit blüht* reflect how the euphoria of the initial revolts of 1848 was superceded by the disillusionment of defeat when a death-like peace returned and the Germans reverted to timidity and servility (3). An 1848 version of the song "Die Gedanken sind frei" encapsulates this contradiction between rebellion and retreat. From the political defiance of "Und ob man mich barg / Im finsteren Kerker / Die Mauern sind stark, / Der Geist aber stärker [. . .]," the emphasis shifts to the finding of sanctuary in an inner world of dreams, privacy, and home comforts: "Ich liebe den Wein, / Mein Mädchen vor allen; / Die tut mir allein / Am besten gefallen, / Bei einem Glas Weine, / Bin ich nicht alleine, / Ich denke dabei: / Die Gedanken sind frei" (4). In this respect, the implied claim of the song — that one's statements can be censored but one's thoughts cannot — is ironic given that retreat into inner seclusion is precisely what censorship promotes.[2] Few songs encapsulate the double-edged condition of rebellion and retreat as well as this one. One that does, however, is Ferdinand Freiligrath's "Trotz Alledem," an adaptation of Robert Burns's "A Man's a Man for a' That." While wistfully reflecting how the winter wind has cooled down the euphoria of the March uprising, the song nonetheless ends with a defiant "trotz alledem," lauding the capacity of mankind to resist tyranny. Despite setbacks, the brotherhood of mankind will not be subdued: "Wir sind das Volk, die Menschheit wir! [. . .] Trotz alledem und alledem, / [. . .] Ihr hemmt uns, doch ihr zwingt uns nicht! / Unser die Welt, trotz alledem!" (11). This chapter will examine how this contradictory condition of hope and disillusionment, rebellion and retreat in the songs of the *Vormärz* and 1848 became a source of identification for protest singers in both the GDR and West Germany who themselves were grappling with their own elusive utopias.

The Song Tradition of 1848 in West Germany: The Kröhers, Rohland, and Süverkrüp

In West Germany from the 1960s onwards, the revived folk song inspired a renewed interest in the songs of the *Vormärz* and 1848. Singers identified with the basic gesture of rebellion in the satirical *Spottlieder*, the parodies of authority and servility and the anti-army songs. Above all, the interest in the 1848 songs lay in the discovery of something new: distinct from the tradition of folk song that had been co-opted by the Nazis and was now viewed as Nazi-tainted, the 1848 songs represented a "low" tradition of oppositional art. This was significant in a young Federal Republic where opposition was struggling to find political and cultural expression. These songs were, however, not readily accessible. School books did not contain information about protest movements and their songs.[3] Examples of the tradition of the German democratic folk song were to be found, however, in Wolfgang Steinitz's GDR collection *Deutsche Volkslieder demokratischen Charackters aus 6 Jahrhunderten*.[4] And libraries and city archives contained numerous pamphlets ("Flugblätter") of *Vormärz* and

1848 songs. It was in such archives that the Swabian Peter Rohland (born 1933) and the twins from Pirmasens Hein and Oss Kröher (born 1927) set about researching and thus reclaiming a lost cultural inheritance. Rohland and the Kröhers stemmed from the *Jugendbewegung*, whose refounding in 1945 after being banned by the Nazis heralded the beginning of a revival of the German folk song.[5] The focal point of this revival was the Burg Waldeck folk song festival held annually in Hünsrück from 1964 through 1969, which brought together different streams of singers: on one hand the "politically committed *Liedermacher*, who had developed out of the Easter march [anti-nuclear] movement, and those who came from cabaret," and on the other hand "the new folk singers who brought with them the tradition of the *Jugendbewegung*" (Blühdorn, 128). Rohland and the Kröhers incorporated the democratic folk songs they had rediscovered in their repertoires. As Oss Kröher remembered in 2004, the singing of such songs often brought tears to the eyes of older workers;[6] such was the degree of severance from proletarian tradition in Germany caused by the Third Reich.

The particular relationship that West German singers formed with the 1848 tradition is reflected in recordings and publications from the 1960s up to the early 1980s. Here, attention will focus on two albums: Peter Rohland's mid-1960s recording *48er Lieder — Lieder deutscher Demokraten*[7] and the Düsseldorfer Dieter Süverkrüp's (born 1934) *1848: Lieder der deutschen Revolution*[8] from 1974. Both clearly identify with the spontaneous spirit of democracy, rebellion, and disrespect for authority that the 1848 songs embody. This identification on the part of the postwar generation has to be viewed in connection with the perception right up to and beyond the student uprisings of 1968 that the legacy of the Third Reich had not been dealt with in West German society. Conservatism and social conformity was still entrenched, and former Nazis still enjoyed positions of power in government and industry.

Several of the songs from the two aforementioned records and many more besides were documented in 1983 in a book by Barbara James and Walter Mossmann entitled *Glasbruch 1848: Flugblätterlieder und Dokumente einer zerbrochenen Revolution* (1983).[9] The commentaries of Mossmann, a veteran of the 1960s Burg Waldeck festivals, and James, a folk-song specialist from The German Volkslied Archive in Freiburg, set these songs in an historical and political context. Particular importance is attached to the role of the wandering craftsmen (*Gesellen*) of the *Vormärz* as mediators of subversive song. Many had fled to Paris after the 1830 July revolution in France and joined political associations such as Das deutsche Volksverein, which was banned in Germany (81). Alongside the law of 1835 that banned the writers of *Junges Deutschland* (including Heine, Gutzkow, Laube, Wienbarg, and Mundt) another law forbade craftsmen traveling to countries that tolerated political associations (85). Subversive songs such as "Bürgerlied" spread the idea of equality and anticipated the day when the tables would be turned on the ruling gentry and military. This song was recorded by both Rohland and Süverkrüp and was popular in the West German folk and political song movement:

> Ehrt doch den Handwerksmann,
> Und auch den Bauersmann,
> Arm oder reich!
> Gleich gebaut, wie auch ihr,
> Und von derselben Zier,
> Darum sind Menschen wir
> Alle uns gleich. [. . .]
>
> Darum ihr liebe Herrn
> Mit Ordensband und Stern,
> Nehmt euch in Acht!
> Rachetag bricht einst an,
> Dann zieht der Bauersmann,
> Wie auch der Handwerksmann
> Muthig zur Schlacht. (91–92)[10]

Another type of song that found resonance in the West German scene was that which dealt with the passive, uncritical *Bürger*. Adolf Glassbrenner's "Der gute stammelnde Untertan," for example, sung by Rohland, is a humorous parody of unquestioning loyalty to prince and police. In one stanza the innocuous word "teuer" is sung instead of the anticipated rhyme "Teufel." In this way the singer mocks the behavior of the loyal *Bürger* he is merely pretending to be: "Ich bin ein guter Untertan, das duldet keinen Zweifel! / Mein Fürst, das ist ein guter Mann, / oh, wär er doch beim Teu. . .-ren Volke immer, / so käm' es niemals schlimmer" (10).

Further songs from the 1848 tradition reflect the breakdown in respect for the rulers. For example, the anonymous "Bürgermeister Tschech," sung by Süverkrüp, laughs at the 1844 assassination attempt by the mayor of Storkow on Kaiser Friedrich Wilhelm IV: "Hatte je ein Mensch so'n Pech / wie der Bürgermeister Tschech, / daß er diesen dicken Mann / auf zwei Schritt nicht treffen kann."

There were also songs of social protest. In the period of industrialization and technological advance that characterized the *Vormärz*, unemployment became the reality for many. As James and Mossmann depict, much of the working class — weavers, carpenters, tailors, cobblers, glaziers — lived in conditions approaching slums (38). In 1847 there were food riots in numerous German cities, as depicted in the poem "Der Krawall in Stuttgart vom 3. Mai 1847" (41). The suffering of the weavers, who famously revolted in 1844 in Silesia, is documented in the anonymous song "Das Blutgericht." This became a standard in the repertoire of many folk groups in the West German revival of the 1970s:

> Hier im Ort ist ein Gericht,
> viel schlimmer als die Vehme,
> Wo man nicht erst ein Urtheil spricht,
> Das Leben schnell zu nehmen.
> Hier wird der Mensch langsam gequält,
> Hier ist die Folterkammer,
> Hier werden Seufzer viel gezählt
> als Zeuge von dem Jammer [. . .] (63)

Soldiers were another social grouping who endured harsh conditions and long years of duty with no pension to look forward to. In an anonymous song from an 1848 pamphlet, a soldier complains: "Steh ich in finstrer Mitternacht / zu Altenburg auf Postenwacht, / so denk ich oft: Gott sei's geklagt, / was wir Soldaten sind geplagt!" (104). "Brudermord" from the same year is written from the perspective of a soldier lamenting the command to shoot on his own people (106). Such disquiet was reflected during the Baden uprising of May 1849, when soldiers mutinied and went over to the side of the rioters. Anti-military songs on Peter Rohland's record include "O König von Preußen" from around 1800, which decries the tortuous existence in the Prussian army: "O König von Preußen, / du großer Potentat, / wie sind wir deines Dienstes / so übermäßig satt." This was a popular song in the West German folk scene against a backdrop where many young men moved to West Berlin to be exempt from the eighteen months of military service that were obligatory in all other locales.

It is significant, however, that expressions of utopianism, rebellion, and protest are counterbalanced by songs containing the narrative of defeat. There is resigned self-parody in a song by Fallersleben, sung by Rohland, which questions the will for revolutionary success of a country dominated by philistines:

> Ausgelitten, ausgerungen
> hast du endlich, deutsches Herz.
> Gut, daß er einmal verklungen,
> dieser deutsche Freiheitsmärz.
> Gut, daß wir geworden kühler,
> wie es zum Dezember paßt.
> Unsre freiheitstrunkenen Wühler
> waren uns von je verhaßt. (18)

Similar resignation in the aftermath of defeat is reflected by Georg Herwegh's "Mein Deutschland, strecke die Glieder," also sung by Rohland. Using the metaphor of sleep it mocks the retreat into renewed subordination:

> Mein Deutschland, strecke die Glieder
> Ins alte Bett, so warm und weich;
> Die Augen fallen die nieder,
> Du schläfriges Deutsches Reich
> Hast oft geschrien dich heiser —
> Nun schenke dir Gott die ewige Ruh'!
> Dich spitzt ein deutscher Kaiser
> Pyramidalisch zu. (15)[11]

The parody is significant for a 1960s audience in the light of the perceived atmosphere of conservative restoration and cultural stagnation that gripped an affluent West Germany in the years after the *Wirtschaftswunder*.

The brutal consequences of revolutionary defeat are documented in songs such as the famous "Badisches Wiegenlied" written by the revolutionary Ludwig Pfau. After two months of democracy in Baden the Prussian military re-established its rule and embarked upon a campaign of reprisals. On one hand this resulted in renewed retreat and stagnation, as reflected in the metaphor of sleep: "Schlaf mein Kind, schlaf' leis' / da draußen geht der Preuss', / und wer nicht schläft in guter Ruh' / dem drückt der Preuss' die Augen zu / schlaf mein Kind, schlaf leis.'"[12] On the other hand this repression resulted in a wave of emigration which produced yet another narrative for songs. Many *Auswanderer-Lieder* are testimony to the fact that from 1849–54 one million left Germany mostly for America, fleeing poverty and repression.[13]

The songs of the *Vormärz* and 1848 revolution reflect the varying aims and agendas of the various protagonists. On one hand, the idea of a proletarian people as actor in its own destiny emerges in lyric for the first time. On the other hand, the image of a *Deutschland* seeking to define itself and torn between old and new, feudalism and democracy, the thinkers and the philistines is also prevalent. The theme of the *deutsche Misere,* Germany's recurring inability to shape its own democratic destiny, would continue in political song in East and West Germany right up until the demise of the GDR in 1990, particularly in the much-publicized *Deutschland-Thematik* of Wolf Biermann.[14]

While Peter Rohland's 1848 album, recorded prior to his premature death in 1966, reflects the initial exuberance of rediscovery of a forgotten tradition, Dieter Süverkrüp's *1848: Lieder der deutschen Revolution*, released in 1973, has a more direct political agenda. The happenings of 1968 — the radicalization of the student movement led by Rudi Dutschke and the Extra-Parliamentary Opposition (APO) — had shaken West Germany out of the cultural and political complacency of the Adenauer era. In this respect Süverkrüp's album reflects the mood of the West German Left in the aftermath of 1968. Despite the disappointment that the radical aims of the student movement had not been realized, West German society under the Brandt SPD government had evolved into a new liberal era, and communists such as Süverkrüp believed revolutionary change could be taken further. This spirit is captured in an extract from Heinrich Heine's *Deutschland. Ein Wintermärchen:* "Ein neues Lied, ein besseres Lied, / o Freunde, will ich Euch dichten! / wir wollen hier auf Erden schon / das Himmelreich errichten." The obstacles to such social change are the topic of songs such as Georg Herwegh's "Wohlgeboren," which parodies the political indifference of the bourgeoisie: "Du sollst, verdammte Freiheit, mir / die Ruhe fürder nicht gefährden! / Lisette, noch ein Gläschen Bier, / ich will ein guter Bürger werden." Other parallels with the contemporary situation exist on a more abstract level. While "Das Blutgericht," excerpted above, expresses the historical class antagonism between bosses and workers, the depicted inhumane treatment of the weavers hardly reflect workers' conditions in West Germany in the 1970s. The same applies to "Das Hungerlied," a song portraying the misery of the famine years of the mid-1840s. But more direct allusions to contemporary West German reality, where, for example, Communist Party members endured the *Berufsverbot,* are evident in "Lied der Verfolgten" and "Der erste Berliner Kommunistenprozeß."

It is significant that Süverkrüp's musical settings for the 1848 songs are more optimistic than Rohland's. The major as opposed to minor keys, the sprightliness of march or courtly dance rhythms encourage action, discourage resignation. There is little sense of the melancholic contemplation of defeat. This is apparent in the aforementioned "Badisches Wiegenlied," which deals with the aftermath of the suppression of the revolution in Baden. But compared to other interpretations, Süverkrüp's musical composition, with its brisk and lively rhythm and particularly its dissonant bridge section, sounds more agitative. This reflects the dialectical aspect of Eisler's theory of composition for political song, whereby music by means of association of style can be a conveyor of meaning and thus serve as a weapon of agitation in the class struggle. The music appears geared towards the rebellious sentiment of the final verse, in which it is predicted that the Prussians will one day be defeated:

> Gott aber weiß, wie lang er geht,
> bis daß die Freiheit aufersteht,
> und wo der Vater liegt, mein Schatz,
> da hat noch mancher Preuße Platz!
> Schrei, mein Kindlein, schrei's:
> Da draußen liegt der Preuß!

This must be contrasted with a well-known musical interpretation of the same song in the GDR by the group Wacholder that emphasized the melancholy of defeat. But firstly we must summarize the history of the 1848 reception in the GDR.

The 1848 Song Tradition in the GDR from Lammel to Wacholder

In the GDR the 1848 songs were initially championed as part of the revolutionary *Erbe* of the workers' state. In 1957 Inge Lammel brought out the pamphlet *Das Lied im Kampf geboren. Heft 1: Lieder der Revolution von 1848*.[15] The selection of twenty-two songs reflects the euphoric spirit propagated by the SED Party in the construction (*Aufbau*) years of the GDR. Texts by Freiligrath, Herwegh, and others stand alongside anonymous texts. Most reflect the pathos of victory, defiance, and the appeal to fight, as in Wilhelm Jordan's "Nicht länger war das Joch zu tragen," Heinrich Bauer's "Aufruf!," and the anonymous "Freiheits-Marsch." Other songs employ the characteristic 1848 slogan "Aufwachen!," for example Freiligrath's "Reveille" and Herwegh's "Frühlingsmorgenruf."

The issue of the defeat of the 1848 revolution, however, is largely left unaddressed in Lammel's selection of songs. This, as mentioned, reflected the positive *Aufbau* mood of the period, one which was to dominate political song in the GDR up until the mid 1970s, especially in the repertoires of the young groups of the state-controlled *Singebewegung*.[16] It is interesting, however, to compare Lammel's omission with the reception of the 1848 songs in the GDR folk scene in the 1980s, when the focus shifted to the theme of defeat. In this later period songs about the despair and trauma of the defeat served as a subtext acknowledging the failure of the socialist dream. By the same token, the emigration songs were sung as a subtext to express desires to leave the republic, or merely to travel to forbidden places, for example in "Auswander-Lied," sung by the group Folkländer: "Ich verkauf' mein gut und Häuselein / Um ein so geringes Geld / Nach Amerika zu ziehen / Einem andern Teil der Welt."[17] The 1848 songs were thus correspondingly revived and sung in order to pass indirect comment on the present.

Compared to the West German Left's more romantic association with the songs of 1848, in the GDR folk scene of the 1980s these songs offered the chance to air dissatisfactions, the expression of which was otherwise prohibited. According to Matthias Kießling of the celebrated Cottbus folk group Wacholder, although the two periods were not directly comparable, the 1848 songs were a great peg on which the GDR singers could hang a multitude of different political grievances ("hervorragender Aufhänger, mit dem man alles loswerden konnte").[18] There was an unspoken understanding ("stillschweigendes Einverständnis") with the audience, who knew exactly how to interpret the subtext of the songs. Censors were hesitant to intervene because these were in essence historical texts relating to what the GDR considered as its own revolutionary heritage.

In 1984 Wacholder produced a program of songs entitled "Trotz Alledem. 1848 Revolutionslieder."[19] This as-yet-unpublished *Liedertheater* program contained interpretations of songs by Freiligrath, Fallersleben, Herwegh, Heine, Weerth, Karl Ludwig Pfau, and other anonymous writers. It was significant that the Berlin poet Glassbrenner also featured the Brandenburg dialect in some of his texts, offering a further point of identification for the Cottbus group and their audience. A carefully and audaciously chosen selection, it said just as much about political repression in the GDR as it did about the 1848 revolution. The basic optimism of the opening "Trotz alledem" is followed by a host of songs of protest, bitter denunciation, satire, and parody. Directed and choreographed by Karin Wolf, formerly of the Dresden *Liedertheater* group Schicht, the songs were sung and performed ambiguously, as if they could also be referring to the GDR. Contemporary themes to which the songs were relevant included the undemocratically elected government, the obsession with hierarchy, bureaucracy, and the military; the stifling effects of censorship and secret police observation; and the widespread emigration.

The anonymous "Blutgericht," already mentioned in the context of the West German folk revival, curses rulers who are not accountable to anyone for their actions on earth:

> Wenn ihr dereinst nach dieser Zeit
> Nach eurem Freudenleben
> Dort sollt in jener Ewigkeit,
> Sollt Rechenschaft ablegen
> [. . .]
> Ihr Schurken all, ihr Satansbrut,
> Ihr höllischen Kujone,
> Ihr fresst der Armen Hab und Gut,
> Und Fluch wird euch zum Lohne.

The song "Die alte Leier" (The Same Old Story) by Glassbrenner denounces figures of state authority and their obsession with titles: "Hofrat, Stadtrat, Registrator, / Landrat, Kriegsrat, Auskulator / Supernumerarius, / Geht die alte Leier, / Titel sind nicht teuer!" It scorns submissive citizens who dance to the tune of officialdom: "Ganz ergebne, treue, schlechte, / Tiefste, untertänige Knechte, / Demutsvoll und erfurchtsvoll, / Nein, sie klingt denn doch zu toll, / Die verdammte Leier, / Hol euch all der Geier!" The last line is emphasized by the cast singing it in unison. Servile behavior is similarly the theme of Freiligrath's "Schwarz-Rot-

Gold," which criticizes people's toleration of hated rulers: "Das ist noch lang die Freiheit nicht / Sein Recht als Gnad zu nehmen / [. . .] Auch nicht, daß die ihr gründlich haßt, / Ihr dennoch auf den Thronen laßt."

Another relevant theme of the production is censorship and the role of the secret police. "Sah ein Fürst ein Büchlein stehn" by Lebrecht Dreves (1816–70) parodies the authority's fear of subversive literature. A video recording of a performance in the Akademie der Künste in East Berlin in 1984 revealed the significance of this theme for a GDR audience.[20] Seeing their own situation clearly mirrored in the surreptitious exchange of politically controversial books, they laughed heartily at the lines: "Und der gute Fürst verbot / Büchlein in dem Lande, / Büchlein aber litt nicht Not, / Ging recht ab wie warmes Brot, / Ging von Hand zu Hande." Fallersleben's "Unsere Fürsten" is performed in such a way as to allude to Stasi observation in the GDR, its effects on freedom of speech and the unchanged relationship (despite socialism) between master and servant: "Schlimmer wird es jetzt von Tag zu tage, / Schweigen ist nur unser einzig Recht. / Untertanen ziemet keine Klage, / Und gehorchen muß dem Herrn der Knecht." The lines "Unsre Brüder werden ausgewiesen / Mehr als das Recht gilt Polizei" would be interpreted as a sly reference to the unlawful confinement of GDR political prisoners who subsequently were pushed out to West Germany.

Wacholder's treatment of the theme of the military is significant. Songs such as "Ich bin Soldat, doch bin ich es nicht gerne" had been popular in the folk scene since the late 1970s.[21] A rigorous military service was compulsory in the GDR, the expression of pacifism was outlawed, the issue of national defense (*Landesverteidigung*) being particularly sensitive. In 1982 the unofficial peace movement, known under the slogan of *Schwerter zu Pflugscharen,* had been banned. Indeed, according to Kießling, the theme of *Landesverteidigung* was even more delicate than that of emigration. In 1982 and 1983, Wacholder, alongside Karls Enkel, had been part of the *Hammer-Rehwü,*[22] which had been banned in Wacholder's hometown of Cottbus for allegedly pacifist lyrics.[23] Now in "Trotz Alledem" the group sang Herwegh's "Die Arbeiter an ihre Brüder," which criticizes the military for spending money that could be used to improve workers' conditions, and for propping up corrupt governments:

> Ach, wenn sie euch nicht hätten
> Wär alles wohlbestellt
> Auf euren Bajonetten
> Ruhrt die verkehrte Welt
> [. . .]
> Durch euch sind wir verraten,
> Durch euch verkauft allein;

Wann stellt ihr, o Soldaten,
Die Arbeit endlich ein?

As in Rohland's borrowings from the 1848 song tradition in 1960s West Germany, here too Wacholder chooses songs that utilize the metaphor of sleep, denoting a land in stagnation. This had a particular resonance in the post-Biermann period in the GDR which is generally viewed as a time of stagnation. Herwegh's "Wiegenlied," for example, sarcastically invites Germany to "sleep on" in the comfort of its religion and literary icons:

Laß jede Freiheit dir rauben
Setze dich nur zur Wehr
Du behälst ja den christlichen Glauben
Schlafe, was willst du mehr?
Und ob man dir alles verböte
Doch gräme dich nicht zu sehr
Du hast ja Schiller und Goethe
Schlafe, was willst du mehr?"

The theme of sleep also arises in the aforementioned "Badisches Wiegenlied." Wacholder's musical accompaniment evokes the melancholy mood of dashed ideals and the retreat into an private, inner world. Compared to Süverkrüp's version, which is geared towards the twist in the final verse where the tables will one day be finally turned on the rulers, these lines are sung somewhat sarcastically by Wacholder's Matthias Kießling as if what they express is merely a distant, elusive, utopian dream. This reflected the pessimism in the GDR in the early 1980s, when no one could have foreseen the changes that were to come later in the decade.

Such melancholy was not unique to Wacholder, but rather was also reflected in the music of singers such as Hans-Eckardt Wenzel and the early Stephan Krawczyk. In fact it was widespread throughout the GDR folk scene. The sweet harmonies of the music — played by wooden recorders, violins, mandolins, concertinas, hurdy gurdies, and guitars — combined with the chosen textual themes often accentuated this mood, as if of an harmonious collective longing. It was not intentional on the part of the singers and musicians, but was an unconscious expression of the hopelessness of their political situation. Moreover, it promoted a distinctive GDR folk sound.

Kießling recalled in 2003 how "Das Badische Wiegenlied" had been extremely popular for Wacholder in the GDR folk scene.[24] In "Trotz Alledem" the group sing another such hit, "Auswanderlied," originally popularized by Folkländer on their 1981 LP *Wenn man fragt, wer hats getan. . . .* This is performed here in a montage with another emigration song, Fallersleben's "Halleluja." Such songs allowed them to express the widespread longing in the GDR for travel.

Wacholder's "Trotz Alledem" ended with two assessments of the defeat of 1848. The first, "Achtzehnter März," was written by Georg Herwegh in 1873, the second, an adaptation of Freiligrath's "Trotz Alledem" by Hans-Eckardt Wenzel and Steffen Mensching in 1984. Herwegh's song laments the betrayal of the proletariat, whose plight had not improved despite German unification, but prophesizes that March 1848 will happen again: "Noch sind nicht alle Märzen vorbei, / Achtzehnhundert-siebzig und drei!" Wenzel and Mensching's adaptation of Freiligrath's song the only contemporary text in the production, unambiguously relates the subject matter of 1848 to the betrayal of the concept of proletarian revolution in the GDR:

> Zu früh, zu spät, wie immer schon,
> Genug wars nie, trotz alledem,
> Verlachten wir die Rebellion
> Der Bürger heut, trotz alledem,
> Trotz alledem und alledem,
> Trotz Wagner, Weerth und Bakunin,
> Uns schlägt der kalte Winterwind
> Noch ins Gesicht, trotz alledem.

To achieve a more universal context and to appease the censors, the song laments the lack of progress in the world since 1848, referring to Third World misery, and appears to blame the US nuclear arms program: "Das alte Brot verfault im Müll, / Trotz Afrika und alledem / Verhüllt in exquisiten Müll / Sind traurig wir trotzalledem. / Trotz Pershing II und alledem; / Wir machten gerne wohnlich uns / Die Erde uns trotz alledem." As Kießling recalls, however, the "und alledem" after "Pershing II" was intended as a sneaky reference to the Soviet SS-20 rockets. As he modestly conceded: "Die [im Publikum], die es merken wollten, haben es schon gemerkt." This supports Kießling's assertion that the treatment of the 1848 material was more of a game, "mehr Spaß als Widerstands-kampf," in an attempt to see how far one could push it with the censors.[25] The song concludes that, as in 1848, only the people can free themselves: "Trotz Dummheit, List und alledem, / 's ist keiner außer uns, der uns / Befreien könnt, von alledem." The celebratory champagne is still lying unopened, the revolution of "März und Marx" has still not been achieved in the GDR or anywhere else.

The Artistic Debate Surrounding Political Lyric: Biermann, Karls Enkel, and the Legacy of Heine

The period of the *Vormärz* and the 1848–49 revolution produced a wealth of oppositional literature and song in both "high" and "low" categories. However, one of the great distinctions of the literature of this period is the blurring of the boundary between these categories. Poetry for the first time took on a practical, agitative function in the form of song, which had a mobilizing effect on the political revolution.[26] Forerunners of the political *Gebrauchslyrik* poets of the twentieth century, *Vormärz* poets were able to both lend expression to and simultaneously engage in the political process (Stein, 211). Poets now broke with the dogma of the classical and romantic traditions that poetry and politics were aesthetically incompatible (236). Examples of the idea of art as a weapon in the struggle for emancipation appeared in numerous illustrated pamphlets (*Flugblätter*). They included Georg Herwegh's "Die Partei": "Ihr müßt das Herz an eine Karte wagen, / Die Ruhe über Wolken ziemt euch nicht; / Ihr müßt euch mit in diesem Kampfe schlagen, / Ein Schwert in eurer Hand ist das Gedicht."[27] In "Frühlingsmorgenruf," Herwegh calls on the German people to wake up: "Die Sonne, der wir lang' geharrt, / ist endlich aufgegangen; / [. . .] Wo ist ein Herz, das ruhig schlägt, / wenn solch ein Tag die Schwingen regt? / Ihr Völker, wachet auf!"[28] Other liberal lyricists of the *Vormärz* took his emotional identification even further, unleashing "Kräfte für diesen Kampf durch Mobilisierung der Gefühle (Liebe, Haß, Begeisterung, Empörung)"[29] often with the use of drastic-sounding metaphors laden with fighting spirit. The anonymous "Der Deutschen Echo" urges: "Zersprengt die Ketten, / Bekämpfet jeden Fürstenhund!"[30] Ludwig Seeger's "Rache" proclaims: "Heraus, du Menschenschlachter, raus! / [. . .] Da steht er, ein verlorner Mann, / Geknickt der blutige Tyrann!" (6).

On one hand therefore, the practical, agitative function of the songs of the *Vormärz* and 1848 created a model for the political *Gebrauchslyrik* of Erich Mühsam in the early twentieth century and the *Kampflieder* of Brecht and Eisler in the late 1920s and 1930s. On the other, a debate emerged as to whether this operative form of political song was blunting the contradictoriness of the political reality. The lyric of Heine, for example, reflected greater ambiguity, as displayed in *Deutschland. Ein Wintermärchen*'s ironic depiction of the unresolved conflict between democratic and philistine Germany. Such ambivalence was supported by Heine's introduction of more avant-garde, modernist formal elements. This debate on the effectiveness of agitative verse was still being contested over 120 years later in the 1960s, in both postwar German states.

In West Germany, for example, Franz Josef Degenhardt had become popular in liberal bourgeois circles for his ironical, grotesque caricatures of West German society. At the height of the radical student movement in 1968, however, he rejected this approach and embraced the new slogan "Zwischentöne sind bloß Krampf im Klassenkampf." Reminiscent of the *Kampflied* theory of Hanns Eisler in the late 1920s, Degenhardt's new songs were greatly simplified and intended to reflect the aims of the proletariat in its class struggle. While this aesthetic (also represented by Dieter Süverkrüp) was rejected by other Burg Waldeck singers such as Reinhard Mey and Christoph Stählin, it did set the agitative tone for West German *Liedermacher* for the next decade. By the late 1970s, however, the militant Waldeck veterans were dislodged by Konstantin Wecker and Udo Lindenberg, who rejected their "Humorlosigkeit und Verbissen-heit."[31] This was reflected by a more ambiguous lyrical and musical form. Wecker's advocacy of anarchy, his rejection of bourgeois values and the state apparatus was supported by a hedonistic lyrical and montage-based musical approach consisting of influences from rock music, opera (Carl Orff), and political theater (Hanns Eisler and Kurt Weill).

In the GDR this conflict was also apparent. The poetic ambivalence of the songs of Wolf Biermann and later of Wenzel and Mensching could be contrasted, for example, with the agitative dogma of the Oktoberklub and other state-sponsored groups of the *Singebewegung*. In this respect it was in the plebeianism and montage technique of the *Vormärz* poet Heinrich Heine that Biermann and Wenzel and Mensching found much inspiration.

Heine had represented a more avant-garde direction in *Vormärz* lyric that existed alongside the emotive, patriotic political poetry of Herwegh, Freiligrath, Fallersleben, and others. In the 1840s a debate emerged on *Tendenzlyrik* and literary technique in political song, one that was to be reignited over a hundred years later in the political song scenes of the two Germanies. While identifying with the aims of Freiligrath and Herwegh, Heine criticized these poets as political folk singers who assumed the role of enlighteners (Stein, 239). He found that the unquestioning identifica-tion with the "we" was dubious, that politically-correct emotions were but a blunt tool in the dissecting of political reality. Unambiguous subjec-tivity (typical of the literary production of the isolated poet in German classicism) was no longer relevant. A new form was needed to respond to the new contradictions of a changing society. Heine therefore adopted a technique that combined subjectivity with distance by the use of sensual-ity, irony, and association (Stein, 240). A new dynamic was thereby formed with the revolutionary content, allowing ambivalences and contradictions to be reflected. As Stein has pointed out, in *Deutschland. Ein Wintermärchen* (1844) Heine combined popular balladesque verse with a journalistic approach and set reality against fairy tale and dream, creating a poetry geared towards social change at a time when a new dynamic was emerging in the relationship between thought and action (227). This is expressed in *Deutschland. Ein Wintermärchen* in the *Doppelgänger* motiv of the poet and his mummified, axe-wielding guest. The axe is the weapon that will put into practice what the poet has in mind. Heine's guest states: "Ich bin dein Liktor, und ich geh / Beständig mit dem blanken / Richtbeile hinter dir — ich bin / Die Tat von deinem Gedanken."[32] In the dream the guest chops up the skeletons of superstition embodied by the holy three kings, who represent the forces of reaction and the past. With the axe of stanzas 6 and 7 as well as with his "Leier" from stanza 27, the poet is going to put his ideas into practice. By stating this is the same "Leier" as used by Aristophanes,[33] his ironic-subversive predecessor from the theater of Greek antiquity, he links himself with the profane, dialogic tradition (which Bakhtin calls the carnivalesque[34]). The distancing gained by such dualisms (displayed also in his dialogue with Hammonia) allows Heine an ambivalence. He can express the necessity of freeing German democratic aspirations while not denying the extent of the *deutsche Misere* which forms an everpresent counterpoint. This image of the negative, reactionary Germany is expressed in Hammonia's ominous projection of the country's future, which she invites the narrator to view in the vile-smelling magic kettle. Moreover, as Meier-Lenz states, the use of the *Doppelgänger* motif contains a further contradiction: the axe man is depicted as a threatening figure, reflecting a fear of revolutionary action if it results — as in the case of France — in the tyrannical regime of a Robespierre (1977, 31). This, nonetheless, does not diminish Heine's belief in the necessity of the implementation of revolutionary ideas in deeds.

Wolf Biermann's *Deutschland. Ein Wintermärchen*

In the GDR the argument over form was part of the wider debate in literature, where the dominant Socialist Realism, as defined by Georg Lukács, forbade formalism. Rather it embraced the totality, proportion, and objectivity reflected in the aesthetic norms of classicism. Brecht, for example, had been accused of formalism for his *Urfaust* production in 1952 and Eisler for his opera libretto *Johann Faustus* in 1953.[35] In the political song scene of the 1960s this debate centered around Wolf Biermann. A former pupil of Eisler's, Biermann was banned from performing in 1965. His songs linked into the tradition of Heine and François Villon with their grotesque, sensual imagery and satirical send-ups of officialdom. This contrasted with the state-sponsored *Singebewegung* in the GDR, whose showpiece group Oktoberklub became infamous for singing the type of pathos-laden song featured in the aforementioned Inge Lammel collection.

Biermann's identification with Heine is confirmed by his own *Deutsch-land. Ein Wintermärchen* from 1972.[36] This tale with interspersed songs relates how Biermann, like Heine, was censored, living in an inner exile and traveling back over a border, in this case from the GDR, to visit his mother in Hamburg. Parallels are also evident in the formal approach, which combines ballad and *Reisebericht,* irony and plebeian language, all within a structure of four-line verses with frequent enjambments and un-usual rhymes.[37] In a departure from the model, Biermann breaks up the stanza structure with the insertion of four songs that — similarly to the defamiliarizing function of songs in Brecht's Epic Theater — provide an extra level of commentary complementing the main subject matter. With this aesthetic approach, Biermann, like Heine, rejects the political *Ten-denzpoesie* of the time, in his case the state-sanctioned agitation poetry embodied by Johannes R. Becher and the trivial propaganda lyric of the *Singebewegung.* Instead, he embraces the dialectical approach to poetry and music of Brecht and Hanns Eisler.[38] This allows a dialogic interplay of ideas, thereby avoiding dogma. Like Heine, Biermann sets hope for demo-ratic change against the historical condition of the *deutsche Misere.* The latter is expressed in images of border guards, the Wall, and other legacies of Stalinism. As with Heine, it is significant that the utopian aspect (Bier-mann's aspirations for a communist united Germany) is set within the form of the fairy-tale.[39] The fantastic elements (for instance the encoun-ters with Hammonia and Ernst Thälmann) as well as the Villonesque profanities have the function of relativizing the utopian content and pro-moting an atmosphere of comic ambivalence. This allows a critique of Stalinism without diminishing Biermann's basic socialist stance.[40] An ex-ample is provided by the poet's dialogue with the dead Thälmann, leader of the German Communist Party from 1925–33 and, as such, a figure as-sociated with Stalinism. The dialogue enables Thälmann to undergo a transformation to professing his belief in a new reformed socialism. The Biermann narrator figure berates him: "Ach Teddy, merkst du nicht? Du bist / Schon selbst total verrostet / Und ahnst nicht, was dein Stalin uns / Gekostet hat und kostet."[41] Thälmann is consequently brought around to the standpoint:

> So alt ich bin, so tot ich bin
> Dann müssen wir *beide* eben
> Von vorn anfangen und länger nicht
> An altem Plunder klebn
> Denn unser Menschheitstraum, er bleibt
> Trotz all der Niederlagn
> Und scheitern wir, dann werden wir
> Es noch und nochmal wagn!" (59)

Karls Enkel's "Die komische Tragödie des 18. Brumaire"

The absence on Wacholder's "Trotz Alledem" of 1848 songs displaying the utopian fighting spirit was indicative of a general trend since the 1970s. The public had become immune to what they considered to be SED propaganda, and this was reflected in the decline of the *Singebewegung* from the early 1970s onwards. Many groups developed new techniques of performance that would more convincingly reflect the contradictory reality of the GDR. Groups such as Schicht, Brigade Feuerstein, and Karls Enkel pioneered *Liedertheater*. In the case of Karls Enkel this new direction was influenced by Piscator's proletarian revue, Brechtian song theater, and the slapstick clowning of commedia dell'arte. Led by Hans-Eckardt Wenzel and Steffen Mensching, the group broke free from the *Singebewegung* in 1979 and began experimenting with modernist theatrical techniques under the direction of Heiner Maaß at the Berliner Volksbühne. Among the treatments of the 1848 revolution by GDR groups in the 1980s, their *Liedertheater* program "Die komische Tragödie des 18. Brumaire des Louis Bonaparte"[42] was the most directly critical of the GDR. A plebeian, Heinesque, ironic ambivalence was evident in the production, which projected the significance of the defeated utopian aims of 1848 onto present-day reality. A striking leitmotif is the treatment of the "revolutionary dead." Here they were not alone in the GDR. As Karen Leeder has written, the official honoring of the dead in the GDR was so endemic that Heiner Müller spoke of "einer Diktatur der Toten über die Lebenden."[43] In view of this, Karls Enkel set out to honor the dead in such a way as to critically examine conditions in the present.

The production is a musical and theatrical montage of texts from Marx's account of the failed uprisings in Paris in 1848 interspersed with texts by Heine, Hölderlin, and by Wenzel and Mensching themselves. For this writing duo, the legacy of the revolutionary dead of history was a reminder of present-day failures. Quoting from Marx's *Der achzehnte Brumaire*,[44] the cast members exclaim in unison: "Die Tradition aller toten Geschlechter lastet wie ein Alp auf dem Gehirn der Lebenden."[45] In their black waistcoats, top hats, and faces painted white like skullcaps, the cast represents these "tote Geschlechter" from the 1848 Paris uprisings. The defamiliarizing montage of texts accentuated by the performance techniques — the constant breaks, the pregnant pauses, the changes in tempo and the choice of musical settings — draw the audience's attention to the parallels between past and present. The image of a betrayed proletariat of 1848 thus merges with that of workers in the GDR of 1983, who, it is implied, are similarly being betrayed.

In the opening scene the cast sits on the stage littered with the debris of the failed uprising. The Wenzel and Mensching texts, reminiscent of

Herwegh's "Der achzehnter März," convey how the historical struggle
has brought the workers no closer to their goals. In "Komm unter die
großen Brücken der Seine": the group sings: "Es gibt nichts Neues unter
dem Mond / [. . .] Die Stadt spie uns aus / Wir frieren und warten noch
immer." And in their melancholy adaptation of Strauß and von Gilm's
"Stell auf den Tisch die duftenden Reseden," Wenzel and Mensching
bring the events of 1848 into the present: "Alles umsonst [. . .] / Was
bleibt sind Tote, Daten, ein paar Lieder, / Ein schöner Traum, ein nicht
erfüllter Zweck." With resigned irony the group sings, to a funeral march
organ accompaniment, an adaptation of Marx's prediction for future proletarian revolutions:[46] "Sie werden sich nicht kostümieren /Und nicht er-
sticken in Phrasen, /Sie werden sich selbst kritisieren [. . .] /Sie werden
sich korrigieren [. . .]" But the tragedy of history flips over into comical
farce as the cast presents an updated adaptation of Marx's lines from
Brumaire: "Hegel bemerkt irgendwo, daß alle großen weltgeschichtlichen
Tatsachen und Personen sich sozusagen zweimal ereignen. Er hat vergessen, hinzuzufügen: das eine Mal als Tragödie, das andere Mal als Farce"
(15). In a cheeky allusion to the recurring farce of history — implying
that Louis Bonaparte and the political charlatans of 1848 would be
equally at home in the GDR — they sing the following lines to an appro-
priately light-hearted tango accompaniment: "Das ist ein altes Stück mein
Kind / Der Stoff ist bekannt aber neu sind die Stars / Das eine Mal als
Tragödie, das and're Mal als Farce."

"Die komische Tragödie" was the first *Liedertheater* program in
which Wenzel and Mensching combined popular forms such as puppetry
and clowning with philosophical analysis. The use of clownesque surreal
dialogues and robust slapstick was a technique pioneered by the early
Brecht, for example, in the *Badener Lehrstück.*[47] Brecht had been influenced by the Munich clown Karl Valentin. Such a montage of the high
and the low captures the essence of Karls Enkel's approach. In the puppet
scene, for instance, philosophical remarks by Marx are juxtaposed with the
grotesquely-portrayed death of Louis Bonaparte while in exile in London.
The scene, in which the puppets make degrading references to Bonaparte
using imagery that Mikhail Bakhtin would describe as relating to the
"lower bodily stratum" (1984, 21) has echoes of the ritual humiliation of
the king in carnival. The Bonaparte puppet, for example, urinates while
his entourage speak of the vile state of his inner organs. According to director Heiner Maaß, the Bonaparte figure was meant to symbolize the
GDR leader Erich Honecker, although this reference was not spelled out
and was missed by most of the audience.[48]

This duality of the exalted and the ridiculous is summarized in "Die
komische Tragödie" in a string of quotations from Heine's *Das Buch Le
Grand* connecting the world of politics to a theatrical farce: "[. . .] und

auf dieser großen Weltbühne geht es außerdem ganz wie auf unseren Lumpenbrettern, auch auf ihr gibt es besoffene Helden, Könige, die ihre Rollen vergessen, Kulissen, die hängengeblieben." Similarly, the clowns, played by Wenzel and Mensching, exclaim: "Aber das Leben ist im Grunde so fatal ernsthaft, daß es nicht zu ertragen wäre ohne solche Verbindung des Pathetischen mit dem Komischen." This ironically reflects the survival technique of Wenzel and Mensching in the GDR: their *Narrenfreiheit* enabled them to laugh at the more unbearable aspects of reality and protected such a comical treatment of Marx from censorship. They allude to this artistic freedom in another extract from Heine:

> Die grauenhaftesten Bilder des menschlichen Wahnsinns zeigt uns Aristophanes nur im lachenden Spiegel des Witzes, den großen Denkerschmerz, der seine eigene Nichtigkeit begreift, wagt Goethe nur in den Knittelversen eines Puppenspiels auszusprechen, und die tödlichste Klage über den Jammer der Welt legt Shakespeare in den Mund eines Narren, während er dessen Schellenkappe ängstlich schüttelt.[49]

In his essay "Chiron oder die Zweigestaltigkeit," Wenzel sheds light on what he regards as the significance of the plebeian aesthetic of Heine. There is clearly a strong subtext in this essay. Wenzel is also alluding to the possibilities of a plebeian aesthetic in GDR poetry and song as a more meaningful alternative to that which celebrated the GDR state. Wenzel historicizes the split in poetic styles (between the written and the spoken or sung word) that characterized the *Vormärz:* "Der Riß, der nach Heine durch das Herz des Poeten geht, geht auch durch die Poesie."[50] In such times leading up to revolution a "Plebejisierung" of poetry takes place whereby poets react to social forces and present a view from below ("ein Blick von unten"). This is a rejection of an inward-looking, overly refined, aesthetic literature (as is characteristic of the *Vormärz*) which has become socially meaningless and restorative (Wenzel, 97). Brecht described these two strains in literature as "pontifikale und profane Dichtung," Hölderlin representing the pontifical and Heine the profane.[51] In an interview after the fall of the GDR, Wenzel related this argument to his own profane approach to political songwriting in the GDR:

> In der DDR, auch in der Singebewegung gab es natürlich eine hochpontifikale Kunst, die das Feiern, den Gottesdienst des Sozialismus stark betonte und wenig mit der Profanität der Leute zu tun hatte.[52]

Plebeian, ironic gesture was particularly apparent in the songs of the *Hammer-Rehwü* of 1982, written by Wenzel and Steffen Mensching.[53] Key examples are the opening number "Du, laß dich nicht bescheißen!"

or the revue's leitmotif "O wir tragen unser Schicksal mit Geduld / An der ganzen Scheiße sind wir selber schuld!" Another example is the poem "Égalité," which mocks the privileged existence of leading politicians:

> Sie hocken auf den Toiletten
> Über den Knien wie du, die Hosen
> Heruntergelassen, ohnmächtige Machtvolle Körper [. . .]
> Ohne Auftrag, in der Einsamkeit
> Der Kacheln der Zelle, allein mit ihren
> Realpolitischen Därmen."[54]

The "Plebejisierung" Wenzel speaks of is reminiscent of Bakhtin's claim that a carnivalization of consciousness takes place in society prior to social upheaval.[55] The peaceful revolution in 1989 in the GDR could not have been predicted in 1982, and protest song in the GDR cannot be compared to that of the *Vormärz*, not merely because of the lengths *Liedermacher* were prepared to go to disguise their criticism in metaphors in order to avoid prohibition.[56] But it is significant that the critical *Liedermacher* of the GDR were highly popular. They played to packed club audiences throughout the 1980s, enjoying an elevated status as the bearers of unofficial tidings, the critical subtexts of their songs serving as a substitute for the censored newspapers and mainstream media.

The various narratives of the protest-song tradition of the *Vormärz* and 1848 — that of rebellion, patriotism, defeat, and emigration — provided points of identification for politically-engaged singers in West Germany and the GDR at different points in the histories of the two republics. In the mid 1960s Peter Rohland revived the 1848 song tradition reflecting a younger generation's search for democratic cultural roots. A decade later Dieter Süverkrüp in West Germany and the *Singebewegung* in the GDR displayed an unambiguous identification with the revolutionary fighting spirit of the 1848 *Kampflieder*. In the 1980s GDR folk groups such as Wacholder and Folkländer — in a cat and mouse game with the censors — identified with their lyrical forebears' satirical attacks on German bureaucrasy and philistinism and with the emigration narrative. In the area where political song overlapped with high literature, poet Heinrich Heine was a source of inspiration. Wolf Biermann adapted Heine's *Deutschland. Ein Wintermärchen* to express the historical condition of the *deutsche Misere*. In the 1980s Hans-Eckardt Wenzel and Steffen Mensching's group Karls Enkel, too, dealt with the narrative of revolutionary defeat. Influenced by Heine, they, like Biermann, used a plebeian, ironic approach to expose the contradictions of a socialism that had degenerated into Stalinism.

Notes

[1] *1848 . . . weil jetzt die Freiheit blüht: Lieder aus der Revolution von 1848/49,* CD (Südwest Records/Deutsches Volksliedarchiv, 1998). Subsequent notes refer to page number from CD booklet.

[2] See the theme of self-censorship in Beate Müller, ed., *Zensur im modernen deutschen Kulturraum* (Tübingen: Niemeyer, 2003).

[3] See Max Nyffeler, *Liedermacher in der Bundesrepublik Deutschland* (Bonn: Internationes, 1983), 40.

[4] Wolfgang Steinitz, *Der große Steinitz, Deutsche Volkslieder demokratischen Charackters aus 6 Jahrhunderten,* 2 vols. (Berlin DDR: Akademie Verlag, 1955 and 1962).

[5] Annette Blühdorn, *Pop and Poetry — Pleasure and Protest: Udo Lindenberg, Konstantin Wecker and the Tradition of German Cabaret* (Bern: Peter Lang 2003), 127.

[6] Oss Kröher speaking at the podium discussion "Burg Waldeck und die Folgen — Songfestivals in Deutschland," Die Wabe, Berlin, 29 February 2004.

[7] Peter Rohland, *48er Lieder — Lieder deutscher Demokraten* (Teldec, 1967; reissue, CD: Thorofon, 1998). Subsequent notes refer to page number from CD booklet.

[8] Dieter Süverkrüpp, *1848: Lieder der deutschen Revolution* (Pläne, 1974; reissue, CD: Conträr, 1998).

[9] Barbara James and Walter Mossmann, *1848: Flugblätterlieder und Dokumente einer zerbrochenen Revolution* (Darmstadt: Luchterhand, 1983).

[10] This is a different song from the "Bürgerlied" on Peter Rohland's 1848 LP.

[11] See also Nyffeler, "Die Festivals auf der Burg Waldeck," 43–44.

[12] Printed in James and Mossmann, 130.

[13] This narrative was particularly picked up on by the GDR folk groups, which is dealt with later in this chapter.

[14] See D. P. Meier-Lenz: *Heinrich Heine. Wolf Biermann. Deutschland. Zwei Wintermärchen* (Bonn: Bouvier, 1977), 69–79.

[15] Inge Lammel, ed., *Das Lied im Kampf geboren. Heft 1: Lieder der Revolution von 1848* (Leipzig: VEB Friedrich Hofmeister, 1957).

[16] See chapter 8 of this book on political song in the GDR.

[17] Folkländer, *Wenn man fragt, wer hat's getan . . .* LP (Amiga, 1982)

[18] Personal interview with Matthias Kießling, 26 November 2003.

[19] Wacholder, "Trotz Alledem. 1848 Revolutionslieder," unpublished manuscript and video (Berlin: Das Liedzentrum der Akademie der Künste der DDR, 1984). Subsequent unreferenced quotations from songs are from this production.

[20] See video of *Trotz Alledem.*

[21] See Lutz Kirchenwitz, *Folk, Chanson und Liedermacher in der DDR* (Berlin: Dietz Verlag, 1993), 90.

[22] Karls Enkel, Wacholder, and Beckert & Schulz, "Die Hammer-Rehwü," unpublished manuscript and video, collected by Karin Wolf (Berlin: Akademie der Künste der DDR, Liedertheater-Dokumentation, Forschungsabteilung Musik/ Liedzentrum, 1982). *Die Hammer-Rehwü,* CD (Nebelhorn, 1994).

[23] See chapter 8 of this book on political song in the GDR.

[24] Interview with Kießling.

[25] Interview with Kießling.

[26] Peter Stein, "Vormärz," in Wolfgang Beutin et al., eds., *Deutsche Literaturgeschichte: Von den Anfängen bis zur Gegenwart* (Stuttgart: Metzler 1994), 250.

[27] Georg Herwegh, *Herweghs Werke: Gedichte eines Lebendigen* (Berlin: Deutsches Verlagshaus Bong, 1909), 122.

[28] Published in Lammel, *Das Lied im Kampf geboren,* 18.

[29] Stein, "Vormärz," 239.

[30] Published in Lammel, *Das Lied im Kampf geboren,* 33.

[31] Thomas Rothschild, "Liedermacher," in Heinz Ludwig Arnold, ed., *Politische Lyrik* (Munich: Edition Text und Kritik, 1984), 9.

[32] Heinrich Heine, *Deutschland. Ein Wintermärchen,* in *Heine Werke,* vol. 2 (Berlin/Weimar: Aufbau Verlag, 1974), 107

[33] Heine, *HW,* vol 2, 159.

[34] See Bakhtin's comments on Heine's awareness of the ambivalent carnivalesque tradition in *Rabelais and His World* (Bloomington: Indiana UP, 1984), 252.

[35] Wolfgang Emmerich, *Kleine Literatur der DDR-Geschichte,* revised edition (Leipzig: Kiepenheuer, 1997), 123.

[36] Wolf Biermann, *Deutschland. Ein Wintermärchen* (Berlin: Verlag Klaus Wagenbach, 1972).

[37] Meier-Lenz, *Deutschland. Zwei Wintermärchen,* 86–91.

[38] See Meier-Lenz, *Deutschland. Zwei Wintermärchen,* 93. See the next chapter for an analysis of the influence of Eisler's music on Biermann.

[39] Jay Rosellini, *Wolf Biermann* (Munich: Beck, 1992), 63.

[40] See Meier-Lenz, *Deutschland. Zwei Wintermärchen,* 93.

[41] All quotations from Wolf Biermann in this book are copyright © Wolf Biermann and are used by permission. Here: Biermann, *Deutschland. Ein Wintermärchen,* 56.

[42] Karls Enkel, "Die komische Tragödie des 18. Brumaire oder Ohrfeigen sind schlimmer als Dolchstöße. Nach Karl Marx," unpublished manuscript and video, collected by Karin Wolf (Berlin: Akademie der Künste der DDR, Liedertheater-Dokumentation, Forschungsabteilung Musik/Liedzentrum, 1983).

[43] Heiner Müller, "Das Böse ist die Zukunft," in *Jenseits der Nation* (Berlin: Rotbuch Verlag, 1991), 75. Quoted in Karen Leeder, *Breaking Boundaries: A New Generation of Poets in the GDR* (Oxford: Clarendon, 1996), 122.

[44] Karl Marx, *Der achtzehnte. Brumaire des Louis Bonaparte* (Berlin: Dietz Verlag, 1974).

[45] Karls Enkel, "Die komische Tragödie," taken from Marx, *Der achtzehnte Brumaire*, 15.

[46] See Marx, *Der achtzehnte Brumaire*, 15.

[47] See the clowns' dialogue in Brecht's *Badener Lehrstück* in *Die Stücke von Bertolt Brecht in einem Band* (Frankfurt am Main: Suhrkamp, 1978), 238.

[48] Personal interview with Heiner Maaß, 23 March 1994.

[49] Karls Enkel, "Die komische Tragödie," here quoted from Heinrich Heine, *Das Buch Le Grand*, in *Reisebilder* (Munich: Goldmann, 1982), 262.

[50] Hans-Eckardt Wenzel, "Chiron oder die Zweigestaltigkeit. Ein Essai," in *Lied vom wilden Mohn. Gedichte* (Halle and Leipzig: Mitteldeutscher Verlag, 1984), 95.

[51] In his *Arbeitsjournal 1938–1955* Brecht wrote: "Sofort nach Goethe zerfällt die schöne widersprüchliche Einheit, und Heine nimmt die völlig profane, Hölderlin die völlig pontifikale Linie." Bertolt Brecht, *Arbeitsjournal* (Frankfurt and Main: Suhrkamp, 1977), 103.

[52] Personal interview with Wenzel, 9 March 1994.

[53] See chapter 8 of this book on political song in the GDR.

[54] "Égalité," *Die Hammer-Rehwü*. Also published in Steffen Mensching, *Erinnerung an eine Milchglasscheibe. Gedichte* (Halle and Leipzig, Mitteldeutscher Verlag, 1984), 12.

[55] Mikhail Bakhtin, *Rabelais and His World*, 49.

[56] Although the *Hammer-Rehwü* was in many ways an exception to that rule in terms of the directness of its criticism. See chapter 8 of this book on political song in the GDR.

2: Mühsam, Brecht, Eisler, and the Twentieth-Century Revolutionary Heritage

David Robb

IN MARCH 1873, *two* years after German unification, Georg Herwegh wrote the poem "Achtzehnter März" for the twenty-fifth anniversary of the 1848 revolution in Vienna. The poem laments the revolution's failure while simultaneously prophesizing that its legacy would live on in future revolutions:

> Achtzehnhundert vierzig und acht,
> Als im Lenze das Eis gekracht,
> Tage des Februars, Tage des Märzen,
> Waren es nicht Proletarierherzen,
> Die voll Hoffnung zuerst erwacht,
> Achtzehnhundert vierzig und acht?
>
> Achtzehnhundert vierzig und acht,
> Als du dich lange genug bedacht,
> Mutter Germania, glücklich verpreußte,
> Waren es nicht Proletarierfäuste,
> Die sich ans Werk der Befreiung gemacht?
> Achtzehnhundert vierzig und acht?
>
> Achtzehnhundert vierzig und acht,
> Als du geruht von der nächtlichen Schlacht,
> Waren es nicht Proletarierleichen,
> Die du, Berlin vor den Zitternden, bleichen,
> Barhaupt grüßenden Cäsar gebraucht,
> Achtzehnhundert vierzig und acht?
>
> Achtzehnhundertsiebzig und drei,
> Reich der Reichen, da stehst du, juchhei!
> Aber wir Armen, verkauft und verraten,
> Denken der Proletariertaten —
> Noch sind nicht alle Märzen vorbei,
> Achtzehnhundert siebzig und drei.[1]

Yet again we see here the utopian sentiment alongside the disappointment of the *deutsche Misere*, the recurring failure of Germany to alter the political status quo from within. This double-edged condition would mark the German political song throughout the twentieth century, from the Spartakus movement in 1919 to the anti-fascist campaigns of the 1930s and from the 1968 student movement in West Germany to the 1989 *Wende* in the GDR.

Thematically the continuance of this tradition is apparent in recurring poetic motifs of the *Liedermacher* from the 1960s up to the 1990s. On another level, however, the early twentieth century represented a time of groundbreaking innovation in terms of literary form and performance techniques. These innovations had a lasting influence on the genre of political song. The appropriations by East and West German *Liedermacher* of the political song *Erbe* of the early twentieth century and the Weimar Republic will form the focus of this chapter.

Utopia and Defeat 1: The Legacy of Erich Mühsam

The history of the early twentieth-century German cabaret has been well documented in books such as Peter Jelavich's *Berlin Cabaret*[2] and Alan Lareau's *The Wild Stage: Literary Cabaret of the Weimar Republic*.[3] German cabaret was based on the original "Chat Noir" model of Paris in the 1880s and 1890s. Embodied by the figure of Aristide Bruant, creator of the "Chanson realiste," the French blueprint was a combination of song, satire, and entertainment. Many political lyricists in Germany saw the cabaret as a medium with which to earn money as well as to disseminate political thought. In the German political cabaret of the early twentieth century, Erich Mühsam (1878–1934), alongside Frank Wedekind (1864–1918), played a substantial part in the renewal of balladesque satire in the tradition of Heinrich Heine.[4] In his early bohemian years in Berlin, Mühsam performed in Germany's legendary first cabaret *Überbrettl* (1901–2) and later in Die elf Scharfrichter in Munich. Along with Wedekind, Christian Morgenstern, Otto J. Bierbaum, and Arno Holz, he was one of the most influential cabaret writers of his day. Mühsam's songs were more radically satirical than those of his colleagues, as were his pieces in the magazines *Simplicissimus* and *Der wahre Jakob*. In "Lumpenlied" from 1912 he identifies with the dispossessed, who are set in opposition to the *Bürger* and the *Philister:*

> Kein Schlips am Hals, kein Geld im Sack.
> Wir sind ein schäbiges Lumpenpack,
> auf das der Bürger speit.
> Der Bürger blank von Stiebellack,
> mit Ordenszacken auf dem Frack,
> der Bürger mit dem chapeau claque,
> fromm und voll Redlichkeit.[5]

Mühsam's most famous cabaret song was "Der Revoluzzer" from 1907. Since the 1860s a unified workers' movement had been organizing itself: workers' associations and clubs had formed, demanding rights that had been promised but not carried through in 1848, such as free elections. This had culminated in the formation of the Social Democratic Party (SPD) in 1869. The gradual institutionalization of this party, however, necessitated a compromise with the system, which left radicals such as Mühsam dissatisfied. His song "Der Revoluzzer" parodies the half-hearted revolutionary approach of the SPD in the figure of the "Lampenputzer" who does not want his street lamps damaged by the building of barricades (see Kauffeldt, 165–67):

> War einmal ein Revoluzzer,
> Im Zivilstand Lampenputzer;
> Ging im Revoluzzerschritt
> Mit den Revoluzzern mit.
>
> Und er schrie: "Ich revolüzze!"
> Und die Revoluzzermütze
> Schob er auf das linke Ohr,
> Kam sich höchst gefährlich vor.
>
> Doch die Revoluzzer schritten
> Mitten in der Straßen Mitten,
> Wo er sonsten unverdrutzt
> Alle Glaslaterne putzt.
>
> Sie vom Boden zu entfernen,
> Rupfte man die Gaslaternen
> Aus dem Straßenpflaster aus,
> Zwecks des Barrikadenbaus
>
> Aber unser Revoluzzer
> Schrie: "Ich bin der Lampenputzer
> Dieses guten Leuchtelichts.
> Bitte, bitte, tut ihm nichts!
>
> Wenn wir ihn' das Licht ausdrehen,
> Kann kein Bürger nichts mehr sehen,
> Laßt die Lampen stehn, ich bitt!
> Denn sonst spiel ich nicht mehr mit!"
>
> Doch die Revoluzzer lachten,
> Und die Gaslaternen krachten,
> Und der Lampenputzer schlich
> Fort und weinte bitterlich.

Dann ist er zu Haus geblieben
Und hat dort ein Buch geschrieben:
Nämlich wie man revoluzzt
Und dabei doch Lampen putzt.[6]

In its parodic role characterization, "Der Revoluzzer" is — despite its greater balladesque simplicity — a forerunner of the *Rollengedicht* of Franz Josef Degenhardt in the late 1960s. In "Verteidigung eines Sozial-demokraten vor dem Fabriktor," for example, Degenhardt uses the inter-play between third-person narrator and character role-play to parody a Social Democrat politician who is persuading workers not to strike:

und heute
guck dir das doch mal an
wohnzimmer teppich
couch sessel
alles was du willst
auto sogar
die kinder arbeiten verdienen
und dann kommt ihr ARBEITER DU BIST AUSGEBEUTET
[. . .]
ich sag dir so geht das nicht
[. . .]
sagt der alte ewige sozialdemokrat und spricht und spricht
und spricht und spricht
bloß ändern das will er nicht[7]

In general, however, Mühsam rated his own cabaret work as trivial (Kauffeldt, 148). Of more importance to him were his non-satirical *Kampflieder* targeted specifically at an audience of revolutionary workers. In their pathos and choice of metaphors, these Mühsam texts show inspiration from the songs of 1848. The hymnic rhetoric — similar to that of Freiligrath and Herwegh — is meant to enthuse the reader and lis-tener (Kauffeldt, 147). Mühsam was inspired by the communicative folk style of the *Kampflieder* of 1848 and their practical use in the context of revolution. He was to bemoan the lack of such songs during the German uprisings of November 1918.[8] A forerunner of Brecht and Hanns Eisler, Mühsam's *Kampflieder* had the express purpose of enlightening the pro-letariat. In 1912 he wrote in the journal *Kain:*

Das ist nämlich der Sinn alles Werbens und aller Agitation: in stim-mungsverwandten Intelligenzen Gedanken zu wecken, Gefühle zu Überzeugungen zu erweitern und Sehnsüchte mit dem Drange zur Tat zu erfüllen.[9]

In "Generalstreikmarsch," as Diana Köhnen writes, the collective "we," as well as the highly accessible structure of four-line verse, alternating rhymes, and refrain, point to its intended use in the daily political struggle (163–64): "Wir waren lang genug die Knechte, / wir wollen unsre Herrn nicht mehr! / Wir setzen uns für unsre Rechte, / für unsre Freiheit nun zur Wehr" (Mühsam 1906, 1). The song agitates for a general strike as a response to the Russian Revolution of 1905. The relationship to 1848 is evident in the depiction of the master-servant opposition and in the metaphors of a sleeping people who are to be woken up by the revolutionaries: "Schläft denn das Volk? Wir woll'n es wecken. / Heh! Arbeitsmann, Rebell, Wach auf!" (1906, 1). Drastic metaphors such as blood-sucking and the slaughterhouse (later used by Brecht) are similarly borrowed from the style of *Vormärz* poetry: "Sie saugen uns das Blut vom Leibe, / Sie greifen frech nach unserm Glück / Daß man das Volk zur Schlachtbank treibe, / das ist das Ziel. — Was kost' das Stück?" (1906, 1).

A decade later the reverberations in Germany of the Russian Revolution of October 1917 presented a more immediate context for Mühsam's *Gebrauchslieder*. "Räte-Marseillaise," for example, relates to the daily political struggle leading up to the Bavarian revolution in April 1919, and directly appeals to the masses:

> Wie lange Völker, wollt ihr säumen?
> Der Tag steigt auf, es sinkt die Nacht.
>   Wollt ihr von Freiheit träumen,
> das schon die Freiheit selbst erwacht?
>   Vernehmt die Rufe aus dem Osten!
> Vereinigt euch zu Kampf und Tat!
> die Stunde der Befreiung naht!
> Laßt nicht den Stahl des Willens rosten![10]

As in 1848, after the euphoria of rebellion came the analysis of failure. When the short-lived Soviet Republic of Bavaria was toppled on 13 April, Mühsam, a member of the Revolutionary Workers' Council, was arrested and jailed until he was granted amnesty in December 1924. Texts he wrote during this period take stock of the defeat. In "Ruf aus der Not" of October 1919, a poem reminiscent of Freiligrath's "Die Toten an die Lebenden" (see Köhnen, 170), Mühsam appeals to the dead revolutionaries Marat and Bakunin to inspire renewed revolt. An image of the *deutsche Misere* is presented again in political lyric with respect to a betrayed people:

> Marat! Bakunin! Steigt aus eurer Gruft hervor!
> Wacht auf, schaut um euch, staunt, empört euch,

lebt und helft!
Oh, unerhört in aller Menschheit Freiheitskampf,
seht sterben in Verrat des deutschen Volkes
Glück!
Marat! Bakunin! Gebt mir Geist von eurem
Geist! (1920, 86)

Requiems to Liebknecht and Luxemburg (1928, 206) and Sacco and Vanzetti (1928, 208) continued in this vein. Mühsam believed nothing fundamental had changed since 1848 and saw himself as part of that same literary tradition, as the reference to "Herwegh, Weerth und Freiligrath, / Pfau und Heinrich Heine" in "Der freie Geist"[11] indicates. Köhnen explains the significance of Mühsam's reference to the dead revolutionaries:

> Das Beispiel der toten Revolutionäre soll die Überlebenden mahnen, die Revolution zu vollenden. Die Beschwörung revolutionär-anarch-istischer Vorbilder, wie auch den pathetischen, stark mit Metaphern überfrachteten Stil des Gedichts kann man als Versuch verstehen, den revolutionären Elan der Arbeiter erneut zu entfachen. (183)

Mühsam's revolutionary ideals were never realized. In 1934 he was brutally murdered by the Nazis in the Oranienburg concentration camp. Forty years later in the GDR, however, his legacy survived in the work of singers who also saw themselves as part of the same literary protest tradition as Herwegh and Heine, which by now also included Mühsam and Brecht. Wolf Biermann, for example, conjured up an image of bygone revolutionaries in "Der Hugenottenfriedhof" from 1969. Like Mühsam's "Der freie Geist," this song laments the passing away of the revolutionary verve associated with icons of the past. In the song Biermann strolls past socialist dignitaries such as Brecht, Hanns Eisler, and John Heartfield, who lie buried in the Berlin "Hugenotten" cemetery. As the chorus "Wie nah sind uns manche Toten, doch / Wie tot sind uns manche, die leben"[12] suggests, the example of the dead revolutionary artists is a reminder to the living leaders that their so-called revolution in the GDR was a phony one.

As explored in the last chapter, the evoking of such iconic images of revolutionary heritage had the aim of questioning the GDR's self-image as the historical continuity of the revolutionary *Arbeiterbewegung*. As Karen Leeder writes of Steffen Mensching's early poem "Traumhafter Ausflug mit Rosa L.," the subject's erotic but unfulfilled encounter with the dead Spartakus revolutionary Rosa Luxemburg serves to depict "how far the present falls short of revolutionary aspirations of the past" (1996, 127). Idealistic, youthful, and vibrant images of the heroine standing barefoot among the red poppies in a Polish field clash with the theme of funerals ("Marmor, Schleifen und Lilien") and official remembrances

("Kränzen und Märschen des Winters"),[13] which is all that revolutionary heritage had come to amount to in the GDR.

Mühsam himself was the "dead revolutionary" conjured up in Karls Enkel's *Liedertheater* program "Von meiner Hoffnung laß ich nicht — Der Pilger Mühsam"[14] in 1980. As in Mensching's poem mentioned above, the motif of funeral and remembrance features strongly. This was controversial. SED Party functionaries would have preferred that such an official remembrance of Mühsam focused on his utopian *Kampflieder*.[15] But examples of those are interspersed with poems relating to death and defeat, as well as playful cabaret texts that lent themselves to ironical present-day interpretations. An example of the latter is Hans-Eckardt Wenzel's rendition of Mühsam's satirical poem "Das Volk der Denker" from 1925, which forms the highpoint of the program. Wenzel's ironic facial expressions and gestures indicate clearly the significance of this text to the present day. It parodies the complacency and ultimate naivety of comrades who believe in the historical inevitability of the communist utopia:

> [. . .]
> Die Zukunft kommt! Von selbst und ungerufen!
> Nur eine Serie von Entwicklungsstufen
> steht noch bevor. — So lehrt's die Theorie.
> Du liest und lernst. Den Rücken krumm gebogen,
> durchwühlst du Heft um Heft und Band um Band.
> O armes Volk! Von aller Welt betrogen,
> betrügst du selbst dich um dein Sehnsuchtsland.

But it is the funeral motif that provides the aesthetic focal point of the program, which begins and ends with Mühsam's poem "Ehrung der Toten." In the lines "Menschen laßt die Toten ruhn / und erfüllt ihr Hoffen!" yearning for utopian change is relativized by the image of death. The members of the cast, wearing black funeral dress, carry the coffin onto the stage, and Mensching, leader of the funeral procession, announces: "Wir möchten jetzt mit den Trauerfeierlichkeiten beginnen." Here arises an irresolvable contradiction: they celebrate Mühsam's life, but in emphasizing his funeral — the coffin remains on stage for the duration of the show — Karls Enkel mourns the loss in the socialist present of the utopianism that Mühsam stood for.

The contradiction runs throughout. Inherent in the title of the Mühsam poem "Von meiner Hoffnung laß ich nicht" was the belief of the group's leaders Hans-Eckardt Wenzel and Steffen Mensching in the struggle for change. This spirit is, however, constantly relativized by the context of performance, that is, by the reality of the political impotence of the individual in the GDR. In "Gesang des jungen Anarchisten," for example, they sing with a hint of irony: "Von Gesetzen nicht gebunden, /

Ohne Herrn und ohne Staat — / frei nur kann die Welt gesunden, / Künftige, durch eure Tat." Stefan Körbel's interpretation of "Der Gefangene" alludes to similar restrictions in the present. In emphasizing the refrain, "Sich fügen, heißt lügen," he mirrors the historical parallel of the dangers of social conformism.

In light of the above, the GDR can be viewed as being at a historical standstill: just as Mühsam had protested that nothing had changed since 1848, Karls Enkel boldly questioned what had changed for the better in the GDR. This is the implied message of Wenzel's rendition of "Kalender 1913": "Im Jahre achtundvierzig schien / die neue Zeit heraufzuziehn / Ihr, meine Zeitgenossen wißt, / daß heut noch nicht mal Vormärz ist."

The funereal motif is never far away. Karls Enkel's reciting of Mühsam's German translation of "The Internationale" was significant on two levels. Despite severe beatings by Nazi *Sturmabteilung* (SA) guards during his captivity, Mühsam had refused to sing the popular Nazi song "Das Horst-Wessel-Lied" (also known as "Die Fahne hoch," from its first line) and had sung "The Internationale" instead.[16] Here it is sung unaccompanied as a lament, Wenzel beating out a slow rhythm on the sound board of his guitar. The lines are separated by long theatrical pauses, creating an alienation or defamiliarization effect. This provokes the audience to view the protesting sentiments of the song in terms of their present-day validity: "Vom Staat und vom Gesetz betrogen, / in Steuerfesseln eingeschnürt, / so wird uns Gleichheit vorgelogen / vom Reichen, der kein Elend spürt."

The production climaxes with the juxtaposition of the "Soldatenlied" with the funeral of Mühsam. The song urges soldiers — again with a controversial subtext in the GDR context — to turn their weapons against the rulers and to free the world. Such rebelliousness is, however, countered by despondency in Mensching's announcement of the funeral procession: "Die Revolution ist vorüber. Räumen Sie die Straßen auf. Wir wollen mit den Trauerfeierlichkeiten beginnen." The production thus ends in an unresolved contradiction. While the positive perspective on the future is sustained, it is held in check by the all-pervading image of death.[17]

Despite intermittently coming into conflict with the authorities, such attempts by Karls Enkel to give the proletarian and literary *Erbe* a renewed significance for the present day were welcomed by the critical intelligentsia of the literary establishment. Influential figures such as Wolfgang Heise from the *Kulturwissenschaft* department at the Humboldt University in Berlin, where group members Wenzel, Mensching, and Stefan Körbel were studying, frequently gave good references to fend off potential bans or censorship.[18] Heise was also a prominent member of the Kulturbund der DDR, which sponsored two of the group's productions: "Deutschland meine Trauer. Ein Johannes-R.-Becher-Abend" (1981)[19] and "Die komische Tragödie des 18. Brumaire nach Karl Marx" (1983).[20]

In West Germany such delving into the proletarian past was perceived as having much less cultural significance. In 1986 Dieter Süverkrüp and Walter Andreas Schwarz released a record of Mühsam songs entitled *Ich lade Euch zum Requiem*. It is clear that Mühsam's requiem for his dead revolutionary colleagues had different connotations for a West German audience than for one in the GDR. The final verse proclaims: "Das Heut' erkennt das Gestern nicht, / trotz Ruhmeskranz und Seelenmessen. — / Wer Zukunft schuf, bleibt unvergessen. / Erst die Geschichte hält Gericht." In the GDR, these lines were dripping with irony even as late as the 1980s because of the hollowness of the state's claims to be the continuation of this past — the dead revolutionaries had indeed effectively been forgotten. In the West German version, on the other hand, there is no intended irony, only the invoking of a tradition in a country where radical socialism has ceased to play a major cultural role. By 1986, the heady days of student rebellion were long gone. Süverkrüp and Schwarz's modest motivation is to keep the spirit alive "für die, die auf dem beschwerlichen Weg in die Zukunft Mühsams Idealismus brauchen als Stärkung und Bestätigung," as the CD booklet informs us.

In the course of the 1980s, however, dealing with the concept of utopia became questionable even for a GDR audience. Karls Enkel's approach was dismissed by the young avant-garde "Prenzlauer Berg" poets of the 1980s and accused of being a new form of didacticism for daring to deal *at all* with an utopian discourse that had long lost its relevance (Leeder 1996, 40). We shall later examine this accusation with regard to Karls Enkel's treatment of the Spanish Civil War in its *Liedertheater* production "Spanier aller Länder" in 1985. First let us look at some of the aesthetic categories of the early twentieth-century political song that influenced the genre from the 1960s onwards.

The Aesthetics of Resistance: The Grotesque

The end of censorship that occurred with the fall of the *Kaiserreich* in late 1918 and the continued political turmoil of the 1920s resulted in a creative climate of artistic experimentation that initiated a golden age of political song. Max Reinhardt revived the Schall und Rauch cabaret in Berlin in December 1919. Wedekind and Mühsam's mantel as the leading satirical songwriters of prewar cabaret was now taken over by Kurt Tucholsky, Walter Mehring, and Erich Kästner.

One of the techniques used and developed in the literary cabaret milieu was the grotesque. Horror stories with elements of the macabre had been a historical feature of the sensationalist *Moritat* variety of the street ballad. The shock effect of this ballad type had been exploited by Frank Wedekind in the satires he performed at the turn-of-the-century cabaret Die elf

Scharfrichter in Munich. These included the provocatively anti-bourgeois "Der Tantenmörder," for which he was taken to court:[21]

> Ich hab' meine Tante geschlachtet,
> Meine Tante war alt und schwach;
> Ich hatte bei ihr übernachtet
> Und grub in den Kisten-Kasten nach.
>
> Da fand ich goldene Haufen,
> Fand auch an Papieren gar viel
> Und hörte die alte Tante schnaufen
> Ohn' Mitleid und Zartgefühl.
>
> [. . .]
>
> Ich hab' meine Tante geschlachtet,
> Meine Tante war alt und schwach;
> Ihr aber, o Richter, ihr trachtet
> Meiner blühenden Jugend-Jugend nach.[22]

In the Weimar Republic Walter Mehring used this shock technique, for example, in "Die kleine Stadt," where he exposes the hypocrisy of social attitudes towards single mothers, the song ending with the ominous hint of a tragic ending for mother and child.[23] Brecht used it in "Von der Kindesmörderin Marie Farrar" from *Hauspostille*. Here the macabre subject matter of infanticide is contrasted starkly by the moral of the refrain: "Doch ihr, ich bitte euch, wollt nicht in Zorn verfallen / Denn alle Kreatur braucht Hilf von allen."[24]

The shock effect could be intensified by the use of directly grotesque imagery as in Brecht's song "Legende des toten Soldaten." He had written this as a satire of the German *Heldenballade* when he was a medical student in a military hospital at the end of the First World War. In this satire of the concept of "Treue über den Tod hinaus" (see Riha, 63–75), the military authorities deem the corpse of a soldier fit to return to battle. Brecht's grotesque comic perspective portrays a dead, stinking, and decaying soldier goose-stepping at the front of a military parade. This is reminiscent of a trait of the grotesque in the history of painting such as the tradition of the *Totentanz,* in which a procession of skeletons are depicted dancing towards the grave. Combined here with a satirical poetic distance the grotesque element exposes the hypocrisy of the rulers and military and the pointlessness of war. With the image of the dead soldier Brecht addresses the concept of the interchangeability of men in war.

Forty years later in the GDR the young Wolf Biermann encountered the literary and theatrical *Erbe* of Brecht while an apprentice at the Berliner Ensemble. Risking the wrath of the SED, which presumed to dictate how Brecht's heritage was to be interpreted, Biermann appropriated several aesthetic aspects of Brecht in his writing as well as in his performance techniques, using these to criticize the GDR. For example, he, too, played on the image of the grotesque body. "Soldat, Soldat," an anti-war song from 1963, is reminiscent of Brecht's "Legende des toten Soldaten" in referring to the facelessness and interchangeability of soldiers: "Soldaten sehn sich alle gleich / lebendig und als Leich" (Biermann, 103). His "Ballade vom Mann, der sich eigenhändig beide Füße abhackt," also from 1963, parodies the self-defeating policies of the SED: a man steps in a pile of feces and finds a solution in chopping off his foot:

> Es war einmal ein Mann
> der trat mit seinem Fuß
> mit seinem nackten Fuß
> in einen Scheißhaufen.
>
> Er ekelte sich sehr
> vor seinem einen Fuß
> er wollt mit diesem Fuß
> kein Stück mehr weitergehn
>
> Und Wasser war nicht da
> zu waschen seinen Fuß
> für seinen einen Fuß
> war auch kein Wasser da
>
> Da nahm der Mann sein Beil
> und hackte ab den Fuß
> den Fuß hackte er ab
> in Eil mit seinem Beil (98–99)[25]

He cuts off the wrong foot and then, in his rage, cuts off the other one too. Biermann, who was expelled from the Party in 1963, makes the parallel clear: "Es hackte die Partei / sich ab so manchen Fuß / so manchen guten Fuß / abhackte die Partei." But at this early stage in his career, Biermann still holds onto the possibility of reform, singing that unlike this man's, the Party's foot can still grow back on: "Jedoch im Unterschied / zu jenem obigen Mann / wächst der Partei manchmal / der Fuß schon wieder an" (99).

It is highly likely that Biermann's grotesque imagery in "Ballade vom Mann" was influenced by the dismemberment of the character Herr Schmitt by two clowns in Brecht's play *Das Badener Lehrstück vom Einverständnis*. This had been intended as an abstract portrayal of the brutality of power relationships in capitalist society — in short: to demonstrate that people do not help one another. The slapstick was an example of Brecht's alienation technique, also known as the estrangement or defamiliarization effect (*Verfremdungseffekt*), which he developed in his theater productions throughout the 1920s and 1930s. The intention was to use artificial (un-naturalistic) performance techniques to prevent the audience's identification with the characters and thereby keep its attention focused on the political message.

This alienation technique is evident in Biermann's "Ballade vom Mann." We see it in the song's function as a parable (here of how the Party cuts its own nose off to spite its face); in the aforementioned grotesque lyrical imagery; but also on the level of performance: in the singer's exaggerated fricative on every repetition of the word "Fuß" and the jarring elongations of certain vowels, for example, the "ei" in "Partei." These guide the audience towards the parodic intent.[26]

A further example of Biermann's use of the grotesque can be found in relation to his identification with the figure of François Villon. This will be dealt with in chapter 3 on "Narrative Role-Play."

In the 1980s Wenzel and Mensching, too, used strong elements of the grotesque. Their clown costumes — Wenzel appeared as a white clown with painted, fat, red lips and Mensching as a dark Mephisto figure — immediately created a grotesque, alienating milieu for their songs and scenes. In traditional folk culture, according to Mikhail Bakhtin, the clown's large, red-painted mouth is a symbol of the carnivalesque grotesque body "that swallows the world and is itself swallowed by the world."[27] In this, it symbolizes transformation; the unfinished; the never completed. When Wenzel and Mensching made use of this fair-ground tradition, this heightened the alienation effect in their — for GDR standards — highly risky portrayals of political leaders. As mentioned, Mensching's 1982 poem "Égalité" from the *Hammer-Rehwü*[28] is a mocking degradation of political leaders sitting on the toilet. In the *Liedertheater* program "Altes aus der Da Da eR"[29] from autumn 1989 (adapted for film by Jörg Foth in 1990[30]) Wenzel and Mensching grotesquely caricature the aging Politbüro. In one scene, the duo, in clown masks and costumes, sprinkle powder on each other's hair, bow their heads and shoulders, and transform into decrepit old men. Wenzel, in a traditional carnivalesque inversion whereby objects are employed in an arbitrary topsy turvy fashion, uses his guitar as a walking stick. With mock pathos they perform the tragicomedy of the soon-to-be deposed leaders, singing: "Eh du dich versiehst mein Freund / Ist die Zeit verronnen/ Und vom Glücke dieser Welt / Hast du nichts gewonnen / Ja, ja, ja, ja / Weißt ja wie gut ich dir bin." The clowns continue to relentlessly lampoon the GDR political hierarchy in the song "Undank ist der Welten Lohn," singing with ironical self-pity of the personal tragedy unfolding:

Ich hab mich nie gebremst für meinen Staat
Regierte viel parteilich Tag und Nacht
Jetzt bin ich alt und ernte den Salat
Das alte Eisen wird nun ausgelacht
Bin selber schuld das hab ich nun davon
Undank ist der Welten Lohn.

Montage Technique

Singers such as Wolf Biermann, Wenzel and Mensching, and Konstantin
Wecker were also highly influenced by the montage technique that had
been pioneered in the Weimar Republic. The montage aesthetic was a reflection of the ambiguous, hybridic nature of the political song between
high and low culture that was particularly evident in the early Weimar
cabarets. The concept of *Gebrauchsmusik* and *Gebrauchslyrik* (music and
lyrics "for use") was widespread. It encompassed the ideals of practicality,
usefulness, relevance, didacticism, and utilization of modern technology
(Cook 1988, 21). In a modern, fast-moving, urban world, where communication could not be taken for granted, music and words were now
written with a particular target audience in mind and with a specific purpose, for example, for political enlightenment or agitation. Montage was a
major communicative technique in this respect.

Montage was pioneered in Berlin dada, cinema, and cabaret. The dada
movement had been founded at the Cabaret Voltaire in Zurich in 1916
by artists and writers such as Hugo Ball, Tristan Zara, Hans Arp, and
Richard Huelsenbeck. Due to the dadaists' rejection of bourgeois values
in general (particularly militarism) figures such as John Heartfield and
George Grosz had aspects in common with the communists. But the
communists distrusted dada because of its rejection of logical systems of
thought. In fact the dadaists were essentially apolitical, as this 1924 poem
by Kurt Schwitters indicates:

Was ist Wahnsinn?

Wahnsinn läßt sich teilen.
Wahnsinn ist dividierbar und multiplizierbar.
Man lernt Wahnsinn am besten kennen, wenn man sich von
    ihm entfernt.
Wahnsinn ist Politik.
Dada ist gegen Politik, weil gegen Wahnsinn.
Politik steht im Weichbild unserer Zeit.
Möge selbiges Bild bald weichen und unserer Zeit freien
    Raum lassen.[31]

Dada was intended, according to Ball, to be apolitical, whimsical, spontaneous, foolish, and should represent "a farce of nothingness."[32] In the wider cultural picture this latter aspect was in tune with the nihilism of Brecht and the poets returning from the war. The randomness of the dadaist montage principle in art and poetry reflected — in the wake of the slaughter of the First World War — the fragmentation of modern life devoid of sense or purpose. There emerges a dislocated relationship to time and history. The senseless catastrophe of the war had shattered the illusion of progress and temporal continuity embedded in the ideals of the Enlightenment. The principle of randomness, breaks, and interruptions was a major strategy in the montage-based dada art of John Heartfield and George Grosz and in the poems of their Berlin colleague Walter Mehring.[33] With its reportage style, Mehring's "Achtung Gleisdreieck," for example, refers to the chaos of the famous triangular station junction in Berlin where trains and people converged and departed: "Jeder in / Anderer / Richtung und / Achtung! Das /Gleisdreieck."[34] The poem is a montage consisting of image fragments of different aspects of Berlin city life: forms of entertainment, modes of transportation, and political sloganeering, none of which have much in common with each other apart from their random simultaneity in the big city (Jelavich 1996, 146–47). Mehring's "Berliner Simultan" (1920), sung by Rosa Valetti, was typically dadaesque in its approach, with frivolous, throw-away lines such as: "Her mit dem Scheck! / Schiebung mit Speck / Komm, süsse Puppe! / Is' alles schnuppe." Such references to black marketeering appear amidst a collage of random, fastflowing images from public life, which among other things point to the rise of the far right and anti-Semitic violence: "Das Volk steht auf! Die Fahnen raus! [. . .] Die Reaktion flaggt schon am DOM/ Mit Hakenkreuz und Blaukreuzgas — / Monokel contra Hakennas' / — Auf zum Pogrom / Beim Hippodrom!" (Mehring, 78–79).

If modernist art after the First World War reflected a crisis; a break with cultural traditions and assumptions, it is interesting to look at GDR lyric and song from the mid-1960s onwards. For example, the significance of the use of montage in GDR *Liedertheater* must be viewed in terms of the general trend in GDR literature of this period to reflect discontinuities and ruptures. After the conviction of the *Aufbau* period of the 1950s and early 1960s, the SED's claim of continuity with the revolutionary tradition was becoming increasingly problematic. For many critical writers, history could no longer be viewed in the traditional Marxist sense "as a rationally transparent, dynamic, and linear process, which would ultimately lead to the communist goal" (Leeder, 108). Rather, from the latesixties onwards, there was the acute sense of being "out of step," of a "gap in time."[35] This idea of a break with cultural tradition was expressed by an adoption of modernist, anti-realist literary techniques by writers such as Christa Wolf, Heiner Müller, and Volker Braun. But it was younger writers, those "born into"[36] this historical standstill, who experienced its contradictions most keenly. In the poetry of Steffen Mensching, Hans-Eckardt Wenzel, Uwe Kolbe, Jörg Kowalski, and others, this resulted in a "subjective acquisition" of history (Leeder, 115). The montage aesthetic behind this approach is reflected in Steffen Mensching's poem "London, fünfzehnter März dreiundachtzig" (1982) in which the poet adapts a telegram sent by Friedrich Engels announcing the death of Karl Marx:

> Gestern mittag, 2 Uhr 45. Das stärkste Herz
> Das ich gekannt,
> Hat ausgeschlagen. Die Menschheit ist um
> Einen Kopf kürzer. Lokalgrößen
> Und kleine Talente, wo nicht Schwindler,
> Bekommen freie Hand [. . .]

In Mensching's presentation of Engel's call to keep up the utopian struggle there is a subjective slant: the poet's basic optimism is tinged with an ironic sadness bordering on resentment. It reflects the skepticism that was felt at the time regarding postponing a "life in the now" for the sake of a future utopian goal:

> [. . .] Ja
> Der endliche Sieg bleibt sicher, aber Umwege,
> Lokale und temporäre
> Verirrungen werden anwachsen. Nun — wir
> Müssens durchfressen. Wozu
> Anders sind wir da. Unsere Courage verlieren
> Wir darum noch nicht. Dein Engels. (1984, 24)

This poem was recited by Mensching in Karls Enkel's *Liedertheater* production "Die komische Tragödie des 18. Brumaire" in 1983. Reminiscent of the group's treatment of Erich Mühsam, it was accompanied by music in the style of a funeral lament. The montage effect is clear in the convergence of two time levels: the one reflects Engel's sadness at the death of Marx in 1873; the other reflects contemporary sadness at how, 100 years later in 1983, Marx's ideas had not been realized.

Musical Montage

The montage-based use of music by performers such as Biermann, Wenzel and Mensching, and Konstantin Wecker can also be traced back to the 1920s. Montage was a feature of the trend of *Neue Sachlichkeit* (New Objectivity) in literature, music, photography, and art. This entailed sobriety, detachment, and a non-expressionistic matter-of-factness, and was evident in the lyric of Brecht, Tucholsky, Mehring, and Kästner. In the world of serious music, *Neue Sachlichkeit* was pursued in the *Zeitoper* (Opera for Our Time) composed by Kurt Weill, Paul Hindemith, and Ernst Kreneck in the late 1920s. Like *Gebrauchsmusik, Zeitoper* recognized the gulf between composer and the modern musical audience and sought to create music for the members of that wider audience.[37] *Zeitoper* renounced the dramatic, expressionistic model of Wagnerian opera and incorporated features of the genres used in revues, such as popular song (including the sentimental German *Schlager* variety), American jazz, and modern dance-steps such as the Charleston. It also made use of new technology (slide projections, film clips, and elaborate new stage settings) which had been pioneered in the political theater of the communist director Erwin Piscator (Cook 1988, 34–39).

In Weill's collaboration with Brecht on *Die Dreigroschenoper* in 1928 and *Aufstieg und Fall der Stadt Mahagonny* in 1929, the music took on a new political function. Here, the concept of *Zeitoper* was combined with Brecht's emerging theory of alienation effects (*Verfremdungseffekte*). Music, text, and performance now had to shake audiences out of their passive consumption of art, to lead them to a critical awareness of its themes. Weill's compositions supported Brecht's satire on the illusionist consumer paradise represented by the city Mahagonny. A musical montage technique was employed in which elements of opera, popular ballads, jazz, and sea chanty (as well as rhythmic influences from Stravinsky) formed dissonances with one another or created tension with the content of the lyrics to create an alienation effect.[38]

The legacy of Weill and Hanns Eisler (whose theory of the dialectical interplay between text and music will be dealt with below) continued to be a major strategy in the revived political song from the 1960s onwards. This was particularly so in the GDR, where the proletarian musical heritage was most heavily nurtured. While Wolf Biermann did not write Eislerian *Kampflieder* — his ballads, *Moritaten,* and *Spottlieder* reflected an altogether more subjective style[39] — he had learned, as one of Eisler's most famous pupils, "daß die Musik nicht nur ein Transportmittel sein soll."[40] Biermann's songs illustrate the Eislerian practice of using music to promote dialogic interplay between different textual levels. In "Enfant perdu" from 1969, Biermann's lament for Florian Havemann, son of the political dissident Robert Havemann, who had abandoned the GDR for the West, the church tonality of the harmony in the minor key expresses the sadness of loss (Kühn, 89). This mood is abruptly broken up, however, by a change in rhythm to a staccato pulse, as Biermann acknowledges the fact that for many in the GDR emigration is never far from their thoughts: "Abgang ist überall" (217).

The use of music to support parody is evident in Biermann's 1965 song "Acht Argumente für die Beibehaltung des Namens Stalinallee." Here the singer mocks the changing of the name of the street to Karl-Marx-Allee after the revelations of Stalin's crimes at the Soviet Union's Twentieth Communist Party Congress in 1956. For Biermann the name should stay as a monument to the legacy of the Stalinism, which had so corrupted the GDR:

> Es steht in Berlin eine Straße
> Die steht auch in Leningrad
> Die steht genauso in mancher
> Andern großen Stadt
>
>> Und darum heißt sie auch STALINALLEE
>> Mensch, Junge versteh
>> Und die Zeit ist passé
>> [. . .]
>
> Die weißen Kacheln fallen
> Uns auf den Kopf ja nur
> Die Häuser stehen ewig!
> (in Baureparatur!!)
>
>> Auch darum heißt das Ding STALINALLEE
>
> Karl Marx, der große Denker
> Was hat er denn getan
> Daß man sein' guten Namen
> Schreibt an die Kacheln dran?!
>
>> Das Ding heißt doch nicht KARL-MARX-ALLEE
>> Mensch, Junge, versteh:
>> STALINALLEE (160–62)

The air-pumping effect of the harmonium conjures up the sound of a carousel and street party celebrations (Kuhn, 124). Through this use of music Biermann caricatures the abandon with which the Party renames streets and towns in order to manipulate history.

The influence of Weill and Eisler is also evident in the music of Konstantin Wecker in West Germany. Musical montage was a means of expressing contradiction and ambiguity. This can be contrasted with the monotony of the music of some of the more militant Burg Waldeck *Liedermacher* (such as the later Degenhardt), for whom music became subordinated to the political statement. But Wecker's message was also political: in a response to increased police surveillance of alleged political deviants following the activities of the Red Army Faction in the late 1970s Wecker wrote

"Hexeneinmaleins": "Immer noch werden Hexen verbrannt / auf den Scheitern der Ideologien. / Irgendwer ist immer der Böse im Land / und dann kann man als Guter / und die Augen voll Sand / in die heiligen Kriege ziehn!" (1978). This song is a montage of rock and classical musical styles. The Carl Orff-influenced operatic motifs support the idea of a hunt, thereby underscoring the theme of the *Hexenjagd,* or witch-hunt. As Matthias Henke observes:

> Expressive Rhythmik, vielseitiger Einsatz der Stimme (geflüstert, gerufen, gesungen, solistisch, im Chor) und der ikonographische Gebrauch der Instrumente (Orgel und Trommel als Symbol für Kirche und Militär) lassen aus den Texten die Schreie der Gequälten hören.[41]

Wecker's song "Einen braucht der Mensch zum Treten" from 1984 also reflects a modernist aesthetic of disruption. Wecker uses the chorus, in a way reminiscent of an Eisler *Lehrstück-Lied* (Henke 1987, 212), to disrupt the conventional song structure, having it burst in unexpectedly and repeatedly. This defamiliarization, also caused by starkly contrasting musical accompaniments throughout the song, intends to draw attention to the textual content: how feelings of inadequacy are often at the root of social ills such as xenophobia: "Es gibt ein ganz probates Mittel / Um den Alltagsfrust zu überstehen / Dazu braucht man keinen Doktortitel / Man löst mit einem Türken das Problem."[42]

In the post-Biermann generation in the GDR Karls Enkel was another example of a younger generation using montage to express dissent from the dogmas of cultural tradition. Here, too, music could have a supportive or an ironic, undermining function. Forms with certain associations (folk, pop, waltzes, marches, tangos, classical string-quartets) formed a dialectical relationship with lyrical content. An example was Wenzel's performance of the previously quoted poem "Égalité" in the *Hammer-Rehwü* of 1982. The rococo string arrangement with its rather prudish associations supports the mock innocence of the white clown Wenzel's delivery. This is, however, contradicted by the profanity of the text, which, in carnivalesque fashion, brings the lofty world of leading politicians down to the level of what Bakhtin terms "the bodily lower stratum."[43] Similarly in Karls Enkel's Goethe program "Dahin! Dahin!"[44] of 1982, defamiliarizing, festive klezmer and folk accompaniments of Goethe's poetry were juxtaposed with more conventional Schubertian arrangements. In this way they alerted the audience to a plebeian dimension in Goethe's work hitherto unacknowledged in GDR literary reception of the poet (Robb 1998, 39–40).

Agitprop Revue

Montage was also an important aspect of the agitprop revue of the 1920s, elements of which were revived in the political song scenes of both the Federal Republic and the GDR. In the 1920s agitprop revue had been distinct from the bourgeois literary cabaret in that it had overtly revolutionary aspirations. A major player was Erwin Piscator, a war veteran and Communist Party member who had founded the first proletarian theater in Berlin in 1920. He staged the *Roter Rummel* revue in Berlin in support for the KPD election campaign of 1924. It was a multimedia event comprising songs and sketches. The action was augmented by film or slide projections, in keeping with the montage aesthetic of the age. In the scenes the players acted out various social roles, for example, the policeman, the worker, and the capitalist. They directly engaged the audience and agitated with political slogans and arguments that demonstrated the power relationships of the class conflict.[45]

In the late 1960s in West Germany a variation of this agitprop tradition — as opposed to established political cabaret acts like Wolfgang Neuss and Hanns Dieter Hüsch — was practiced by the group Floh de Cologne.[46] Stemming from the radical student movement, their first album in 1968 was a collaboration with Dieter Süverkrüp entitled *Vietnam*. All royalties were transferred to a foundation to benefit the Vietnamese. With their montage of rock music, political lyrics, humor, and lunacy, they became known as the German answer to the American rock groups The Fugs and Mothers Of Invention.[47] The sleeve of their album *Fliessbandbabys Beat Show* shows a nineteen-point step-by-step guide to becoming politically active. Their most acclaimed album was *Profitgeier* (1971), "a highly imaginative rock opera" executed at a furious tempo, in which "the group members acted as different characters or proclaimed political views on the class-divided society."[48]

Floh de Cologne performed several times at the annual Festival des politschen Liedes in East Berlin. But their form of agitprop rock theater was too politically direct to be practiced by GDR groups. From the mid-1970s onwards a new form known as *Liedertheater,* distinct from GDR cabaret,[49] was pioneered by groups such as Schicht, Brigade Feuerstein, and Karls Enkel. Disenchanted with the limitations on the political song form imposed by the censorship in the GDR,[50] they used parodic techniques from 1920s proletarian revue to expose contradictions in their own society. A technique employed by Erwin Piscator in the 1920s was that of dismantling ("Demontage"), whereby well-known quotations are cut up and satirically recast. This is evident in the *Hammer-Rehwü* of 1982, where, for example, Spencer Davis's 1960s rock hit "Keep on Running" becomes "Halt zur Stange," the motto of a social conformist or "Mitläufer" and Zarah Leander's "Es wird einmal ein Wunder geschehen," from the 1942 film *Die große Liebe,* is transformed into a parody of the utopian delusions of the GDR leadership and their love affair with the socialist ideal: "Es wird einmal ein Wunder geschehn, / Und dann werden tausend Märchen wahr. / Ich weiß, so schnell kann keine Liebe vergehn, / Die so groß ist und so wunderbar."

Similarly the opening song, "Du, laß dich nicht bescheißen," constitutes a play on the line "Laßt euch nicht verführen" from Brecht and Weill's *Mahagonny.*" The new version laughs at the utopian belief in a future communist paradise and implies that the government uses people as mere objects in the pursuit of that goal. The parodic hybrid functions by adapting the original *Mahagonny* lines "Laßt euch nicht verführen / Zu Fron und Ausgezehr. / Was kann euch Angst noch rühren / Ihr sterbt mit allen Tieren / Und es kommt nichts nachher"[51] to become: "Du, laß dich nicht einwickeln / Von Liebe, Fron und Ehr / Wir sind Verbrauchsartikel / Und sterben wie Karnickel. / Und es kommt nichts nachher."[52]

Although it appropriated the form and structure of the proletarian revue, the *Hammer-Rehwü* turned the whole concept on its head. Rather than propagating socialism, it made fun of the symbols of GDR authority, namely the general, the dictator, and the worker (see Robb 1998, 55). And in a clear distancing from the didacticism of proletarian revue, the cast declares to the audience in the epilogue that there will be no moral:

> Ihr aber, die ihr nutzlos rumgesessen / Mit euren fiesen Füßen, dicken Bäuchen, / Schiefgegrinsten Fressen, / Was sagt ihr nun? / Was nehmt ihr mit ins Heim? / [. . .] Mein Freund, ich will nicht sagen, du bist bös / Doch etwas dümmlich hockst du hier / Nervös, auf deinem Stuhl, / Weil die Moral, es ist fatal, / Nicht mitgeliefert wurd in diesem Fall.

The Political Song Theory of Hanns Eisler

Despite the satirical provocation of the literary chanson, it seldom proposed a revolutionary solution to society's ills. Furthermore, the fact that it was targeted at a bourgeois taste group (Jelavich, 134–35) undermined its political effectiveness, according to Benjamin, who wrote in 1931 that "linke Melancholie" had merely become a marketable commodity within a bourgeois avant-garde milieu.[53] By 1929 Brecht was departing from the subjective approach of his *Hauspostille* poem collection and was increasingly writing songs for the political use of a mass audience. He began collaborating with Hanns Eisler, a composer who shared Brecht's own increasingly Marxist beliefs. Eisler conceived a theory of the political song that combined current modernist aesthetics with a revolutionary ideological stance. In the mid-1920s he had been influenced by the Soviet avant-garde and was impressed by the agitprop group Blaue Blusen, which made current problems tangible by means of photography, film, and radio.[54] Working with the Berlin group Das rote Sprachrohr, Eisler learned to use music to represent political concerns. He found that "music, if intelligently used, was in a position effectively to indicate the relationship between the various topics and to intimate the emotional level" (Betz 1982, 65). This approach to composition — geared towards agitation and enlightenment of a proletarian audience — contrasted to that of bourgeois music, which Eisler believed was composed for passive consumption, for the purpose of recovery and reproduction.[55] Within this broad category of "bourgeois music," serious music, such as Schönberg, was a means of entertainment for an educated elite, while popular music such as the *Schlager* merely served to dull the minds of the masses (Eisler 1973, 178). Proletarian music therefore had to rid itself of all trappings of bourgeois music. This included the melodic logic and harmony of the *Schlager* and *Volkslieder,* which Eisler believed to be corrupt in their encouragement of passivity and conformity (170).

Eisler's approach mirrored Brecht's theory of Epic Theater in that actors had to preserve distance, that is, not lose themselves in their roles. In this respect the affectation of bourgeois music, as reflected in the personality cult of a conductor, had to be replaced in the militant songs by a "kalte Grundhaltung" that helped impart the political message (170). The words should be presented rhythmically and precisely, as if in a lecture. For Brecht and Eisler this particular attribute was to be found in the singing style of Ernst Busch.

In short, workers' music should be challenging, should not promote conformity, but should be as transparent as possible. Its first aim should not be to revel in its own artistry, but to demonstrate a particular *Gebrauchswert.* As Betz states, "beauty, aesthetic charm and enjoyment were no longer the highest aim [of the music], but were pressed into its service" (82). To these ends, the technique of musical montage was used to communicate the Marxist vision of social dialectics and the class struggle, as illustrated in the discussion of songs that follows.

Eisler's composition for Tucholsky's "Lied der Wohltätigkeit" is a montage of cabaret chanson, marching rhythms, and jazz counterpoints. The song, which was sung by Ernst Busch, is laden with sarcasm. It protests at the hypocrisy of the capitalists, who pretend to be working in the interests of the proletariat:

> Sieh, da steht das Erholunggsheim
> Einer Aktiengesellschaftsgruppe;
> morgens gibt es Haferschleim
> und abends Gerstensuppe,
> und die Arbeiter dürfen auch in den Park

Sie reichen euch manches Almosen hin
Unter christlichen, frommen Gebeten;
sie pflegen die leidende Wöchnerin,
denn sie brauchen ja die Proleten.
Sie liefern auch einen Armensarg.

Gut, das ist der Pfennig
und wo ist die Mark?

The lighthearted, almost decadent, cabaret aspect of these verses and chorus underline the parody of Tucholsky's lyrics — exposing the sham of the capitalists' good intentions toward the workers. A dialectic tension, however, is continually created by the accompanying march pulse and the jazz inflections. Changes in tempo are used to highlight certain ideas and insights. In the third and final section, the cabaret music subsides, to be replaced entirely by an agitative march rhythm as Busch shouts the emphatic conclusion:

Proleten fallt nicht auf den Schwindel, rein!
Sie schulden euch mehr als sie geben.
Sie schulden euch alles, die Länderei'n,
die Bergwerke und die Wollfärberei'n. . .
sie schulden euch Glück und Leben!
Nimm, was du kriegst! Aber pfeif auf den Quark.
Denk an deine Klasse und die mach stark![56]

Similarly, Eisler's composition for Brecht's "Solidaritätslied" from 1931 constitutes a montage of agitative text, march rhythms, modal ecclesiastic music, and popular jazz. The march provided urgency, the jazz inflections were inserted to increase accessibility, and the collective associations of church music were used to promote class consciousness (Betz, 80). "Solidaritätslied" became the theme song for Brecht and Eisler's *Kuhle Wampe* (1932), a film starring Ernst Busch, which clearly illustrates the milieu of the mass workers' gathering for which the *Kampflied* was conceived. The text itself contains distinct echoes of the militant songs of 1848 and those of the early Mühsam in its call to break the chains of tyranny and overturn the master-slave relationship:

Unsre Herrn, wer sie auch seien
Sehen unsre Zwietracht gern
Denn solang sie uns entzwein
Bleiben sie doch unsre Herrn.
[. . .]
Proletarier aller Länder
Einigt euch und ihr seid frei.

Eure großen Regimenter
Brechen jede Tyrannei!

This, however, is combined with a more purposeful, less romantic vision within the structure of an organized world solidarity movement: "Vorwärts und nicht vergessen / Worin unsre Stärke besteht! / Beim Hungern und beim Essen / Vorwärts, nie vergessen/ Die Solidarität."[57]

Utopia and Defeat 2: The Legacy of the Anti-Fascist Movement and the Spanish Civil War

With the coming to power of the Nazis in 1933 Eisler was unable to properly test the intended effects of the *Kampflied* that he had envisaged in his theory. With the exodus from Germany of left-wing artists including Brecht, Eisler, and Busch, it now remained to be seen how songs could contribute to the international anti-fascist movement. The history of the particular relationship between Brecht, Eisler, and Busch in the early years of exile has been well documented in Albrecht Dümling's *Laßt Euch nicht verführen: Brecht und die Musik.*[58] It was in this period — up until he was arrested by the Nazis in Belgium in 1940 — that Busch made an international name for himself on his journeys between Amsterdam, London, Moscow, and Barcelona as the singer of the anti-fascist song.

Busch was originally a metal worker who had joined the Kiel Arbeiterjugend in 1916 at age 16. After taking singing and acting lessons he became an actor in the Kiel Stadttheater, later moving to Berlin in 1927, where he found roles in Erwin Piscator's Theater am Nollendorfplatz. He greatly impressed as a singer and was invited by Edmund Meisel to sing his settings of Walter Mehring lyrics. Brecht invited him to play Constable Smith in *Die Dreigroschenoper* at the Theater am Schiffbauerdamm in 1928. A year later he worked again with Hanns Eisler in Piscator's production of Mehring's play *Der Kaufmann von Berlin*. Mehring was later to say of Eisler: "[sein] bestes Instrument war Ernst Busch."[59] Busch also performed in the cabarets, where he sang workers' songs such as Julien Arendt's "Seifenlied," Erich Weinert's "Roter Wedding," and David Weber's "Stempellied." Eisler wrote the music for these and often accompanied Busch on the piano.

Busch fled from Nazi Germany to the Netherlands in March 1933, where he performed radio broadcasts specifically targeted at an anti-fascist audience within Germany. In the summer of 1933 Brecht and Eisler compiled a new book entitled *Lieder, Gedichte, Chöre*. With songs such as "Ballade vom Baum und den Ästen," "An die Kämpfer in den KZ Lagern," and "Ballade vom SA-Mann" they hoped to invigorate the anti-fascist resistance. As Dümling writes, it was intended, somewhat idealistically, that the book could be smuggled into Germany to resistance fighters. Three thousand copies were printed, but it is likely that few reached their intended destination (394).

In 1935 Busch went to Moscow, where he worked with lyricist Erich Weinert and played for German communist exiles. He performed on the radio station Komintern, which, with 500 kilowatts of power, was broadcast all over the world. Later, on the eastern front, the Red Army played Busch's singing over public address systems to spread propaganda among the German troops. Author Heiner Kipphardt, confirming the quality of Busch's singing, which had so impressed Brecht and Eisler, recalls as a young German soldier hearing Busch's voice: "Die Stimme verjagte meine Apathie [. . .] Diese Stimme wußte, daß [. . .] die Wahrheit triumphieren würde."[60]

In July 1936 workers and left-wing intellectuals from around the world joined together in the International Brigades to fight against General Franco's overthrow of the democratically-elected socialist government in Spain.[61] In his Moscow exile, Busch began compiling the volume *Canciones de las Brigadas Internacionales,*[62] which appeared in Spain in 1937. It contained Spanish Republican songs such as "Bandera Roja" (best known for its Italian version "Bandiera Rossa") and compositions from Eisler and Paul Dessau, among a host of international worker's songs in several languages. The songs reflected the utopian spirit of the International Brigade fighters, as exemplified by Dessau's "Spaniens Himmel" (otherwise known as "Die Thälmann-Kolonne"):

> Spaniens Himmel breitet seine Sterne
> Über unsre Schützengräben aus
> Und der Morgen grüßt schon aus der Ferne,
> Bald geht es zu neuem Kampf hinaus.
> Die Heimat ist weit, doch wir sind bereit
> Wir kämpfen und siegen für dich: Freiheit. (1937)[63]

The self-sacrifice and resolve of the brigade is evident in Busch's "Lincoln-Bataillon": "In dem Tal dort am Rio Jamara / Schlugen wir unsre blutigste Schlacht / Doch wir haben auf Tod und Verderben / Die Faschisten zum Stehen gebracht" (1937). Erich Weinert's song "Jaramafront" proclaims how the battle of Jamara will serve as a model for the world revolution to come: "wenn die Stunde kommt, /[. . .] Wird die ganze Welt zur Jaramaschlacht." And Busch's "Die Herren Generale" evokes, to the tune of the Spanish folk song "Mamita Mia," a new era in which the chains of servitude will be broken: "Und alle deinen Tränen / mamita mia, / die werden wir rächen. / Und alle unsre Knechtschaft / mamita mia, / die werden wir brechen." Busch journeyed from Moscow to Spain in February 1937 for the publication of *Canciones,* and he himself sang for the brigades. In 1938, under wartime conditions in Barcelona, Busch recorded *Discos de las Brigadas Internacionales,* songs that Jürgen Schebera described as "Höhepunkte kämpfender Kunst unseres Jahrhunderts." In a tribute to Busch, who died in the GDR in 1980, Schebera rated *Canciones* on par with Picasso's *Guernica* in terms of its artistic contribution to the Spanish Civil War.[64]

This musical legacy of the Spanish International Brigade was carried on in the GDR, initially by the workers' choirs and from the mid-1960s onwards by the FDJ-sponsored *Singebewegung.* An altogether more provocative relationship to the Spanish *Kampflieder* was established in 1975 by Wolf Biermann with his recording *Es gibt ein Leben vor dem Tod.* Initially the project had been inspired as a critical response to the GDR's diplomatic recognition of Franco's Spain. But there was a more general cultural criticism: the utopian spirit of the songs of the International Brigade clashed with the stagnation of the socialist ideal in the GDR. Biermann emphasized the irony of this in his performance of Dessau's "Spaniens Himmel." Having long been a compulsory item at FDJ or Party meetings, the song had lost any association with freedom for the average citizen of the GDR. Biermann's response was to parody it, singing it as a slow dirge as opposed to a vibrant, optimistic march. He sang as if he were a cold, frightened young soldier stumbling over words that, according to Biermann, would have been remote to the immediate reality of war in any case. There is a non-commitment: words such as the usually declamatory "Freiheit" tail away at the end of lines or are not sung at all, as in the case of the "nicht" in "Mit uns stehn Kameraden ohnegleichen, / Und ein Rückwärts gibt es für uns nicht." He remembers: "Ich hatte dieses Lied durch meine Interpretation dermaßen gegen den Strich gebürstet, daß es für die Wissenden im Osten eine herzerfrischende Provokation gegen die herrschende Ideologie war, in den Augen der Obrigkeit ein Sakrileg."[65] A comment from Otto F. Riewoldt illustrates the tensions between Biermann and the West German Communist Party (DKP) of the time, whose members mistrusted Biermann's criticism of the GDR. Riewoldt says his approach was in keeping with the defeatist mood among socialist intellectuals of the time: "Biermanns kommunistische Utopie [nährt] sich von Niederlagen, Trauer um die verraten Revolution, Lob der toten, gescheiterten Revolution."[66] This comment foreshadowed the controversy that surrounded Karls Enkel's 1985 program "Spanier aller Länder," with its treatment of the themes of utopia and defeat.

If the 1983 production "Die komische Tragödie des 18. Brumaire" had expressed Karls Enkel's identification with the defeated Parisian proletariat of 1848, 1985's "Spanier aller Länder"[67] explored the group's relationship to the failure of the International Brigade. In this *Liedertheater* production, a collaboration between the group and the well known musician and veteran of the Spanish campaign, Eberhard Schmidt, utopian fighting spirit is again balanced against death and defeat. The heroism of writers who fought on the Republican side is highlighted. This is countered with a mood of melancholy that is conveyed through the medium of montage. As Mensching shouts out "Gestern alles Vergangene [. . .] Doch heute der Kampf" from W. H. Auden's "Spanien 37," the cast, dressed in the uniforms of the International Brigade, sing Schubert and Uhland's "Frühlingsglaube" quietly in the background. The pathos of the fighting spirit is doubly relativized, the optimistic refrain "Nun muß sich alles wenden" from "Frühlingsglaube" contradicted by the sadness of the singing. In this way a moment of revolutionary history is projected onto the contemporary GDR.

Again, mirroring the narratives of the songs of the *Vormärz* and the 1848 revolution, the utopian aspirations of the International Brigade are countered with images of sleep and death. Rilke's "Schlußstück" is adapted as follows: "Groß ist der Tod / Wir sind die seinen / Lachenden Munds / Wenn wir uns mitten im Leben meinen / Wagt er zu weinen / Mitten in uns." A dialogue between Wenzel and Mensching, playing the roles of Don Quixote and Sancho Pansa, relates the dangerous similarity of death and sleep. As they watch the sleeping Republican fighters in the valley below, Quixote observes: "Ein einziges böses Ding hat der Schlaf [. . .] daß er namlich dem Tode so ähnlich sieht, denn zwischen einem Schlafenden und einem Toten ist nur ein geringer Unterschied." Here Walter Benjamin's idea that Western society had not yet awoken from the dream of the nineteenth century[68] is applied to the GDR. With echoes of the Biedermeier period, it relates to the retreat en masse into the inner self that Wenzel and Mensching felt so characterized their own society. Through this technique of association, the GDR appears as a land in slumber.

"Spanier aller Länder" finishes with the internment of the International Brigade fighters in the Gurs concentration camp. Don Quixote acknowledges this defeat in his final speech. As in "Die komische Tragödie," the levels of past and present blend together and the GDR appears as bereft of any utopian perspective. The ghosts of revolutionary ancestors still weigh heavily, but Wenzel and Mensching's sense of responsibility toward them cannot be fulfilled because of the constraints of their time. As the "Jetzt noch nicht" sentiment in Mensching's poem "Für Peter Weiss" provocatively reflects, the GDR in 1985 was simply not yet ready to confront the taboos of the past.[69] As if to underline this fact, the concluding words "Jetzt noch nicht" were omitted from the published version of the poem:

Einmal, später, irgendwann
werden wir die Siegel der Archive brechen.
Beieinander sitzend dann
Das nie Ausgesprochene aussprechen.

[. . . .]

Irgendwann, hoffentlich bald, aber später,
Werden wir die ganze Wahrheit ertragen.
Nennen werden wir Helden Helden
      Verbrechen Verbrechen

Nacheinander werden wir zu Wort uns melden,
das Schweigen brechen,
das taktische dumpfe beredsame Schweigen.
[. . .]
Einmal, später, jetzt noch nicht.[70]

By the same token, the fact that Karls Enkel did not challenge taboo subjects more openly earned them fierce criticism from their audience. Many felt the depiction of the International Brigade's heroism amidst spirited marching music and pathos-laden songs such as "No pasaran" and "Santa Barbara" overshadowed the level of contradiction presented in the clowns' dialogues or in the treatment of the defeat. In retrospect Mensching confessed to having been too much in awe of the sacred socialist heritage that the International Brigade and Eberhard Schmidt represented: "Spanien [war] für uns etwas Hehres [. . . .] Es war sehr schwer für mich, an dieses Heiligtum frech heranzugehen."[71] Wenzel explained they had overestimated their audience's continuing readiness in 1985 to embrace the basic concept of utopia at all:

Aller bisheriger plebejischer Protest/Karneval bei *Karls Enkel* basierte auf der stillschweigenden Übereinkunft, daß es nicht um konservative Weltmodelle geht, die als unausgesprochene Utopie in den Köpfen existierte. Dieser Zustand war, als wir "*Spanier*" produzierten, vorbei [. . .] Das naive Experiment wurde nicht mehr zugelassen.[72]

No matter how challengingly and creatively Karls Enkel treated the theme of utopia in "Spanier aller Länder," by 1985 it was in essence already too late to present it to a critical GDR audience. This was an indication of how rife disillusionment was in the final few years of the state's existence.

In conclusion, the combination of literary movements and revolutionary flashpoints from 1900 until the late 1930s inspired a wealth of German protest song. This formed both a thematic and stylistic reference point for the revived political song of the 1960s onwards. On an artistic level, avant-garde techniques developed for song, agitprop theater, and cabaret in the 1920s were acquired and exploited by the new *Lieder-macher*. As in the Weimar Republic, diverging artistic forms reflected differences in approach to the issue of revolution. Cabaret chanson and *Kampflied* reflected the opposition between literary satire and didactic agitation. This was later mirrored in the diverging approaches of, for example, Wolf Biermann and the *FDJ-Singegruppen*, Konstantin Wecker and the Burg Waldeck activists, as well as in the different approaches to political revue of Floh de Cologne and the GDR *Liedertheater* groups. Finally, on the thematic level, the political song movements of the *Vormärz* and 1848, the Weimar Republic, West Germany, and the GDR — for all their differences — are connected by a common strand in which the gesture of rebellion is juxtaposed with the despair of failure. And here the importance of the relationship between content and form becomes evident: the contradictoriness embodied in the recurring theme of *deutsche Misere* demanded an ambiguity of approach — to music and text — which the artistic techniques developed in the earlier part of the twentieth century facilitated.

Notes

[1] Georg Herwegh, "Achtzehnter März," in *Herweghs Werke. Erster Teil. Gedichte eines Lebendigen* (Berlin: Deutscher Verlagshaus Bong & Co., 1909), 142–43.

[2] Peter Jelavich, *Berlin Cabaret* (Cambridge, MA and London: Harvard UP, 1996).

[3] Alan Lareau, *The Wild Stage: Literary Cabaret of the Weimar Republic* (Columbia, SC: Camden House, 1995).

[4] Rolf Kauffeldt, *Erich Mühsam Literatur und Anarchie* (Munich: Fink Verlag, 1983), 147.

[5] Erich Mühsam, *Der Ruf,* Heft 1, 1912, 1–2. Quoted in Kauffeldt, *Erich Mühsam,* 152–53.

[6] Erich Mühsam, *Der Krater. Gedichte* (Berlin: Morgen Verlag, 1909), 142–43.

[7] Franz Josef Degenhardt, "Verteidigung eines Sozialdemokraten vor dem Fabriktor" in *Im Jahr de Schweine 27 Neue Lieder mit Noten* (Hamburg: Hoffmann und Kampe, 1970), 32–33. Other songs by Degenhardt from the early 1960s such as "Rumpelstilzchen" and "Wölfe mitten im Mai" from *Spiel nicht mit den Schmuddelkindern* (Reinbek bei Hamburg: Rowohlt, 1969, 15–17 and 28–32) show an influence from the grotesque ballad style of Christian Morgenstern, a cabaret contemporary of Mühsam.

[8] Diana Köhnen, *Das literarische Werk Erich Mühsams* (Würzburg: Königshausen & Neumann, 1988), 171.

[9] Mühsam, "Generalstreik!" in *Kain,* II, 5, 1912, 65. Quoted in Köhnen, *Das literarische Werk Erich Mühsams,* 170.

[10] Mühsam, "Räte-Marsellaise" in *Brennende Erde: Verse eines Kämpfers* (Munich: Kurt Wolff Verlag, 1920), 73. See Köhnen, *Das literarische Werk Erich Mühsams,* 176–79).

[11] *Welt am Montag,* 27 July 1925. Quoted in Kauffeldt, 270.

[12] Wolf Biermann, "Der Hugenottenfriedhof" (1969), in *Alle Lieder* (Cologne: Kiepenheuer & Witsch, 1991), 215. All subsequent references to Biermann unless otherwise stated concern this book.

[13] Steffen Mensching, "Traumhafter Ausflug mit Rosa L.," in *Erinnerung an eine Milchglasscheibe. Gedichte* (Halle and Leipzig: Mitteldeutscher Verlag, 1984), 14–15.

[14] Karls Enkel, "Von meiner Hoffnung laß ich nicht — Der Pilger Mühsam," unpublished manuscript and video, collected by Karin Wolf, archive of the Akademie der Künste der DDR, Berlin, Liedertheater-Dokumentation, Forschungsabteilung Musik/Liedzentrum, 1980. All subsequent unreferenced quotations from this program can be found in the above unpaginated manuscript.

[15] See chapter 8 of this book on political song in the GDR for the reactions of the GDR Stasi to this production.

[16] F. C. Weiskopf, quoted in concert program for *Von meiner Hoffnung laß ich nicht.*

[17] The treatment of the "revolutionary dead" by Karls Enkel has been addressed in David Robb, "Reviving the Dead: Montage and Temporal Dislocation in Karls Enkel's Liedertheater," in *Politics and Culture in Twentieth-Century Germany,* ed. William Niven and James Jordan, 143–61 (Rochester, NY: Camden House, 2003). For an account of Wenzel and Mensching's respective tributes to Mühsam in their own poems see Karen Leeder, *Breaking Boundaries: A New Generation of Poets in the GDR* (Oxford: Clarendon, 1996), 87–88.

[18] See chapter 8 of this book on political song in the GDR.

[19] Karls Enkel, "Deutschland meine Trauer — neun Arten einen Becher zu beschreiben. Ein Johannes-R.-Becher-Abend" unpublished manuscripts and tape recording, collected by Karin Wolf, archive of the Akademie der Künste der DDR, Berlin, Liedertheater-Dokumentation, Forschungsabteilung Musik/Liedzentrum, 1981.

[20] Karls Enkel, "Die komische Tragödie des 18. Brumaire. Oder Ohrfeigen sind schlimmer als Dolchstöße. Nach Karl Marx," unpublished manuscript and video, collected by Karin Wolf, archive of the Akademie der Künste der DDR, Berlin, Liedertheater-Dokumentation, Forschungsabteilung Musik/Liedzentrum, 1983.

[21] See Riha, *Moritat, Bänkelsong, Protestballade,* 16.

[22] Frank Wedekind, "Der Tantenmörder," in *Gesammelte Werke,* vol. 1 (Munich: Georg Müller Verlag, 1920), 107.

[23] See chapter 3 of this book, "Narrative Role-Play as Communication Strategy in German Protest Song."

[24] Bertolt Brecht, "Von der Kindesmörderin Marie Farrar," in *Gesammelte Werke,* vol. 8 (Frankfurt am Main: Suhrkamp, 1967), 176.

[25] All quotations from Wolf Biermann's lyrics in this book are copyright © and used by permission of Wolf Biermann.

[26] Biermann, "Ballade vom Mann," on the live CD *Es geht sein' sozialistischen Gang* (CBS, 1977).

[27] Mikhail Bakhtin, *Rabelais and His World* (Bloomington: U of Indiana P, 1984), 317.

[28] Karls Enkel, Wacholder, and Beckert & Schulz, "Hammer-Rehwü," unpublished manuscripts and video, collected by Karin Wolf, archive of the Akademie der Künste der DDR, Berlin, Liedertheater-Dokumentation, Forschungsabteilung Musik/Liedzentrum, 1982. CD *Hammer-Rehwü von 1982* (Nebelhorn, 1994).

[29] Wenzel and Mensching, "Altes aus der Da Da eR," unpublished manuscript and video, collected by Karin Wolf, archive of the Akademie der Künste der DDR, Berlin, Liedertheater-Dokumentation, Forschungsabteilung Musik/Liedzentrum, 1989.

[30] Wenzel and Mensching, *Letztes aus der Da Da eR,* directed by Jörg Foth (DEFA, 1990). The various textual versions of the Altes and Letztes revue series are published in Wenzel and Mensching, *Allerletzes aus der Da Da eR/ Hundekomödie,* edited by Andrea Doberenz (Halle and Leipzig: Mitteldeutscher Verlag, 1991).

[31] Kurt Schwitters, "Was ist Wahnsinn?" in *Eile ist des Witzes Weile: Eine Auswahl aus den Texten* (Stuttgart: Reclam, 1987), 51.

[32] Hugo Ball, *Flight Out of Time: A Dada Diary* (New York: Viking, 1974), 65. Quoted in Roy F. Allen, "Zurich Dada, 1916–1919: The Proto-Phase of the Movement" in Stephen C. Foster, ed., *Dada/Dimensions* (Ann Arbor: UMI Research Press, 1985), 7.

[33] Mehring, Grosz, and Heartfield, together with composer Friedrich Hollaender, produced and performed a puppet show called "Einfach Klassisch" for the opening Schall und Rauch cabaret in December 1919.

[34] Walter Mehring, *Chronik der Lustbarkeiten: Die Lieder, Gedichte und Chansons 1918–1933* (Düsseldorf: Classen Verlag, 1981), 117–18.

[35] Marilyn Sibley Fries, ed., *Responses to Christa Wolf: Critical Essays* (Detroit: Wayne State UP, 1989), 47.

[36] Leeder, 4. Here Leeder is referring to Uwe Kolbe's term "Die Hineingeborenen," also the title of his poetry collection: *Hineingeborenen: Gedichte 1975–1979* (Berlin and Weimar: Aufbau, 1980).

[37] Susan C. Cook, *The Opera for a New Republic: The Zeitopern of Krenek, Weill, and Hindemith* (Michigan: UNI Research Press, 1988), 30–31.

[38] Ronald Sanders, *The Days Grow Short: The Life and Music of Kurt Weill* (London: Weidenfeld and Nicolson, 1980), 145–53.

[39] Georg-Friedrich Kühn, "Kutsche und Kutscher. Die Musik des Wolf Biermanns," in Heinz Ludwig Arnold, ed., Wolf Biermann (Munich: Edition Text und Kritik, 1980), 111.

[40] Biermann, in *Frankfurter Rundschau* (30 December 1972), 5.

[41] Matthias Henke, *Die großen Chansonniers und Liedermacher: Verflechtungen, Berührungspünkte, Anregungen* (Düsseldorf: ECON, 1987), 212.

[42] All quotations from Konstantin Wecker's lyrics in this book are copyright © and used by permission of Konstantin Wecker/Management Konstantin Wecker.

[43] See Mikhail Bakhtin, *Rabelais and His World*, 23. See references to the carnivalesque in the work of Biermann and Karls Enkel in chapter 3 of this book, "Narrative Role-Play as Communication Strategy in German Protest Song."

[44] Karls Enkel, "Dahin! Dahin!" unpublished manuscript and tape recording, collected by Karin Wolf, archive of the Akademie der Künste der DDR, Berlin, Liedertheater-Dokumentation, Forschungsabteilung Musik/Liedzentrum, 1982.

[45] See Christa Hasche, "Bürgerliche Revue und 'Roter Rummel.' Studien zur Entwicklung massenwirksamen Theaters in den Formen der Revue in Berlin 1903–1925." Diss. (Berlin: Humboldt University, 1980).

[46] For a wider examination of agitprop rock see Annette Blühdorn, *Pop and Poetry — Pleasure and Protest: Udo Lindenberg, Konstantin Wecker and the Tradition of German Cabaret* (Bern: Peter Lang, 2003), 135–37.

[47] http://digilander.libero.it/mguitarweb/KrautRock/F1.htm.

[48] http://digilander.libero.it/mguitarweb/KrautRock/F1.htm.

[49] See Joanne McNally, "Shifting Boundaries: An Eastern Meeting of East and West German 'Kabarett,'" *German Life and Letters* 54: 2 (2001).

[50] See chapter 8 of this book, "Political Song in the GDR."

[51] Bertolt Brecht, *Aufstieg und Fall der Stadt Mahagonny* (1928), in *Die Stücke von Bertolt Brecht in einem Band* (Frankfurt am Main: Suhrkamp, 1987), 214.

[52] The "Du" at the start of the first line is also a blatant reference to the banned Wolf Biermann song "Du, laß dich nicht verhärten, in dieser harten Zeit." From "Ermutigung," *aah-ja!* (CBS, 1974). Because Biermann's songs were strictly forbidden in the GDR it is possible that the reference was not understood by everyone, even though the *Hammer-Rehwü* audience consisted of many insiders of the *Liedermacher* scene.

[53] Walter Benjamin, "Linke Melancholie" in *Lesezeichen, Schriften zur deutschsprachigen Literatur* (Leipzig: Reclam, 1972), 255. For an analysis of this dispute see also Annette Blühdorn, *Pop and Poetry*, 114–15.

[54] Albert Betz, *Hanns Eisler Political Musician*, translated by Bill Hopkins (Cambridge: Cambridge UP, 1982), 62.

[55] Hanns Eisler, "Unsere Kampfmusik" in *Musik und Politik: Schriften 1924–1948* (Leipzig: VEB Deutscher Verlag für Musik, 1973), 169.

[56] Ernst Busch, "Das Lied der Wohltätigkeit," on CD *Merkt ihr nicht: Ernst Busch singt Tucholsky/Eisler* (Barbarossa, 1997).

[57] Bertolt Brecht, *Gedichte* (Leipzig: Reclam 1976), 112.

[58] See Albrecht Dümling, *Laßt Euch nicht verführen: Brecht und die Musik* (Munich: Kindler, 1985), 391–428.

59 Karl Siebig, *"Ich geh mit dem Jahrhundert mit."* Ernst Busch: Eine Dokumentation (Reinbek bei Hamburg: Rohwohlt, 1980), 59. Quoted in Dümling *Laßt Euch nicht verführen*, 307).

60 Siebig, *"Ich geh mit dem Jahrhundert mit,"* 181. Quoted in Dümling, 411.

61 This section on songs of the Spanish Civil War contains excerpts from David Robb, "Clowns, Songs and Lost Utopias: Reassessment of the Spanish Civil War in Karls Enkel's 'Spanier aller Länder,'" *Debatte: Review of Contemporary German Affairs* 11, 2 (2001): 156–72.

62 Ernst Busch, ed., *Canciones de las Brigadas Internacionales* (Madrid: Im Auftrag der 11. Internationalen Brigade, 18 July 1937).

63 Also on CD Ernst Busch, *Lieder der Arbeiterklasse & Lieder aus dem Spanischen Bürgerkrieg* (Pläne, 1967).

64 Jürgen Schebera, "Ernst Busch auf Schellack," on CD booklet for Ernst Busch, *Der rote Orpheus: In originalaufnahmen aus den dreißiger Jahren* (Edition Barbarossa, 1996).

65 Wolf Biermann: *Der Sturz des Dädalus* (Cologne: Kiepernheuer & Witsch, 1992), 44.

66 Otto Riewoldt, "Wir haben jetzt einen Feind mehr" in Arnold, *Wolf Biermann*, 26.

67 Karls Enkel, "Spanier aller Länder," unpublished manuscript and cassette recording, 1985, collected by Karin Wolf, archive of the Akademie der Künste der DDR, Berlin, Liedertheater-Dokumentation, Forschungsabteilung Musik/Liedzentrum 1985.

68 See Rolf Tiedemann, ed., in Walter Benjamin, *Das Passagenwerk* (Frankfurt am Main: Suhrkamp, 1983), 20–21.

69 Unlike Weiss, who had tackled the theme of the Stalinist purges in the International Brigade head-on in his monumental novel *Die Ästhetik des Widerstands*, the three volumes of which had been published in West Germany in 1975, 1978, and 1981. A limited edition came out as a single volume in the GDR in 1983.

70 See also Steffen Mensching, "Für Peter Weiss," in *Tuchfühlung. Gedichte* (Halle and Leipzig: Mitteldeutscher Verlag, 1987), 20.

71 Personal interview with Mensching (21 February 1994).

72 Wenzel, letter to David Robb (12 October 1997).

3: Narrative Role-Play as Communication Strategy in German Protest Song

David Robb

O F ALL THE COMMUNICATIVE strategies the twentieth century political song has employed, one of the most creative and effective has
been that of narrative role-play. It provides a good example of how *Gebrauchslyrik* (as discussed in chapter two) has functioned by playing to the
knowledge and cultural styles and tastes of a target audience. With the
term narrative role-play I mean, first, variations on the literary *Rollengedicht* or dramatic monologue, in which the singer assumes an identifiable role, impersonating the language, mannerisms, and characteristics of
known social types. An example of this is Franz Josef Degenhardt, who, as
a representative of West German alternative culture in the 1960s, parodied conventional figures of the establishment in his songs. Second, I refer to the narrative identities constructed by singers and performers either
by means of literary association (for example Wolf Biermann's frequent
references to Villon, Brecht, Hölderlin, and Heine) or by association with
certain political ideas or stances (for example, Ernst Busch or Gerhard
Gundermann embodying the proletarian worker or Konstantin Wecker's
identification with anarchy and hedonism). Unlike the *Rollengedicht* of
Degenhardt, these role-plays are frequently non-ironic and equate the
singer with the role itself, although aspects of society can still be parodied
from the standpoint of that role. A variation on this is the role-play of
Hans-Eckard Wenzel and Steffen Mensching, who in their performances
in the 1980s as a duo or with the group Karls Enkel assumed the ironic
masks of clowns, which they used to present an alternative vision of GDR
society in their songs.

In all of the above examples of narrative role-play, performance techniques, including delivery style, language register, and musical accompaniment, are used to support the role-play and hence the political ideas or
stances conveyed. The audience's recognition of these roles and stances is
assumed, which therefore entails the audience having a developed political, historical, or literary awareness. This reflects the unique essence of the
German political song, transcending conventionally perceived boundaries
of high and low culture: it can often make considerable intellectual de-

mands on its audience while at the same time employing structures and styles of "popular" musical forms such as chanson, street ballad, and folk or pop song to convey its political message. Despite this ambiguity the political song remains a protest form, appropriating aspects of high and low culture as a means of asserting countercultural identity against that of the dominant culture. In this chapter I will examine how this is achieved with regard to narrative role-play in the songs of some of the most prominent political singer/songwriters in West and East Germany from the 1960s up until the 1990s. To examine the source of their influences, it is first necessary to return to the artistic experimentation of the Weimar Republic.

Narrative Role-Play in the Weimar Republic

In the years following the First World War the rise of mass culture brought with it the "blurring of the distinctions between high and low, art and commerce, the sacred and the profane" (Frith 1998, 32). This supported Walter Benjamin's claim of the democratic potential of mass technology.[1] As Simon Frith writes: "In short, the rise of 'mass culture' meant new forms of social activity, new ways of using aesthetic experience to define social identity" (1998, 34). Echoing Benjamin, Hanns Eisler saw the potential of the mass-orientated *Kampflied* to resolve the opposition between consumer and producer of music.[2] Eisler used sophisticated compositional techniques, but at the same time subverted classical music's notions of hierarchy, scholarship, and the rituals it constructs around the musical event. In place of this, he promoted collectivity: the wall between artist and audience should be pulled down; everyone should participate. In this respect the rituals of the mass singing event more closely resembled those of the folk music world.

Frith, a leading sociologist in the field of pop music, has distinguished three main musical discourses — classical, folk, and pop — with reference to Pierre Bourdieu's sociological model of taste groups (1998, 36). In this respect it is significant to note that the *Kampflied* has aspects in common with all three of these distinctions: it has the serious compositional aspirations of classical music; it aims to promote a communality akin to the folk scene (for example, in its use of modal ecclesiastic elements to promote feelings of collectivity, as discussed in chapter two); and in its orientation toward a modern mass audience it makes use — often in the form of montage — of popular musical genres such as jazz, chanson, and marching songs.

Unlike twentieth century popular song, it is clear that the *Kampflied* was not devised in the first instance as a commercial commodity, but rather as a weapon in the class struggle. But whereas modern protest pop, according to Frith, tends to contain slogans (for instance, Springsteen's

"Born in the USA") (1998, 165) as opposed to developing an intellectual argument, Brecht and Eisler's *Kampflied* attempted to have *both:* the philosophical arguments were presented (albeit simplified for the genre) alongside highly singable refrains such as "Vorwärts und nicht vergessen" in "Solidaritätslied" (1931) or "Drum links zwei drei" in "Einheitsfrontlied" (1934). The latter presents the problem of proletarian hunger in the first verse and uses the chorus to present the solution: the worker should not sit around, but should take action by joining the workers' united front to defeat capitalism:

> Und weil der Mensch ein Mensch ist
> Drum will er was zu essen, bitte sehr!
> Es macht ihn ein Geschwätz nicht satt
> Das schafft kein Essen her
>
> Drum links, zwei, drei!
> Drum links, zwei, drei!
> Wo dein Platz, Genosse, ist!
> Reih dich ein in die Arbeitereinheitsfront
> Weil du auch ein Arbeiter bist[3]

The performance posture of Brecht and Eisler's favored singer, Ernst Busch — the antithesis of the bourgeois conductor or "Lied" singer with his unaffected proletarian style — further enhanced the popular image of the *Kampflied*. On this level we can see that Brecht and Eisler clearly understood the communicative dynamics of pop music. According to Frith, "the issue in lyrical analysis is not words, but words in performance. Lyrics, that is, are a form of rhetoric or oratory; we have to treat them in terms of the persuasive relationship set up between singer and listener" (1998, 166). With his film-star looks and stage presence, Busch became an identification model for his audience, a proletarian pop star with a narrative, an attitude, and style.

The chanson of the literary cabarets of the 1920s also featured narrative role-play. The broad term "Chanson," derived from the French word, had parodic, socially critical connotations in German. Musically, too, it is influenced strongly by the French cabaret song, for example, of Aristide Bruant, the original star of the Montmartre cabarets of the late nineteenth century, and, more recently, of George Brassens. But in political song circles) the word "Chanson" has also been used as a generic term that encompasses virtually the whole spectrum of popular song forms with political content, as is evident in Tucholsky's call in 1919 for a new German political Chanson, or "Couplet" as he called it (Riha, 103), or in Peter Rohland's similar call at the early Burg Waldeck festivals in the 1960s. In particular the forms subsumed under Chanson include the traditional

Bänkellied (street ballad) and the *Moritat* (sensational ballad). The latter category included songs about whores, outlaws, tramps, and other socially marginalized figures, as featured strongly in the pre-First World War cabaret lyric of Frank Wedekind and Christian Morgenstern. In this respect, unlike the *Kampflied,* the literary chanson generally has a strong ironic-satirical dimension in the tradition of Heinrich Heine, Wedekind, and the cabaret songs of Erich Mühsam.

A specific type of song within the category of literary chanson was the dramatic singing/role-playing monologue known as *Rollengedicht*. Famous examples of the *Rollengedicht* from German literary history include Goethe's "Schäfers Klagelied" and Heine's "Lied des Gefangenen." Cabaret artists of the 1920s now experimented with this model, presenting recognizable social types from everyday life and the worlds of politics, business, and fashion, often in the form of caricature or parody. Joachim Ringelnatz's "Kuttel Daddeldu" (1920), for example, portrayed a drunken seaman whose nihilism, hedonism, and philandering were well-received by the lost generation of soldiers returning from the war.[4]

> Wie Daddeldu so durch die Welten schifft,
> Geschieht es wohl, daß er hie und da
> Eins oder das andre von seinen Kindern trifft,
> Die begrüßen dann ihren Europapa:
> "Gud morning! — Sdrastwuide! — Bong Jur, Daddeldü!
> Bon tscherno! Ok phosphor! Tsching — tschung! Bablabü!"
> Und Daddeldu dankt erstaunt und gerührt
> Und senkt die Hand in die Hosentasche
> Und schenkt ihnen, was er so bei sich führt,
> — Whiskyflasche,
> Zündhölzer, Opium, türkischen Knaster,
> Revolverpatronen und Schweinsbeulenpflaster,
> Gibt jedem zwei Dollar und lächelt: "Ei, ei!"
> Und nochmals: "Ei, Ei!" — und verschwindet dabei.[5]

This mood reflects the nihilistic, pessimistic consensus of young poets in the post-First World War period. The mindless slaughter of the war had exploded the myth, cherished since the Enlightenment, of rational, progressive development of society. The widespread disillusionment among young poets such as Brecht, Erich Kästner, and Kurt Tucholsky reflected a world that had lost the certainties and securities associated with their pre-war childhoods. In Brecht's poem "Ballade vom armen B. B." from 1921, which appeared in the famous *Hauspostille* collection, this is expressed in the line: "Wir sind gesessen, ein leichtes Geschlechte / In Häusern, die für unzerstörbar galten."[6] There is an indifference and coldness in this poetry. The individual is portrayed as having lost his moral substance: "In mir habt ihr einen, auf den könnt ihr nicht bauen" (261). The subject is living for the moment with little hope in a better future: "Und nach uns wird kommen: nichts Nennenwertes" (262). The subject withdraws into a life of hedonism; tobacco, brandy, and women and conveys an indifference toward life in general.

For disillusioned young soldiers returning from the war, the style, role-play, and attitude expressed in "Kuttel-Daddeldu" were crucial means of communication. This anticipates Frith's description of the contemporary pop song: "All songs are implied narratives. They have a central character, the singer, a character with an attitude, in a situation" (1998, 169). Role-play is thus a technique that is used to establish identity between performer and a specific social "taste group." While the German political song shares this aspect of the pop song, many *Rollengedichte* of the 1920s established the connection between singer and audience member like "Kuttel-Daddeldu" via ironic role-play, but also contained serious political content. This is a unique feature of the twentieth-century German political song, one that is overlooked by Frith when he draws a clear line of distinction between pop and the tradition of the critical chanson and theater song. He writes:

> The [pop] singer is playing a part, and what is involved is neither [. . .] the equation of role and performer as in chanson [. . .] nor critical commentary (as in German theater song) but, rather, an exercise in style, an ironic — or cynical — presentation of character *as* style. (1998, 171)

It is clear that Frith has an oversimplified idea of the chanson, based on the example of Edith Piaf (or even Ernst Busch). He is not aware of the great tradition of irony in German political chanson. One sees in the songs of Kurt Tucholsky and Walter Mehring from the 1920s a creative combination of both critical commentary and ironic role-play. Often the trick was to lure the audience with a display of popular style, for example, by donning a characteristic costume or quoting the style of speech of a known social type. Tucholsky's "Schiffer-Lied" (1924) achieves its political effect by introducing such a recognized role and then unexpectedly comparing this with a known politician. The song begins harmlessly in the style of Ringelnatz's "Kuttel-Daddeldu" with the story of an unfaithful seaman:

> Der Seeman schifft sich ins Meer hinaus,
> ihm ist so leicht zu Sinn.
> Marie weint sich die Augen aus,
> er segelt rasch dahin.
> > Er sitzt in der Kombüse
> > und stochert im Gemüse

und denkt sich: Wenn Marie nicht ist, na, dann ists eine Negerin.
    Der hat
in jeder Stadt 'ne Braut — !
Die erste für die Seele,
die zweite fürs Gemüt;
die dritte wegen Hopeldibopp
auf Nacht wenns keiner sieht!

But in a twist the third verse suddenly introduces the figure of Gustav Streseman, the SPD party leader, who is depicted in the same opportunistic vein as the seaman, willing to make deals with anyone:

Mensch, unser Gustav Streseman
das ist wohl ein Filou!
Er meiert sich bei jedem an
und singt was Schöns dazu.
    Er steht am Wasserglase
    und redet durch die Nase,
mal rechts durchs Loch, mal links durchs Loch — der Junge ist atout!
    Der hat
in jeder Stadt 'ne Braut — ![. . .][7]

As Riha comments, the political parody works by equating the cheap literary role, the cabaret mask of the seaman, with the political role of Streseman in the Weimar Republic (1975, 92). In "Schiffer-Lied" therefore we see how the chanson can function to de-heroicize the protagonist, to bring the world of the ruling classes down to street level. The style of expression also corresponds with Tucholsky's theories on *Gebrauchslyrik,* whereby the singer of political chanson had to know the language of the street in order to employ it as a point of identification with the intended audience. For this reason many of the songs were sung in the Berlin dialect. Brecht and Mehring also recognized the importance of street attitude for communication.

Another example of such ironic role-play is Trude Hersterberg's rendition of Mehring's "Die kleine Stadt" (1924). Here she adopts the role of a small town floozy who has given birth out of wedlock. Hesterberg, who founded the legendary Wilde Bühne cabaret in Berlin in 1921, uses her seductive stage persona as bait to draw the audience into her narrative:

[. . .]
Es sind in meinem Städtchen
Die Gassen so beengt,
Drum sind die Männer und Mädchen
Auch alle so beschränkt!

Ich würd, gäb's nicht die Herrn vom Rat,
Die einzige Jungfrau sein:
So klein
So klein
So klein ist meine Stadt

Es lebt dort ein Apotheker,
Ein Bäcker und ein Schmied,
Es lebt dort ein alter Quäker
Der stets auf Tugend sieht!
Ich weiß nicht, wen zum Vater hat
Mein herziges Kindelein:
So klein [. . .][8]

Via the technique of irony, accentuated by the frivolous cabaret music, critical comment is passed on the small-mindedness of the character's environment. In a recorded performance from 1928 Hersterberg giggles with feigned innocence after the lines "Ich würd, gäb's nicht die Herrn vom Rat, / Die einzige Jungfrau sein," emphasizing her character's fun in breaking such small town taboos.[9] There is, however, a defamiliarizing twist at the end — accentuated by a darker, more melodramatic piano accompaniment — where the woman hints that she is ready to take her own and her baby's life: this provides a grotesque contrast with the innocence of Hersterberg's delivery in such a way as to expose the social injustice of the situation.

Ich schäme meines Kindes mich,
Weil ich keine Wiegen hab —
Mein Stübchen ist so winzig,
So winzig als ein Grab!
Ich halte ein Kissen ihm parat
In meinem Totenschrein:
So klein
So klein
So klein ist meine Stadt [. . .]

West German *Liedermacher:* Degenhardt and Wecker

The ironic *Rollengedicht* was rediscovered during the protest song movement in West Germany in the 1960s. Focal points were the annual Easter Marches and the Burg Waldeck song festivals held from 1964 through 1969, where a new generation of songwriters including Dieter Süverkrüp, Walter Mossmann, and Franz Josef Degenhardt emerged. They were protesting against issues ranging from the bomb and Vietnam to the failure of the denazification process in the Federal Republic.[10] Despite the economic success of the Federal Republic in the 1950s and early 60s, intellectuals and students felt marginalized amidst a perceived climate of restoration and cultural stagnation.

Franz Josef Degenhardt

Born in 1931 in Schwelm and a doctor of law, Franz Josef Degenhardt created a sensation at the first Burg Waldeck festival in 1964 with his political chansons. In Degenhardt's early songs social conformity and the image of uniform wealth propagated by the media are countered by the skeptical view of the social outsider. This was a current theme in the literary world: Heinrich Böll's *Ansichten eines Clowns* (1963) portrayed a hypocritical society through the eyes of the main character, the clown Hans Schnier, and Günter Grass's *Die Blechtrommel* (1959) exposed the unresolved legacy of National Socialism in West Germany through the disarming observations of the dwarf Oskar Matzerath. In his chansonesque ballad "Rumpelstilzchen" from 1963 Degenhardt plays the role of the anarchic outsider who has come to create disorder: "Es ist gut, daß niemand weiß / daß ich Rumpelstilzchen heiß."[11]

Degenhardt's ironic identification with Rumpelstilzchen is an artistic device to communicate with the like-minded, intellectual outsiders that constitute his audience. To distinguish this social grouping from others, it is useful to apply Bourdieu's concept of "cultural capital"[12] defined as the dominant class's "accumulation of cultural knowledge and experience — through education," which it in turn uses as a weapon of taste distinction (Frith 1998, 9). Since the Burg Waldeck generation rejected the conservative consensus of the establishment, it is clear that their group distinctiveness rested rather on what Sarah Thornton terms "subcultural capital."[13] In 1963, however, theirs was as yet a passive, intellectual protest. It had not yet been channeled into what would become the Extra-Parliamentary Opposition (APO) in 1967, the non-party-affiliated political movement comprised of students and intellectuals who were dissaffected with the Grand Coalition of the Social Democratic Party (SPD) and Christian Democratic Party (CDU) from 1966 to 1969.[14] It is significant therefore that the gesture of non-conformity in "Rumpelstilzchen" was not transmitted via an overt political message, but via the upside-down imagery that constitutes the narrative of Rumpelstilzchen's fairy-tale world. Everything is the opposite of the commonly perceived image of West German prosperity, propriety, and order: a burning school, a drunken cemetery watchman laughing over an open grave:

> Wenn morgens schon die Schule brennt,
> wenn ein Pfarrer aus der Kirche rennt,

ein Schutzmann in die Pfütze fällt,
ein Hund durch ein Museum bellt,
wenn der Friedhofswächter, der niemals trinkt,
noch am offnen Grab an zu lachen fängt,
wenn der Mond sich vor die Sonne schiebt,
und ein Greis ein Mädchen von siebzehn liebt,
da habe ich, mal kaum, mal viel, die Hand im Spiel.
Ich bin mit jedem blutsverwandt,
doch bleibt mein Name ungenannt.
es ist gut, daß niemand weiß,
daß ich Rumpelstilzchen heiß.

Images from the fringes and undersurfaces of society — the rail embankments, car scrapyards, and derelict places where truant children build their dens — abound. It is no accident that Degenhardt refers to "der bucklige Oskar" beating his drum. The disorder that Grass's dwarf creates in *Die Blechtrommel,* undetected from his position "below" is likewise a protest at the falsehoods of society:

Am Bahndamm, wo der Zug verkehrt,
der von Schilda nach Schlaraffia fährt,
wo Kinder ihre Höhlen baun,
weil sie sich nicht nach Hause traun,
wo der Rattenfänger von Hammeln pfeift,
wo der Ziegenjunker die Scheren schleift,
wo der Wind durch tote Autos fegt,
wo der bucklige Oskar die Trommel schlägt,
da zünde ich am Abend dann meine Feuer an.
Ich tanze, bis der Mond aufgeht,
und sing' dazu mein altes Lied:
Es ist gut, daß niemand weiß,
daß ich Rumpelstilzchen heiß.

In Degenhardt's early *Rollengedichten,* the depiction of non-conformity in an asocial character becomes a narrative convention, the medium of identification between performer and audience. In "Spiel nicht mit den Schmuddelkindern" from 1965, a middle-class boy's development is examined against the background of an underprivileged fringe existence. Here Degenhardt's insights into the class-character of Adenauer society contradict the view that a prosperous West Germany had dissolved class boundaries.[15] The constant opposition of "Proletenviertel" and "Oberstadt" implies the necessity of being in the right class and playing by its rules. The refrain, which urges the ceasing of contact with the scruffy kids, provides an ironical counterpoint:[16] "Spiel nicht mit den Schmud-

delkindern / sing nicht ihre Lieder / Geh doch in die Oberstadt /
mach's wie deine Brüder" (1969, 45). The boy's untidy tendencies are
beaten out of him and he climbs up the social ladder. The underworld is,
however, never far away from his superficial existence and, after a fall from
grace, it becomes his permanent home until he dies:

> Und eines Tages hat er eine Kurve glatt verfehlt.
> Man hat ihn aus einem Ei von Schrott herausgepellt.
> Als er später durch die Straßen
> hinkte, sah man ihn an Tagen
> auf 'nem Haarkamm Lieder blasen,
> Rattenfell an Kragen tragen.
> Hinkte hüpfend hinter Kindern,
> wollte sie am Schulgang hindern
> und schlich um Kaninchenställe.
> Eines Tages in aller Helle
> hat er dann ein Kind betört
> und in einen Stall gezerrt.
> Seine Leiche fand man, die im Rattenteich rumschwamm.
> Drum herum die Schmuddelkinder bliesen auf dem Kamm:
> "Spiel nicht mit den Schmuddelkindern,
> sing nicht ihre Lieder.
> Geh doch in die Oberstadt,
> mach's wie deine Brüder."

In this subversion of the conventional German balladesque portrayal
of a hero we see a further trait of Degenhardt's narrative. As in Brecht's
famous 1918 war satire "Ballade des toten Soldaten,"[17] there is a defamiliarizing function: the hero becomes an anti-hero who no longer invites
the listener's emotional identification, but rather provokes him or her to
question (Vormweg 1972, 33).

The fairy-tale guise of Degenhardt's early songs was enhanced by his
light-hearted, melodic accompaniment in the style of the French chanson
singer George Brassens. If this functioned as a protective cabaret mask, a
safe medium through which to deliver a subtle political message to a middle-class taste group, the mask was gradually stripped off throughout the
mid-sixties as Degenhardt targeted his songs more and more toward the
increasingly politicized students and intellectuals in the APO.[18] In "Adieu
Kameraden" from 1965, Degenhardt symbolically renounces his friends
who do not share his developing political awareness. "Väterchen Franz"
(1966) sees him breaking with his role as the drunken chronicler and re-
nouncing the pure entertainment value of his cabaret-like art. The text
"Wenn der Senator erzählt" (1967) subtly addresses the fact that former
Nazis were still occupying positions of financial and political power. Per-

formed in the style of *Sprechgesang* (alternating between spoken and sung parts), it is an example of a typical Degenhardt *Rollengedicht* that functions by means of the singer donning a character mask and — via an ironic self-exposure — revealing that character's hypocrisy or self-interest (von Bormann 1978, 5–6). For students and intellectuals in the 1967–68 period of revolt, the narrative of the capitalist senator with Nazi connections was instantly recognizable as that of their political adversaries in the establishment. In a "them and us" climate in which Herbert Marcuse's idea of "the Great Refusal" had many adherents, this was the cultural knowledge that united the youth against a generation whose members were still reluctant to speak about their roles in the Third Reich.[19]

In "Wenn der Senator erzählt" the accumulation of the senator's wealth in the steel industry is traced from the Kaiserreich through to the Weimar Republic, the Third Reich, and up to the present. Faced with the destruction of his factories in the war, he turns the land on which they had stood into a holiday park with the help of the currency reform of 1948 and the blessing of an old friend in the government (here it is implied that the friend is an old Nazi):

> Und als er dann morgens auf der Straße stand,
> neblig war's und kalt,
> da mußte der Senator plötzlich so richtig lachen.
> Er hatte eine gute Idee:
> "Wie wäre es" sagte der Senator,
> "wenn man aus dem Wackelsteiner Ländchen
> ein Ferienparadies machen würde?"
> Gesagt, getan.
> Verkehrsminister angerufen — alter Kumpel aus schwerer Zeit.
> Ja, und dann ist aus dem Wackelsteiner Ländchen
> *das* Wackelsteiner Ländchen geworden,
> wie es jedermann heute kennt.
> Und dann hat der Senator noch ein Hüttenwerk
> auf das Wackelsteiner Ländchen gestellt,
> Ja, wenn der Senator erzählt.

The satirical perspective of the narrative ("Ja, ja, ja, ja, ja, wenn der Senator erzählt"), underlined by the false innocence of the peaceful string quartet music (Jungheinrich 1972, 50), is enhanced by Degenhardt's skillful parodic quotation, whereby the senator effectively digs his own grave by revealing his blatant opportunism. A similar technique is employed in "vatis argumente" from 1967, a father's tirade against the student leader Rudi Dutschke, whereby, due to Degenhardt's distancing technique, nothing the father says may be taken seriously:

lieber Rudi Dutschke
würde vati sagen
wissen sie was das hieß
studieren damals
keine bücher kein brot kein bier
ja
da hatte keiner
flausen im kopp
die welt verbessern
und so
in alten kommisklamotten
paarmal gewendet
so sind wir herumgelaufen
aber gewaschen haben wir uns
und wenns keine seife gab
mit sand
jawohl mit sand

Everything is reduced to his mantra: "ÄRMEL AUFKREMPELN ZUPACKEN AUFBAUEN," which betrays that throughout his life the father has been no more than a conformer, far from the rebel against the Hitler Youth he claims to have been. Via the ironic technique of role-play, Degenhardt exposes the reactionary mentality of a broad section of middle-class society:

lieber Rudi Dutschke
würde vati sagen
[. . .]
mir paßt hier auch manches nicht
das können sie mir glauben
als ich so alt war wie sie
ich habe mir auch nichts gefallen lassen
hatte immer krach
mit dem fähnleinführer
dem spieß
um ein haar und
ich wär bei der strafkompanie gelandet
aber bei aller aufsässigkeit
wenn not am mann war
da hieß es doch
ÄRMEL AUFKREMPELN ZUPACKEN AUFBAUEN

In Degenhardt's parody of the father's expressions we see a parallel with pop's use of language as a means of establishing identity. Using the word "language" to mean a social-cultural grouping's particular use of jargon, slang, and dialect in opposition to the dominant language in a given culture,[20] Frith writes: "Songs can be used to explore the relationships of *different* languages — and in pop terms this has often meant challenging linguistic hierarchies, subverting the way words are used to dominate [. . .]" (1998, 169). We have already seen this in the *Gebrauchslyrik* of the cabaret songs of Mehring and Tucholsky in the 1920s, which used dialect and street language to convey its countercultural message. In Degenhardt's "vatis argumente," however, the distinctiveness of the student generation asserts itself purely in its rejection of the father's clichés; in its parody of the cultural mainstream's ideological and moral appropriation of concepts such as "Aufbauen," "Sauberkeit," and "russische Kriegsgefangenschaft":

> lieber Rudi Dutschke
> würde vati sagen
> [. . .]
> wissen sie was das heißt
> RUSSISCHE KRIEGSGEFANGENSCHAFT
> na schön
> 47 zu hause da war nichts
> buchstäblich gar nichts
> ja da half kein jammern und wehgeschrei
> da hieß es ganz einfach
> ÄRMEL AUFKREMPELN ZUPACKEN AUFBAUEN

The contrast between the rebelliousness of the young generation and the conventionality of its forebears is further cemented by the rock-music accompaniment in the style of the Doors. Degenhart's technique of *Sprechgesang* reminds one of the possibilities of rap to use spoken form to present an argument, which is more difficult in pop songs because of the tight melodic structures.[21]

What is significant about Degenhardt's songs before 1968 is that their identity-shaping function arose more from the satirical depiction of mainstream conservative society than in a presentation of the language and arguments of a unified target audience. This was a reflection of the protest movement itself: there was unanimity on what was to be rejected but much less agreement on how to change it. As the protest movement intensified in 1968 against the backdrop of the Vietnam conference in February in Berlin, the assassination attempt on Rudi Dutschke, and the passing of the Emergency Laws, Degenhardt's songs became more militant and direct in their demands for change. After the controversial fifth Burg Waldeck song festival in May 1968, where militant spectators attempted to dictate who should have access to the microphones, Degenhardt himself went on the offensive, embracing Marxist ideology and advocating a *Volksfront* between SPD and DKP to overthrow the capitalist system. His political transformation entailed a further change of artistic form. With echoes of Hanns Eisler's theory of the *Kampflied* from the early 1930s, Degenhardt came up with the maxim "Zwischentöne sind bloß Krampf im Klassenkampf" (1969, 113–15), thereby distancing himself from the subtle nuances of his earlier songwriting. From now on his songs were no longer for the aesthetic gratification of an educated audience, but for explicit agitation. This resulted in his music becoming harder-edged, his texts less ironic and more dogmatic. In the song "Monopoly," for example, the construction of a political argument dominates at the expense of musical and lyrical artistry.[22] The brand of role-play Degenhardt adopted in the early 1970s tended toward that of model socialist figures as exemplified in the songs "Mutter Mathilde" and "Rudi Schulte." An exception to this trend was a double A-side single featuring the highly melodic "Sacco and Vanzetti" and the witty *Rollengedicht* "Befragung eines Kriegdienstverweigerers," which in 1972 reached number one on the West German pop charts. This reflected both the commercial potential of the political song genre in the early Brandt era and the controversial extent of the issue of military service. But in general, Degenhardt's new, agitative, outright Marxist narrative was unpalatable for a mainstream audience. Nonetheless, throughout the 1970s and 1980s he continued to play to a sizeable countercultural taste group of ardent followers who saw him as the master of the agitprop chanson.

Konstantin Wecker

The ideological dogma and stridency of such Burg Waldeck veterans was rejected in the late 1970s by a new generation of *Liedermacher* that included Konstantin Wecker[23] (born 1947 in Munich). Releasing his first album in 1973, Wecker finally achieved his breakthrough in 1977 with the album *Genug ist nicht genug,* which won the Deutscher Kleinkunstpreis and included the hit song "Willy." Thematically Wecker's songs must be assessed against the failures of 1968 and the resulting disillusionment regarding socialist utopias and rational solutions based on the ideals of the Enlightenment. Jürgen Habermas, for example, wrote of opaque, bureaucratic societies controlled by mass media and technology and characterized by arms proliferation and unemployment.[24] As Inke Pinkert-Saeltzer writes, Wecker responded to the climate of pessimism by advocating the smashing of social norms that underlie the behavioral patterns on which such systems depend (1990, 256). To this end he developed a narrative in which he played the role of an anarchist. His songs confronted order with chaos, the numbness of existence with a hedonistic lust for life. Only in the transgressing of traditional norms, as Wecker believed, lay the possibility of change. In his 1981 song "Schafft Huren, Diebe, Ketzer her," for example, he sang "Schafft Huren, Diebe, Ketzer her / und macht das Land chaotisch, / dann wird es wieder menschlicher / und nicht mehr so despot-isch."[25] His philosophical approach was influenced by Marcuse's principle of *Eudämonismus,* whereby the happiness of the individual is a condition for the well-being of mankind (Pinkert-Saeltzer, 267–87). Indeed self-realization is a key issue in Wecker's entire work, as Blühdorn remarks with regard to the close link between his songs and his life (2003, 278).

Wecker's narrative also embraces socially marginalized outsiders: prostitutes (as in the song "Ich liebe diese Hure," 1978), alcoholics, and the homeless. But his realistic character portrayals differ markedly from the grotesque balladesque figures of the early Degenhardt. Wecker does not distance himself ironically from these figures, but instead identifies fully with their fringe status. He makes their case and valorizes their moral decay as a form of resistance (Pinkert-Saeltzer, 265). In his 1981 song "Endlich wieder unten," referring to an alcoholic in the railway station toilet at five in the morning, he states: "Nur die sich mißtrauen / brauchen Normen zum Sein / und verteilen als Schuld / was sie sich nicht verzeihn."

The outsider figures Wecker's songs promote also include the political *Andersdenkenden.* His hit "Willy" from 1977, one of his many songs sung in Bavarian dialect, relates the brutal killing of a former 1968 student activist who dared to speak out against prevailing Nazi sentiment in a typical German pub. The song "Hexeneinmaleins" (1978) is a response to increased police surveillance of alleged political deviants following the activities of the Rote Armee Fraktion in the late 1970s:

> Immer noch werden Hexen verbrannt
> auf den Scheiten der Ideologien.
> Irgendwer ist immer das Böse im Land
> und das kann man als Guter
> und die Augen voll Sand
> in die heiligen Kriege ziehn!

In the above respects the *Gebrauchslyrik* of Wecker — similarly to that of Tucholsky — can be seen as a means of establishing a communicative narrative. As Blühdorn writes, his lyrics forge a common bond with the audience not only in terms of political opinion but also in terms of lifestyle: "They deal with the socio-political realities of Germany, and support the listener in coping with the demands and problems of her or his everyday life" (312).

GDR *Liedermacher*: The Oktoberklub, Biermann, Wenzel, and Gundermann

In 1967 the Free German Youth (FDJ) hijacked the autonomous Berlin Hootenanny-Klub and forced it to change its name to the Oktoberklub, in memory of the Russian Revolution. The group, comprised of teenagers and young adults, became a showpiece for the state's emerging mass *Singebewegung*. When members began writing their own songs in the late 1960s, the only type of song allowed was what was termed "DDR-konkret": songs reflecting the everyday concerns and problems of young people and workers. A distinct narrative emerged, one demanding commitment and loyalty to the ideologies and principles of the socialist fatherland. As in socialist realist literature, an exemplary role-play was demanded. A blatant example of this is Oktoberklub member Reinhold Andert's "Das Lied vom Klassenkampf" (1968) in which a young activist demonstrates his ideological conviction to a young colleague whom he attempts to convert to the socialist cause:

> Ich werde das Buch heut zu Ende lesen
> Damit ich's dir morgen geben kann
> Wir können es auch gemeinsam lesen
> Weil man es dann besser verstehen kann[26]

The Kurt Demmler text "Lied vom Vaterland" (1969) — in prescribed fashion — expresses the "we" narrative role-play of the collective youth of the GDR in its praise of the emancipatory achievements of both youth and state:

> Und was haben wir selber an unserm Vaterland?
> Wir haben, daß wir Herren sind und Herrn aus eigner Hand
> Und Herrn über uns selber und über die Natur,
> und mühen uns und arbeiten und arbeiten nicht nur.
> Ja, das haben wir selber heut an unserm Vaterland:
> Wir haben endlich ein Gesicht
> und endlich auch die Zuversicht —
> dies Land ist von Bestand.[27]

The *Liederbücher* of the youth radio show DT64 between 1969 and 1974 ensured that these songs had the widest possible circulation. Despite being ordained from above, it is clear that in the early years the *Singebewegung* enjoyed a fair degree of popularity, not least because it encouraged the participation of everyone — not just a select few. But the wishful thinking in such songs as the one above was not going to convince youths in the long term and, as we will see in chapter 8, on the

GDR, by 1973 at the latest the popularity of the *Singebewegung* began to decline drastically.

The political songs of the *Singebewegung* reflected the ideology of the dominant culture and as such form an exception among the types of songs dealt with in this chapter. In the 1960s and 1970s there existed alongside the *Singebewegung*, however, an alternative culture of critical *Liedermacher*. These included Wolf Biermann and Bettina Wegner, both of whom were subject to censorship and performance bans. And from the mid-1970s onwards the *Singebewegung* itself began producing singers and groups such as Schicht, Brigade Feuerstein, and Karls Enkel who endeavored to expose the gap between ideal and reality.

For many singers a subversiveness emerged in their creative and often playful approach to the canons of dominant culture. In schools and universities the ruling Party, the SED, required a celebration of the German literary and revolutionary *Erbe* to which the GDR state laid claim. This included the humanist and classical literary tradition as well as lower traditions of theater and song. Writers, too, had to be respectful toward this inheritance. But a dialectic emerged: the government's endeavors to force the sacred canon on the population (for example, the writings of Goethe, Heine, Marx, and Brecht and the history of revolutionary movements) were matched by the creative acquisition of this *Erbe* on the part of young authors, playwrights, and songwriters. This would invariably constitute a subtle reinterpreting of this inheritance in such a way as to challenge the SED's rose-tinted portrayal of the GDR's achievements. In the *Liedermacher* scene this process reflected a tacit oppositional consensus between songwriters and their audience.

Wolf Biermann

As the son of a communist Jew murdered in Auschwitz, Wolf Biermann[28] was initially feted by the GDR establishment. His brand of art was a montage of various styles from high and low culture. Musically his influences ranged from Eisler (who had discovered the young singer at the Berliner Ensemble in the late 1950s) and the international protest song to the French chanson and the German street ballad. His lyrical influences ranged from Hölderlin to the more plebeian poetic traditions of François Villon, Heinrich Heine, and Bertolt Brecht. In his use of motifs and imagery from these poets we encounter a subversive and creative approach to the dominant literary heritage, a game that was played by performers and audience alike. Biermann communicated his views through the use of literary role-play. In many songs he identifies strongly with Villon, the anarchic fifteenth-century vagabond poet, in others with Heine, the censored exile, or Hölderlin, the innerly torn alien in his own country.

With his references to Villon, Biermann was latching onto a tradition in German political song. Earlier in the twentieth century Villon had been a role model for poets such as Brecht and Walter Mehring. The latter was a prominent cabaret lyricist in Berlin in the 1920s with strong links to the Dada movement. Reopening the Schall und Rauch cabaret as master of ceremonies in December 1919, Mehring invoked the figure of Villon in his declaration of war on all aspects of society: "Rire, jouer, mignonner et baiser [. . .] Il n'est trésor que de vivre à son aise."[29] Villon's poetry celebrated anarchic freedom, and a hedonistic attitude to life, and this functioned as a central motif of many cabaret *Rollengedichte*. Displaying a disrespect of institutions and convention, Mehring wrote in "Die Vier auf der Walze" for the 1924 revue *Europäische Nächte:* "Wir brauchen keinen Staat. Und zum Minister / Erkennen eine Vogelscheuche wir!"[30] In typical Villonesque style the song is coarse and vulgar: "Und ehe als Englein wir im Himmel fliegen: Beschlafen wir des Teufels Großmama / Halle-lu-ja. . . . . ." (242).

An aspect of social rebellion is expressed in this ribald approach. It is also reflected in the young Brecht's identification with the vagabond poet in the poem "Vom François Villon." It depicts the hedonistic and dangerous lifestyle of Villon in coarse language and profane body imagery: "Er mußte Menschen mit dem Messer stechen / Und seinen Hals in ihre Schlinge legen. / Drum lud er ein, daß man am Arsch ihn leckte / Wenn er beim Fressen war und es ihm schmeckte." It ends with Villon dying on the run from the police. Yet Brecht concludes that Villon's spirit will never die and that he even managed to find enjoyment in his death:

> François Villon starb auf der Flucht vorm Loch
> Vor sie ihn fingen, schnell, im Strauch, aus List —
> Doch seine freche Seele lebt wohl noch
> Lang wie dies Liedlein, das unsterblich ist.
> Als er die viere streckte und verreckte
> Da fand er spät und schwer, daß auch dies Strecken
>   schmeckte. (1967, 38–39)

Such Villonesque activities as defecation, beatings, cursing, and laughter are popular motifs of the carnival of the Middle Ages as defined by Mikhail Bakhtin in *Rabelais and his World*.[31] These activities had an antiauthoritarian, utopian aspect in their symbolism of a world temporarily turned on its head with the "suspension of all hierarchical precedence" (10). Included in this is the motif of the grotesque body, which, according to Bakhtin, symbolizes a world that is not fixed or constant but continually renews itself (1984, 303–67). For Bakhtin,

[t]he sexual series functions [. . .] to destroy the established hierarchy of values via the creation of new matrices of words, objects and
phenomena [. . .] [T]here is a heroization of all the functions of the
life of the body, of eating, drinking, defacation and sexual activity
(1981, 192).

Of course, the carnival was a temporary event — the "official" world
with all its rules and taboos reasserted itself after the festivities were over.
But there is a moment of rebellion captured in these images and motifs
which, as Bakhtin writes, is to be found to varying degrees in the history
of literature and popular forms of theater and poetry.[32] It is clear that poets such as Heine and Brecht were aquainted with and had respect for this
alternative "low" tradition. Brecht made use of the corporeal motif in
Baal and in his early poems. Biermann made no secret of his admiration
for Villon, Heine, and Brecht and consciously embraced this profane poetic tradition. While professing loyalty to the ideals of the GDR state, he
adopted an impudent, plebeian tone to address how these ideals were being corrupted.

The depiction of women in Biermann's songs of the early 1960s con-
forms to this profane tradition, again reminiscent of Heine and Brecht, which
accentuates the sensual, bodily image of women. The symbolism of renewal
and transformation inherent in such imagery clashes with the rigidity of
GDR state policy and ideology. In "Lied auf das ehemalige Grenzgänger-
Freudenmädchen Garance" (1961) he sings about the prostitute who is
forced to give up her occupation because of the building of the Berlin
Wall. This, the song implies, is her downfall, not her sexual promiscuity:
"Aber du, Garance, bist die Schönste! / Die Unzucht hat deinen Leib
nicht gefressen / Die Unzucht nahm nicht deine Lieblichkeit."[33]

In "Die alten Weiber von Buckow," Biermann presents an image of
old wives standing in the rain cursing the GDR state because they cannot
buy fish, while the young fishmonger is in bed with his girlfriend: "Ein
Fischer jung und stark / — ein junges Weib von Buckow / Verschläft mit
ihm bis acht / Das hat die Weiber von Buckow / So bös und nass gemacht" (Biermann, 68). Such imagery in the work of Bierman was the antithesis of the requirements of Socialist Realism and led to the charges of
literary decadence that contributed to his being banned from performing
and publishing in 1965.

In "Ballade auf den Dichter François Villon," vibrant language and
imagery of the body clashes with the images of GDR officialdom. The
profanity is used as a means of creating distinction — it contrasts here
with the reverential tones with which socialism was treated in the GDR
media and public life. Biermann, in typically immodest fashion, begins the
song by establishing the line of heritage from Villon through Brecht up to

himself. He alludes to the watchful, intrusive eyes of the GDR secret police (Stasi) as he shelters his grotesquely decaying guest Villon in his flat:

> Mein großer Bruder Franz Villon
> Wohnt bei mir mit auf Zimmer
> Wenn Leute bei mir schnüffeln gehn
> Versteckt Villon sich immer
> Dann drückt er sich in' Kleiderschrank
> Mit einer Flasche Wein
> Und wartet bis die Luft rein ist
> Die Luft ist nie ganz rein
>
> Er stinkt, der Dichter, blumensüß
> Muß er gerochen haben
> Bevor sie ihn vor Jahr und Tag
> Wie'n Hund begraben haben
> Wenn mal ein guter Freund da ist
> Vielleicht drei schöne Fraun
> Dann steigt er aus dem Kleiderschrank
> Und trinkt bis Morgengraun
>
> Und singt vielleicht auch mal ein Lied
> Balladen und Geschichten
> Vergißt er seinen Text, soufflier
> Ich ihm aus Brechts Gedichten

There is further grotesque imagery in Biermann's description of Villon's fat wife Margot, who makes him curse, and in the way he ingratiates
himself with his superiors: "Die Eitelkeit der höchsten Herrn / Konnt
meilenweit er riechen / Verewigt hat er manchen Arsch / In den er mußte
kriechen" (121). Villon's carnivalism forms a counterpoint to rigid authority. The stinking Frenchman drinks wine and vodka and struggles with
the "Sklavensprache" of the Party newspaper. When he is shot at while
walking along the Berlin Wall, red wine flows from his wounds. He coughs
up the lead cartridges, spits, and curses. The fact that the police can only
find his skeleton in Biermann's cupboard is significant: the spirit of Villon
will always haunt the authorities — he is synonymous with the utopian
spirit of the carnival crowd and its subversion of hierarchy.

While the Villon narrative lay at the basis of many of Biermann's *Spottlieder,* another type of narrative related to the divided Germany and the
plight of the artist in the face of the historical *deutsche Misere.* Biermann's
sense of alienation was complex: he was a West German who as a communist youth had gone of his own free will to the GDR, which now rejected
him. He constructed his *Deutschland* narrative by appropriating poetic

motifs and imagery from Hölderlin and Heine, who themselves had had a tortured relationship to their country. Here Biermann plays the historical role of the artistic outsider, a concept that the GDR literary public — for whom literature was an escape from the thoroughly politicized everyday life in their country — could well relate to. The *Erbedebatte,* which previously had focused on Goethe and Schiller, was extended in the 1970s to encourage, as Karen Leeder writes, "a renewed interest in the historical reality and life and times of [. . .] those more marginalized figures associated with Romanticism."[34] This was reflected in poems dedicated to Hölderlin by Volker Braun, Heinz Czechowski, and Biermann. In two particular songs Biermann moves away from the antagonistic satire of his *Spottlieder* to a more melancholic contemplation mirroring his personal alienation. In "Es senkt das deutsche Dunkel" from 1967, the darkness overcomes him "weil ich mein Deutschland / So tief zerrissen seh / Ich lieg in der bessren Hälfte / Und habe das doppelte Weh" (198). In "Das Hölderlin-Lied" of the same year Biermann identifies with the author of the fiercely socially critical *Hyperion* (Leeder, 131–32). Its subtitle "So kam ich unter die Deutschen" stems from the main character Hyperion's "Scheltrede." Torn between high poetic ideals and painful reality, Hyperion sees his problem mirrored in a Germany where artists are outnumbered by philistines.[35] Similarly, in Biermann's GDR the bureaucrats alienate those who believe in the humane values of socialism: "In diesem Lande leben wir / wie Fremdlinge im eigenen Haus." In the final verse Biermann sings: "ausgebrannt sind die Öfen der Revolution" (198–99): the revolutionary rhetoric of the Party has become empty and meaningless. All that is left is stagnation and a peace "of enforced stasis and repression," one that "has betrayed the revolutionary ideal" (Leeder, 132).

This historicization of the German conflict between the intellectual and the philistine is also a feature of Biermann's adaptation of Heine's epic poem *Deutschland. Ein Wintermärchen.* In his rhyming couplets and satirical language Biermann adopts the role of Heine, who had been forced by the German censorship of the time to cross the Rhein to exile in France. Biermann crosses the River Spree (in a train high over the Berlin Wall) back to West Germany on a family visit in the early 1960s, posing the question: "Was eint die Deutschen eigentlich / Trotz Stacheldraht und Minen / Was ist an dem zerrissnen Volk / Noch unteilbar geblieben?" (1977, 106). He answers: "[. . .] Wir bleiben was wir waren: Das deutsche Volk, ein wenig Volk / von Denkern und Barbaren."[36]

At the time some criticized the political impotence of Biermann's use of Heine and Hölderlin as a paradigm of his own existence in the GDR.[37] But in a situation where intervention was futile and censorship was rife, Biermann's was a realistic form of resistance. The creative use of literary and mythological figures of history in GDR literature (for example, by

Heiner Müller, Volker Braun, Franz Fühmann, and Christa Wolf) was widespread. It functioned as a tool for establishing a narrative code of communication with the public. In this way, artists and audiences voiced a silent protest by constructing an alternative social identity via aesthetic experience.

The *Deutschland* theme continues in Biermann's reference to the mythological figure of Icarus, which he, like Bettina Wegner,[38] uses as a symbol of political impotence and crushed ideals. In 1976 Biermann adopted the narrative role of "Der preußische Ikarus" in the song by the same name. The title refers to the steel emblem of the eagle on the Wei-dendammbrücke over Berlin's River Spree. Biermann compares it to the mythological Icarus, who flew up to the sun but fell to the ground when the sun melted the wax that held his wings together. But unlike the Greek Icarus, the Prussian Icarus is not flying anywhere; it is painfully heavy and rooted to the ground, its wings made of gray iron. This is a metaphor for GDR socialism: fixed, unchanging, and stagnant:

> Da, wo die Friedrichstraße sacht
> Den Schritt über das Wasser macht
> da hängt über der Spree
> Die Weidendammerbrücke. Schön
> Kannst du da Preußens Adler sehn
> wenn ich am Geländer steh
>
> dann steht da der preußische Ikarus
> mit grauen Flügeln aus Eisenguß
> dem tun seine Arme so weh
> er fliegt nicht weg — er stürzt nicht ab
> macht keinen Wind — und macht nicht schlapp
> am Geländer über der Spree

The third verse becomes personal, practically prophesizing his immi-nent exile to the West — the hated state machinery is going to drag him over the edge:

> Und wenn du wegwillst, mußt du gehen
> Ich hab schon viel abhaun sehn
> aus unserm halben Land
> Ich halt mich fest hier, bis mich kalt
> Dieser verhaßte Vogel krallt
> und zerrt mich übern Rand

And then Biermann himself will become a tragic Icarus who crashes to the ground, his utopian dreams finally dashed:

dann bin ich der preußische Ikarus
mit grauen Flügeln aus Eisenguß
   dann tun mir die Arme so weh
dann flieg ich hoch — dann stürz ich ab
mach bißchen Wind — dann mach ich schlapp
   am Geländer über der Spree (285)

Hans-Eckhardt Wenzel and Steffen Mensching

The most striking example of narrative role-play in the post-Biermann generation of *Liedermacher* in the GDR was that of Hans-Eckardt Wenzel and Steffen Mensching, who inhabited roles as clowns. Having begun in the *FDJ-Singebewegung* with the group Karls Enkel in the late 1970s, they took the group to new heights of artistic experimentation in the early 1980s. In a state where the expression of "otherness" was a delicate matter, they spoke to a taste group of *Andersdenkenden* through the medium of the clown's mask. In the climate of censorship, the mask presented the possibility, as Wenzel himself put it, "auszusteigen ohne weggehen zu müssen."[39] This temporary opting out was the implied narrative of Wenzel and Mensching's songs, attractive for the frustrated intellectuals who made up their audience. Via the use of the clown masks and costumes and clownish antics Wenzel and Mensching took their audience into a world of surreal subversion where they could momentarily forget their political impotence. Supporters of reform, Wenzel and Mensching believed nonetheless in the ideals of socialism, and in this respect inhabited a sociocultural milieu distinct from that of the dissident Prenzlauer Berg poets, who rejected the socialist cultural *Erbe* that so preoccupied Wenzel and Mensching in their songs, poems, and *Liedertheater* productions.[40]

Wenzel and Mensching first took on the guise of the clown figure in the *Hammer-Rehwü* of 1982, a co-production of their *Liedertheater* group Karls Enkel, the folk group Wacholder, and the duo Beckert & Schulz.[41] In this production they contrasted the serious world of politics with a festive world of mockery and ridicule of the GDR experience. While the worker was the hero of Piscator's *Roter Rummel* revue (on which the *Hammer-Rehwü's* form and structure was based), the hero of the *Hammer-Rehwü* is undoubtedly the clown. In "Berlin-Lied," the Spree flows past the Palast der Republik. The carefree attitude of three anglers on the river clashes with the seriousness of the apparatus of power: the general who tries to recruit them to the army, the politicians passing by in their black limousines, and the official who threatens to call the police to clear the area of such "schmutzige[n] Leute." In the final verse, Wenzel assumes the role of a fish in the river protesting against being caught by the anglers. The subtext clearly relates to the wish of the unofficial alternative culture in the GDR to be left alone by officialdom. The taboo issue of *Republikflucht* is cheekily alluded to in the notion of the fish who threatens to swim out to the North Sea. Wenzel also throws in the hushed-up theme of pollution, which in 1982 was beginning to become an issue for the alternatively minded:

> Lieber Angler vorm Komitee,
> Nein, ich will nicht in Gelee.
> Laßt mich leben, liebe Leute,
> Sucht euch eine andre Beute.
> Haken weg, ich bin nur ein armes Vieh
> Und stink viehisch nach Chemie,
> Ich will lieb sein, wie die Bürger hie,
> Sonst sag ich den Genossen vis-à-vis
> Daß ich in die Nordsee flieh.
> Lala, Lala, Lala, Laa

In the chorus, even the Wall is derided: "Kleine Fische, große Fische / Kleine Haken, große Haken / Nicht aus Stahl und Pappmaché / Nein, aus Wasser ist die Spree" (1982). From the clown's carnivalesque standpoint all authority is temporary, while the Spree, on the other hand, is eternal. The video recording by the East Berlin Akademie der Künste of a *Hammer-Rehwü* performance in 1982 shows the audience's clear delight at the comical expression of such taboo subjects.[42]

Toward the finale of the revue, Dieter Beckert, in the costume of an army general, sings "Bleib erschütterbar doch widersteh,'" a text by the West German Peter Rühmkorf, set to music by Beckert and Wenzel. Later he is joined on stage by the clown Wenzel. The song is sung in a sober, matter-of-fact manner, every syllable accentuated in the refrain "Bleib-er-schütt-er-bar-doch-wid-er-steh'" The insistent, pulsing rhythm of the violins, cello, and bass provides an atmosphere of tension slowly driving the song forward. The text is used here to refer to pressing issues of that period in the GDR that remained taboo in public: destruction of the environment, compromising one's values through conformity, and the dangers of submissiveness in the face of political oppression:

> [. . .]
> Die uns Erde, Wasser, Luft versauen
> — Fortschritt marsch! mit Gas und Gottvertrauen
> Ehe sie dich einvernehmen, eh
> du im Strudel bist und schon im Solde,
> wartend, daß die Kotze sich vergolde:
> Bleib erschütterbar — und widersteh!

Schön, wie sich die Sterblichen berühren
Knüppel zielen schon auf Hirn und Nieren,
daß der Liebe gleich der Mut vergeh. . .
Wer geduckt steht, will auch andre biegen.
(Sorgen brauchst du dir nicht selber hinzufügen;
Alles, was gefürchtet wird, wird wahr!)
Bleib erschütterbar.
Bleib erschütterbar — doch wiedersteh!

In the current political climate in the GDR this text was highly controversial and contributed to the revue being banned in Cottbus in March 1983. In 1982, due to the intensification of the deployment of nuclear weapons in both East and West Germany, people had been arrested for being members of the unofficial peace movement (known under the title *Schwerter zu Pflugscharen*). In this respect Wenzel's clownish antics at the end of the song were highly significant and as such illustrate how he constructed his own narrative role-play: Beckert symbolically discards his military jacket at the end of the song and walks off stage; Wenzel, in his full circus clown costume and mask, then picks it up and, with a look of disgust on his face, ceremoniously drops it on the ground again. This scene demonstrates how gestures and costumes can sometimes be more effective than words, which are vulnerable to censorship.

Although Wenzel later reached a wider audience with his two Amiga LPs *Stirb mit mir ein Stück — Liebeslieder* and *Reisebilder,* his clown productions with Mensching (including the legendary *Da Da eR* series, which they performed as a duo intermittently from 1982 to 1990) were never published or recorded until after the fall of the Wall and remained popular only among a limited group of insiders. The conditions and constraints that *Liedermacher* such as Wenzel and Mensching had to endure will be dealt with later, in chapter 8 on the GDR.

Gerhard Gundermann

Another GDR *Liedermacher* was Gerhard Gundermann. But Gundermann, a driver of an excavator truck ("Baggerfahrer") in a coal mine by day, was a very different kind of protest singer from Biermann and Wenzel and Mensching, who were highly educated and influenced by literature. Touted as the "Springsteen des Ostens" or "Dylan des Tagebaus" in the 1990s, he had already made a name for himself in the *Liedertheater* group Brigade Feuerstein. With origins, like Wenzel and Mensching, in the state-controlled *Singebewegung,* his proletarian style and wit culminated in a distinctive narrative: that of the self-educated worker, street-wise and committed to socialism. His critical approach, however, resulted in him being expelled from the Party and subsequently from the Stasi, where he had been an informer in the early 1980s. Songs from that period such as "Vater du bist müde" (1988), written by fellow Brigade Feuerstein member Alfons Förster, express their generation's loss of faith in the aging GDR leadership.[43] The song "Hoy Woy" (1986) is a tribute to Gundermann's industrial home town of Hoyerswerda: "hoy woy, / dir sind wir treu, / du blasse blume auf sand. / heiß, laut, / staubig und verbaut, / du schönste stadt hier im land." The final verse, however, conveys the insistence that even loyal workers are not going to be duped by the political propaganda slogans on the walls:

> deine grauen häuser werden nicht bunt
> wir reiben uns an dir nur die pinsel wund
> deshalb gucken wir nicht mehr auf die wände,
> sondern leuten auf gesichter und hände,
> deshalb, daß wir augen haben,
> die sich nicht ablenken lassen von fassaden,
> deshalb können wir nie voll andacht stehn,
> nein, wir müssen immer dahinter sein,
> wie in
> hoy woy [. . .]

In "Lancelots Zwischenbilanz" (1986) Gundermann refers to the exclusion from political participation of anyone who, like himself, diverged from the official line. Although he still calls himself a communist, his utopian dreams have not been realized and his red carnation has withered "in einem kalten winter." The second stanza reflects his disappointment at the lack of genuine news in the state-controlled newspapers:

> mein halbes leben steh ich an der weltzeituhr.
> und ich bin nicht mehr so jung.
> und ich warte und ich warte.
> und die rote nelke trag ich immer noch am helm.
> obwohl sie mir in
> einem kalten winter verdorrte.
>
> und diese zeitung halt ich noch in der hand,
> obwohl ich sie schon nicht mehr lesen kann.
> und starre in den nebel —
> wann kommt der mann,
> der mir sagt: wir brauchen dich,
> jetzt bist du dran!
>
> und ich weiß nicht, ob ich noch springen kann,
> bis an eine kehle.

und ich weiß nicht, ob ich noch singen kann,
bis in eine seele.
und ich weiß nicht, ob ich noch starten kann,
bis in die Welt.
und ich weiß nicht, ob ich noch warten kann,
bis die Welt mich zählt.

With the "Warten" motif, which will be dealt with further in chapter 8, the song echoes the theme of "a passive and alienated waiting" (Leeder, 53) as expressed in texts of the 1980s such as those of Heiner Müller and Wenzel. In his narrative of the "Baggerfahrer," Gundermann overlaps with that of the literary elite, indicating how common political concerns transcended taste-group distinctions in the GDR. After unification and up until his premature death at the age of 43 in 1998, he continued to play to a large following, successfully pitching his songs at an East German former communist section of society whose cherished ideals had been dashed.[44]

The hybrid of high and low culture that constitutes the political song genre was an effective means of communication with target audiences in the Weimar Republic and again after its revival from the 1960s onwards. Musical and narrative techniques pioneered in the early years of popular mass culture, such as the montage of the *Kampflied* or the ironic role-play of the chanson, were reappropriated from the 1960s onwards to parody the dominant culture of both the FRG and the GDR. In the cases of Biermann, Degenhardt, Wenzel and Mensching, and Wecker, high poetic imagery or philosophical content exist side-by-side with low musical and performance techniques from the street ballad to the popular rock song. In particular the narrative role-play of the singer — portraying social figures such as the outsider, the artist, the anarchist, or the clown — has functioned as a medium of identification for countercultural taste groups.

Notes

[1] See Walter Benjamin, *Das Kunstwerk im Zeitalter seiner technischen Reproduzierbarkeit* (Frankfurt am Main: Suhrkamp, 1966). This was a contradiction of Adorno's assertion that the mass cultural industry merely enslaved the people.

[2] Hanns Eisler, "Die Arbeitermusikbewegung" in *Musik und Politik: Textkritische Ausgabe* (Leipzig: Deutscher Verlag für Musik, 1982), 180.

[3] Bertolt Brecht, "Einheitsfronlied,"in *Gedichte* (Leipzig: Reclam, 1976), 111.

[4] Karl Riha, *Moritat, Bänkelsong, Protestballade: Zur Geschichte des engagierten Liedes in Deutschland* (Frankfurt am Main: Fischer, 1975), 81–84.

[5] Joachim Ringelnatz, "Kuttel-Daddeldu," in *Kuttel-Daddeldu* (Munich: Kurt Wolff Verlag, 1923), 36.

[6] Bertolt Brecht, "Vom armen B. B." in *Gesammelte Werke* vol. 8.: *Gedichte 1* (Frankfurt am Main: Suhrkamp, 1967), 262.

[7] Kurt Tucholsky, "Schiffer-Lied," in *Kurt Tucholsky Chanson Buch* (Reinbek bei Hamburg: Rowohlt, 1983), 277–81. See also Riha's analysis of this song, *Moritat, Bänkelsong, Protestballade*, 90–92.

[8] Walter Mehring, "Die kleine Stadt," in *Chronik der Lustbarkeiten: Die Gedichte, Lieder und Chansons 1918–1933* (Düsseldorf: Classen Verlag, 1981), 212–14.

[9] Trude Hersterberg, "Die kleine Stadt," on CD *Ramona Zundloch. Musikalisches Kabarett in klassischen Interpretationen von 1921–1933* (Edition Berliner Musenkinder, 1999).

[10] See Keith Bullivant and C. Jane Rice, "Reconstruction and Integration. The Culture of West German Stabilization 1945 to 1968" in Rob Burns, ed., *German Cultural Studies* (Oxford: Oxford UP, 1995), 213.

[11] Franz Josef Degenhardt, *Spiel nicht mit den Schmuddelkindern: Balladen, Chansons, Grotesken, Lieder* (Reinbek bei Hamburg: Rowohlt, 1969), 15–17. All quotations from Degenhardt's lyrics in this book are copyright © and used by permission of Franz Josef Degenhardt.

[12] Pierre Bourdieu, *Distinction: A Social Critique of the Judgement of Taste* [1979] (London: Routledge, 1984).

[13] Sarah Thornton, *Club Cultures: Music, Media and Subcultural Capital* (Cambridge: Polity, 1995).

[14] See Bullivant and Rice, "Reconstruction and Integration," 235–43.

[15] This view had been further encouraged by the SPD's Godesberg Program of 1959, where, in order to make itself electable, the Party had distanced itself from its working class roots by ommitting references to Marxism in its program and dropping demands for the nationalization of industry.

[16] Heinrich Vormweg, "Degenhardt dichtend," in Heinz Ludwig Arnold, ed, *Franz Josef Degenhardt. Politische Lieder 1964–1972* (Munich: Edition Text und Kritik, 1972), 35.

[17] Bertolt Brecht, "Legende des toten Soldaten" (1918), *Gesammelte Werke Band 8* (Frankfurt am Main: Suhrkamp, 1967), 256.

[18] See also Alexander von Bormann, "Franz Josef Degenhardt" in Heinz-Ludwig Arnold, ed. *Kritisches Lexikon zur deutschsprachigen Gegenwartsliteratur* (Munich: Edition Text + Kritik, 1978), 5.

[19] Bullivant and Rice, "Reconstruction and Integration," 241–43.

[20] The subvertion of cliches of the dominant "language" through other "languages" is well expressed by Mikhail Bakhtin in the *Dialogic Imagination* (Austin: U of Texas P, 1981). Using the term "heteroglossia" to mean "the base condition governing the operation of meaning in any utterance" (428), Bakhtin writes, "on the lower levels, on the stages of local fairs and at buffoon spectacles, the heteroglossia of the clown sounded forth, ridiculing all "languages" and dialects; there developed the literature of the *fabliaux* and *Schwänke* of street songs, folksayings, anecdotes, where there was no language center at all, where there was to be found a lively play with the "languages" of poets, scholars, monks, knights and others,

where all "languages" were masks and where no language could claim to be an authentic, incontestable face." 273.

[21] See Frith, 169.

[22] Franz Josef Degenhardt, "Monopoly," LP *Die Wallfahrt zum Big Zeppelin* (Polydor, 1971).

[23] For a fuller picture and analysis of Wecker and his work, see Annette Blühdorn's chapter 6 in this volume, "Konstantin Wecker — Political Songs between Anarchy and Humanity."

[24] Jürgen Habermas, *Die neue Unübersichtlichkeit* (Frankfurt am Main: Suhrkamp, 1985), 143. See Inke Pinkert-Saeltzer, "Die literarische Verarbeitung der bundes-republikanischen Wirklichkeit nach 1968 in den Texten des Liedermachers Konstantin Wecker," dissertation (New York University, 1990), 252–53.

[25] Konstantin Wecker, "Schafft Huren, Diebe, Ketzer her." Unless otherwise stated, all songs by Wecker appear on the compilation CD *Konstantin Wecker* (Polydor/Zweitausendeins, 1997). All quotations from Wecker's lyrics in this book are copyright © and used by permission of Konstantin Wecker/Management Konstantin Wecker.

[26] Oktoberklub, "Das Lied vom Klassenkampf," on LP *Unterm Arm die Gitarre* (VEB Deutsche Schallplatten, 1968).

[27] Kurt Demmler, "Lied vom Vaterland," in *DT64 Liederbuch* (1969), 48. Quoted in Holger Böning, *Der Traum von einer Sache: Aufstieg und Fall der Utopien im politischen Lied der Bundesrepublik und der DDR* (Bremen: edition lumière, 2004), 210.

[28] For a fuller treatment of Biermann and his work, see Peter Thompson's chapter 7 in this volume, "Wolf Biermann: Die Heimat ist weit." All quotations from Biermann's lyrics in this book are copyright © and used by permission of Wolf Biermann.

[29] Walter Mehring, *Neues Ketzerbrevier, Balladen und Songs* (Cologne and Berlin: Kiepenheuer & Witsch, 1962), 21. Quoted in Riha, 1975, 78.

[30] Walter Mehring, "Die 4 auf der Walze" (1924), in *Chronik der Lustbarkeiten*, 240.

[31] See Mikhail Bakhtin, *Rabelais and his World* (1984), 263–69.

[32] Mikhail Bakhtin, *The Dialogic Imagination*, 273.

[33] Wolf Biermann, "Lied auf das ehemalige Grenzgänger-Freudenmädchen Garance," *Alle Lieder* (Cologne: Kiepenheuer & Witsch, 1991), 57–58. Unless otherwise stated all references to Biermann are to this volume.

[34] Karen Leeder, *Breaking Boundaries: A New Generation of Poets in the GDR* (Oxford: Clarendon, 1996), 130.

[35] See Friedrich Hölderlin, *Hyperion* (1797/99; Munich: Goldman, 1981), 286.

[36] For further analysis see Veit Sorge, *Literarische Länderbilder in Liedern Wolf Biermanns und Wladimir Wyssozkis* (Frankfurt am Main: Peter Lang, 1998), 44–49. See also Jay Rosellini, *Wolf Biermann* (Munich: Beck, 1992), 69.

[37] Otto F. Riewoldt, "Wir haben jetzt hier einen Feind mehr" in Heinz Ludwig Arnold, ed., *Wolf Biermann* (Munich: Edition Text + Kritik, 1980), 11.

[38] See Bettina Wegner, "Ikarus," CD *Die Lieder 1978–8* (Buschfunk, 1997).

[39] Wenzel in an interview with Jens Rosbach, "Zwei Clowns," Deutschland-Radio (15 March 1998).

[40] Leeder writes of the antipathy of certain underground poets toward Wenzel and Mensching as a result of their adherence to utopian socialist ideals in her *Breaking Boundaries,* 40.

[41] Karls Enkel, Wacholder, and Beckert & Schulz, "Die Hammer-Rehwü," unpublished video from 1982, collected by Karin Wolf, archive of the Akademie der Künste der DDR, Berlin, Liedertheater-Dokumentation, Forschungsabteilung Musik/ Liedzentrum. CD *Hammer-Rehwü* (Nebelhorn, 1994).

[42] For further reading on the *Hammer-Rehwü* see David Robb, *Zwei Clowns im Lande des verlorenen Lachens: Das Liedertheater Wenzel & Mensching* (Berlin: Ch. Links, 1998), 51–70.

[43] Gerhard Gundermann, "An Vater." This and subsequent Gundermann songs in this chapter appear on the album *Männer, Frauen und Maschinen,* LP (Amiga, 1988).

[44] See the final chapter of this volume, "The Demise of Political Song and the New Discourse of Techno in the Berlin Republic."

4: The Burg Waldeck Festivals, 1964–1969

Eckard Holler

The Cultural Momentum of the *Jugendbewegung* in the Early 1960s

A T THE UNIVERSITIES OF THE Federal Republic in the first half of the 1960s there was a widespread type of student that was non-conformist, had a strong aspiration for independence, and was less interested in a bourgeois career than a self-determined life — preferably as a free artist and bohemian. The style for males was smoking a pipe, sporting a beard, and wearing parkas and long scarves in winter, jeans and wooden clogs in summer; for female students it was long hair, pullovers, and trousers. A preoccupation with the Nazi past led to far-reaching conflicts within families and an inner opposition to "society," which many tried to escape from for as long as possible. Hitchhiking was a popular means of travel because of its association with the feeling of boundless freedom. Hitchhiking journeys led through Europe to the North Cape or to Scotland, Istanbul, Cape Sunion, or even to Vienna or Paris for a quick breakfast; the romanticized self-image was that of a "noble vagabond" standing apart from society. Serving one's mandatory eighteen months in the military was frowned upon. Those who wanted to avoid military and community service went to study in West Berlin, where the draft did not apply due to the special status of the city. Günter Grass's *Die Blechtrommel* became a cult book, its antihero Oskar Matzerath wreaking chaos among the marching columns with the counter rhythms of his drum, and Enzensberger's poem "Was habe ich verloren in diesem Land" encapsulated the self-image of the individual. Writing poems and essays, thinking up satirical dialogues for cabaret groups, sitting in cafés, discussing aesthetics and planning a "lyric week" or the opening of a cabaret theater in a disused, empty cinema — such activities filled up the semester more easily than attending lectures. Small publishing houses like the Eremitenpresse of V.O. Stomps enjoyed a great reputation and magazines like *Konkret, Pardon,* and *Akzente* shaped one's self image and political and aesthetic horizons. The first half of the 1960s was for many a bohemian time in which placing oneself in opposition to the despised *Spießer* society celebrating its own economic miracle was the main goal.

Many youth felt affiliated to what Helmut Schelsky termed in 1957 the "skeptical generation."[1] But by the 1960s many were already searching for new challenges. Anything remotely conservative, let alone right-wing, was challenged vociferously. New forms of political engagement "from below" that offered possibilities for practical activity — such as the Easter Marches — were excitedly discussed. In the mid-1960s these formed a bridge for the transition from being a "skeptical" outsider to participating in actions such as the Kampagne für Abrüstung (Campaign for Disarmament) and, later, the Außerparlamentarische Opposition (Extra-Parliamentary Opposition), known as the APO. As the 1960s progressed, concepts like "Kollektiv," "Masse," and "Bewegung" lost their negative connotations and formed the consciousness of a new generation whose role model was no longer the social outsider, but rather the "Genosse" (comrade). And in the shaping of this consciousness the new *Liedermacher*, not least Peter Rohland, Wolf Biermann, Dieter Süverkrüp, and Franz Josef Degenhardt played a pioneering role.

The *Jugendbewegung* in the Emerging *Liedermacher* Scene

The forming of the network of friends, acquaintances, and musicians that organized the first Burg Waldeck festivals can in many respects be traced back to connections within the *Jugendbewegung*.[2] In the early 1960s there emerged in many parts of the Federal Republic, above all in university towns, informal, private and semi-public meeting points, intellectual circles, and student work groups. These were often run by people who had originally come from associations of the Bündische Jugend (the youth movement of the Weimar Republic, which had reformed after the Second World War). They had discarded the movement as "infantile" and "escapist" and were looking for new challenges for members who were now of student age. An example of this was the development of the Baslertorturm in Karlsruhe-Durlach, a youth club of the Deutsche Jungenschaft e.V. This was an autonomous youth association in the tradition of the youth organization dj.1.11[3] from the 1920s and 30s. It had been revived after 1945 and now ran groups in the big cities. From 1963 onwards "turmgespräche" were held in the tower and a small literary and political magazine was brought out.[4] Among the themes discussed were the the politics of the *pläne* magazine, the pros and cons of taking part in the Easter Marches, the question of political engagement "from below," and not least the role of youth opposition in the period of National Socialism.[5] The participants liked to see themselves as descendants of the Scholl siblings and the illegal youth opposition of the dj.1.11. The tower also held discussions on the lyrics of Paul Celan and the Karlsruhe poet Walter

Helmut Fritz and on the dramatic theories of Brecht. Performances were staged of Brecht's *Ausnahme und die Regel* and Peter Weiss' *Nacht mit Gästen*. It was possible to hear tape recordings of Wolf Biermann that had been smuggled over from the GDR, and the singer Peter Rohland stayed over one night in 1963 during his first tour performing Yiddish songs.

Another place of cultural significance in Karlsruhe was the "Atelier" of the painter Peter Bertsch (known as "der fuchs"), where modern art and graphics were discussed and Shrove Tuesday was celebrated with a three-day festival called "der schnarpf." This featured the new breed of political singers known as *Liedermacher,* including Roland Eckert, Walter Mossmann, and Christof Stählin. In December 1963 the first of a series of annual events featuring *Liedermacher* and singers was held in the jazz club in Pforzheim under the title "Improvisation." It was broadcast live by the SDR youth-radio program. Among those taking part were Hein and Oss Kröher, Peter Rohland, Hanno Botsch, Nono Breitenstein, Walter Stodtmeister, Christof Stählin, and Michaela Weiß.

One song from the performance, "Lob des Omnibus" by Walter Mossmann, reflects the mood of the time in the *Jugendbewegung*. The song comes from a 1964 song pamphlet of the Bund deutscher Jungenschaften. This was a dynamic youth association that had dominated intellectual youth circles in the first half of the 1960s until it fell apart after being condemned by the student movement in 1968 for lack of political engagement. The song uses the 7/8 rhythm of Greek folk music and conveys the feeling of the trips to Greece that were popular among youth groups at the time and were viewed as an alternative to the new West German mass tourism. Like other songs of Mossmann's peers it was written to be sung by large groups in the youth associations. The latter's new philosophy rejected the old style of wandering (*Wandervogel*) songs and demanded the embrace of the modern world while at the same time retaining the naivety of the folk song.

Lob des Omnibus (Jubellied)

Südwind, Nordwind gleich den Schwalben und den Lerchen, trugt den Ikarus.
Flüstert im Platanenlaub ihr jenes Märchen überm Omnibus.
Wollte zu hoch und fiel, dein Kind, armer Dädalus
Halten wir uns fest, wo wir sind, auf dem Omnibus.

Südwind, Nordwind, nenne uns der Trinker Paten: Pate Romulus.
Er hat Rom erbaut, wir tun nur kleine Taten auf dem Omnibus.
Ihm gab die Wölfin Milch und Kraft (nach dem Livius),
Uns der Ziegenschlauch Rebensaft auf dem Omnibus.

Südwind, Nordwind treibt die Sterne schon zu Paaren, komm o
    Pegasus.
Komm und bringe uns das Lied, nach dem wir fahren — mit
    dem Omnibus.
Ist auch dein Flügel arg geflickt, kläffe wie Zerberus,
Bis wir in Staub und Qualm entrückt im Jubel — Omnibus.[6]

In Bonn-Bad Godesberg *Jugendbewegung* members Siegfried Maeker and
Burkhard Schaeder formed a "folkloristischer Arbeitskreis" (folklore study
group) and a skiffle band[7] after meeting each other while hitchhiking in
Greece in the summer of 1962. They put on their first folk concert in the
autumn of that year in the small auditorium of the Beethovenhalle in
Bonn-Bad Godesberg. Other than themselves it featured musicians they
had met on their travels such as the English folk-singing duo Colin Wilkie
and Shirley Hart, and Peter Rohland, whom Maeker knew from the
Jugendbewegung. These concerts continued until 1967. Reflecting the intellectual dimension of the newly emerging folk and political song scene
in Germany, the activities in Bonn-Bad Godesberg also included a philosophy study group that dealt with, among other topics, Albert Camus
and modern existentialism.

Peter Rohland

The Haus Seebe[8] in Berlin where Peter Rohland (1933–66) lived was a
center for new ideas and activities. After his *Abitur* in 1954 Rohland, a
classically trained bass baritone, had taken his guitar and hitchhiked to
Greece on an eight-month journey of self-discovery that led as far as the
Iraq-Kuwait border. In the late 1950s in Berlin he began a singing career
performing German and international folk songs, initially in modest en-
gagements in pubs and small cabaret theaters. Alongside his activities as a
singer he held a leading function in the Schwäbische Jungenschaft and
later in the Deutsche Jungenschaft e.V. From 1953 he had organized annual trips to Greece and became acquainted with Greek folk culture. In
Greece he had learned to play bouzouki and learned a range of local
songs and dances. His enthusiasm had led to a wave of modern Greek
singing and dancing in the *Jugendbewegung*. By the early 1960s he began
discovering Israeli folk song and dance and propagated these in his circles.
In 1962 he went for three months to Paris, where he sang in the chanson
cellars on the left bank of the Seine and came home with the idea of establishing a festival to further a renaissance of a German *Chanson* akin to
the satirical and political model known in France. He quickly succeeded in
creating a chanson wave in the *Jugendbewegung*. His chanson program
"Vertäut am Abendstern" emerged at the end of 1962 containing songs

of *Jugendbewegung* writers such as Werner Helwig, Wolfgang Münch, Manfred Hausmann, and Bastel Losch. In the autumn of 1962 he performed it in public and produced an EP of the same name with Thorofon, the small publishing house of the *Jugendbewegung*.

"Ich schaukle meine Müdigkeit" is an example of a chanson from Rohland's "pre-critical" period, which still reflected the world outlook of the *Jugendbewegung*. While it documents his transition from a *bündisch* singer and singing master to a *chansonnier*, it nonetheless reflects the difficulties he had to overcome. The song, written by Werner Helwig in 1934, conjures up an archaic, static time of past happiness. It is retrospective and melancholy and views the present and future negatively with its perspective of imminent destruction.

> Ich schaukle meine Müdigkeit
> und denk, es wär die beste Zeit
> zum Schlafen gehen.
>
> Ich mach mein altes Zelt bereit,
> such süßes Moos der Üppigkeit;
> die Stunden stehn.
>
> Das Holz im offnen Feuer kracht.
> Die Flamme küßt mich schattensacht.
> Und Träume wehn.
>
> Da denke ich in meine Nacht
> wie wir zu Zeiten gut gelacht,
> die Sterne stehn.
>
> Die Sterne stehn im alten Stand.
> Der Tod hält uns in kalter Hand.
> Die Freunde gehen.
>
> Zick und Floh sind aus der Zeit,
> sie bechern goldne Ewigkeit.
> Die Schnitter mähn.
>
> Die Schnitter mähen nah zu mir.
> Ich aber singe für und für
> und wills nicht sehn.[9]

The program of "Vertäut am Abendstern" is an example of the backward-orientated, escapist mentality that was widespread in the 1950s *Jugendbewegung* and constituted an alternative world for many of its adherents. Its theme, also echoed in other songs in the cycle, completely ignores the questions that were being asked by the West German youth of the time, which were geared toward a critical re-evaluation of the recent German past. Due to its ahistorical and apolitical intention the program "Vertäut am Abendstern" did not further the chanson cause among contemporary critically minded musicians — contrary to Rohland's expectations. It was also judged ambivalently by the *Jugendbewegung* itself — and after Rohland's untimely death in early 1966 from a cerebral hemorrhage this led to an argument between the publishers of his songs. Axel Hauff, editor of the "Edition Peter Rohland," rejected Rohland's planned fifth LP entitled "Lieder der Matrosen." It featured the five songs from the *Vertäut am Abendstern* EP alongside cowboy songs and others from the *Jugendbewegung,* the quality of which was in some cases judged to be "miserabel."[10] Helmut König published these, however, in 1977 as the fifth record of the Thorofon Complete Works, under the title *Lieder von anderswo.*[11]

Rohland's interest in politics and the democratic folk song began in Berlin in the early 1960s. There he was confronted with the Nazi past and anti-Semitism by friends who studied at the Free University and who had relations with the German-Israeli student group (Diss) and the Sozialistischer Deutscher Studentenbund (Socialist German Students Association, SDS). He also participated in discussions on Marxist theory and continuing undemocratic tendencies in West German society. Impressed by these, Rohland developed a critical and realistic folk song concept that included oppositional songs from the 1848 revolution, songs of repressed minorities, and songs from the anti-Nazi resistance. Also operating in the Seebe house in Berlin was Diethart Kerbs, an up-and-coming art and cultural studies expert who similarly had held a leading position in the *Jugendbewegung.* He was interested in the relationship between art and society, supported an undogmatic socialism ("des dritten Weges"), and was looking for opportunities to lead the *Jugendbewegung* out of its fruitless preoccupation with itself and give it a more contemporary orientation.

During his stay in Paris in spring 1962 Rohland was not only inspired to reflect on a new German chanson, but also had the idea of compiling a program of both historical and modern Yiddish songs. Together with musicians Hanno Botsch and Gesine Köhler he collected songs of the Eastern European Jews and arranged them as modern folk songs. For his concerts he worked out explanatory notes for every song. His program "Der Rebbe singt" in 1963 brought him his artistic breakthrough in West Berlin and the Federal Republic. With these songs Rohland met head-on with the latent will among the student youth and the intelligentsia to make amends for the crimes of the Nazis. He became the first German singer to break through the heavy postwar silence ("das bleierne Schweigen") over the Nazis' persecution of Jews and to make a gesture of reconciliation.[12] He performed the program over fifty times on tour and broadcast it on both radio and TV. Being the sensitive topic that it was, Rohland was unable to entirely avoid controversy. Some Jewish commentators criticized him for the singing of the Jewish partisan song "Shtil, die Nacht ist oys-geschenrt." This was a more modern as opposed to a traditional Yiddish song and had been written by the Jewish poet and resistance fighter Hirsh Glick in 1943 to commemorate the uprising in the Vilna ghetto. Among the responses was the complaint that Glick would not have wanted a German to sing this song. Rohland was alleged to have overstepped "eine unsichtbare Grenze [. . .] die ihm als Deutschen gesetzt sei."[13]

His second program consisted of "Landstreicherballaden" (vagabond ballads), which he had come across partly in old songbooks and partly from tramps themselves.[14] With his third program in 1965 Rohland became the most celebrated singer of the nascent student movement in West Berlin. The program consisted of songs of the German revolution of 1848, which he arranged as chansons on the guitar and set to music sometimes in collaboration with others. His fourth program was made up of songs and ballads of François Villon (in the translations of Paul Zech) for which he composed the music himself. A fifth program "Deutsche Volkslieder — entstaubt und unverblümt" was uncompleted. Peter Rohland died in 1966 just as his singing career was taking off at a national level. His complete works were released in 1977 on five LPs and now is available on CD.

The First Burg Waldeck Festival, 1964: Chanson Folklore International — "Junge Europäer singen"

The idea for the festival had been fermenting with Peter Rohland since his stay in Paris in the spring of 1962. This had led to discussions in Berlin with people such as Oss and Hein Kröher, Jan Weber, and Diethart Kerbs. In the autumn of 1963 the idea of an international chanson gathering at Burg Waldeck was gathering steam in the wake of discussions in the student work group of the Arbeitsgemeinschaft Burg Waldeck (ABW). The concept formulated by Diethart Kerbs envisaged a workshop of singers and *Liedermacher* in the style of the literary Gruppe 47: participants would sing and discuss their songs and explore the possibilities of a renaissance of the German chanson. The term *Chanson*, which Peter Rohland had introduced, reflected an artistic orientation toward the French chanson. It was agreed that the revival[15] of the German *Chanson* should be differentiated from German *Schlager* as well as from opera and classical singing ("keine Maria Callas und kein Freddy Quinn") and should at the same time constitute a break from the group singing of the *Jugendbewegung*.

But despite general unanimity of purpose, there were varying agendas. Rather than chanson, the sibling duo Oss and Hein Kröher favored the creation of a "Bauhaus für Folklore" where Germans could contribute to the Anglo-American folk revival. Others in the ABW work group focused more on politics and, for example, discussed the news of the arrests of guitar-playing singers at anti-Vietnam-war demonstrations in the USA. Differences notwithstanding, these varying agendas were all encompassed within the aims of the festival, and as the New Year of 1964 dawned, the festival idea was finalized in discussions at Burg Waldeck, the title "Chanson Folklore International" decided upon, and Whitsun 1964 fixed as the date for the first festival.

In his opening speech "Gesang zwischen den Fronten" Diethart Kerbs formulated the aesthetic agenda of the gathering. Politically he positioned the organizers as supporters of peaceful coexistence in Europe between the two sides in the Cold War. The festival had the air of a weekend conference, with lectures, discussions, and studio concerts. There was communal singing with the reknowned European folk song expert Sepp Gregor and a morning cembalo concert by music students from Detmold. But Waldeck also had the character of an open-air festival with its three concerts held on a makeshift wooden stage with a PA system in front of a sloping field.

The Anglo American folk revival was represented by a contingent of Americans resident in West Germany, including Carol Culbertson, Karen Litell and Russ Samson as well as the English folk duo Colin Wilkie and Shirley Hart, who had played on the English folk club and festival circuit up until 1962, but were now resident in Germany. Wilkie was responsible for acquainting the German guitarists with the new finger-picking technique now prevalent in Anglo-American folk circles. Other acts at the festival were Peter Rohland with his Yiddish songs, Oss Kröher with songs from the Steiermark, the young Reinhard Mey singing chansons, the folk singer Michaela Weiß from Israel, and Hai och Topsy from Sweden. But the most important feature in the eyes of the festival organizers and the media was the advent of the new German singers with their contemporary, self-penned, and socially critical songs.

At the first Burg Waldeck festival in 1964 the German *Liedermacher* were hailed as a great new phenomenon. Singer and guitarist Franz Josef Degenhardt performed his songs such as "August der Schäfer" and "Rumpelstilchen" and immediately stood in the center of discussion. Born 1931 in Schwelm in Westfalia, Degenhardt was, following his law studies, a lecturer at the Institute for European Law at the University of Saarbrücken. He had already made his mark in 1963 with a Polydor LP of his own chansons entitled *Zwischen Null Uhr Null und Mitternacht*. With the Burg Waldeck festivals, which he took part in from the beginning and where he was generally judged by festival and fans alike to be the most important *Liedermacher,* he became known to a wider public. He came from a Catholic, anti-fascist background in Westphalia and had been a member of the SPD since 1961.[16] With his songs, which became more political and concrete with every year, he both reflected and shaped the development of the Burg Waldeck festivals between 1964 and 1969. In the beginning he sang songs about suspicious characters on the edge of society whose life stories clashed with the successes of the *Wirtschaftswunder* propagated by the media. In these early songs he expressed the widespread feeling among intellectuals of a vague but unmistakable uneasiness with the social order of the Adenauer period. In the song "Rumpelstilzchen" from 1963 (already quoted from by David Robb in chapter 3) he uses the fairy-tale figure as a symbol for the brittleness of the existing order:

> Wenn morgens schon die Schule brennt,
> Wenn ein Pfarrer aus der Kirche rennt,
> ein Schutzmann in die Pfütze fällt,
> ein Hund durch ein Museum bellt,
> wenn der Friedhofswärter, der niemals trinkt,
> noch am off'nen Grab an zu lachen fängt,
> wenn der Mond sich vor die Sonne schiebt,
> ein Greis ein Mädchen von siebzehn liebt,
> Da habe ich, mal kaum, mal viel, die Hand im Spiel.
> Ich bin mit jedem blutsverwandt, doch bleibt mein Name ungenannt.
> Es ist gut dass niemand weiß, dass ich Rumpelstilzchen heiß.
> Hemba hemba he, hemba hemba he.
> [. . .][17]

The partly mysterious, partly threatening allusions in Degenhardt's early songs were followed by an increasingly direct social critique and political commentary with each year that he performed at Waldeck. From "Rumpelstilzchen" in 1964 one can chart his development to "Spiel nicht mit den Schmuddelkindern" (1965), where he makes a more direct, more open criticism of a social climber, through to his lament at the misuse of the German folk-song tradition by the Nazis in "Die alten Lieder" (1966) right up to the political agitation of "Zwischentöne sind nur Krampf — im Klassenkampf" in 1968. In this way Degenhardt was always in step with the development of the 1968 movement, his annual appearances at the Waldeck festivals reflecting the changing state of its political consciousness. He was in close personal contact with the leading representatives of the student movement (for example, Rudi Dutschke and Gaston Salvatore), which occasionally influenced his songwriting directly, for example, in the song "vatis argumente,"[18] in which Degenhardt ironically adopts the roleplay of a "father" who is scandalized by the attitudes and actions of the Dutschke generation. In the late 1960s Degenhardt renounced his academic career in order to become a lawyer for the APO and to become a professional political *Liedermacher*.

Another of the new breed of political singer who performed at the first Waldeck festival was Dieter Süverkrüp. Born in 1934, Süverkrüp came

from a communist background in the Ruhr. He was a graphic artist who
performed on the side as a singer and jazz guitarist, working additionally
with the author and translator Gerd Semmer, who was active in the *Demo-
kratischer Kulturbund*. He had come into contact in the early 1960s with
the magazine *pläne*, a journalistic project that stemmed from the left wing
of the *Jugendbewegung*.[19] When *pläne* branched out into the record market in 1961 its first release was an EP by Süverkrüp featuring songs from
the French Revolution translated into German by Semmer.[20]

Süverkrüp sang out against the nuclear arms race and the threat it
posed as well as the anti-communism that was widespread in the Federal
Republic. He became known for political children's songs such as "Bagger-
führer Willibald" and for songs such as "Erschröckliche Moritat vom Kryptokommunisten," which satirizes bourgeois attitudes toward communists:

Wenn die Sonne bezeichnenderweise im Osten
und rot hinter Wolken aufgeht,
das ist dann die Zeit, da er flach wie ein Tiger
aus härenem Bette aufsteht.
Er wäscht sich nur ungern und blickt in den Spiegel
mit seinem Mongolengesicht,
er putzt sich die Zähne mit Branntwein und trinkt einen
Wodka — mehr frühstückt er nicht.
Dann zieht der Kommunist die Unterwanderstiefel an,
und dann geht er an sein illegales Untertagewerk ran.
Huhu, huhu . . .!

Und dann fletscht er die Zähne, die Hand hält er vor,
denn das darf ja kein Mensch niemals sehn.
Um neun Uhr zehn frißt er das erste Kind (blauäugig,
blond) aus dem Kindergarteehn.
Um elf brennt die Kirche, es drängen sich hilfsbereit
Feuerwehr, Bürger und Christ.
Derweil diskutiert er mit Schwester Theres',
bis die auch für den Weltfrieden ist.
     Der Kommunist ist so geschickt, dagegen kann man nicht!
     Und zu Mittag schreibt er gar noch ein politisches Gedicht.
     Huhu, huhu . . .!
[. . .][21]

At the first Waldeck festival Süverkrüp sang songs satirizing political
naivety ("Leute greift zur Feuerpatsche, stellt den Tütensand bereit"[22]),
sang translations of songs of the French Revolution ("Ah, das geht ran"[23]),
and was celebrated as by far the most "brazen" singer of the gathering.
Süverkrüp was one of the few *Liedermacher* in the early 1960s who had

clear sympathies with the Communist Party (KPD), which was banned in the Federal Republic.[24] Unlike the artistically refined songs of Degenhardt, which functioned as parables of society, Süverkrüp's songs were distinct in their clarity and directness. This, however, did not yet correspond to the tastes of the student milieu, which in the early to mid 1960s still preferred the subtlety of Degenhardt, with the result that Süverkrüp was slightly adrift of public interest at the early Waldeck festivals and never felt particularly at home there.

Another protest singer who performed at the first Waldeck festival was Fasia Jansen (1929–97). Born of a German mother and Liberian father in Hamburg, Jansen, being a "non-Aryan," endured SS brutality and concentration camp labor, from which she contracted a heart condition. Accompanied by the Conrads at Burg Waldeck in 1964 she sang out against the atom bomb ("Geht auf die Straße und schreit Feuer! Feuer, unsre Erde wird verbrannt"[25]) and performed other political songs in a skiffle and blues style. Her version of Wolf Biermann's "Ballade vom Briefträger William L. Moore aus Baltimore," a song identifying with the American civil rights campaign against the persecution of blacks, became the most popular song of the festival.

From the first Waldeck festival onwards Biermann was always present in spirit despite never being allowed by the GDR authorities to play there. Born in Hamburg in 1936, Biermann was already in the early 1960s the epitome of the new political *Liedermacher*[26] and a figure of identification for the unorthodox left in both West and East Germany. As the son of communist and Jewish parents — his father was murdered in 1943 in Auschwitz — in 1953 he moved with the blessing of Margot Honecker[27] from the Federal Republic to the GDR to fulfill the legacy of his father and to participate in the building of socialism. In 1961, with friends, he converted an empty cinema auditorium into a theater (which they called the Berliner Arbeiter- und Studententheater, or b.a.t.) in which to put on their own performances. The theater was, however, closed by the authorities in 1963, and his play "Berliner Brautgang," which dealt with the building of the Wall, was banned. In autumn 1964 the SDS organized a tour of the Federal Republic, where tape recordings of his songs were already circulating. His mid-1960s collaborations with the West German cabaret performer Wolfgang Neuss, both in musical concerts and in the pages of the satirical magazine *Neuss-Deutschland* were legendary. In December 1965 he was banned by the GDR authorities from traveling, performing, and publishing, but was still able to further his career by publishing in the West. Chausseestraße 131 in East Berlin, where Biermann lived, was an important address for non-conformist intellectuals in the capital city of the GDR.

Biermann acknowledged François Villon, the vagabond French Renaissance poet, as his role model, and provoked the anger of the SED with bold and rebellious criticism of GDR socialism. He sang against German petit bourgeois narrowmindedness and prudishness, and for an unbureaucratic socialism. His song "Soldat, Soldat" became an object of lengthy contention with the SED regarding the "correct" attitude — in accordance with party lines — toward bourgeois pacifism and revolutionary force in the international class war:

> Soldat, Soldat in grauer Norm,
> Soldat, Soldat in Uniform,
> Soldat, Soldat, ihr seid so viel,
> Soldat, Soldat, das ist kein Spiel.
> Soldat, Soldat, ich finde nicht,
> Soldat, Soldat, dein Angesicht.
> Soldaten sehn sich alle gleich,
> lebendig und als Leich.
> [. . .]

The first Waldeck festival was judged an unexpectedly great success by its organizers, by the musicians themselves, and by the members of the media who were present. Many cited the high number of young German singers and the variety of themes dealt with in the songs. In Franz Josef Degenhardt, the media had discovered a new German *Chansonnier* of the highest caliber. It was decided that a second festival in an extended form would be held the following year. The event had enjoyed a comparatively large media resonance with the presence of three German radio stations (SDR, SWF, and WR) producing a full range of music programs, which spread the news of what was the first German chanson festival. The record company Polydor had also been present recording concerts and signing artists.

Peter Rohland did not have the central role at the first Waldeck Festival that he, as co-initiator of the festival, expected to have. One reason lay in the fact that he was not able to perform his new program of "Landstreicherballaden" because his partner Schobert Schulz canceled his appearance at the last minute. Rohland was also unable to maneuver himself into an authoritative position in the chanson debate, which he had initiated three years before, because his Yiddish songs were evaluated as folk songs rather than chansons, and the audience and media only had a secondary interest in folk. Moreover, promising record contract negotiations for an LP of his Yiddish songs failed due to the question of the authenticity of his performance style. A positive outcome for him, however, was the signing of a deal with Polydor for his LP *Landstreicherballaden,* which was released in 1965. The new *Liedermacher* found another important contact in the journalist Susanne Feijal from Sender Freies Berlin. In late 1964 she produced the television program *SFB-Liederfestival,* which featured the most important Waldeck singers and continued for several years.

The Second Burg Waldeck Festival, 1965

At the second Waldeck festival, held from 26 May to 1 June 1965, the number of performing soloists and groups doubled to thirty-two and the number of visitors increased fivefold to 2,000. Television crews from the public channels were present this time alongside the broadcasting vans of the radio stations. The festival was again dominated by the question "what is a chanson?" There were two lectures about this, one from the singer's perspective by Franz Josef Degenhardt and the other by his brother, the sociologist Martin Degenhardt. Diethart Kerbs had already started the discussion in his opening speech with a definition that found broad acceptance: "Ein Chanson ist ein Lied, das nicht im Chor gesungen werden kann." This formulation was well received because it hit upon the anti-fascist mood, which identified collective singing with the Nazis and judged solo singing in front of an audience as a democratic alternative.

In this second year of the festival, workshop concerts were arranged in the small hall to go alongside the big concerts on the open-air stage. A big tent was put up where one could escape the constant rain. The festival newspaper *piep-in* appeared on each of the three days, commenting on the festival goings-on and causing considerable excitement.

At this second festival, the rediscovery of the German democratic folk-song tradition was gathering momentum. The twins Oss and Hein Kröher (born 1927) from Pirmasens were, alongside Peter Rohland, at the fore-front of this. A groundbreaking event of the 1965 festival was Rohland's workshop of songs from the 1848 revolution. This can be seen in retro-spect as having given the initial spark for the German folk revival. The music academic Gisela Probst-Effah established that two of the songs sung by Rohland, "Das Bürgerlied" and "O König von Preußen," appeared only a few years later, at the highpoint of the folk movement in the 1970s, in the repertoires of almost every folk singer.[28] In his workshop Rohland ex-plained the origins of the texts in relation to the democratic song tradi-tion in Germany and commented on their contemporary political relevance. He advocated that this new, "realistic" German folk song should replace the old romantic concept with its nationalistic overtones:

> Wir müssen diesen Begriff endlich berichtigen. Deutsche Volkslieder haben weder mit "Volksseele" noch mit "ewigen Werten" etwas zu tun. Es sind einfach Lieder, die den ganzen Aspekt menschlichen Lebens umfassen.[29]

Rohland felt that the folk-song tradition should no longer be syn-onymous with banal songs such as "Blümlein rot und weiß und blau," but should also take into account songs stemming from freedom move-ments in German history. One of these was the "Bürgerlied" from the years leading up to the 1848 revolution. It is a call for social unity to further political progress and combat the forces of reaction:

> Ob wir rote, gelbe Kragen
> Helme oder Hüte tragen
> Stiefel tragen oder Schuh;
> Oder ob wir Röcke nähen
> und zu Schuh'n die Drähte drehen,
> das tut, das tut nichts dazu.
>
> Ob wir können präsidieren
> oder müssen Akten schmieren
> ohne Rast und ohne Ruh;
> Ob wir just Collegia lesen,
> oder aber binden Besen,
> das tut, das tut nichts dazu.
>
> Ob wir stolz zu Rosse reiten
> oder ob zu Fuß wir schreiten
> fürbaß unserm Ziele zu;
> Ob uns Kreuze vorne schmücken
> oder Kreuze hinten drücken,
> das tut, das tut nichts dazu.
>
> Aber ob wir Neues bauen
> oder Altes nur verdauen,
> wie das Gras verdaut die Kuh;
> Ob wir in der Welt was schaffen,
> oder nur die Welt begaffen,
> das tut, das tut was dazu.
>
> Ob wir rüstig und geschäftig,
> wo es gilt zu wirken kräftig,
> immer tapfer griefen zu;
> Oder ob wir schläfrig denken:
> "Gott wird's schon im Schlafe schenken,"
> das tut, das tut was dazu!
>
> Drum ihr Bürger, drum ihr Brüder,
> alles eines Bundes Glieder,
> was auch jeder von uns tu —
> Alle, die dies Lied gesungen,
> so die Alten wie die Jungen,
> tun wir, tun wir denn dazu![30]

The focus of attention, however, was the new German *Liedermacher/ Chansonnier* Franz Josef Degenhardt and his most recent program of songs "Spiel nicht mit den Schmuddelkindern." These undertook a more direct social critique than his songs of the previous year. Over the coming years the term "Schmuddelkinder" ("scruffy kids") was to enter the popular language as a ironic synonym for those involved in the *Liedermacher* scene. The protagonist is a middle-class child who is continually warned against fraternizing with the riff-raff: "Spiel nicht mit den Schmuddelkindern, / sing nicht ihre Lieder. / Geh doch in die Oberstadt / mach's wie deine Brüder."[31] The song was interpreted on one hand as a criticism of social opportunism and conformity[32] and on the other as showing sympathy with proletarian children whose upbringing, unlike the majority of the Burg Waldeck participants and spectators, were not constrained by shallow bourgeois convention.[33]

Walter Mossmann (born 1941) was the festival's unexpected new success. He was a political science student from Freiburg and had come to Waldeck via the *Jugendbewegung*. In his husky voice he sang his own songs in the style of the French chanson, songs that stood out for their contrariness and power of association. After the following year's festival, Ann Thönnissen was to write in *TWEN:* "Was Mossmann bringt, ist von intellektueller Schärfe, widerhakig, schmerzhaft, bösartig, plattenreif. Ich bin beeindruckt, wittre Morgenluft, höre: Ist das endlich das neue deutsche Lied?"[34]

A whole line-up of young, intellectual, male and female *Liedermacher* also drew attention. Kristin Bauer-Horn (born 1936), a female advocate of the chanson, was praised for poetic songs that dealt with everyday situations. Guitar-playing Reinhard Mey (born 1942) from the Berlin student scene sang his "Hymne an Frau Pohl," in which he rents a room from the chaste landlady Frau Pohl for 80 marks per month: "alles inclusive, außer Liebe."[35] Walter Hedemann (born 1932), a school teacher from Hamlin, sang to his own piano accompaniment songs about stereotypical aspects of German life such as "deutscher Wald," "deutsche Mädel," and "deutscher Sang." with ironic references to how the specter of National Socialism was never far away, for example, in the form of the West German right-wing radical party, the NPD: "Ich kann mich nicht entschließen, NPD zu wählen. Ich weiß nicht, das ist bei mir so 'n Tick."[36] In an indication of the debates to come at Waldeck, Hedemann met with controversial reactions. Klaus Budzinski found his songs banal and misguided, while Hanns Dieter Hüsch praised them for their irony.

The 1965 festival also presented a workshop of songs by Wolf Biermann. The GDR authorities had not granted him an exit visa to travel to Waldeck, but had had a tape recording of new songs smuggled over the border. The group of Anglo-American folk singers centered around Colin

Wilkie and Shirley Hart was also present. This year it was strengthened by the English folk singer John Pearse, the black blues singer Al Curtis, and the young Charly McLean, son of a Scottish noble and war general. Karl Wolfram also made a big impact with his hurdy gurdy and Middle-High German *Minnesang*, and Aviva Semadar impressed with her Israeli, German, and international folk songs. Also present was the Spanish émigré duo Juan Esteller and José Suarez, who sang songs against the Franco dictatorship.

If the previous year had in some respects given the impression of an open-air weekend conference with workshops, the second Waldeck meeting was more of a typical song festival. This development, which the organizers would have preferred to avoid, took on its own momentum as the number of visitors grew to two thousand and it began to ressemble a mass event: the stage was bigger, the stage equipment better, and the longer open-air concerts were now the focal point. The atmosphere was still largely unpolitical to the extent that artists with a political agenda such as Dieter Süverkrüp, Fasia Jansen, and Juan Esteller and José Suarez began to question their further participation.

The idea was raised to open Burg Waldeck the whole year round to support and help professionalize chanson activities, but due to financial problems this never proceeded beyond discussion. Concrete plans did emerge, however, for the bimonthly magazine *Song* for chanson, folk, and street ballad. It was run by the organizers of Burg Waldeck under the editorial leadership of Rolf Gekeler and first appeared at the 1966 festival.[37]

The Third Burg Waldeck Festival, 1966

The 1966 festival, held over Whitsun from 26–30 May, was overshadowed by the sudden death of Peter Rohland from a brain hemorrhage shortly before the festival. Diethart Kerbs remembered Rohland in his opening speech. The number of artists and groups had risen to above fifty; the number of spectators to above three thousand. The capacity of the grounds had now been reached.

Yet another German *Liedermacher* was discovered at this third meeting, in the figure of Hannes Wader (born 1942) from Berlin. Accompanying himself on the guitar, he sang songs about love, loneliness and wanderlust. A characteristic of Wader's was that he — unlike the other Waldeck *Liedermacher* — was influenced equally by the French chanson and by the American folk song. His model was Georg Brassens, and he had learned finger-picking from watching American street musicians in Berlin. Also appearing for the first time was the Mainz cabaret artist Hanns Dieter Hüsch (1925–2005), who performed despite many reservations about guitarists and the open-air conditions. He played songs on the piano in the small "Sälchen" of the Schwabenhaus and was so impressed by the festival atmosphere that he returned to the festival in the years that followed, becoming one of the core group of artists. Another debut act which was to appear again at later Waldeck festivals was the duo Wolfgang "Schobert" Schulz (1941–92) and Lothar "Black" Lechleitern (born 1942).

The 1966 festival also saw a new wave of young protest singers in the style of the early Bob Dylan with guitars and harmonicas singing out against the Vietnam war and social hypocrisy among other things. These included Andreas Merkel, Nono Breitenstein, and Christopher and Michael. Their protest songs attracted the interest of the media, but were strongly criticized by the festival leadership and by many of the established Waldeck artists on aesthetic grounds. In his opening speech on "Chanson und Konsum," Kerbs had dealt with the commercialization of the new "Chanson." Now with all the media fuss about the protest song he saw his worst fears realized. In his festival reflections in *Song*, Hanns Dieter Hüsch found fault with the lack of self-awareness of the young protest singers. He accused Nono Breitenstein of being clichéd and Christopher and Michael of being tantamount to schmaltz.[38] But this critique was challenged by the cabaret expert Klaus Budzinski, who, also writing in *Song*, turned the tables on Hüsch by noticing a bourgeois lack of commitment in his songs that was out of place at Waldeck. Budzinski praised the readiness of the protest singers to sing out against injustice.[39] The debates over the protest song continued in *Song*, where Dieter Süverkrüp and Schobert Schulz argued the merits of the song "Protest gegen den Protest oder — wie schön, daß es die Bombe gibt," with which Schulz had won the first prize in the song competition of South German Radio (SDR). Süverkrüp described the text as "confused" and the argument against protest as "petit-bourgeois." Schulz criticized Süverkrüp in turn for having neither competence nor a sense of humor.[40] This first controversy surrounding the theme of political engagement in song lyrics provided a mere foretaste of conflicts at the later Waldeck festivals.

The song that received the most attention at the 1966 festival was Degenhardt's "Die alten Lieder." It posed the question why Germans were embarrassed to sing their own folk songs in front of foreigners. In his song, Degenhardt named three songs that could no longer be sung: "Ein Heller und ein Batzen," "Feinsliebchen, du sollst nicht barfuß gehn," and "Wildgänse rauschen durch die Nacht," and blamed the death of the German folk song on the "braune Horden" of the Nazis, the "Stiefel" of the German Army, and a misguided cultivation of the folk-song tradition by the "Lehrer" and the "Kurzbehoste" of the youth organizations. This song was frequently cited in the media as an example of the songs sung at Waldeck.[41]

Wo sind eure Lieder, eure alten Lieder?
Fragen die aus andren Ländern, wenn man um Kamine sitzt,
mattgetanzt und leergesprochen und das high-life-Spiel ausschwitzt.

Ja, wo sind die Lieder, unsre alten Lieder?
Nicht für'n Heller oder Batzen mag Feinsliebchen barfuß ziehn
und kein schriller Schrei nach Norden will aus einer Kehle fliehn.

Tot sind unsre Lieder, unsre alten Lieder.
Lehrer haben sie zerbissen, Kurzbehoste sie verklampft,
braune Horden totgeschrien, Stiefel in den Dreck gestampft.
Tot sind unsre Lieder, unsre alten Lieder.[42]

For many, the highpoint of the festival was the spontaneous singing of "We Shall Overcome" by the crowd and the on-stage musicians at the close of the nightly Hootenannies, which expressed their feelings of solidarity and hopes for a common future.

In 1966 the festival was at its pinnacle. From the press it received exuberant reviews full of superlatives. Many big German papers and youth magazines were present with their own correspondents. The *Frankfurter Allgemeine Zeitung* dedicated a whole page to the festival, claiming to have discovered "a new generation," which it set in a historical context alongside other great generations of Germans. The youth magazine *OK* declared Waldeck to be the German Newport (after the prominent American folk festival). The hour-long live ZDF broadcast from the Waldeck field, which was specially outfitted with artificial bushes in which cameras were positioned, also reflected the significance that the media attributed to the event.

For many artists, glittering careers as professional singers beckoned. They received record contracts and embarked on publicized tours. The Waldeck festival was no longer a workshop in the original sense, but had instead become a display of prominent artists before a large public with the inevitable separation of artist and audience that this involves. The spectrum of artists had greatly increased, not least due to performers from Italy, Poland, Great Britain, Belgium, Switzerland, and the Netherlands. Two singers of the previous year, Dieter Süverkrüp and Fasia Jansen, who represented the strand of politically committed song, had not returned due to doubts about the political seriousness of the festival. This was regretted, but in no way did it dampen the general euphoria.

The Conflict between the Nerother Wandervogel and the Arbeitsgemeinschaft Burg Waldeck

One historically and culturally significant aspect of the Burg Waldeck festivals, although largely unrelated to political song, was the bitter feud between the Arbeitsgemeinschaft Burg Waldeck (ABW) and the Nerother Wandervogel (NWV). During the 1966 festival, this conflict between the two youth groups, both of which had built their huts on the Burg Waldeck, escalated. The NWV appeared to feel threatened by the success of the ABW's event, and some suspected that the burning down of the festival's wooden stage two weeks after it ended was the work of the NWV.[43]

Legal disputes over the ownership of the Burg Waldeck land had impeded the work of the ABW since the 1950s and constitute an independent chapter in the history of the *Jugendbewegung* after 1945, not least because they were also a reflection of ideological differences within the movement. Acts of sabotage, generally attributed to the NWV but never proven to be its work, constantly threatened the Waldeck festivals from 1966 through 1969.

In the early 1920s the brothers Karl and Robert Oelbermann had formed a *Wandervogel* association named the Nerother Wandervogel. It acquired a plot of land around the ruins of the Burg Waldeck and established itself there. The association became known for its long trips abroad lasting months or even years to places as far afield as South America and India. The roots of the dispute with the ABW lay in the occupation of Burg Waldeck by the Nazis in 1933. The Nazis had banned the NWV despite the Oelbermann brothers' sympathies with National Socialism. To protect the land of the NWV the youth association had ownership transferred to Arbeitsgemeinschaft Burg Waldek e.V. This had been formed in July 1934 as a "bündische Tarnorganisation" specifically for this transfer. Robert Oelbermann was arrested in February 1936 and sent to the Dachau concentration camp, where he died in 1941. Karl Oelbermann (1896–1974) survived the Nazi period in exile in South Africa. After the war the newly re-formed ABW assumed ownership of the land on Burg Waldeck. When Karl Oelbermann returned in the 1950s, he revived the NWV and confronted the ABW, initiating legal proceedings against it in 1957, which, after several trials, ended unsuccessfully for the NWV in 1978. The new ABW was granted all rights to the land the old ABW had owned. Because the NWV, however, had in the meantime acquired further plots of land on Burg Waldeck, the area was now — and remains today — divided up between the two groups based opposite one another in a state of permanent hostility, their respective plots separated partly by barbed wire.

The festivals in the 1960s were disturbed by various actions of sabotage, including the aforementioned arson of the concert stages. At the

1967 festival car tires were slashed and electric cables for radio and TV recordings cut. The tap of the main water supply for the village of Dorweiler and the festival grounds was turned on, with the result that the water ran out. In 1968 the main stage was even blown up, and the manager of the ABW endured physical attacks. Violence continued into the 1970s, to the point where people spoke of the "Intifada of the NWV." After the final court judgment of 1978, the ABW's main building, the Säulenhaus, was burned down. The sabotage abated, but the court judgment in favor of the ABW was always viewed by the NWV as a legitimization of a National Socialist injustice.[44]

On a political and cultural level the conflict represented two opposing interpretations of the *Jugendbewegung* tradition. After the war the ABW had joined up with the Schwäbische Jungenschaft, a successor organization of the avant-garde dj.1.11. In 1954 this gave birth to the Burgjungenschaft, which quickly encompassed other West German groups with similar leanings to the NWV.[45] In the early 1960s the "Studentische Arbeitskreis" of the ABW emerged out of the Burgjungenschaft and occupied itself with Marxist theories and the reappraisal of the Nazi past. The Nerother Wandervogel on the other hand continued as a traditional youth association in the style of the 1920s *Jugendbewegung* and re-emerged strongly in the 1950s and 1960s at Burg Waldeck. They criticized the "Americanization" of German youth and rejected the politicization of a song festival that they had initially been well disposed to.

The conflict became a point of intense debate within the German *Jugendbewegung* about ways of dealing with the legacy of National Socialism. At Burg Waldeck this assumed the character of a political conflict between the left and right wings of the movement. While the ABW tended towards the "new left" and to a renunciation of conservative traditions within the *Jugendbewegung*, the NWV strengthened its traditional leanings and tended politically towards the "new right."[46]

The Fourth Burg Waldeck Festival, 1967: "Das engagierte Lied"

For the 1967 festival, held from 24 to 28 May, a new stage was built, a metal pipe construction based on a design by the sculptor Eberhard Fiebig. To avoid the predicted mass invasion, the festival was moved to the second weekend after Whitsun. Also the festival theme was narrowed down to focus on "Das engagierte Lied" and the number of artists was reduced. The success of these measures was limited, however, because yet again the capacity of the grounds was overstretched: three thousand people came to attend the concerts and lectures given by forty-two different groups, solo performers, and speakers.

In a development that reflected the gradual politicization of the festival, the artists were all asked to answer four questions about the politically engaged song and their own artistic commitment:

1. Hat das engagierte Lied über seinen aktuellen Erfolg hinaus Bestand?
2. Wie verhält sich künstlerische Qualität zu Direktheit und Überzeugungsfähigkeit der Aussage?
3. Kann das engagierte Lied auf Abläufe seiner politischen und sozialen Umwelt einwirken?
4. Korrumpieren Erfolg und Einbeziehung in die "Kulturindustrie" die Funktionen des gesellschaftlich engagierten Liedes?

In addition, the organizers, this year the team of Rolf Gekeler, Jürgen Kahle, and Alf Schumann with the support of the political scientist Arno Klönne, stated in the festival program: "The fourth festival should openly discuss not only the difficult questions of our society, but also the difficult questions about the form of artistic engagement."[47] The festival theme was their reaction to the increased political focus of the artists, audience, and media. This development, however, did not only win them friends. Hanns Dieter Hüsch criticized the festival theme for hanging over the artists like the sword of Damocles over the delightful hills and dales of Hunsrück.[48]

As well as the usual figures of Degenhardt, Schobert and Black, Hedemann, Bauer-Horn, Wader, Mossmann, Mey, and Hüsch there were also several first-time appearances including the author Erich Fried and the gypsy jazz group Schnuckenack Reinhardt. The GDR was "officially" represented in the form of the Brecht singer Hermann Hähnel and by Inge Lammel and Erna Berger from the Institut für Arbeiterlieder of the Akademie der Künste in East Berlin. They presented a workshop on Wolfgang Steinitz's research on the German democratic folk song. In the discussions, however, they were asked uncomfortable questions about Wolf Biermann and the suppressed *Liedermacher* scene in the GDR, questions which they — perhaps understandably — dodged or were not able to answer. In addition Hähnel was harshly criticized for his emotional rendition of Brecht's songs, which was felt to be inappropriate. A unprecedented event was the concert of the Pole Alex Kulisiewicz, who performed in the clothes of a concentration camp prisoner. With broken voice and alarming authenticity he sang songs he had gathered as an inmate at Sachsenhausen. After the war he had written down from memory seven hundred pages of songs and texts in four languages.[49]

In 1967 the first activists from an increasingly politicized student movement arrived at Burg Waldeck. They succeeded in making life difficult for the festival organizers, confronting them for using German Army assistance in building a big tent and for making arrangements with the NATO air base in Hahn to cancel fighter-jet training flights for the duration of the festival. A major row blew up concerning the plan of the Voggenreiter publishing house to bring out — together with the ABW — a compilation LP of the festival. It was discovered that Voggenreiter had published a Hitler Youth songbook in the Nazi period and was currently the publisher of a German Army songbook. This resulted in several artists withdrawing from the LP project.[50] On top of this, the ABW had to endure the ongoing probems with the Nerother Wandervögel as well as a complaint by the Bischöfliches Ordinariat in Mainz regarding a song by Schobert and Black that allegedly insulted the Pope. The affair was initiated by the NWV and led to legal wranglings that remained unresolved, but kept the ABW busy for a long time.

The Influence of the 1968 Movement on the Burg Waldeck Festivals

To understand the further development of the Burg Waldeck festivals it is necessary to summarize the development of the student movement and the Extra-Parliamentary Opposition or APO in 1967 and 1968. It is important to note the extent to which the singers and large sections of their public were politicized by the events of that period. As a result the basic conditions for putting on a song festival suddenly changed from one year to the next.

A large number of political events at home and abroad occurred in the year between the 1967 and 1968 festivals. Among these was the death of Benno Ohnesorg on 2 June 1967 at a demonstration in Berlin against the Shah of Iran (who was viewed as a supporter of American foreign policy and whose own brutal regime was supported by the US) and the assassination attempt on Rudi Dutschke, leader of the student movement, on 11 April 1968. The motives of the perpetrator, the young laborer Josef Bachmann, were never properly cleared up. These events resulted in the expansion and radicalization of the Socialist German Students Association and culminated in the violent Easter riots of 1968 in protest against the conservative Springer Verlag, whose newspapers such as the *Bild* were virulently anti-student, and indeed were blamed by the students for the attack on Dutschke.

Other significant events between 1967 and 1968 included the formation of a Grand Coalition on 26 November 1967 between the Christian-conservative CDU and the social-democratic SPD, an alliance that reinforced perceptions that there was no effective opposition in the Federal Republic. Also unpopular was the passing of the Emergency Laws in 1968, which gave the government the power to intervene as it saw fit in a state emergency. To some this was reminiscent of Hitler's Enabling Act of 1933. A big demonstration against these laws on 11 May 1968 was unable to prevent their passing through parliament. In the foreign political arena, the US was intensifying its war in Vietnam with the bombing of North Vietnam and the use of napalm against the civilian population in the summer of 1967. Other events included the murders of Che Guevara on 9 October 1967 in Bolivia and Martin Luther King on 4 April 1968 in the USA. These all had a galvanizing effect on the oppositional movement in Germany, as did the May 1968 disturbances in Paris and the French general strike, which took place immediately before the 1968 Burg Waldeck festival.

Another factor influencing the consciousness of the young people was the hippie movement with its talk of sexual revolution, which came to the fore in the summer of 1967 in the USA, the so-called Summer of Love. This had an effect on the form that demonstrations were to take in Germany. The SDS had already imparted an anti-capitalist, socialist content to the demonstrations. Added to this now came the new social fringe group theory of Herbert Marcuse and ideas for new pleasure-orientated forms of demonstration ("Ho-Tschi-Minh-Hop," go-ins, sit-ins, teach-ins, occupations of podiums and stages). Suddenly questions of revolutionary social change were discussed passionately and new radical organizations were formed. The movement spread beyond the universities and reached its climax in May 1968 with the transformation of the SDS into an "action group movement" under the slogan "From Protest to Resistance." It was the beginning of a "red decade"[51] not only in Germany, but worldwide too. It was in this politically turbulent situation that the fifth Waldeck festival took place.

The Fifth Burg Waldeck Festival: "Lied 68"

The focus of the 1968 festival, held from 12 to 17 June 1968, was the American protest song rather than the French chanson. The festival's new director Rolf Gekeler had visited the Newport Folk Festival in the USA in 1967 and booked the prominent singers Phil Ochs, Odetta, and Guy Carawan for Waldeck.[52] The festival, with its fifty-one artists, eight speakers, and its neutral slogan "Lied 68" was planned according to the model of the previous years. However, as a result of the shooting of Rudi Dutschke in April and the May unrest in France it took a different course. As soon as the festival started there began to be disruptions of concerts of singers whose songs were perceived as not sufficiently political. Reinhard Mey and Hanns Dieter Hüsch were the first two victims. Their performances were disrupted by catcalls and other distractions by the audience. Instead of being allowed to sing, they were forced — in the style of a Maoist People's Court — to sit on the stage and provide justifications for their texts. The agitators were mostly members of the SDS and pupils of the Aktionszentrum Unabhängiger und Sozialistischer Schüler (AUSS). They did not agree with the festival concept and believed that the participating artists should be more clearly in line with the APO's political agenda and that their songs should reflect this. On Saturday afternoon a meeting was called for AUSS and SDS members and sympathizers. An action group (Basisgruppe Waldeck-Festival) was formed, and promptly came up with a theory on the role of the chanson in the song movement, criticizing the unpolitical stance of the festival organizers and the commercialization and lack of political relevance of the festival. The action group believed that the festival had turned into a meeting place for "singende Fachidioten." Its theories were disseminated in a leaflet that also called for Franz Josef Degenhardt's main concert on Saturday evening to be changed to a "teach-in." During the occupation of the stage, red flags and Vietcong flags were waved and the theories of the leaflet read out over the microphone. This culminated in the slogan: "Stellt die Gitarren in die Ecke und diskutiert."

The following text from the action group's leaflet was read out by myself, Eckard Holler, the author of this chapter. The black-and-white argumentation and the heightened tone of the wording corresponded to the atmosphere of the day: there was a feeling that the revolution was nigh and that it was imperative not to waste time by singing. All like-minded people were challenged to take part in these political changes, which were perceived to be "an der Zeit." The festival organizers were criticized for not recognizing the signs of the times and for their insistence that the singing should continue. However, for the co-authorship and reading out of this statement I was severely criticized, even by friends, and there are still people to this day who hold this action against me. The statement ran as follows:

Thesen zur politischen Funktion der Chanson- und Liedbewegung

1. Das Waldeck-Festival hat keine politische Bedeutung mehr. Es hat sich zu einer Tagung für singende Fachidioten entwickelt. Sänger werden bei revolutionären Aktionen nicht mehr benötigt. Bei Sit-in, Go-in, Teach-in wird heute sinnvollerweise nicht gesungen, sondern diskutiert in der Absicht der konkreten Aktion.

2. Die Chansonbewegung war nur eine Vorstufe der theoretischen Bewußtwerdung, wie die Musik der Theorie stets nur vorgeordnet ist. Sie kann nur ein ästhetisches Bewußtsein schaffen, selbst wenn das Lied durch die Verbindung der Musik mit dem Text der Theorie eine gewisse Strecke Wegs entgegengehen kann.

3. Die Chansonbewegung gehörte vor ca. 4 Jahren — als die Waldeck-Festivals entstanden — zu den avanciertesten Positionen der

revolutionären Theorie-Praxis. Heute ist die Negation dieser Position notwendig, wenn wir einen Schritt weiterkommen wollen.

Das ästhetische Bewußtsein muß sich als theoretisches rationalisieren. Das System der repressiven Gesellschaft wird nicht durch Lieder verändert.

4. Die Chansonbewegung sinkt im Augenblick ihrer Negation zur partiell-reaktionären Position herab. Sie zieht Kräfte ab, die an der Front dringend gebraucht werden. Ihre Beibehaltung ist ein Versuch, den Prozeß an einer Stelle zu stoppen und zur Sub- oder Kontrastkultur zu verdinglichen. Auch als Kontrastkultur aber ist sie in das System integriert und wird von ihm freundlich getätschelt — wie die Fernseh- und Rundfunkaufnahmen zeigen. Der APO hingegen wird die geforderte Sendezeit vom Establishment verweigert.

5. Die Waldeck hat die Chance verpaßt, mit der ihr zuströmenden Jugend zusammenzuarbeiten, als sie 1966 in elitärer Selbstüberschätzung die sogenannten "Gammler" durch Erhöhung des Eintritts und Einschränkung der Werbung bewußt abwimmelte, und hat sich stattdessen vom Establishment kaufen lassen. Zugleich hat sich das Festival zum narzißtischen Selbstzweck verengt.

6. Wenn das Festival noch einen ernsthaft — politischen Sinn haben soll, sind statt der Großkonzerte Teach-ins über die konkreten Probleme der antiautoriären Bewegung zu veranstalten. Also: Stellt die Gitarren in die Ecke und diskutiert!

7. Es ist unmoralisch, daß eine sich für engagiert haltende Jugend ästhetisiert, während ihre Altersgenossen von der Polizei zusammengeschlagen und erschossen werden. Am Ende des letztjährigen Festivals wurde Benno Ohnesorg in Berlin erschossen, am Tage vor Beginn des diesjährigen Rudi Dutschke gerade wieder aus dem Krankenhaus entlassen. Am Mittwoch wurden in Frankreich alle progressiven Jugend- und Studentenverbände verboten und Demonstrationen generell untersagt, was in Bonn als beispielhafte Maßnahme aufgenommen wurde. Wir erinnern daran: die Verabschiedung der NS-Gesetze hat auch für das Waldeck-Festival eine neue Situation geschaffen.

8. Da die Festival-Veranstalter ihren ästhetischen Eskapismus nicht aufgeben wollen und Teile des Publikums beim "ersten deutschen Chansonnier" und "König der Waldeck" nur die Selbstbefriedigung suchen, rufen wir heute abend zum Go-In bei Franz Josef Degenhardt auf, um das Konzert in ein Teach-in umzufunktionieren. Wir fordern Degenhardt zur Stellungnahme zu diesen Thesen auf.

Franz Josef Degenhardt showed solidarity with the action group. He emphasized the importance of discussion and left the stage after only a few songs (which included "vatis argumente," "Das Ereignis am Mond-falterfluß im Mai 1968," and "PT aus Arizona") to make room for the teach-in. Walter Mossmann also shortened his set, but managed to sing "Drei Kugeln auf Rudi Dutschke," which Wolf Biermann had sung to Mossmann over the telephone and asked him to play in his absence.

In 1968 Dieter Süverkrüp returned for the first time since 1965 to perform together with the agitprop rock cabaret group Floh de Cologne. They caused consternation with political phrases that some people were not yet accustomed to on subjects such as the Vietnam war. One of these songs, "Jack Miller," written by Floh de Cologne member Markus Schmidt, was a bitter, grotesque satire of profiteering from the barbarism of war. It indeed set out to shock with its apparent direct equation between "evil capitalist entrepreneur" and "American soldier":

> Jack Miller ging nach Vietnam,
> ging hin zum Heiligen Krieg,
> weil er von jedem Mann vernahm:
> "Die Freiheit führt zum Sieg."
> Zum Abschied küsst' er seine Braut.
> Die sagte: Sende mir,
> da ich dir schließlich angetraut,
> nach Haus ein Souvenir.
>
> Kaum war die erste Woche hin,
> verschickt er sein Paket,
> 'ne Schädelwunde war darin
> vereitert und vernäht,
> verbrannte Haut von einem Kind,
> der Tripper einer Hur',
> ein Schädel angefault und blind
> und eine Nabelschnur.
>
> Und Jenny macht' 'nen Laden auf,
> verkauft da die Effekten.
> Und alle kaufen da zu Hauf
> die Toten und Verreckten.
> Denn schließlich hat man ja Moral,
> man weiß als guter Christ,
> der beste Kommunist ist mal
> der tote Kommunist [. . .].[53]

The Viennese writer Rolf Schwendter attracted attention with his "Anti-Lieder," which he beat out on a child's drum, prompting associations with Oskar Matzerath from Grass's *Blechtrommel*. With his particular style of *Sprechgesang* he lectured on latent fascism and his own "theory of subculture."[54] He caused a scandal among the *Liedermacher* with his attack on Reinhard Mey, who had written a text that Schwendter judged to be latently fascistic and which he tore to pieces in a satirical performance. The lyrics went:

> Und für mein Mädchen würd' ich,
> verlangte sie's von mir,
> honorig, ernst und würdig, von höflicher Manier.
> Ich würde für ihre Liebe Gendarm oder Soldat
> und würde im Getriebe des Staats ein kleines Rad
> und ein Kapazitätchen — ich würd' es für mein Mädchen.[55]

Despite these controversies, the focus of public attention at the festival was the American political singers Carawan, Odetta, and Ochs. Their concerts were not interrupted and were immensely popular. Other concerts, too, provided fun and contrasted with the seriousness of the debates about the political status of the song. One example was the nonsense group Insterburg & Co from Berlin who, far from being booed off as was expected, managed to enthuse a midnight audience with their ridiculous lyrics. One interpretation of this unexpected reaction was that it was evidence that the Waldeck audience of 1968 was only superficially politicized. Bernhard Lassahn had a more plausible explanation, pointing out that "Blödel-Barden" like Insterburg & Co and Schobert & Black were beneficiaries of the same political polarization to which the more subtle lyricists ("Zwischentöner") like Hüsch or Mey had fallen victim. This corresponded, in Lassahn's view, to the dialectical law by which the highest intellectual standard — as demanded by the political singer — had its necessary opposite in complete simplicity.[56]

As a final political gesture, the singers and audience passed a resolution of solidarity for the opponents of the Gaullist regime in France. The festival organizers looked on in despair, believing that this was one step too far. At the festival finale on the Sunday "The Internationale" was sung by everyone, and Burg Waldeck was proclaimed an "International Center of Resistance."

In many respects the 1968 Waldeck festival had run out of control. The four to five thousand spectators by far exceeded the capacity of the grounds. Considerable damage to the fields outside the actual festival grounds resulted and was made even worse by the rainy weather. The Dorweiler villagers were particularly annoyed that the village sign and the church were spray-painted with hammers and sickles. Because of this and the generally negative impression left by the hordes of "layabouts," a tension arose between the ABW and the inhabitants, calling into question the continuation of the festival.

The internal festival balance sheet did not look good either. The organizers lost control of the 1968 festival not only politically, but financially as well (due to the flight costs of the US singers). Now critical voices within the ABW gained the upper hand and forced a compromise by which the work group would no longer act as organizers of the event, but would rent the ground to a project group from the Mainz Republikanischer Klub, which continued the festival under the direction of Rolf Schwendter and according to a new concept: "alternative culture."

It is fitting to close this section with the text of Degenhardt's "Zwischentöne sind bloß Krampf im Klassenkampf." Alongside the slogan "Stellt die Gitarren in die Ecke und diskutiert," this song, which Degenhardt first sang at the Essen Song Days (25–29 September) reflected the battle-readiness of the time and as such was characteristic for the development of the political song in Germany in 1968:

Manchmal sagen die Kumpanen jetzt, was soll denn dieser Scheiß?
Wo sind deine Zwischentöne? Du malst bloß noch schwarz und weiß.
Na schön, sag ich, das ist ja richtig, aber das ist jetzt nicht wichtig.
Zwischentöne sind bloß Krampf — im Klassenkampf.

Auch die alten Kunden klagen, wo ist Ihre Poesie?
Dinge bilderreich umschreiben, andeuten, das können Sie.
Na schön, sag ich, das ist ja richtig, aber das ist jetzt nicht wichtig.
Schöne Poesie ist Krampf — im Klassenkampf.

Einen Scheißhaufen zu malen, das nutzt gar nichts, der muss weg.
Und trotz aller schönen Künste stinkt der Dreck nach Dreck.
Dass er da liegt, ist nicht richtig, dass er weg muss, das ist wichtig.
Alles andere ist Krampf — im Klassenkampf.

Und um es genau zu sagen, ohne alle Poesie.
Weg muss der Kapitalismus, her muss die Demokratie.
Ja, genau das ist jetzt richtig, alles andre nicht so wichtig.
Alles andre ist Krampf — im Klassenkampf.

Und der Dichter, der poetisch protestiert in seinem Lied,
Bringt den Herrschenden ein Ständchen und erhöht ihren und seinen
    Profit.
Und genau, das ist nicht richtig, und genau das ist nicht wichtig.
Protestieren ist bloß Krampf — im Klassenkampf.

Vom Protest zum Widerstand, doch dabei bleiben wir nicht stehn,
denn wir müssen bald vom Widerstand zum Angriff übergehn.
Ja, genau das ist jetzt richtig, alles andre nicht so wichtig.
Alles andere ist Krampf — im Klassenkampf.[57]

The Sixth Burg Waldeck Festival, 1969:
"Gegenkultur"

The 1969 Waldeck Festival, held from 10 to 15 September, had one hundred performers and around five thousand spectators. The musical focus was no longer the *Liedermacher* with their acoustic guitars, but the new German underground rock groups like Checkpoint Charlies, Tangerine Dream, and Guru-Guru. The new festival concept included the participation of political groups affiliated with the student movement and the APO. Among those officially invited were the Sozialdemokratistischer Hochschulbund (SHB), a German Communist Party (DKP) group affiliated with the magazine *Kürbiskern*, and various Marxist-Leninist groups. The plan was to have a festival with theory workshops in the daytime and concerts in the evenings.[58] The festival disintegrated, however, into a workshop festival for the politicized participants and an underground rock festival for the hippies, who danced through the night around the big campfires to the music of the bands.

The festival concept envisaged working out a common alternative cultural strategy for the Left. This failed due to festival director Rolf Schwendter's false assumption that all left-wing groups would be willing to work together in a network. But the anti-authoritarian student movement as characterized by Rudi Dutschke had already fallen apart by 1969. With this the action group concept had become obsolete. Instead the strategy discussions were determined by various political cadre organizations of Marxist-Leninists who had emerged from factions in the student movements. They attacked Schwendter's idea of "alternative culture" bitterly as an unpolitical, leftist "quagmire." The emergence of these factions was apparent among the festival spectators and prevented any political unity. Instead a leaflet war was waged in the course of which left-wing groups cursed each other as "Revisionisten" or "wild gewordene Kleinbürger" and attacked the Waldeck festival in general for being politically unfocussed and disorganized. The *Liedermacher* present (Wader, Mey, Degenhardt, and Eva Vargas) played no role. Degenhardt did not sing; Mossmann, who in the meantime had joined the Freiburg SDS, was only involved politically.

The pivotal player in the whole festival, as both theoretician and singer, was Rolf Schwendter, who again beat out his "Anti-Lieder" on his child's drum. A typical song of his was "Ich bin noch immer unbefriedigt" based on "Satisfaction" by the Rolling Stones.

> Chorus:
> Ich bin noch immer unbefriedigt,
> ich bin noch immer unbefriedigt,

ich bin noch immer unbefriedigt,
und deshalb muss ich schrein, schrein, schrein.

Die Zeitschriften krakeelen von früh bis spät,
über die anscheinend befreite Sexualität.
Doch außer einem bißchen Ersatzlust
Hab' ich von allem nichts gewußt.

Man hält mich dumm und hält mich wie ein Tier.
Man hält mich zum Narren: "Konsumier!"
Das wird dir nicht gelingen, mein lieber Mann.
Das Zeug, das ist bald schrottreif: und was dann?

Die, die da herrschen, die haben ein Alibi.
Ihr Alibi heißt Freiheit, und heißt Demokratie.
Doch ist das demokratisch, wie ich's begreif,
wenn man mich in vier Jahren mal zur Wahlurne schleift?

Die Herrschenden, die sagen: Ich tu, was ich tun kann.
Doch was bieten mir die Herrschenden schon an?
Statt Umwälzung nur eine ganz kleine Reform,
streng nach althergebrachter Norm.[59]

The lingering image of the festival was that of the traveling hashish sellers with their handcarts peddling their wares among the crowds. The chaotic atmosphere of the festival was reflected by an event staged by the First Vienna Working Group in which the cast laid out an opulent meal as part of their open-air performance. The audience did not know how to react, and proceeded to wreck the whole installation. Nobody knew in the end what the point had been. In the end the 1969 "alternative culture" festival remained a much-disputed experiment. With it the series of festivals on Burg Waldeck came to a close.

Assessing the Waldeck Festivals of the 1960s

The Waldeck festivals began with a practical and theoretical orientation towards the French chanson. This orientation was, however, rather abstract because the artists who were held up as models (Brassens, Ferré, Brel, etc.) were never invited to play (not least because of the cost involved). French chanson singers, when they did make it to Waldeck, found little reception and did not feel at home in the open-air setting. On the other hand the Anglo-American singers, who had imported the folk revival to Germany, made their presence felt from the beginning. Degenhardt, Rohland, Mey, Süverkrüp, and Mossmann began as representatives of a German chanson based on the French model. In the course of the festivals they came into competition with singers identifying themselves with the Anglo-American folk and protest model. In this respect Hannes Wader formed an exception in his successful combination of both directions within his style.

With the years the American influences increased as the festival became more commercialized. This reached its peak in 1968 when star figures of the folk scene were flown over from the USA. This was seen by many, however, as an infringement of the hitherto accepted festival policy, particularly so because it did not seem to accord with the festival's original central motive: Peter Rohland's intention to create a relevant, contemporary German "Chanson."

Nonetheless the 1960s did see the birth of a "new German song" ("neues deutsches Lied") as an artistic genre. Burg Waldeck with its concerts and workshops on the theme of German chanson and political song undoubtedly provided the setting for this. This was helped by the close personal friendships that arose between the student work groups of the ABW and the artists themselves. The comfortable, familiar atmosphere at the first festivals was a motivating factor for the many singers to attend and to perform their new material, despite not being paid. In the end the Waldeck festivals brought about not so much the revival of the German "Chanson," as the creation of a German "Liedermacherlied" that stood somewhere between folk song and chanson. The more political examples of this were to play a major role in the *neuen sozialen Bewegungen* and other political intitiatives which were to emerge in the Federal Republic of the 1970s. But it could be said that Burg Waldeck's greater legacy, after the fashionable trend of protest song in the late 1960s and early 1970s had passed, was the strong presence of "das neue deutsche Lied" in pop and rock music in Germany of the 1970s and beyond.

Translated by David Robb

Notes

[1] See Helmut Schelsky, *Die skeptische Generation: Eine Soziologie der deutschen Jugend* (Düsseldorf: Eugen Diederichs, 1957).

[2] Die Jugendbewegung was formed in 1896 as an anti-bourgeois youth organization with romantic leanings. The period up until the First World War was known as the *Wandervogel* phase, in which youths would organize hikes in the countryside as a conscious alternative to life in the towns and cities. After the war the organization was reformed as Die bündische Jugend. It was still based on the ideals of the Pfadfinder (Scouts) and the Wandervögel, but the reformed organization had a greater socio-political agenda than before as a result of losing many of its prominent members in the war. In 1933 many of its associations were subsumed by the Hitlerjugend. Others disbanded in protest or continued illicitly. After the

Second World War some of the associations of the Jugendbewegung reformed. See: http://de.wikipedia.org/wiki/Jugendbewegung.

[3] The dj. 1.11 (deutsche Jungenschaft 1. 11) was formed on 1 November 1929 in Stuttgart as a splinter of the "Deutschen Freischar" of the youth leader Eberhard Koebel (known as "tusk," 1907–55). In the Third Reich it was part of the youth resistance. After 1945 various successor organizations emerged that still exist today. See Walter Z. Laqueur, *Die deutsche Jugendbewegung* (Cologne: Verlag Wissenschaft und Politik, 1962).

[4] *turmgespräche. Blätter für kritisches Gegenwartsverständnis* 1–15 appeared between October 1963 and March 1969.

[5] See Harry Pross, *Jugend Eros Politik: Die Geschichte der deutschen Jugendverbände* (Bern: Scherz, 1964).

[6] From *schrift 22. Liederheft* 2, December 1964, 62.

[7] Skiffle was an eclectic style of music combining elements of jazz, blues, folk song, and rock-and-roll. It was popularized in the UK in the mid 1950s by musicians such as Lonnie Donegan. It was played chiefly on guitars and improvised percussion instruments such as washboards. See Michael Brocken, *The British Folk Revival* 1944–2002 (Aldershot: Ashgate, 2003), 67–88.

[8] This was the house of the widow Frau Seebe, where Rohland lived during his stay in Berlin. She allowed him to practice his music with friends and have regular meetings late into the night, and generally lead a bohemian lifestyle.

[9] Peter Rohland, "Ich schaukle meine Müdigkeit," on *Vertäut am Abendstern*, EP-Thorofon 1963.

[10] Letter from Axel Hauff to Eckard Holler, 14 February 1996. See Eckard Holler, "Peter Rohland — Volksliedsänger zwischen bündischer Jugend und deutschem Folkrevival," in *puls 24. Dokumentationsschrift der Jugendbewegung*, April 2005, 33.

[11] Peter Rohland, *Lieder von anderswo*, LP (Thorofon, 1977). Ten youth movement songs including two previously unreleased songs also appear on the Rohland CD *seh ich Schwäne nordwärts fliegen* (Thorofon, 2001).

[12] See Rita Ottens, "Der Klezmer als ideologischer Arbeiter," in Gisela Probst-Effah, *Lieder gegen "das Dunkel in den Köpfen": Untersuchungen zur Folkbewegung in der Bundesrepublik Deutschland* (Essen: Die Blaue Eule, 1995).

[13] Schalom Ben Chorim, in *Yedioth Ahronot* (Tel Aviv), 26 February 1965.

[14] See Holler, "Peter Rohland — Volksliedsänger zwischen bündischer Jugend und deutschem Folkrevival," 24.

[15] Revival in the sense that the political song of the 1920s written by people such as Kurt Tucholsky and Walter Mehring had also been termed *Chanson*, already then with a specific reference to the French satirical cabaret song.

[16] Degenhardt was expelled from the SPD in 1971 for supporting a common front with the communists and became a member of the DKP in 1978.

[17] Franz Josef Degenhardt, "Rumpelstilzchen," on LP *Zwischen Null Uhr Null und Mitternacht, Bänkelsongs 1963 von und mit Franz Josef Degenhardt* (Polydor 1963). All quotations from Degenhardt's lyrics in this book are copyright © and used by permission of Franz Josef Degenhardt.

[18] Bernhard Lassahn, *Dorn im Ohr: Das lästige Liedermacher-Buch* (Zurich: Diogenes 1982), 198.

[19] This became the mouthpiece of the Easter March movement against the atom bomb when the British Easter marches spread to West Germany in 1960.

[20] This was followed in 1963 by the release of *Ostersongs 1962/63* featuring Süverkrüp and Fasia and the Conrads. The same year saw the first EP by Hanns Dieter Hüsch, *Carmina urana: Vier Gesänge gegen die Bombe*. In 1965 *pläne* released their first LP, a compilation of various artists *Lieder des europäischen Widerstands gegen den Faschismus*.

[21] Dieter Süverkrüpp, "Erschröckliche Moritat vom Kryptokommunisten" on LP *Die widerborstigen Gesänge des Dieter Süverkrüp* (Pläne, 1967).

[22] From Gerd Semmer and Dieter Süverkrüp, "Luftschutzlied" in Annemarie Stern, *Lieder gegen den Tritt* (Oberhausen: Asso-Verlag, 1972), 326.

[23] German translation of "Ça ira" by Gerd Semmer in Stern, *Lieder gegen den Tritt*, 52.

[24] Süverkrüp was later to join the DKP (Deutsche Kommunistische Partei) after it was formed in 1968.

[25] Gerd Semmer and Fasia Jansen, "Verbrannte Erde in Deutschland" in Stern, *Lieder*, 322.

[26] The term "Liedermacher" was coined by Biermann, inspired by the example of Brecht's "Stückeschreiber." Occasionally the alternate term "Dichtersänger" is used.

[27] Margot Honecker had been a friend of Biermann's parents in the KPD in Hamburg before the Second World War.

[28] Gisela Probst-Effah, *Lieder gegen das "Dunkel in den Köpfen": Untersuchungen zur Folkbewegung in der Bundesrepublik Deutschland* (Essen: Die Blaue Eule, 1995), 18.

[29] Peter Rohland, quoted in Probst-Effah, 18.

[30] Peter Rohland, "Bürgerlied," on *Lieder deutscher Demokraten*, LP (Teldec, 1967); CD (Thorofon, 1998).

[31] Franz Josef Degenhardt, *Spiel nicht mit den Schmuddelkindern: Chansons* LP (Polydor, 1966).

[32] Heinrich Vormweg, "Degenhardt dichtend" in, *Väterchen Franz: Franz Josef Degenhardt und seine politischen Lieder,* ed. Heinz-Ludwig Arnold (Reinbek bei Hamburg: Rowohlt Taschenbuch, 1975), 46.

[33] Thomas Rothschild, *Liedermacher* (Frankfurt am Main: Fischer Taschenbuch, 1980), 54.

[34] http://www.walter-mossmann.de/WM_Chronologie/wm_chronologie.html.

[35] Reinhard Mey, "Hymne an Frau Pohl," in *Von Anfang an* (Bonn: Voggenreiter, 1977), 43.

[36] See Hotte Schneider, *Die Waldeck: Lieder Fahrten Abenteuer* (Berlin: Verlag für Berlin Brandenburg, 2005), 334.

[37] Gekeler's team for the first issue included Martin Degenhardt, Diethart Kerbs, Arno Klönne, Niklas Trüstedt, Dimitrij Werschbizkij, Bernhard Wette, Franz

Zeithammer, and Volker Zinser. In 1967 and 1968 the festival program books came out as a special edition of *Song*.

[38] Hanns Dieter Hüsch, "Eindrücke vom Festival Chanson Folklore International '66," in *Song* 3, 1966, 54–56.

[39] Because of his publications on cabaret Budzinski was regarded as "Kabarettpapast." See Klaus Budzinski, *Die öffentlichen Spaßmacher* (Munich: List-Verlag, 1966.)

[40] Dieter Süverkrüp, "Protest gegen den Protest" in *Song* 4, 1967, 46–50. Schulz's answer in *Song* 5, 1967, 52.

[41] Bernhard Frank, "Ja, wo sind die Lieder, die alten Lieder," in *FAZ* supplement "Bilder und Zeiten," 11 June 1966, unpaginated.

[42] Franz Josef Degenhardt, "Die alten Lieder," on LP *Der Senator erzählt* (Polydor 1968).

[43] For the perspective of the NWV see Nerohm, *Die letzten Wandervögel: Burg Waldeck und die Nerother Geschichte einer Jugendbewegung* (Baunach: Spurbuch, 1995). For the perspective of the ABW see Hotte Schneider, *Die Waldeck: Lieder, Fahrten, Abenteuer* (Stuttgart: Verlag Berlin-Brandenburg, Berlin 2005).

[44] Nehrohm, *Die letzten Wandervögel*, 140.

[45] These huts (Salamander-Hütte, Schwabenhaus, Wiesbadener Hütte, and Berliner Hütte) had an important communication function at the festival.

[46] See Nerohm, *Die letzten Wandervögel,* and Schneider, *Die Waldeck: Lieder, Fahrten.*

[47] Quoted from the festival program, 1967, 4.

[48] Hanns Dieter Hüsch, "Burg Waldeck 67," in *Song* 5 (1967): 5.

[49] The papers of Alex Kulisiewicz (1918–82) are held in the Holocaust Museum in Washington; a 2,200 page manuscript by Kulisiewicz about the concentration camp songs is at the Stiftung Brandenburgische Gedenkstätten.

[50] The original planned festival documentation was finally realized in 2004 as a double CD, *Burg Waldeck Festival 1967* (Wedemark 2004). It was based on the LP *Burg Waldeck Festival 1967* (Xenophon/Voggenreiter-Verlag, 1967) which appeared in 1967.

[51] See Gerd Koenen, *Das rote Jahrzehnt* (Frankfurt am Main: Fischer, 2002) and *68 — Eine Weltrevolution*, booklet and CD-ROM, ed. Brigitte Walz-Richter, Rainer Wendling (Berlin and Zürich: Edition 8 — Assoziation A, 2001).

[52] It caused disquiet in the ABW that Gekeler had promised to pay these artists' flight costs. Until now it had only been the ABW's practice to give the artists free room and board. When possible, organizers would help artists book other concerts in the area and provide them with media contacts.

[53] Floh de Cologne & Dieter Süverkrüp, "Jack Miller," on LP *Vietnam — für fünf Sprech- und Singstimmen Streicher, Bläser, Orgel, Baß, Schlagwerk, Klavier und Gitarren* (pläne, 1968)

[54] See Rolf Schwendter, *Theorie der Subkultur* (Cologne: Kiepenheuer & Witsch, 1971).

[55] Reinhard Mey, "Und für mein Mädchen," on LP *Ich wollte wie Orpheus singen* (Chanson-Edition Reinhard Mey, 1967).

[56] This phenomenon is analyzed by Bernhard Lassahn in *Dorn im Ohr*, 259

[57] Franz Josef Degenhardt, "Zwischentöne sind bloß Krampf im Klassenkampf," on LP *Degenhardt live* (Polydor 1968).

[58] An example of the political lectures was journalist Günter Wallraff's reportage of his secret work with the Hamburg firm Blohm & Voss in which he uncovered illegal arms deals with Argentina and Turkey.

[59] Rolf Schwendter, "Ich bin noch immer unbefriedigt," in *Lieder zum freien Gebrauch* (Berlin: Rotbuch Verlag, 1980), 59.

5: The Folk and *Liedermacher* Scene in the Federal Republic in the 1970s and 1980s

Eckard Holler

The Left-Wing Positioning of the *Liedermacher* in the 1970s

THE PROTAGONISTS OF THE student movement underwent a process of politicization during the events of 1968/1969. A profound change in behavior and consciousness took place, which in turn influenced perspectives on careers and life in general. What had been a naïve nonconformity prior to 1968 became a more radical opposition as a result of the head-on conflict with the state. Student opposition was additionally given a sharper focus by the study of philosophy, particularly Marxism. The short euphoria of revolution, however, was followed by the hangover of political defeat. Some reacted to this by becoming dropouts or members of the RAF (Rote Armee Fraktion). Many others became supporters of a dual strategy by which one embraced the idea of — in the words of Rudi Dutschke — "a long march through the institutions." These took part in the building of an "alternative" society, which in the coming years was to emerge from a network of various social projects at roots level including folk clubs and festivals. While convinced of what Ernst Bloch termed "die Invariante der Richtung" (the invariant direction) toward socialism, supporters were nonetheless prepared for a long, confrontative coexistence with "bourgeois society."

The radicalization of the 1968 protagonists was particularly apparent in the folk and *Liedermacher* scene, which consciously positioned itself left of the SPD. Franz Josef Degenhardt, who had been a member of the SPD since 1961, was expelled from the Party in 1971 for siding with the DKP (Deutsche Kommunistische Partei) in the Schleswig-Holstein regional election. He, alongside fellow *Liedermacher* Hannes Wader, joined the DKP in the late 1970s. It should be said, however, that the DKP's activities in the *Liedermacher* scene — the result of successful political campaigning with cultural funding — far surpassed the general public relevance of the Party. The festivals of the Party newspaper *UZ* (*Unsere Zeit*) and those of the Sozialistische Deutsche Arbeiterjugend (SDAJ) were mass events whose cultural significance resonated beyond the respective organizations. Singers and groups were offered a platform in front of large audiences without having to become Party members. The Pläne label and publisher also looked after tour management, taking on many non-communist artists if they were prepared to fulfill certain minimal conditions. It saw itself as a facilitator of a left-wing alliance (despite a leaning toward the DKP) and through this achieved a strong influence. The DKP's leverage was such that events such as the Tübingen Festival had to justify themselves against criticism from DKP members within the Tübingen folk scene.[1]

The role of the DKP was, however, not undisputed. Walter Mossmann, under the influence of the student movement, had become a supporter of the anti-authoritarian wing of the Socialist German Students Association. In the 1970s, after a long artistic break, he performed in the anti-nuclear movement as a singer of *Flugblattlieder* and supporter of a socialism of "the Third Way." As a vehement opponent of the DKP, he articulated a widespread feeling in the folk and *Liedermacher* scene that the Party was dogmatic, conservative, and incompatible with the "New Left" with which many identified. Hanns Dieter Hüsch is an example of an artist who fell victim to the dogma of the DKP. In the 1960s he had taken part in the Easter Marches against the bomb side by side with communists. Subsequently he had felt himself unfairly victimized by the 1968 movement for being "bourgeois" and "individualistic," and had abstained from performing in Germany for one year. While many other influential *Liedermacher* adopted clear political positions, Hüsch withdrew from politics and concentrated in his performances on his hallmark ironic observations and witty word-plays. In 1970, due to criticism of his individualism as well as his position on the Prague Spring, he annulled his contract with the DKP-influenced label Pläne.

The Third Way[2] position gained additional support due to the popularity of Wolf Biermann. During his conflicts with the SED in the GDR he had successfully portrayed himself as a "true communist" while at the same time an influential critic of Eastern Bloc communism. Through his performance and travel ban as well as the release of his records in the West he had become the most famous political singer in Germany. After his expatriation from the GDR in 1976 he had quickly established contact with the folk and *Liedermacher* scene of West Germany and become a leading, albeit controversial political figure. In many respects his concerts united the left. An emotional identification with Biermann extended even into the ranks of the officially pro-GDR DKP. Sympathy with Biermann here was evident from the proceedings to expel Party members who criticized his expatriation from the GDR. In fact it was only a small, isolated core of DKP functionaries who adopted a strong position against him. In many towns his concerts were public gatherings for the alternative, green, and left spectrum. A high point was his "Es grünt so grün" concerts at the Tübingen Festival of 1980, where he sang the praises of the Green Party, which had just been founded. His participation at the peace demonstrations in the 1980s, however, led to criticism, particularly when he rejected the Krefeld Appeal[3] and was identified by the DKP as a political opponent. It is also worth mentioning that even in the Federal Republic the GDR continued to agitate against Biermann, for instance exercising its influence to prevent acts from the socialist countries from appearing on the same bill with Biermann: two Hungarian folk groups, for example, were not allowed to perform at the 1980 Tübingen Festival simply because Biermann was playing.

Another political grouping influencing the *Liedermacher* scene was that of the so-called Marxisten-Leninisten (later known as the K-Gruppen). They assumed a dominant position immediately after the collapse of the student movement, espousing a revolutionary theory aligned to Maoism and combating petit-bourgeois modes of behavior. In many university towns student committees were quickly taken over by Marxist-Leninist party groups, which were distinguished by their strong rhetoric against the DKP and Moscow line, which they viewed as revisionist. At the same time they attempted to develop a class consciousness among the industrial working youth by distributing pamphlets and newspapers while at the same time complying with trade union requirements. Even if the ML phase was only a transition period for many, it was not without significance. The Marxist-Leninists' activities led to the formation of long-lasting alliances. A few of the K-Gruppen joined the Green Party in the late 1970s; others went on to found the Marxist Leninist Party of Germany (MLPD) in 1982.

The alternative cultural scene also profited from the K-Gruppen: Trikont in Munich and Eigelstein in Cologne were music publishers with an ML past, who in the 1970s and 1980s promoted groups from a similar political background. The federally-sponsored Lindenhof Theater in Melchingen in the Swabian Alb had its origins in an ML apprentice group at the Tübingen Technical College, which in the mid-1970s had generated interest with a play entitled "Klassenspiel."

The left wing of the SPD also played a constitutive role in the folk and *Liedermacher* movement. Despite the negative image the SPD generally had in the scene, Dieter Dehm-Lerryn, who belonged to the Marxist Stamokap wing of the party, succeeded in exercising considerable influence as a record producer and tour manager. He worked not only for Wolf Biermann, Zupfgeigenhansel, BAP, Klaus Lage, BOTS, and other important singers and groups, but also influenced the cultural activities of the SPD and even wrote a new party anthem, "Das weiche Wasser bricht den Stein." Alongside this, Dehm developed a widely discussed thesis based on Antonio Gramsci's concept of the cultural hegemony of the left, in which a new folk music played a central role.[4]

Liedermacher in the Solidarity Campaigns of the 1970s

In the 1970s a wealth of new social movements ("neue soziale Bewegungen") and initiatives emerged in the Federal Republic and West Berlin. They dealt with an extremely wide range of issues, for example, youth centers, apprentices, the *Berufsverbot*,[5] women's rights, squatters, nuclear energy, traffic, the environment, healthy eating, and the Third World.[6] Such initiatives were frequently supported by an alternative scene of *Liedermacher*, folk groups, cabaret artists, and political rock groups. Because many of these musicians had originated from the same milieu as the new social movements it was a matter of course that they showed their solidarity. They performed for no fee, wrote songs about the relevant subject matter, increased public political awareness, and helped raise often substantial sums of money for solidarity funds.[7] The group Kattong, for example, which emerged in 1970, wrote songs about conditions for prison inmates. They gave concerts in prisons and with their program "Lieder vor und hinter Gittern" supported the Aktionen der Strafgefangenenhilfe (ASH, or Campaign to Help Prisoners) for the reform of the penal system. The song "Karriere der Marion S.," written by Frank Baier, imparts feelings of rage and political impotence:

> Schenk mir deine Wut
> Ich kann sie gebrauchen
> Schrei denen ins Gesicht
> Die dir die Knochen stauen
> Was nützt es, wenn du wiederschlägst
> Nur deine Haut zu Markte trägst
> Zu viele, die dich mangeln woll'n
> Zu viele, die dich überroll'n
> Na heul' schon, weil du hilflos bist
> Und schenk' mir deine Wut
> Ich kann sie gebrauchen [. . .][8]

In 1971 there were citizens' initiatives against the energy group VEBA's planned building of a petrochemical factory in the river bend at Orsoy-Rhein. The plan threatened the last channel of fresh air blowing from the West into the Ruhr region. At a rally in June 1971 Kattong sang the song "Rotes Liebeslied" from the back of a lorry to demonstrate their solidarity with the protestors. As the following extract shows, the song was laden with obscenities. It was put on the pornography index and banned from the radio. Distributed as a single by the Young Socialists in the SPD of North Rhine-Westphalia, however, it created much public awareness of the protest and ultimately contributed to the scrapping of the plans for the plant:

> [. . .] ich ging, weil ich für Wärme
> Und auch für Dicke schwärme, mit ihr ins Ufergras
> Der Rhein floß dumpf und träge
> Wir wippten in der Schräge und hatten unsern Spaß
> Wir sind ins Gras gesunken
> Sie hat mich ausgetrunken
> Und so beim Niedersinken
> Begann der Rhein zu stinken
>
> Ein kapitales Schwein
> scheißt in den Vater Rhein
> Es tut auf Uferwiesen
> Chemie die Lieb' vermiesen.
>
> Mein Schatz, es stinkt auch balde
> im schönen deutschen Walde
> Beim Regnen, mußt du wissen
> tun nicht nur Engel pissen [. . .][9]

The singers and groups of the alternative scene also showed solidarity with the trade unions. One example was the during the six-week steel-workers' strike from 28 November 1978 until 11 January 1979, one of the biggest strikes in the history of the German steel industry. Together with the pickets in front of the Thyssen steel works, the Duisburg song group Krempeltiere sang — to the melody of "Von den blauen Bergen kommen wir" — the new text "Mit 35 Stunden geht's voran":

> Wenn wir schuften Tag für Tag in der Fabrik
> Brechen sich viele von uns für euch das Genick
> Ja, ein Menschenschicksal zählt bei euch nicht mit
> Eure Sorgen gelten nur eurem Profit
> Nun schon wieder sagt ihr uns: Ihr zahlt allein
> Da sagen wir zur Arbeitsplatzvernichtung "nein" [. . .]
> Recht auf Arbeit für die Frau und für den Mann
> Schluss mit Arbeitslosigkeit — mit Entschlossenheit
> Packen wir die 35 Stunden an![10]

The group Schmetterling, from Vienna, made a spontaneous excursion from their tour to play at the conference of the Mannesmann IG Metall union representatives in Hüttenheim. Hannes Wader sang at a company meeting of Hoesch, and Wolf Biermann arrived with his guitar at five in the morning at the Thyssen picket line, where the temperature was minus five celsius. "Keiner schiebt uns weg," a spontaneously-written German version of the American civil rights song "We Shall Not Be Moved" became the hit of the steel strike, a folk song sung by everyone:

> Keiner, keiner schiebt uns weg
> Keiner, keiner schiebt uns weg —
> So wie ein Baum beständig steht am Wasser —
> Keiner schiebt uns weg.
> . . . der Kompromiss ist ein Beschiss
> Keiner schiebt uns weg.
> Auch wenn er vom Minister ist
> Keiner schiebt uns weg.
> So wie ein Baum . . .[11]

The *Liedermacher's* solidarity was soon in demand again, this time to support a hunger strike. This was carried out mostly by older inhabitants of the Rheinpreußen mining area in Duisburg in protest against the demolition of their area and the privatization of their housing. The hunger strikers — who averaged sixty years of age — lay on their mats on the stairs of the Duisburg Town Hall for eighteen days and nights until the news came that their houses had been saved; the town of Duisburg was buying the area.[12] During the strike there was an unprecedented display of solidarity that included the political singers Frank Baier with Teewurzellöwe, Ernst Born, Fasia Jansen, Walter Kurowski, and Die Krempeltiere. The striking steelworkers came and tipped a coal container in front of the town hall stairs. The worker poet Richard Limpert from Gelsenkirchen read a poem, "Rheinpreußen ruft Alarm," specially written for the strike. Encouraged by Fasia Jansen, the singers who were present immediately turned the text into song, singing it to the melody of the Easter March song "Eine Bombe ist gefallen."

> [. . .] Ich lieg auf meiner Liege
> Rheinpreußen ruft: Alarm
> Das Fell von einer Ziege
> Hält mir die Nieren warm
> Ein Flugblatt lässt mich wissen
> Der Siedlung droht Gefahr
> Der Mieter wird beschissen
> Wie es schon öfter war.

Die Menschen, die dort wohnen
Die setzen sich zur Wehr
Noch mehr Profit für Drohnen
Die scheffeln immer mehr
Die Hunger-Streiker frieren
Für Wohnrecht und Erhalt
Auch Frauen demonstrieren
Am Rathaus ist es kalt.

Ich muss zur Rathauspforte
Noch ist es nicht zu spät
Was nützen große Worte
Von Solidarität
Mit einem warmen Hintern
Bei fünfundzwanzig Grad
Am Ofen überintern —
Ist Arbeiterverrat.

Gemeinsam wolln wir zeigen
Wir stehen Frau und Mann
Hier darf kein Bürger schweigen
Das geht uns alle an [. . .][13]

Punks and *Liedermacher* Singing for Squatters

Another political cause that engaged the solidarity of *Liedermacher* and rock groups was that of the so-called *Autonomen* (autonomous left-wing youth movement). A wave of squatting actions and street battles throughout West Germany was triggered by violent clashes between police and youths in Zurich on 30 May 1980. The youths had been demonstrating against the luxurious renovation of the Zurich Opera House while funds had been refused for an autonomous youth center.[14] The nationwide disturbances that followed culminated in September 1981 in the death of a demonstrator in Berlin, who was crushed by a bus while running from a police water cannon. This intensified the confrontation between the "autonomous" scene and the state to the point that the SPD politician Peter Glotz warned of an emerging "second culture." The house occupations of the early 1980s followed on from the squatting actions of youths in the early 1970s, which had led to hundreds of self-administered youth centers nationwide. The new protagonists differed, however, in their increased militance, their black attire, the circled symbol "A" standing for "autonomy" and "anarchy," and in their opting-out, "no future" mentality. All this reflected the styles of the newly emerging punk music movement in West Germany. "Jetzt oder nie, Anarchie" by the group Cochise encapsulates the autonomous scene's rejection of the bourgeois state and its police:

> Wir wollen keine Bullen
> Die uns prügeln
> Wir wollen keine Gesetze
> Die uns zügeln
> Wir brauchen keine Städte
> In denen wir ersticken
> Wir wollen keine Bürger
> Die reichen, fiesen, dicken . . .
> Jetzt oder nie, Anarchie [. . .][15]

The wave of house occupations resulted in a series of court actions against the squatters. Here again the *Liedermacher* were asked to show their solidarity. The main priority was to cover the court costs, which in the Ruhr area amounted to around 200,000 DM. With the slogan "Lieder, Reggae, Rock und Dampf — Kohle für den Häuserkampf" the squatters' councils from Bochum, Dortmund, Essen, and Gelsenkirchen approached the regional music scene. Groups and singers including Ape, Beck & Brinkmann, Frank Baier, and Geier Sturzflug took part in two solidarity concerts in late October 1981 in the occupied refectory of Bochum University and the town sports hall of Mühlheim. Many of the songs dealt with police violence against squatters. One example is Ape, Beck & Brinkmann's "Das Haus":

> Das Haus ist zugemauert
> Das Haus stand lange leer
> Es hat bis heut' gedauert
> Wir stell'n es wieder her
> Wir stell'n es wieder her [. . .]
>
> Wir stehen auf der Treppe
> Da bricht die Haustür auf
> Sie bilden eine Kette
> Und stürmen in das Haus
> Helmvisier geschlossen
> Den Knüppel in der Faust
> Wir liegen auf dem Boden
> Und halten's kaum noch aus.[16]

The takings from ticket sales plus the proceeds from the live recorded LP *Schöner Wohnen — Aber fix! — Lieder, Reggae, Rock & Dampf — Kohle für den Häuserkampf* raised enough money to ensure that the trial costs were "halbwegs abgefedert" (Baier 2002, 166).

Liedermacher and Nuclear Protest in West Germany

Of all the solidarity initiatives in the 1970s and 1980s, those against the building of nuclear energy plants were particularly significant. One of the most famous examples in North Rhine-Westphalia was the campaign mounted by the farmer Maas from Hönnepel near Kalkar. Beginning in 1972 he had an ongoing court action against the building of the fast-breeder reactor in Kalkar, the costs of which amounted to 50,000 DM. Many *Liedermacher* and folk groups responded to his call for help. Names such as Saitenwind, Bruno & Klaus, Fiedel Michel, Tom Kannmacher, Kladderatsch, Schmetterlinge, Frank Baier, and Walter Mossmann took part in solidarity concerts — one demonstration on 24 September 1977 was attended by 50,000 people — as well as in the making of the benefit LP *Bauer Maas — Lieder gegen Atomenergie*.[17] In "Lied vom Bauern Mass," written specially for this LP, Frank Baier sang: "[. . .] um den Prozess für uns zu führen / [. . .] / Dafür brauchen wir 'ne Menge Geld / Na und, was macht das schon / Die kriegen wir zusammen / Und wenn wir singen geh'n / In Kalkar soll kein Kraftwerk / Kein Schneller Brüter steh'n [. . .]." In "Hände über Hönnepel" the group Schmetterling sang:

> [. . .] Hände über Hönnepel — Hände überm Land
> Wessen Hände halten hier alles in der Hand
> Deine Hände sind es nicht, die sind von Arbeit rauh
> Die halten hier die Zügel nicht
> Das weißt du ganz genau
> Wir weichen hier nicht mehr zurück
> Sie wissen es nur zu gut
> Bis unser eigenes Geschick
> In eigenen Händen ruht [. . .]

The LP was distributed by the anti-nuclear campaign and enjoyed three pressings, from which virtually all the necessary money was raised. Considered a "Lehrbeispiel für Solidarität und Demokratie," the solidarity campaign enabled Maas to draw out the process until plans to build the nuclear plant were scrapped.

The most controversial of all anti-nuclear protests in the 1970s was that surrounding the village of Wyhl on the Rhine, where the regional government of Baden-Württemberg planned to build an atomic energy plant. The construction was prevented, however, by a large protest movement sustained by the population of the region and supported by student groups and intellectuals. *Liedermacher* and folk groups also played an important role. The variety of the forms of protest and not least the successful prevention of the building of the reactor made Wyhl the cradle of the anti-nuclear movement in Germany.

Until late 1971 the civil use of atomic energy was not a controversial issue, a fact confirmed by among other things the small number of objections against the building of nuclear plants. This changed with the Wyhl protests. The number of objections from all segments of society reached 90,000. The local population was roused not least by plans to transform the so-called *Dreieckland* of Alsace, South Baden, and northern Switzerland into a "second Ruhr region" by building a host of new nuclear plants and chemical factories. This resulted in the formation of diverse, local civil groups, which took part in cross-border activities. The Upper Rhine Action Committee was formed in 1972–73. In 1974 eighteen action groups from South Baden and Alsace joined together to form an alliance. They organized the world's first ecologically motivated construction site occupations in Marckolsheim on 20 August 1974 and in Wyhl on 18 and 23 February 1975. The police's heavy-handed dispersing of the crowd of farmers, winegrowers, housewives, and children led to a mobilization of large sections of the local population and achieved nationwide publicity.

While industry and politicians argued that in view of the oil crisis of 1973[18] it was necessary to expand nuclear energy because "ohne das KKW Wyhl würden in Baden-Württemberg die Lichter ausgehen,"[19] particularly the winegrowers of the region viewed the risks of the atomic and chemical industry as an incalculable threat to their existence. The controversies between the population on one side and the state and industry on the other escalated in an unprecedented way in the Federal Republic. The civil protest in the *Dreieckland* was successful. In the "Offenburger Erklärung"[20] of 1976 the Baden-Württemburg regional government agreed on a moratorium with the nuclear opponents and finally renounced their plans to build the Wyhl plant in 1977 after a negative court decision. At the same time plans for a nuclear plant in Kaiseraugst in Switzerland and a chemical plant in Marckolsheim in France were cancelled. This success was, however, relative, since the construction of the Fessenheim nuclear plant in Alsace and five new ones in Switzerland went ahead regardless.

The intensity of the conflict can be seen in Walter Mossmann's song "In Mueders Stübele." His contribution to the site occupation in February 1975, the song became a kind of anthem for the Wyhl anti-nuclear movement. It was originally a traditional German folk song known to large sections of the population. Mossmann kept the melody, structure, and first verse of the song, but his new text gave it an anti-capitalist slant relating to the situation in Wyhl. The new message was that there was a war, this time not between the French and Germans, but between the "Büren" (farmers) and the "riichen Herren" (rich men) of the nuclear industry. By using an everyday, naïve language, Mossmann connected with

the everyday experiences of his audience in such a way that his analysis of
the conflict and the consequences appeared plausible. The people from
the villages themselves allegedly gave the impetus for the rewriting of the
words:[21]

> In Mueders Stübele, do goht der hm hm hm
> In Mueders Stübele, do goht der Wind.
>
> Der Wind sait d'Wohrhait, nit äso wie d'Zittig sait
> Der Wind sait d'Wohrhait, ich loos em Wind.
>
> Der Wind sait d'Büre, die hän jetzt hm hm hm
> Der Wind sait d'Büre, die hän jetzt Krieg!
>
> Der Krieg der dundret nit, kunnt nit von üswärts
> Der Krieg der kunnt üs dinem aigne Land.
>
> Sind nit d'Franzose, s'isch s große hm hm
> Sind nit d'Franzose, s'isch s große Geld.
> Die riiche Herre hän d'Büre üsbrücht
> die brüche Arbetslitt für die Fabrik.
>
> Wil der Atomstrom der git viel hm hm hm
> Wil der Atomstrom git vil Profit.
>
> Eerscht kunnts Atomkraftwerk und dann kunnt die Chemie
> un bis du "Au" gsait häsch, ischs Ländle hi.
>
> So gohsch zur Arbet für klaine hm hm hm
> So gohsch zur Arbet für klaine Lohn.
> Din Lohn isch immer klai, isch der Profit au groß
> Un kunnt die Krise bisch arbetslos.
>
> Do bisch de Arbet los und bisch de Acker los
> un dine Herre bliebe riich un groß.
>
> So goht im Elsas un in Bade hm hm hm
> So goht im Elsas un in Bade Krieg.
>
> In Mueders Stübele goht erscht en andre Wind
> Wenn mange Litt emol erscht uffgwacht sind![22]

With the spread of the anti-nuclear movement "In Mueders Stübele"
was adapted to fit many different regional contexts. The *Liedermacher*
Ernst Born wrote a version in Swiss German. For the demonstrations
against the Brokdorf nuclear plant on the lower Elbe between 1976 and
1980 the place names were changed and the text translated into High

German. Reno Rebscher wrote a version in Hessian for the protests surrounding the building of the west runway at Frankfurt airport in the early
1980s. "In Mueders Stübele" shows the clear connection between the folk
revival and new social initiatives, which gave the impression at times that
the West German anti-nuclear campaign was indeed a singing movement.

Many of the Wyhl anti-nuclear songs that became known across
Germany came from Walter Mossmann. "Die neue Wacht am Rhein"
(sung to a melody by Phil Ochs), based on a patriotic song from the nineteenth century, acquired an ecological and unifying international slant
due to its new text. The song "S'Bruckelied," written in the Alemannic
dialect, appealed to the population in the *Dreyeckland* for cross-border
solidarity. Following the tradition of the 1848 revolution, Mossmann called
his songs *Flugblattlieder* to emphasize their everyday use value (*Gebrauchswert*) as opposed to being a performance art form for public consumption.
In the anti-nuclear campaign Mossmann represented the type of intellectual political singer who, from a decidedly anti-capitalist position, used
songs to politically enlighten his audience. He held an undogmatic left-
wing viewpoint and found himself in constant battles with other left-wing
groups in the anti-nuclear movement, who, like the K-Gruppen or the
DKP, tried to use the protests for their own ends. His relentless activity as
a singer and publicist was one of the key contributing factors to the Wyhl
protest movement establishing itself as a model for a whole region's self-
determined struggle against the plans of the state and industry.

Volkstümlichkeit, Dialect Songs, and a Clash of Cultures

Another singer involved in the Wyhl protests was Roland Burkhart
(known as Buki). He studied sociology in Freiburg and, as a native of the
Kaiserstuhl area, identified with the people's campaign against industrial
planning. Unlike Mossmann, his concern was not to enlighten an audience about capitalism, but merely to prevent the building of the nuclear
plant in Wyhl. His were the songs with which the people identified most.
His texts were often set to melodies from well-known *Schlager* and drinking songs. An example is the Fasching song "Wenn das Wasser im
Rhein," the original text of which ran:

> Wenn das Wasser im Rhein lauter Wein wär,
> Ja, da würde ich gern ein Fischlein sein.
> Mensch, was könnte ich dann saufen
> Brauchte keinen Wein zu kaufen,
> Denn das Fass vom Vater Rhein wird niemals leer!

Now Burkhart sang:

Wenn das Wasser im Rhein voll Atom wär',
Nein, da würde ich nicht gern ein Fischlein sein.
Mensch, was müsste ich da saufen,
Keine Hausfrau würd' mich kaufen,
Denn das Fass vom KaKaWeh wird niemals leer!

For Burkhart the main criteria of a worthy song were its singability and its intention to express the fears and hopes of the people. Above all he became popular for his *Bekenntnislieder* (confessional songs) in the "we" form. His use of the Alemannic dialect, which was spoken in his home region of Kaiserstuhl, also aided the audience's identification with him. His most popular song was "Mir sin eifach wieder do," sung to the melody of "America latina" by Daniel Viglietti. The song was written in August 1976 for the second anniversary of the Baden-Alsatian civil action and was circulated nationwide in the songbooks of the anti-nuclear movement.[23]

Mir sind eifach wieder do, wänn sie kumme wänn.
Mit wohne schleäßlig do. Mir häns in dr Händ.
Nai! Do wird kai Stei uff dr ander gsetzt fir dä "Affekaschte"
am Rhin. Sunscht wird wieder (bsetzt).

Horche mal ihr Litt am Kaiserstöel weng rum. Was schwätze si?
Was hert mer dänn? Ischs dänn umesuscht gsi, daß mer in dr
Wyhlerwald nüsgsimblet sin fir Existänz un Gsundheit,
Vadder, Möeder, Kind?
Allwäg mir wisse's, frog doch nit so dumm.
Mir wisse, wänn dr Herbscht kunnt, no geht's wieder rund.
Dü nimsch di Schapfe (Gitarre), ich mi Schifferklaveer,
sait Wirti vu Wiswil, un no spiele mir:

[. . .]

Mir sind eifach wieder do, wänn si kumme wänn.
WYHL ISCH DERT UN DO. Mir häns in dr Händ.
Nai! Do wird kai Stei uff dr ander gsetzt fir dä "Affekaschte"
am Rhin. Sunscht wird wieder . . .
Gsunge uffem Platz . . . Gsunge uffem Platz . . .

Despite the national success of his songs Burkhart did not embark on a professional singing career. His dialect songs were so intimately connected with his home region that they seemed to him displaced when removed from that context. With the end of the civil movement in Wyhl his fame became a burden and in 1980 he withdrew completely from the *Liedermacher* scene.[24]

A further point of interest was the collision of two contrasting "folk" cultures during the civil actions in Wyhl. It was by no means just the representatives of the new political folk music — people like Walter Mossmann from Freiburg student circles — who gained a hearing. The traditional *Volkskultur* of the region (as opposed to the Anglo-American-influenced contemporary German *Folk* revival) contributed just as much to the civil protest. This included the men's choir Rheintreue, the Fasching group Remidemis, Die Singenden Winzerinnen vom Breisgau, and the traditional dialect poets Ernst Schillinger and Karl Meyer.[25] Aside from showing each other mutual respect there was in fact very little coming together of *Folk* and traditional *Volksmusik* at Wyhl. In the subsequent development of the anti-nuclear movement, traditional *Volksmusik* ceased to play a role, and remained a peculiarity of Wyhl. Despite the intensity of the conflict, the degree of actual politicization in Wyhl remained relatively small. Many of the interest groups had a one-point agenda in that they were only concerned with the prevention of the nuclear plant. When the regional CDU, under its new leader Lothar Späth, renounced plans for the nuclear plant, it regained its position as the leading party in the area, which had been temporarily lost to the FDP.[26] It should also not be overlooked that there was by no means a uniform rejection of the government's plans. Indeed in the village of Wyhl itself there was a majority in favor of the construction, who, together with the mayor, expected economic advantages from the plant and reacted indignantly and sometimes violently toward the unlawful site occupations of the "Langhaarigen" and "Kommunisten" (Mossmann 1975, 81).

From a folkloristic viewpoint, the use of the Alemannic dialect in the Wyhl anti-nuclear campaign was of interest because this gave an additional stimulus to the dialect renaissance of that period (Probst-Effah 1995, 122). In the mid-1970s there were young *Liedermacher* and poets in all the German-speaking regions performing their own dialect poems and songs.[27] Indeed the dialect song became virtually a side-branch of the German folk revival and for a time played an important role in the discussions on a new regionalism and the appropriation of the concept of *Heimat* by the political left. The controversy over this subject was apparent from the debate on Hannes Wader's LP *Plattdeutsche Lieder* from 1974. Although Wader claimed his interest in the Low German songs was political, some critics accused him of "ein Rückzug aus der Politik ins Privatleben" (Probst-Effah, 146). In later years rock groups like Spider Murphy Gang and BAP were successful with songs in the Bavarian and Cologne dialects respectively.

A peculiarity of the situation in Wyhl was that the Alemannic dialect spoken in the "Dreyeckland" was used as a language of "the people" against the language of those in power while at the same time enabling an alliance across national boundaries. Because the dialect used by the singers from the various parts of this region varied only slightly, it was deemed a supranational, colloquial language. It united the Alsatian performers Roger Siffer, Franz Brumbt, Gérard Walter, Folk de la Rue des Dentelles, Roland Engel, and Franz Keck with Ernst Born from Switzerland and Roland Kroell, Roland Burkhart, and Walter Mossmann from South Baden. On top of that, the Alemannic dialect was used as the common language at all meetings and actions, underlining regional independence against the High German of the enemy, which came from outside. In this way, as the Alsatian poet André Weckmann formulated it, the dialect was appropriate as a weapon to defend the quality of life of the regional *Heimat*.[28]

The Emerging Folk Scene in the Federal Republic

Despite irreconcilable rifts among left-wing activists who had campaigned together in the 1968 movement, the folk and *Liedermacher* scene of the 1970s was still able to present a harmonious image of the "alternative" left spectrum. For the activists this political utopia was influenced by the Eurocommunism that seemed to be becoming reality in countries such as Italy and France, where socialist and communist parties were collaborating. This spirit was in evidence, for example, in the film of the Tübingen Festival of 1977, which ended with the singing of the "Internationale" in Italian. In general, the folk and *Liedermacher* scene had a reconciling function within the left, for which there was a generally perceived need. It contributed considerably to a climactic political change in the Federal Republic, which was visibly expressed in the founding of the Green Party in the late 1970s.

Dieter Dehm-Lerryn's goal of creating a left-wing collaboration that transcended all factions for the purpose of defeating capitalism and imperialism was constitutive for the folk and *Liedermacher* scene in general in the 1970s. It corresponded to the image of a big "folk family," an ideal that was frequently lived out in exemplary fashion at the festivals. Set against this commonly projected utopia, the aforementioned conflicts over the "correct" political line — as ferocious as they were[29] — played a subordinate role at the West German folk festivals. The bulk of the public did not pick up on the factional battles behind the scenes and were not particularly interested in them either.

It is clear that the degree of politicization of the followers of folk music varied considerably. For many it was more a question of alternative cultural identity and lifestyle than of politics. The annual Ingelheim Festival in the 1970s serves as but one example. This 10,000-strong happy "folk family" event promoted an alternative *Lebensgefühl* with its many wine stands set out along the street toward the castle ruins. In many respects this alternative cultural identity went hand in hand with a rejection of the commercialism of pop culture. It is interesting to compare this with Michael Brocken's critique of the folk revivals in Britain in the twentieth century. Brocken questions many of the assumptions that folk communities make about themselves and the traditions they promote, claiming that these are "human constructions and, like the very history of the folk revival itself, products of social agency [. . .] not rediscoveries of the products of nature, but political inventions of particular times and places in the twentieth century."[30] Symptoms of such assumptions are the "sectarian folk-versus-popular dichotomies" in folk discourse (Brocken 2002, 12), also a feature of the West German folk scene. A song popularized by Tom Kannmacher at the Ingelheim Festival, "Wackawacka Boing & Boom Boom Bang," illustrated this. In parodying the onstage posturing of local rock bands, it reflected how the folk community took their alternative, culturally more sophisticated self-image for granted:

> Heute spielt die Spheres of Universe,
> die Anlage ist schon aufgestellt,
> die Musiker ziehn noch einen durch,
> und der Mann am Eingang ist bang um sein Geld.
> Mit Wackawacka Boing & Boom Boom Boom Bang
> Wackawacka Boing Boom Boom [. . .]
>
> Der Schlagzeuger hat zwei linke Füß' und Hände,
> fühlt sich so gut wie Ginger Baker,
> schreit und schmeißt die Stöcke ins Gelände,
> und liest jede Woche den Melody Maker.
> Mit Wackawacka [. . .]
>
> Der Bassist schiebt ne ruhige Kugel,
> denn man kann sowieso nicht hören, was er spielt,
> dafür bewegt sich dieser Mann ekstatisch,
> sexy und grazil.
> Mit Wackawacka [. . .]
>
> Vom Sänger versteh' ich kein einziges Wort,
> das ist auch ziemlich uninteressant,
> den Text hat er nie begriffen,
> so singt er die erste Strophe am laufenden Band.
> Mit Wackawacka [. . .][31]

Kannmacher, however, overlooked the fact that folk music was subject to the same commercial forces as rock music, and that the provincial *Krautrock* that he was parodying contained comparable elements of emancipation to that of the folk world, in its attempt to create an alternative form of artistic and cultural expression.

At the same time — and especially at points of interesection with the *Liedermacher* scene — it is clear there were folk artists who understood the German revival not as a mere rediscovering of "uncontaminated" tradition but rather in terms of its critical potential in the present. Peter Rohland's appropriation of the democratic songs of the 1848 revolution had already demonstrated this. Discussions at the Tübingen Festival in 1976 emphasized, for example, that the generally perceived longing for the past that characterized the folk revival was not escapism into the past, but represented rather a criticism of the present. With reference to Ernst Bloch, it was described as a search for the as-yet-unattained "Zukunft in der Vergangenheit."[32] The motifs on the festival poster by Peter "fuchs" Bertsch, "Bundschuh," and "Friedrich Hecker" alluded to the Peasants' Uprising and the 1848 bourgeois revolution and thus to democratic forces in the folk revival that could not merely be dismissed as "Romantik" or "neue Innerlichkeit."

Generally, however, the folk and *Liedermacher* movement was subject to a trend of depoliticization after the collapse of the student movement. The protests of the 1968 era had to a large extent been diverted into institutional channels by the new reforms of the Brandt and Scheel government. In this way the cadre organizations of the New Left had degenerated into sects[33] and public life had reverted to its normal orderly course. At concerts the traditional divide between performers and audience — which had been questioned in 1968 — was re-established. Concert disruptions and other spontaneous audience activities belonged to the past. This development was bemoaned by the Tübingen Festival in 1975. In its brochure it ascertained that the present festival wave was running in tandem with the trend in depoliticization. Alluding to the disruptions of the 1968 Waldeck Festival, it concluded that, in the face of political impotence, it was now time for the radical youth to give up the slogan "Gitarren in die Ecke" and to once again let the songs do the talking at the festivals: "[E]ine politische Ohnmacht [gibt offenbar] Gelegenheit, die Gitarren wieder aus der Ecke zu holen, in die sie eine sich als radikal verstehende Jugend gestellt wissen wollte." By this it meant the political song scene should not forgo its radicalism, but should adapt to the new conditions of the 1970s.

As stated, there were important strands in the folk scene whose primary interest was folk music and not political song. The first Internationales Folklorefestival (or Interfolk) in Osnabrück in October 1967 had been envisaged as a conscious alternative to the "political" Burg Waldeck Festival. As the festival's organizer Willy Schwenken remembers, however, it was plagued with similar problems to Waldeck, in that due to the general politicization of 1967 the music had to an extent been sacrificed ("die Musik [war] ziemlich den Bach hinuntergeredet worden").[34] With its intention to emulate the Anglo-American folk revival at a German festival, Osnabrück recruited singers from Ireland, Scotland, England, and some from the USA who were regularly appearing in folk clubs in Holland and Belgium. Many of these English-singing artists (including Tucker Zimmermann, The Sands Family, Hamish Imlach, Archie Fisher, and Mike Cooper) appeared on records sold by Schwenken in the early 1970s from his "Folkshop" in Nottuln.

The main priority at the Interfolk Festivals was authentic folk music and an intimate atmosphere. With artistic quality the chief selection criterion and the non-commercial orientation of the performers, Interfolk remarkably withstood the trend toward mass-oriented festivals. But without any state or corporate sponsorship the Interfolk Festival relied on the goodwill of its many helpers and was unable to bring in expensive acts. From 1969 to 1980 it ran twice a year and thereafter once a year up until 1988, when it was discontinued due to lack of funds.

The Interfolk Festival was also pioneering in the German folk revival. Fiedel Michel from Münster, who had first appeared in 1972 as the Rambling Pitchforkers, playing a set of Scottish and Irish folk, won first prize for German songs in 1973 and released their first LP, *Deutsche Folklore,* in 1974.[35] In the mid-1970s they were alongside Elster Silberflug (Heidelberg) and Liederjahn (Hamburg) one of the leading German folk groups. On their first record Fiedel Michel performed sixteen old German songs and dance tunes, among them several socially critical *Volkslieder* such as "O König von Preußen" and "Blutgericht." The latter stemmed from the Silesian weavers' uprising of 1844, which was brutally put down by the Prussian military:

> Die Welt, die ist jetzt eingericht'
> noch schlimmer als die Feme,
> wo man nicht erst ein Urteil spricht,
> das Leben schnell zu nehmen.
>
> Hier wird der Mensch langsam gequält,
> hier ist die Folterkammer,
> hier werden Seufzer viel gezählt
> als Zeugen von dem Jammer.
>
> Die Herren Zwanziger Henker sind,
> die Dierig ihre Schergen,

davon ein jeder tapfer schind't,
anstatt was zu verbergen.

Ihr seid die Quelle aller Not,
die hier den Armen drücket,
ihr seid's, die ihm das trockne Brot
noch von dem Munde rücket.

Kommt nun ein armer Weber an,
die Arbeit wird besehen,
find't sich ein kleiner Fehler dran,
wird's ihm gar schlecht ergehen.

Hier hilft kein Betteln und kein Flehn,
umsonst ist alles Klagen,
gefällt's euch nicht, so könnt ihr gehn,
am Hungertuche nagen.

Nun denke man sich diese Not
und Elend dieser Armen,
zu Hause oft keinen Bissen Brot —
ist das nicht zum Erbarmen?

Ich frage, wem ist wohl bekannt,
wer sah vor zwanzig Jahren
den übermütigen Fabrikant
in Staatskarossen fahren?[36]

Folk dancing was also promoted at the Interfolk Festivals. The dance groups Mauritius and Töätendierk emerged from a workshop with Fiedel Michel and established the regular "Folktanz-Dienstag" in Münster in 1976. Out of this came Ulrich van Stipriaan's book *55 Volkstänze*, which was published by Willy Schwenken's Folkshop Edition and achieved good distribution.[37] Other folk dance groups inspired by Fiedel Michel were Schnappsack and Lilienthal in Göttingen and Hampelmuse in Berlin. For a period of time the latter created a folk dance craze in Berlin with their "Folk-Bällen."[38]

Another center of the West German scene was Münster. This town boasted a folk meeting point as early as 1964–65 in the cellar of the pub Schwarzes Schaf. Three years later Willy Schwenken formed the Münster Folk Club.[39] The club, with its workshops, its discussion forums, its magazine *Folkletter,* and even a "Folk-Picknick" with sessions in the summer, became a model for clubs throughout northwest Germany. Additional support for the folk scene in the northwest (the former British occupation zone) was received from British Armed Forces Radio (BFBS) and by folk clubs in British Army barracks run by culturally-aware officers who organized a wealth of tours of Anglo-American folk singers and groups.[40] On the German side Westdeutscher Rundfunk supported the folk revival alongside its program of traditional *Volksmusik,* and the ubiquitous Schwenken had his own fortnightly evening show *Folksong Panorama.*

Two other significant folk events of the 1970s were the Ludwigs-hafen and the aforementioned Ingelheim[41] folk festivals. While Ingelheim was essentially apolitical, the Ludwigshafen Festival of 1973 was an at-tempt to rekindle the political folk and *Liedermacher* tradition of Burg Waldeck. With a strong media presence it marked the beginning of a new festival era in which the German folk revival prospered. The festival had the atmosphere of a reunion after the "wild" years of the 1968 move-ment. But the basic conditions for folk festivals had changed too much since the 1960s for a revival in the style of Waldeck. Artists were no longer prepared to play for no fee, and there were substantial financial risks, particularly if the festivals were open air. While sponsorship was of-ten obtained from local youth welfare departments, this dependency lim-ited the political independence of the festivals. Additionally these were only rated as "regional" or as "youth events" by the media, and even the big festivals such as Ingelheim, Mainz, and Tübingen never received the media attention of Burg Waldeck.

The Folk and *Liedermacher* Culture in Tübingen: From Idealism to Commercialization

The Club Voltaire e.V. Tübingen was a successor of the Republikanische Clubs of the 1968 period[42] and was comparable to the political and cul-tural clubs prevalent in various towns of Baden Württemberg from 1966 onwards.[43] Due to the special significance of Tübingen in the student movement, the club displayed stronger leftist tendencies than those in other towns. Given the name Club Voltaire at its inception in 1970, the original idea had been for a youth club for school pupils and apprentices.[44] This had come from the Bund Deutscher Pfadfinder (Association of Ger-man Scouts, or BDP) who had been involved in emancipatory youth de-velopment work. The BDP's "mildly progressive" concept, however, was usurped by the new left, and its influence diminished thereafter due to its collaboration with groups such as the Anarcho-Syndikalistische Lehrlings-gruppe and the Sozialistisches Jugendzentrum. These had joined in late 1969 after the closure of the Republikanischer Club Tübingen. Then in summer 1970 the local Tübingen SDAJ, the youth organization of the DKP, became members, this culminating in the BDP leaving the club and handing it over to the SDAJ.

The Club Voltaire was situated in a two-story building in the *Alt-stadt*. Having been at various times in the past a blacksmith's shop, a carpet store, and a dance school, it provided neither refreshments nor even a toilet.[45] In 1972 the club received its own legal charter as the Jugendzentrum Club Voltaire e.V. Between 1971 and 1974 it was perceived largely as an SDAJ club. Alongside SDAJ events it offered a politically unspecific program of events featuring folk and *Liedermacher* concerts and film evenings. These attracted 5,000 spectators in 1973. Particular public interest was generated by the series of lectures "DDR-heute" to which speakers came specially from the GDR. The public mouthpiece of the club was the SDAJ apprentice newspaper *Der Lehrling,* which denounced bad conditions in Tübingen apprentice programs. Divergences in reactions to the threat of *Berufsverbot*[46] — which affected myself in my positions as club leader and local teacher — caused controversy in the club in 1974. After careful consideration I resigned from the SDAJ (which had a close relationship to the DKP) and thus narrowly avoided a *Berufsverbot*. This resulted in a split between the Club Voltaire and the SDAJ in late 1974. My decision was treated as betrayal by some club members who had received a *Berufsverbot* during the years 1970 to 1974. But I was more interested in turning the club into a publicly recognized cultural center. While the communists were offended, many of the club "folkies" who had never been comfortable with the close connection to the communists heaved a sigh of relief.

The club continued its cultural and political activities on an independent and non-profit basis. It saw itself as left wing with a pluralistic emphasis[47] and as a representative of the "Zweite Kultur." With its folk and *Liedermacher* concerts from 1975 onwards the Club Voltaire grew into an active promoter of culture in Tübingen. The split from the SDAJ was criticized by some as a retreat into the realm of culture. But it was greeted by the independent left (which included the figures Ernst Bloch and Walter Jens)[48] as well as by the Tübingen political mainstream as a long overdue step out of isolation.[49] The enormous success of the first Tübingen Festival in 1975 was a breakthrough to public acceptance and respect. In a study from 1986 the local political significance of the Club Voltaire was seen in the fact that:

> er [ist] zu den wichtigsten Geburtshelfern jener beiden neuen Fraktionen zu zählen [. . .], die 1975 und 1980 weit links von der SPD mit zuletzt beachtlicher Stärke in den Tübinger Gemeinderat eingezogen sind — nicht nur auf Kosten der SPD. Hat die DKP vor allem durch die frühere enge Bindung zwischen SDAJ und Club Voltaire Nutzen gezogen, so war der Club Voltaire gegen Ende der 70er Jahre Ort der Begegnung der Grünen und Alternativen Liste und ist nicht ohne Einfluss auf ihr Kulturprogramm geblieben.[50]

The club enjoyed a continuity in personnel over the years and a strong anchoring in the local life of Tübingen. A group of collaborators evolved, mostly musicians, intellectuals, and local folk enthusiasts, including myself and my wife Gretel Holler, the *Liedermacher* and poet Bernhard Lassahn, the musician Fritz Fleischer, and the cultural studies student Angela Wagner.

Of the acts invited to perform at the Club Voltaire there was roughly a fifty-fifty balance between German and international artists, although the folk acts initially came primarily from Ireland and Scotland. The number of concerts rose from twenty-three in 1973 to ninety-six in 1976 and varied thereafter between seventy and eighty a year. As a result the club room with its one hundred seats soon had to make way for larger venues. This reflected the national surge in popularity of the folk scene, which resulted in a growth crisis in the course of the 1970s whereby the scene became split into a small number of successful acts and many more lesser known ones whose concerts invariably ended in deficit. The Club Voltaire adapted to this development by promoting concerts in other available halls in Tübingen. In 1973 it put on big concerts such as Eddie and Finbar Furey in Mensa 1 of the university, which held one thousand seats. From 1977 artists such as Hannes Wader, Wolf Biermann, Günter Wallraff, Zupfgeigenhansel, Hanns Dieter Hüsch, Bots, Schmetterlinge, Konstantin Wecker, Mercedes Sosa, Miriam Makeba, and Gerhard Polt performed in the university's three-thousand-seat Mensa II Morgenstelle. The club room in Haaggasse 26b remained a venue only for occasional cabaret performances, work group meetings, guitar courses, and jazz and women's evenings. The office was occupied from 1978 onwards by one full-time employee year round and during the festivals up to four full-time employees.

The popular and commercial development the folk scene underwent in the 1970s is illustrated by the example of Hannes Wader. Having started his career at Burg Waldeck in 1966, he was filling big concert halls by the early 1970s. In 1976 he did a "back to the roots" tour of the smaller venues and played the Club Voltaire on 15 May.[51] Because the concert was unamplified, it was a very intimate affair and was spoken fondly of in years to come. But there was also a sour aftertaste when Wader kept all the receipts of 840 DM, leaving the promoters' costs of 150 DM uncovered. The grievance was forgotten, however, the following year when he attracted 2,000 people to his concert in Mensa II, bringing in 12,000 DM, from which he received 9,500 DM as a fee. After deduction of all costs the club was left with a 850 DM profit, which more than made up for the deficit of the 1976 concert.

From 1978 to 1987 the Tübingen concerts of Wolf Biermann were promoted exclusively by Club Voltaire, Biermann effectively becoming a political and artistic advertisement for the club. The success of his concerts also helped to stem the continually precarious financial situation due to the general crisis in the West German folk scene. In this respect the cooperation with Dieter Dehm-Lerryn's Kulturladen in Frankfurt was also extremely beneficial. It not only organized Biermann's tours, but also promoted many of the artists in the peace movement of the 1980s.[52] A highpoint of this cooperation was an open-air BAP concert on 11 July 1984 in Tübingen which, with 9,500 spectators, was the biggest single concert in the history of the Club Voltaire.[53]

This concert clarified the development that had taken place in the scene, which in ten years had grown from an intimate folk family into a mass audience. The singers and musicians, who had begun as amateurs with vague ideas, had become professional artists with accelerating careers. The Club Voltaire also had to professionalize its promotional work and increasingly encountered the forces of the music market. The difficult question arose how left-wing political ideas, which the Club Voltaire claimed to represent, could be aligned with the reality of the commercial music business. Whatever political content there was in the songs, the folk music industry in the 1970s and 1980s was promoting its stars to what was, by today's standards, a large niche market. This new commercial reality did not encourage actual political discussion at a roots level as had been the norm at the Burg Waldeck festivals in the 1960s.

The Club Voltaire attempted to address this contradiction by staging an annual festival which began in 1975. For over a decade the Tübingen Festival (as it was called from 1978) was a major event very much in the public spotlight, at which it was possible — in workshops, debates and solidarity actions — to discuss radical left-wing issues relatively unconstrained by the music market.

The Tübingen Festival

In many respects the history of the Tübingen festivals reflected the issues faced by the wider folk scene in the Federal Republic. All the festivals were marked by serious discussions on music and politics. In the first year the trend toward more "private"[54] songs exemplified by artists such as Hanns Dieter Hüsch, Christof Stählin, Kuretitsch-Lassahn-Virch, and Günter Wölfe was discussed. In the festival brochure Franz Josef Degenhardt warned of the dangers of inwardness ("Vorsicht vor privaten Liedern"), maintaining that it was an expression of the depoliticization in the Federal Republic. This argument was countered, however, by the opinion that these "private" songs contributed to a new, intelligent *Unterhaltungsmusik* that formed an alternative to the trivial German *Schlager*.[55]

The second festival acclaimed the great influence of the German democratic folk-song researcher Wolfgang Steinitz on the current folk revival. It also addressed the contemporary relevance of the German folk-song tradition, referring to the utopian aspect of Ernst Bloch's previously mentioned idea of the search for the "Zukunft in der Vergangenheit." Bloch himself, a native of Tübingen, was the inspiration behind several of the festival themes over the years, and quotations from him frequently appeared on festival posters, for example, "Tausend Jahre Unrecht machen noch keine Stunde Recht" in 1976, "Grüne Blätter am Freiheitsbaum" in 1980, "Auf 1000 Kriege kommen nicht 10 Revolutionen" in 1981, and "Was allen in die Kindheit scheint und worin noch keiner war" in 1986. Bloch's wife Karola was a regular and enthusiastic guest at the festivals after the philosopher's death in 1977.

The third festival discussed the need for outside stimulus in order for German political and folk song to avoid stagnating. A contingent of Italian groups (including Stormy Six, Fausto Amodei, and Cantovivo) pointed to possible new directions with performances that were more avant-garde than those of their German counterparts.[56] For the next two years the festival continued to experiment, embracing developments in the alternative music scene such as the emergence of political choirs, cabaret, theater and dance groups. There were also concerts by the successful new political rock groups Schroeders Roadschow, Ton-Steine-Scherben, Schmetterlinge, and Bots, who to a certain extent pushed the folk groups and *Liedermacher* off of center stage.

The theme of the fifth festival was "Hanns Eisler und die zweite Kultur von heute."[57] Inspired by the great composer, an ambitious attempt was made to select examples of a progressive music ("die dem Sozialismus nützt") from the categories of folk, new political song, jazz, rock, and chamber music. Three concerts were dedicated to Eisler, featuring Hinz und Kunst, the Eisler Choir of West Berlin, Sergio Ortega, Frederic Rzewski, and Goebbels & Harth. A special symposium on Eisler explored the current relevance of his theory and asked whether non-commercial popular music was at all possible. This was driven by the concern that the folk and *Liedermacher* scene was spawning commercial rock and pop music rather than "progressive" music in the Eislerian sense.[58]

Such experimentation, however, resulted in a crisis. From 1975 to 1977 the festival crowds had doubled every year, rising from 3,000 to 6,000 and then up to 12,000. The high point was reached in 1978 when the festival sold 16,000 tickets for concerts at fifteen different venues. The following year the main concert was moved from the castle courtyard of Hohentübingen to a specially constructed outdoor area on the outskirts of the town. Costs soared and the character of the festival changed. It was undergoing an identity crisis. The festival volunteers, who had begun as "folkies" with a preference for acoustic music, now had to deal with a full range of musical styles that leaned more toward rock and pop. On top of

that, they were unequipped to deal with some of the problems of a mass festival. These included streakers ("die Nackten") and the so-called "Sponti-
Gruppen" who criticized the prices and climbed over the fences, demanding an "Umsonst- und Draußen-Festival," a free and open-air festival.

The main problem with the 1979 festival, however, was that it was
overladen with acts, and its avant-garde concept was too challenging for
most of the audience. This was evident from the response to the 256-page
festival program, which was left virtually unsold. There was also dissatisfaction with the high price of 38 DM for the festival ticket. The number
of spectators declined to 9,000, which resulted in a deficit of 30,000 DM,
a loss which was cushioned by a Tübingen town subsidy of 38,000 for the
Club Voltaire. The festival was from that point forward included in the
town's annual budgeting plans, with the subsidy being steadily increased
up to the highpoint of 140,000 DM in 1988. This was a significant development particularly in light of the fact that a predominantly left-wing
festival was effectively being encouraged by local government policy. This
provides an example of the SPD government's aforementioned practice of
containing the protest movement by diverting it into institutional channels.

The festival crisis of the years 1978 to 1979 was remedied by a new,
leaner festival structure and a new political concept. It was felt that the
audience base was no longer the folk scene as such, but rather the new
social movements that were gaining momentum at the time. Subsequent
Tübingen festivals had a clearly defined theme reflecting national and international political concerns of the time such as the rise of the Greens
(1980), Nicaragua (1981), the campaign against nuclear rearmament
(1982), apartheid in South Afrika (1983), and the fight for a nuclear-free
zone in the Pacific (1987). The "Nikaragua" festival of 1981, amid
euphoria for the Sandinista revolution, was able to raise 30,000 DM for a
solidarity project in that country. The "Afrika" festival of 1983 culminated in the concert "Freiheit für Nelson Mandela," featuring many groups
from that continent.

Other festival themes included the difficult question of Germany's
Nazi past, which the 1984 festival dealt with via its focus on the Scholl
siblings. The 1985 festival "für das andere Amerika" looked for points of
connection with the US peace campaign and featured representatives of
the American Indian Movement, Floyd Westermann and Binah McCloud.
At the 1986 festival "Heimat und internationale Solidarität" Ernst Bloch's
notion of *Heimat* was promoted in opposition to the conservative concept of the term. Bloch saw *Heimat* as an utopian place that everyone
knows from childhood, but where nobody has ever yet been; a place that
must be created by a restructuring of the world.[59]

The festival's media image was still a potential problem. If in the
1970s controversy had arisen due to the alleged influence of the orthodox

communist DKP, in the 1980s the Club Voltaire and its festival were viewed as friends of the Green Party. The club's support for Walter Schwenninger — a Green candidate from within the club's own ranks — in the 1983 Federal Government election, led to charges that it had mis-used public money and breached its political neutrality. Wolf Biermann, through his acclaimed concerts in Tübingen, became a leading public fig-ure who helped dispel the suspicion of the festival as communist-related, which still emanated from conservative corners.[60] The extent to which this suspicion lingered on was evident in the lack of TV coverage of the festi-val. The first and only TV documentation was a thirty-minute film by Fernsehen-Südwest on the 1985 festival "für das andere Amerika."[61]

The status the festival had acquired by the mid-1980s concealed the precariousness of the financial situation. This became evident at the 1987 festival "Asien und Pazifik — Traum oder Trauma," where the attendance figures plummeted to 5,000, producing a deficit of 100,000 DM. A crisis ensued that was only solved by sacking the paid members of staff and radically curtailing the program.[62] The festival continued on a smaller scale until 1992. Its promotion was then taken over by the "Afro-Brasil Festi-val," a jazz festival that had begun in 1986 and which held the event an-nually on the Tübingen marketplace up until 2004, when it moved to Stuttgart because of complaints due to noise.

The Sociocultural Centers — From Confrontation to Cooperation

In the 1970s the "alternative culture" to which the folk and *Liedermacher* scene belonged was seen as politically suspect, and this made public fund-ing difficult to obtain. Supporters of the cultural organizations involved in promoting the scene even refused to apply for money, on one hand be-cause they thought it was pointless, on the other because they did not want to jeopardize their own autonomy. Nevertheless, in the wake of the 1968 movement, as previously stated, there emerged self-organized po-litical-cultural clubs and new centers of communication which were in great demand as meeting places for social and political groups and initia-tives and especially as venues for all kinds of music and theater groups.

In the late 1960s and into the 1970s public cultural policy had played no part in this new cultural direction, as political leaders in this area saw their responsibility lying only in the traditional bourgeois elite culture and — to a lesser extent — in the traditional *Volkskultur* of the *Heimat* or-ganizations. Generally there was also the perception that the "alternative" culture was a form of youth culture, which fell into the area of responsi-bility of the public youth departments. But by the early 1980s this alter-native cultural scene had expanded to such an extent that clubs had become simply too small. They now sought to set up bigger cultural centers, for which they needed state support.

A change came in the 1980s when the concept of "socioculture," whose central concepts had already been formulated by the Deutscher Städtetag in its study *Wege zur menschlichen Stadt*[63] in 1973, and which had also been much discussed internationally (for example, in France and Norway, and at the UNESCO world conference in Nairobi in 1976), gained a foothold in West Germany. The term socioculture marked a new democratic approach to culture in general, based on the motto "Kultur für alle und von allen." It emphasized culture as practice as opposed to culture as object of contemplation, and was an attempt to revitalize what previously had been considered the domain of the social elite, and to instrumentalize it as a counterpart to commercial mass culture.[64]

At the founding of the Kulturrat, or Cultural Council, of the FRG in November 1982 the Allgemeine Kulturarbeit/Soziokultur was set up as one of its eight departments. This was followed in 1987 by the establishment of the federally sponsored Fonds Soziokultur e.V. within the Kulturpolitischen Gesellschaft, which was active nationwide. Leading politicians in the field of culture (among them Hilmar Hoffmann, Olaf Schwenke, and Hermann Glaser) joined together in the Kulturpolitischen Gesellschaft to push through a broader idea of culture in line with the concept of socioculture. The time was ripe for a collaboration between the politicians and the alternative culture movement: it was only necessary to break down mutual reservations. A precondition for this was that the representatives of alternative culture give up their confrontational stance with regard to the state, to adjust from "Konfrontation zur Kooperation." This step was a difficult one for the "alternatives," since there was a widespread mentality of anarchism in the new cultural centers according to which cooperation with the state was betrayal. In the end, however, the economic need of the cultural centers was so strong that ideological misgivings were laid aside and the offer of public funding accepted.

In the early 1980s the term *soziokulturelles Zentrum* became a collective name for the various forms of new cultural centers. These had often already existed for ten years as self-administrated youth centers or cultural venues (*Kulturkneipen* and *Kulturfabriken*). As early as 1977 a federal association of sociocultural centers had formed in which these new centers (also known as *Kommunikationszentren*) — for example KOMM in Nuremberg, Börse in Wuppertal, Lagerhalle in Osnabrück, Pavillon in Hanover, and Schlachthof in Bremen — cooperated on a loose basis. In 1982 the first regional association, Die Landes-Arbeitsgemeinschaft der Kulturinitiativen und Soziokulturellen Zentren (LAKS) Baden-Württemberg was formed. Representing the interests of its initial fifteen member groups at the regional government level, it was a forerunner of developments in the whole of West Germany. In 1983 the demand for a "15 million DM development program for the creation and support of sociocultural facilities in Baden Würtemberg" led to the first constructive regional political discussions. For their exemplary sociocultural work the Goldener Anker in Pforzheim and the Club Voltaire in Tübingen together received the Prize for Innovation from the Kulturpolitische Gesellschaft in 1985. Also in 1985 the sociocultural centers were given their first hearing in the Baden-Württemberg parliament. This led, thanks to the CDU regional government under Lothar Späth, to a budget item of half a million DM for the sociocultural centers in Baden-Württemberg's two-year budget for 1986 and 1987. In the following years this funding was increased. Administered by LAKS, it reached 3.3 million DM by the 1995 and 1996 budget. The inclusion of these centers in the regional budget reflected the public recognition of sociocultural work. This was confirmed by the inclusion of the centers in the "Kunstkonzeption des Landes Baden-Württemberg"[65] in 1990 and was of particular national significance because the region was governed by the conservative CDU. This signaled that socioculture was not merely "Sozi-Kultur," or lefty culture, as it was occasionally mockingly termed. With the help of regional funds tied to matching local funds, LAKS was able to support numerous cultural initiatives in the towns as well as in the countryside by creating highly efficient sociocultural centers. These included K9 in Konstanz, Gems in Singen, Sudhaus in Tübingen, Merlin in Stuttgart, Vorderhaus in Freiburg, and Tollhaus in Karlsruhe.[66] After the lean years of the 1970s the sociocultural centers became a long-term success story. For the alternative cultural scene, to which the folk groups and *Liedermacher* belonged, this created favorable conditions for financial survival.[67]

After German unification, the Bundesvereinigung soziokultureller Zentren (Federal Association of Socio-Cultural Centers) spread to the East and by the year 2002 had 440 member organizations in fifteen federal regions. In that year 27 million people attended 85,000 cultural events and over 100,000 took advantage of courses, counseling, and group meetings. These figures show that the sociocultural centers are no relic of the 1970s, but in fact, as a focal point of the alternative cultural scene, have become one of the most modern and most utilized institutions in Germany.[68]

Conclusion

The 1970s were an exciting time for all involved in the folk festivals. Above and beyond the songs and the music, they had a profound effect on the climate of public life. The festivals were forerunners of a new model of leisure-time behavior and informal communication that from then on became common in the "open air" environment of the inner towns. They led to a relaxation of lifestyle and loosened up out-of-date formalities such as the question whether one should go to a concert wearing a tie, a sweater, or training shoes. Along with such atmospheric changes in town life, the festivals played a part in the practical implementation of the central concepts of social culture initially formulated by the Deutscher Städtetag in its study *Wege zur menschlichen Stadt* in the early 1970s.

The festivals were part of the legacy of the 1968 movement and showed its enormous democratic potential, which was denied by many of its critics.[69] Due to their peaceful proceedings, joyful, carefree atmosphere, informal singing and dancing in the open-air settings of the town marketplaces, they won sympathy for a scene that had often been scorned for being populated with "Schmuddelkinder" or even violent. In this way they formed a lively counterforce to the anti-communist and anti-terrorist hysteria promoted at the time, which led to the policy of *Berufsverbot* and almost to a national state of emergency in the *Deutscher Herbst* of 1977.

Many festivals only wanted to be "fêtes" at which the "happy folk family" could be among its own kind. This, however, was not all that they amounted to. The example of the Tübingen Festival shows the political interests that preoccupied the folk movement of the 1970s and 1980s. These extended from solidarity with the democratic, anti-dictatorial movements in other parts of the world to contemplation of the future of Germany. As such, it can be said that the initial fear that the folk festivals were becoming depoliticized after the student rebellion of the late 1960s turned out to be unjustified. Rather the festivals formed a focus for all kinds of initiatives later to be known as the new social movements. These were filled with hopes and expectations that were still fantasy in the 1970s but became social reality only a decade later, as was to be seen in the examples of the Green Party and the new sociocultural centers.

The folk scene in Germany is still in evidence, although since the heady days of the 1970s it has once again reverted to being a niche culture with only marginal public visibility. After the *Wende* of 1989 the folk scenes of East and West were unified, from which emerged the annual folk festival in Rudolstadt and the magazine *Folker*. A number of festivals from the 1970s, for example, Ingelheim and Mainz, continued to be held annually with unchanged formats. The old GDR Festival des politischen Liedes in Berlin has been revived under the new circumstances as the Festival Musik und Politik.[70]

It must be said that many of the expectations connected with the German folk revival of the early 1960s were not fulfilled. The rediscovery of the democratic German folk song championed by Peter Rohland and the Kröhers was a mere episode. The chanson, which was the focal point of the first Burg Waldeck festivals of the 1960s, was not even an issue in the German folk revival of the 1970s and 1980s, and remained a marginalized genre. Rohland's challenge in the early 1960s to create a German chanson as an equal alternative to the French chanson of Brassens, Montand, and Ferré was hardly taken up. The folk and *Liedermacher* scene of the 1970s nonetheless played a considerable part in the emergence of rock bands singing in German, which proved that dialects were singable and capable of reaching a wider audience.

From the state's perspective, however, the folk festivals and sociocultural centers could be seen as a successful integration of the alternative cultural scene, which had initially been on a course of confrontation with mainstream society. The potential for innovation within this movement was channelled successfully for the rejuvenation of town life and the enrichment of West German social plurality.

Translated by David Robb

Notes

[1] See Irene Hübner's criticism of the political conception of the Tübingen Festival, in Irene Hübner, *Kulturelle Opposition* (Munich: Damnitz, 1983), 115–23. Hannes Wader cancelled at short notice a contractually agreed concert, giving a political reason, which gave rise to the suspicion of DKP influence.

[2] "Der Dritte Weg" was represented nationwide by "Das Sozialistische Büro" in Offenbach (founded in 1969) and its newspaper, *links.* "Sozialistische Zentren" existed at a regional level.

[3] The "Krefelder Appel" was an appeal against the NATO deployment of new arms, a motion that was unanimously passed by around 1500 various peace groups in Krefeld on 15 and 16 November 1980 and had been signed by around 2.5 million citizens of the Federal Republic by 1982. Despite criticism from the SPD and Deutscher Gewerkschaftsbund (DGB) among others, which described it as "politically unbalanced" and "Moscow friendly," it met with support from wide sections of the community.

[4] See for example Diether Dehm (Lerryn), *Politik live gemacht: Kulturarbeit und politische Praxis.* With a foreword by Günter Wallraff titled "Ästhetik und politisches Bewutsein" (Wuppertal: Peter Hammer Verlag, 1984), 8, 182.

[5] The Berufsverbot for teachers was based on the "Radikalenerlass," the ban on the employment of civil servants considered to be radical. This was passed by the heads of the Federal Government and the *Länder* on 28 January 1972.

[6] See Joseph Huber, *Wer soll das alles ändern: Die Alternativen der Alternativbewegung* (Berlin: Rotbuch Verlag, 1980); Karl-Werner Brandt, Detlef Büsser, Dieter Rucht, *Aufbruch in eine andere Gesellschaft: Neue soziale Bewegungen in der Bundesrepublik* (Frankfurt and New York: Campus Verlag, 1983).

[7] Frank Beier, himself a musician and lyricist, gives a colorful summary of the most important solidarity campaigns in the Ruhr region in the 1970s in "Ruhrgebiet — Leben, Kämpfen, Solidarisieren," in Robert von Zahn, ed., *Folk und Liedermacher*

an Rhein und Ruhr, Musikland NRW, volume 3 (Münster: agenda Verlag, 2002), 129–93.

[8] Kattong, "Karriere der Marion S.," on *Stiehl dem Volk die Geduld,* LP (schwann, 1972).

[9] Kattong, "Rotes Liebeslied" / "Wenn einer Macht besitzt," Single (Eigenverlag/ Juso NRW, 1973).

[10] Krempeltiere, "Mit 35 Stunden geht's voran," in *Teufel, Teufel! Trau keiner Stunde über 35!* (Offenbach: Verlag 2000, 1980), 124.

[11] Various, "Keiner schiebt uns weg," in *Teufel Teufel!,* 116.

[12] In 1984 a cooperative was founded by the Rheinpreußen estate, which signed a lease with the town Duisburg for ninety-nine years.

[13] Frank Baier, "Rheinpreußen ruft Alarm," on *Auf der schwarzen Liste,* LP (pläne 1981). The line "[. . .] auch Frauen demonstrieren" was changed after sharp criticism from the audience ("Du weißt ganz genau, dass bei dem Hungerstreik mehr Frauen in der Kälte saßen als Männer") to the line "[. . .] auch Männer demonstrieren."

[14] See the film *Züri brännt* (Zurich: Züricher Videoladens, 1980).

[15] Cochise, "Jetzt oder nie — Anarchie!" on *Wir wollen leben,* LP (FolkFreaks, 1981); live on *Schöner wohnen — Abber fix!,* LP-Sampler (pass. op, 1981).

[16] Ape, Beck & Brinkmann, "Das Haus," on *Regenbogenland,* LP (FolkFriends, 1981); live on *Schöner wohnen — Abber fix!*

[17] Saitenwind, Bruno & Klaus, Fiedel Michel, Tom Kannmacher, Frank Baier, Walter Mossmann, Kladderatsch, Schmetterlinge, *Bauer Maas — Lieder gegen Atomenergie,* LP (pass. op, 1978).

[18] In 1973 in West Germany the petrol shortage resulting from the Arab oil embargo led for the first time to a ban on driving on Sundays.

[19] A statement by the then-Ministerpräsident of Baden-Württemberg, Hans Filbinger.

[20] On 21 January 1976 it was agreed that all actions be stopped until after the regional election of April 1976 and the national election of October 1976.

[21] Gisela Probst-Effah, *Lieder gegen "das Dunkel in den Köpfen." Untersuchungen zur Folkbewegung in der Bundesrepublik Deutschland* (Essen: Verlag Die Blaue Eule, 1995), 130.

[22] From Walter Mossmann, *Lieder zu Marckolsheim und Wyhl* (31 badisch-elsässischen Bürgerinitiativen, Bürgerinitiative Weisweil e.V., Selbstverlag, 1975), 21.

[23] See *Bremer Liederbuch für KKW-Gegner* (Bremen: Bremer Initiative gegen Atomenergieanlagen, 1980), 242.

[24] See Roland Burkhart (Buki), "Isch säll Fierie üs? Weshalb ich das Liedermachen gesteckt habe," in Walter Mossmann and Peter Schleuning, eds., *Alte und neue politische Lieder* (Reinbek bei Hamburg: Rowohlt, 1980), 378–81.

[25] Karl Meyer was swept off his feet by police water cannon while performing drinking songs and comical rhymes on 20 February 1975. Meyer came from Nimburg-Bottingen and Ernst Schillinger from Ihringen in the Kaiserstuhl area.

[26] The region of Kaiserstuhl was a traditional CDU stronghold. At the regional election of April 1976 voting trends in north Kaiserstuhl swayed between abstaining and voting for the FDP, for whom a leading member of the civil campaign was standing as candidate.

[27] *Liedermacher* and folk groups singing dialect songs included Linnenzworch, Schwabenliesel, Günther Wölfle (all from Swabia), Dieter Beck, Hanns Meilhammer, Biermösl Blosn (all from Bavaria), Bodo Kolbe (Hessen), Töätendirk (from the Münster region), Günter Gall (from the Lower Rhine), Michael Bauer, Anni Becker (both from the Pfalz), and Fiedel Michel, Moin, Liederjan, and Helmut Debus (all Low German).

[28] André Weckmann, "Dialekt als Waffe" (excerpt), in program of the Tübingen Festival, 1977.

[29] An example was an argument with Walter Mossmann about the DKP's alleged influence on the organization team (Club Voltaire) of the Tübingen Festival in 1977. Mossmann complained that the time allotted to his concert against the *Berufsverbot* had been cut due to his critical position toward the DKP.

[30] Michael Brocken, *The British Folk Revival 1944–2002* (Aldershot: Ashgate, 2002), 2.

[31] Tom Kannmacher, "Wackawacka Boing & Boom Boom Bang und andere deutsche Lieder," LP (Songbird 1974.)

[32] See Ernst Bloch, *Das Prinzip Hoffnung* (Frankfurt am Main: Suhrkamp, 1959), 8, 17.

[33] Karl-Werner Brand, Detlef Büsser, Dieter Rucht, *Aufbruch in eine andere Gesellschaft* (Frankfurt and New York: Campus Verlag, 1983), 71.

[34] The description is based on a letter from Willy Schenken sent to this author on 9 July 2003.

[35] Fiedel Michel, *Deutsche Folklore,* LP (Autogramm, 1974).

[36] Fiedel Michel, "Das Blutgericht," from *Deutsche Folklore.*

[37] Ulrich van Stipriaan, *55 Volkstänze — Niederdeutsche Kreistänze und Quadrillen, Polkas, Walzer, Rundtänze* (Nottuln: Folkshop-Edition, 1978).

[38] Florian Steinbiß, *Deutsch-Folk: Auf der Suche nach der verlorenen Tradition* (Frankfurt am Main: Fischer, 1984), 109.

[39] This Münster establishment, which celebrated its thirty-fifth birthday in 2003, is one of the oldest German folk clubs.

[40] See Bernd Hanneken, "Folk in Nordrhein-Westfalen," in von Zahn, ed., *Folk und Liedermacher an Rhein und Ruhr,* vol. 3, 66.

[41] Ingelheim as well as Mainz have enjoyed an uninterrupted festival tradition up until today. The 35th Eurofolkfestival Ingelheim took place from 7–9 July 2006 and the 32nd Open-Ohr-Festival Mainz from 2–5 June 2006 (Whitsun).

[42] "Club Voltaire" and "Republikanischer Club" were the names of the discussion clubs of the 1968 movement which were to be found in every university town. The best known was the Republikanischer Club in Berlin, which was founded in 1967 by Enzensberger among others. The Club Voltaire in Stuttgart existed from 1965 to 1970. The Club Voltaire in Frankfurt was founded in 1962 and still exists today.

[43] For example Club alpha 60 in Schwäbisch Halle, Club Manufaktur in Schorndorf, Club Kuckuckssei in Nürtingen, Club Bastion in Kirchheim, and Club Zelle in Reutlingen.

[44] See newspaper article "Für Schüler und Lehrlinge," *Schwäbischer Tagblatt/ Tübinger Chronik*, 15 May 1970.

[45] It had no bar license. A small toilet was built in 1971.

[46] In Tübingen in the early 1970s around twenty teachers in the DKP, the SDAJ, and the MSB Spartakus were affected by the *Berufsverbot*. "Mitarbeit im Club Voltaire" was one of the findings that cast doubt on one's loyalty to the constitution.

[47] The Club Voltaire strongly rejected the terrorism of the RAF and also kept a distance from the "autonomous" groups. For this reason among others it was criticized by student groups who dominated the student councils at the university as "zu wenig aktuell-politisch."

[48] The independent left-wingers in Tübingen, who had distanced themselves from the Club Voltaire due to the DKP influence, included Karola and Ernst Bloch and Inge and Walter Jens. After the separation from the SDAJ a friendly relationship developed with the two couples. This was evident in the message of greeting from Ernst Bloch and the opening words from Walter Jens at the second Tübingen Festival in 1976. In subsequent years Karola Bloch and Inge Jens supported the festival again and again with their involvement.

[49] As long as the SDAJ dominated the Club Voltaire, the Tübingen Department of Finance denied the club non-profit status, membership of the District Youth Committee was rejected, public funding was not granted, and politicians ignored all invitations to participate in discussions.

[50] Markus Hug, *Kultur- und Freizeitpolitik in der Mittelstadt. Zum Beispiel: Universitätsstadt Tübingen*. Untersuchungen des Ludwig-Uhland-Instituts der Universität Tübingen im Auftrag der Tübinger Vereinigung für Volkskunde, volume 68 (Tübingen: Eigenverlag, 1986), 233.

[51] Wader traveled by motor bike; his guitar was taken in an accompanying car. He refused to stay in the hotel "Hospiz" for reasons of prestige and spent the night at his own cost in "Krone," the most expensive hotel on the square. The 120 tickets were distributed among Club Voltaire members and friends for 7 DM each.

[52] Dieter Dehm-Lerryn, who himself had toured as a *Liedermacher* in 1973, later had under contract with his concert bureau in Frankfurt and as head of EMI Elecrola's Musikant label some of the most successful *Liedermacher* and folk groups (BAP, Klaus Lage, Zupfgeigenhansel).

[53] This concert had a back story in that the club had already put on a concert of the then completely unknown dialect group Wolfgang Niedeckens BAP on 19

December 1979 in Mensa I, which just 100 spectators had attended, resulting in a loss of 2,000 DM. At the BAP concert in 1984 132,000 DM were taken in. After deduction of costs BAP received 69,000 DM and the Club Voltaire 13,000 DM.

[54] The confrontation between "political" and "private" song went back to the Burg Waldeck festivals of 1966 and 1967, when the *Liedermacher* had demanded political engagement on the part of all artists.

[55] The tour promoter Fritz Rau among others maintained in the early 1980s that "Lieschen Müllers Schlager" was dead and had been replaced by the songs of the new German *Liedermacher*.

[56] The festival was documented in an unpublished ninety-minute color video by Utze Beutelspacher and Wolfgang Berlit with a commentary by Bernhard Lassahn, "3. Tübinger- Folk- und Liedermacherfestival 1977." Copies of this video are in the private festival archive of this author and in the Tübingen Stadtarchiv.

[57] Alongside the Eisler concerts other new musical avenues were explored, for example, feminist orientated concerts including Feminist Improvising Group, Ina Deter, Inge Latz & Bonner Blaustrümpfe, Mary Sherburne, and Unterrock. There were also folk groups from Hungary (Kormoran, Unikum, and Makvirag) and Scandinavia (Jan Danielson & Lekstulgat, Lillebjörn Nilsen & Steiner Ofsdal).

[58] The outcome of this festival led to committee member Bernhard Lassahn's resignation. He felt that the potential for alternative music had been exhausted.

[59] See Ernst Bloch, *Das Prinzip Hoffnung* (Frankfurt am Main: Suhrkamp, 1959), 1628. See also Peter Thompson's analysis of Wolf Biermann's use of a Bloch-influenced concept of *Heimat* in chapter 7 of this volume.

[60] As late as 1985 an anonymous report of a CDU regional member of parliament warned of the "communist endeavors" of the Club Voltaire, recommending that it should not receive public funding.

[61] Andrea Morgentaler and Helmut Bürgel, *Das Tübinger Festival: "Das andere Amerika"* (FS-Südwest, 1985). Besides this the only TV coverage of the festival consisted of short news reports.

[62] I was sacked as director after the 1987 festival and resigned from the Club Voltaire. The festival deficit was cleared by cutting personnel costs and by raising the local government support for the festival from 120,000 DM in 1987 to 140,000 DM in 1988.

[63] Deutscher Städtetag, ed., *Wege zur menschlichen Stadt* (Stuttgart: Deutsche Städtetag, 1973).

[64] See Norbert Sievers, *Blick zurück und nach vorn: Zwanzig Jahre Neue Kulturpolitik* (Essen: Klartext, 1994). See also LAKS, ed., *Kulturarbeit und Ästhetik, Beiträge zur Theorie und Praxis der Soziokultur* (Pforzheim: LAKS Baden-Württemberg, 1992).

[65] See Staatsministerium Baden-Württemberg, ed., *Kunstkonzeption des Landes Baden-Württemberg* (Stuttgart: Staatsministerium Baden-Württemberg, 1990), 284–88.

[66] A LAKS brochure from 1998 contains descriptions of forty-eight organizations from all over the region. See LAKS Baden-Württemberg, ed., *Soziokulturelle Ini-*

tiativen und Zentren in Baden-Württemberg. Situation und Perspektiven. LAKS-Schriftenreihe, 4 (Pforzheim: Verlag Pennclub, 2000).

[67] For the recognition of the socio-cultural centers at national level the two-day "Symposium Soziokultur" in 1987 was significant. See Der Bundesminister für Bildung und Wissenschaft, ed., *Soziokultur — Innovation für Kultur, Bildung und Gesellschaft. Dokumentation des Symposiums am 9.-10.10.1987 in Tübingen* (Bonn: Bundesministerium für Bildung und Wissenschaft, 1988). See also Der Bundesminister für Bildung und Wissenschaft, ed., *Vielfalt als Konzeption. Zu der Arbeit soziokultureller Zentren und den Anforderungen an ihre Mitarbeiter* (Bonn: Bundesministerium für Bildung und Wissenschaft, 1990).

[68] See Gerd Spieckermann, "Soziokulturelle Zentren in Zahlen im Jahr 2002. Ergebnisse der Umfrage der Bundesvereinigung," http://soziokultur.de/_seiten/zahlen2002/ from 31 August 2005.

[69] One recalls, for example, the term "linker Faschismus," which Jürgen Habermas used in 1967 to describe the activities of the student movement.

[70] The Festival Musik und Politik, which concerns itself thematically with the political song, took place under the leadership of Lutz Kirchenwitz for the sixth time in 2007.

6: Konstantin Wecker: Political Songs between Anarchy and Humanity

Annette Blühdorn

WHEN IN 1977 THE BAVARIAN singer-songwriter Konstantin Wecker (born 1947) made his breakthrough with his song "Willy," he was at once categorized as a political singer, following in the footsteps of the singer-songwriters of the student movement. As a result, political parties of the left tried to monopolize him, while for the right-wing scene he developed into "eine Haßfigur."[1] "Willy," a talking-blues about the death of a young man who was killed during an argument with neo-Nazis, has always been regarded as a political song.[2] However, Wecker himself has quite a different view of "Willy." The song, he declares, relates to a real event, and also has traces of autobiography. More than a political song, he considers it an emotional expression of an intense personal experience. In an interview in 1998, Wecker explained: "Das Lied 'Willy' ist zwar ein politisches Lied, aber es ist ein innerliches Lied. Es geht um eine, ja eine Liebesbeziehung zu einem Freund und um einen großen Zwiespalt in der eigenen Seele."[3]

The different viewpoints on "Willy" reveal a general peculiarity of Wecker's political songs: although they express criticism of the political system, the key issue of Wecker's thinking and writing has always been the self-determination of the individual, and very clearly of Wecker himself. In his political songs, Wecker is not concerned with political ideologies, which, on the contrary, he disdains. His songs are therefore different from those of political singer-songwriters of the late 1960s and 1970s such as Degenhardt, Mossmann, and Süverkrüp.

It is a characteristic feature of Wecker's political songs that they do not argue ideologically. At the same time, however, they have nothing in common with postmodern cynicism and irony, which since the 1980s has had a strong influence on German popular music, most obviously on the songs of the *Neue Deutsche Welle* and the revival of the German *Schlager*.[4] Wecker's entire thinking is based on a deeply rooted interest in people and broader issues of humanity. Since the mid-1990s Wecker has intensified this humanistic approach, which also led him to a renewed political awareness. His position between the opposites of ideological dogmatism and postmodernist pluralism of values is another special feature and tension of Wecker's political songs.

In his political songs Wecker takes up two different perspectives that create a further field of tension. On the one hand, he shows how the individual's self-determination is restricted by official institutions, ideologies, theories, laws, and societal norms, yet, on the other hand, he makes it clear that individuals adapt too easily to the standardization of the system without fighting for their own needs and wishes. Wecker criticizes both of these aspects in his songs. However, it is interesting to note that his criticism only very rarely leads to political agitation and direct calls for action.

This chapter aims to further elucidate the characteristic features of Wecker's political songs via close readings of selected lyrics. However, the complexity and multidimensionality of Wecker's political songs necessitate a brief summary of his thought and philosophy first.

Biographical and Philosophical Background

The key issue of Wecker's lyrics has always been the self-determination of the individual, which is normally inhibited by external factors such as the power of authorities and institutions, rules and laws, theories and ideologies, as well as social conventions. In 1976, at the beginning of his career, Wecker made this view very clear:

> Wir brauchen keine Führer und Heilsbringer mehr, wir brauchen Menschen, die endlich einmal in der Lage sind, sich eigenständig ihres Körpers und ihrer Gedanken zu bedienen. Menschen, die ihren eigentlichen, ihren eigenen Wünschen nachgehen, lustvolle Menschen, unmoralische und ketzerische Menschen, ein Volk von Faulenzern und Idealisten. [. . .] Leute, die endlich mal "scheiß drauf" sagen, denn dann kommen sie angerobbt von oben, wenn ihre Brötchenmacher das Machen einstellen, wenn die Menschen unter Pflichterfüllung endlich verstehen: höchste Pflicht ist es, sich mit sich selbst zu erfüllen.[5]

This perspective obviously implies a critical view of society, and indeed, throughout his career Wecker has released several political and socially critical songs.[6] Yet, since the release of "Willy" in 1977, he has always rejected the one-dimensional image of being a political singer, and endeavored not to be instrumentalized by political interests. The most obvious turning point in this respect was his album *Liebesflug*[7] in 1981, which Arnd Schirmer referred to as "Weckers Flucht nach innen," and led him to describe Wecker as "ein entrückter Poet."[8] Wecker himself declared with regard to *Liebesflug:*

Das ist ja überhaupt interessant, welche Klischeebilder man eigentlich zu erfüllen hätte. Also der Revolutionär ist angeblich der, der immer revolutionsartige Texte bringt. Ich bin der Meinung, ich war sehr viel revolutionärer, weil ich es gewagt habe, gegen mich selbst und gegen mein eigenes Image zu revoltieren [. . .], weil ich vom politischen Sänger die Wende zum innerlichen, wie man mir vorgeworfen hat, zum innerlichen Sänger gemacht habe. Ich bin der Meinung, ich war nie ein äußerlicher Sänger.[9]

Again and again, Wecker has emphasized that his artistic self-assessment as singer-songwriter and poet does not leave room for political agitation. In full accordance with the position that Hans Magnus Enzensberger expressed in 1962 in his essay *Poesie und Politik,*[10] Wecker argues "daß ein Lied oder ein Gedicht nie aktuell tagespolitisch bezogen sein darf."[11] Wecker has always been more interested in people and their inner conflicts than in politics. In 1992 he affirmed "daß ein politischer Weg keiner ist," explaining that "wenn du dich mit dem Menschen beschäftigst, mehr als mit Parteien und Ideologien, [bist du] immer näher an der Situation dran und weniger verblendet."[12]

In Wecker's view, the individual is in permanent conflict with official rules and authorities. A positive point of orientation and normative yardstick for him is nature. Echoing a long German tradition that critiques a one-dimensional and disempowering modern society, Wecker seeks guidance from nature for the achievement for a better, reconciled society. A large number of his lyrics and poems provide evidence of this reverence for nature. The songs "Nur dafür laßt uns leben" (1982), "Vom Weinstock und den Reben" (1982), "Noch lädt die Erde ein" (1982), "Inwendig warm" (1984), and "Der Baum" (1986) are only some examples.[13]

Wecker's ideal form of social and political organization is a utopian brand of anarchy combined with peacefulness and pacifism. It involves all living creatures as well as inanimate nature, and is thus based on a holistic approach.[14] Anarchy is supposed to maximize the space for every individual to freely develop her or his needs, abilities and identity. In this endeavor, the integrity of other beings, including nature, represents the only limit to otherwise unrestricted personal development. Within this concept, failure is impossible; even if an individual's life may seem a failure when measured against the moral standards of bourgeois society, as for instance with drug addicts, prostitutes, and other social outsiders. Many of Wecker's songs — for instance "Endlich wieder unten" (1981), "Schafft Huren, Diebe, Ketzer her" (1981), and "Wieder eine Nacht allein" (1982) — deal with the experiences of social outcasts whom Wecker aims to give a voice.

Wecker's persona of an introverted, sensitive singer-songwriter and advocate of the individual seems to conflict with his Bacchic macho image, which earned him ambiguous descriptions such as "Liedermacher-

Kraftprotz"[15] or "Vitalo-Grande."[16] Wecker, who never made a secret of the fact that he pursued non-intellectual activities such as bodybuilding, is tall, well built, and athletic; his concerts depend on his enormous power, enthusiasm, and vitality. He is also well known for living life to excess, shown by, for example, his openly admitted contact with prostitutes,[17] and, of course, his extensive drug consumption.

For about fifteen years Wecker was addicted to cocaine. In November 1995, he was arrested at his home in Munich for possession of the drug, and spent two weeks in jail. This marked the end of his drug phase; he has remained clean since then. In September 1996, he was sentenced to two and a half years imprisonment, yet the outcome of the various appeal proceedings was that, on 14 April 2000, Wecker received a twenty-month suspended sentence plus a fine. In practical terms this meant he was free.

For Wecker, this incident was a radical break that changed his life completely. In February 1996 he married his second wife, Annik Berlin, and since then has fathered two sons. In the following years Wecker did not release recordings of any songs to which he had written the lyrics. Instead he concentrated on coming to terms with his drug experience, and put lyrics by other writers to his own music. In 1998 he released his album *Brecht*,[18] as well as various compositions for children, for example, *Es lebte ein Kind auf den Bäumen*,[19] and in 2000 and 2001 his musicals *Minna*[20] and *Schwejk it easy!*[21] In September 2001, six years after breaking with his drug addiction, he released a new album consisting exclusively of his own songs, *Vaterland*.[22] Also, in the period from 1995 to about 2001 Wecker withdrew even more from politics, contrary to his image as political singer-songwriter. This change of emphasis led Arno Frank Eser to state: "Sein Blick richtet sich immer mehr auf die Seele, weniger auf das feindliche Umfeld" (1996, 43).

During the process of quitting drugs and searching for a new orientation in his life, Wecker linked his humanistic approach with spiritual thinking. Coming from a Catholic background, Wecker has always had a certain religious leaning,[23] and some of his lyrics may be read as confirming this inner disposition. Songs such as "Der Schutzengel" (1981), "Wenn unsre Brüder kommen" (1982), "Inwendig warm" (1984), and his poem "Lieber Gott" (1980) provide evidence of the strength and protection he drew from religious belief.[24] After he had quit his drug addiction, he developed, as he calls it, "ein organistisches Weltbild," by which he means "dass alles mit allem verbunden ist — dass der Geist mit dem Körper verbunden ist und der Mensch nicht allein auf der Welt steht, sondern mit den Tieren und Pflanzen verbunden ist."[25] Yet this approach has to some extent always been characteristic of Wecker. His entire thinking and writing — including his interest in politics — is based on a concept of humanity that involves both humans and nature.

Furthermore, as Wecker declared in an interview in 1998, his lyrics always relate back to his own experiences:

> Ich schreibe meine Lieder, ich schreibe über das, was in mir brennt. [. . .] Ich habe das, was ich schreibe, nicht nach den Regeln und Ge- setzen einer Moral und auch nicht als Lehre oder Ideologie, wie es manchmal empfunden wurde, herausgegeben, sondern im besten Sinne des Wortes als Lyrik. Auch wenn's mal politisch war, so war's trotzdem Lyrik, von mir Erfahrenes, das ich weitergegeben habe.[26]

With this statement Wecker emphasized that his interest in politics goes beyond the declaratory reiteration of ideological phrases. Indeed his rather skeptical stance toward theory and ideology surfaces at many places in Wecker's work. In a number of songs Wecker advocates that authentic emotions ought to take priority over cold and strategically calculating rea- son. For example, in "Schafft Huren, Diebe, Ketzer her" (1981), he pleads "geb meinen Bauch zum Denken frei." He criticizes "dieses Überintellek- tualisieren," which he describes as "ein böses Erbe des Jahres 68."[27] The preponderance of theory and ideology prohibits any naturalness and spon- taneity, and thus hinders the self-determination of the individual. With this attitude Wecker echoes the general skepticism toward theory among the immediate post-1968 generation in Germany, which according to Hermann Glaser regarded "Theorie als soziale Kontrolle." Wecker aimed to live and think more in accordance with his emotions ("mehr aus dem Bauch heraus").[28]

Since about 2001 Wecker has openly and frequently engaged in poli- tics, that is to say, he has championed the goals of the anti-globalization and peace movements. This commitment might be motivated by his new role as a husband and father; it might also have its roots in his recovery from his drug addiction and the caesura this meant in his life. Moreover, the American-led "war on terror," with its campaign against "rogue states" and the "axis of evil" represented additional incentives for Wecker to join in the transnational protest movement. But the fact that Wecker's approach to politics disdains all political ideologies makes it different. He pleads for a new holistic and spiritual thinking within politics. He explains that

> der größte Fehler ist, immer ein ideologisches Konzept bereit zu haben, mit dem man glaubt, schon wieder die Welt verändern zu können. Ich denke — und da bin ich mit vielen ehemaligen Linken im Clinch — es muss auch eine andere Spiritualität ins Spiel kom- men. Es braucht eine andere Kraft des Geistes.[29]

As Wecker indicates here, his political thinking distinguishes him from the singer-songwriters of the 1960s and 1970s, that is, from Franz Josef Degenhardt, Walter Mossmann, Wolfgang Neuss, and Dieter Süverkrüp,

who sang and fought in the context of the APO and the student movement for left-wing ideas. Neither is Wecker "ein später Sproß aus der Vereinigung von Liedermachern und Studentenbewegung," as Thomas Rothschild describes him,[30] nor is it appropriate to consider Wecker a political
singer-songwriter and to place him directly next to Degenhardt,
Süverkrüp, Wader, and Biermann, as Inke Pinkert-Saeltzer does.[31] Wecker
shares with the early German singer-songwriter movement the intention
to use songs as a means of enlightenment; however, his political commitment is, unlike that of his predecessors, not based on specific political issues and a particular political ideology but on spiritual thinking and a
humanistic approach to life. It can thus be argued that it is not a political
commitment in the narrow sense, but a deeply rooted interest in people
and their liberation from social and political constraints. Wecker does not
pursue specific political goals with his songs, and he has always endeavored not to be monopolized by any political party or ideology.[32]

While Wecker's political thinking is not directly based on any political
ideology, he does share the utopianism and the progressive beliefs that
have been articulated by leftist protest movements since the late 1960s. In
his song "Prost Deutschland" (1991) Wecker describes himself as "ein
alter Sack / der noch von achtundsechzig träumt, / von Bier und Beifall
aufgeschwemmt, / schon lang den letzten Zug versäumt." Both the postmodernist pluralism of values and the fun culture of the 1980s and 1990s
are foreign to him. On the contrary, due to his renewed political commitment Wecker has more recently been reproached for dragging up outdated ideas from the 1968 generation.[33] In an interview in February 2003,
Hans-Dieter Schütt goes even further by arguing that Wecker's recent
political engagement manifests "einen Anachronismus: den Künstler, der
sich außerhalb seiner Kunst zum Bekenntnis verführen läßt."[34] In his reply
to this statement, Wecker positions himself explicitly between dependency
on ideologies typical of the 1960s and 1970s and the subsequent postmodern pluralism of values:

> Warum sollte man sich nicht zum Guten verführen lassen! Die Post-
> moderne hat alle Standpunkte relativiert, das war ein heilsamer Pro-
> zeß gegen die Behauptungsdiktatur der Ideologien. Aber ich finde es
> furchtbar, daß diese Relativierung zu einer zynischen Übertreibung
> ausgewachsen ist. [. . .]. Inzwischen wird jedes politische Engagement
> als Lächerlichkeit abgestempelt. Mich schreckt das nicht ab. Ich will
> mich bekennen. (50–51)

In brief, Wecker sees himself not mainly as a political singer-
songwriter but as a poet and advocate of the individual. At the same time
Wecker is a child of his time, that is, a late affiliate of the 1968 generation
to whom the postmodern "anything-goes" mentality, which scorns politi-

cal partisanship, is foreign. The following investigation will show how Wecker's convictions have found their expression in his political lyrics.

Wecker's Political Critique

In his songs and poems Wecker persistently criticizes the power that institutions exercise over the individual. His song "Hexeneinmaleins" (1978) deals with this issue extensively. It presents various examples of suppression exerted on individuals by institutions and the ideologies on which they are based: Giordano Bruno and Urbain Grandier were both burned at the stake during the Inquisition for coming into conflict with the Roman Catholic Church; Leo Trotsky was exiled and murdered for countering the authority of the Soviet state; the execution of Sacco and Vanzetti despite the lack of evidence illustrates the power of the judiciary; and the mass murder of the Jews in the Third Reich once more demonstrates the abuse of power by the state. These examples represent a continuous line of oppression of innocent individuals by official authorities from the Inquisition up to the present. Wecker aims to condemn the abuse of power by these authorities, which arbitrarily impose their ideological instruments of domination.

Wecker's symbol for the victim of abuse of power is the witch, and the second part of the song's chorus thus states: "Immer noch werden Hexen verbrannt / auf den Scheiten der Ideologien." Of course, the methods of control have become more subtle in our time, but they still restrict the freedom and personal development of human beings. Yet the call to action on which Wecker concludes remains vague. The demand to "stand up" does not offer much guidance for the political struggle ahead:

> Heute haßt man modern
> die Angst ist die Flamme unserer Zeit
> und die wird fleißig geschürt.
> Sie verbrennen dich mit ihren Zungen und ihrer Ignoranz
> dicke freundliche Herren
> bitten per Television zur Jagd.
> Tausende
> zum Feindbild verdammt
> halten sich fürs Exil bereit.
>
> Die Schlupfwinkel werden knapp, Freunde.
> Höchste Zeit
> aufzustehn!

This song, written at a rather early stage of his career, displays several crucial aspects of Wecker's political thinking. It not only shows his criticism of ideologies; it also shows that Wecker denounces both the institutions and their representatives as well as the people who support the system through their passivity and conformity:

> Als sie Giordano Bruno verbrannten
> sandte sein Gott keine Blitze gegen das Unrecht
> munter flackerte das Feuer
> der Pöbel mußte manchmal husten zwischen zwei Lachern
> so qualmte Giordano
> oder Grandier
> [. . .]
> und das christliche Abendland
> sann befriedigt
> nach weiteren guten Taten
> Was hat dieser Ketzer mit uns zu tun
> flötet unser Jahrhundert
> [. . .]

Furthermore, like no other song of the period, "Hexeneinmaleins" clearly identifies the two state authorities Wecker was to criticize throughout his later work, namely the church and the judiciary. His criticism of the judiciary finds its most obvious expression in his songs "Verehrter Herr Richter" (1982) and "Der Herr Richter" (1988). They condemn a legal system that completely excludes humanistic concerns, working solely on the basis of law and order. Wecker considers unbiased law to be impossible; in his view one individual has no right to judge another. Wecker's attitude toward the law has to be seen against the background of his own experiences. At the age of eighteen, Wecker was arrested for burglary and theft of DM 30,000. He was held in custody for number of months and then sentenced to a one-year suspended sentence and three years' probation. Years later, in 1984, Wecker still found this decision very unfair (Wecker 1984, 240). More recently, Wecker's drug case has confirmed his negative view of the legal system. In his 1996 song "Ebata (Staatsanwälte küßt man nicht)" Wecker portrays a positive utopia in which music softens everyone's heart except for the representatives of the legal system.

Only a few of Wecker's songs focus exclusively on criticism of the church, most obviously his 1979 song "Habemus Papam."[35] Here Wecker exposes the history of the crimes and corruption of the Roman Catholic Church, involving the accumulation of wealth, oppression of minorities and social outsiders, and the abuse of power for political purposes. He criticizes the church for losing sight of its original Christian aims, namely charity and humanity. Wecker also holds the church responsible for restricting and controlling the individual's sexual life. In his poem "Sizilianische Psalmen"[36] he claims that "man muß die Wollust zum Sakrament machen / anstatt sie aus den Kirchen zu verbannen." However, Wecker's disapproval of the church as an institutional power has to be distinguished from his personal attitude toward religion, and since the 1980s Wecker has almost ceased criticizing the church in his poems and songs. The poem "Lieber Gott" (1980) may be seen as a turning point in this development.[37]

While the individual can to some extent avoid contact with the church and certainly conflict with the law, control and regulation by state authorities (and their multi-layered bureaucracy) is for the majority of people direct and unavoidable. Accordingly, Wecker is more concerned with the power of the state than with the church and the judiciary. In his satirical song "Ballade vom Puff, das Freiheit heißt" (1982), Wecker employs the brothel as a metaphor for a world in which the authorities of the state guarantee a life of safety and prosperity, but only at the price of all individual autonomy:

> Kommen Sie in das Puff, das Zukunft heißt
> und Wachstum, Profit und Ordnung!
> Wenn Sie auch einer sind, der aufs Weiterleben pfeift,
> dann sollten Sie das sofort tun.
>
> Wir bieten Ihnen Wohlstand und Sicherheit
> und unverwundbare Seelen.
> Sie geben Ihr Hirn am Eingang ab
> und brauchen sich nie mehr zu quälen.

This place is a "Kloake der Illusionen" that prohibits, first, the individual's self-determination, and second, any criticism of the alienated and unfulfilling life in modern society: "Wer brav ins Töpfchen der Wahrheit scheißt, / hat freies Essen und Wohnen." The drastic tone of these lines reminds us of Brecht, and the correspondence becomes even more obvious in the chorus, which is very similar to Brecht's "Schlußstrophen des Dreigroschenfilms"[38] both in form and content:

> Zwar: Es hat in diesem Leben
> vieles nicht den rechten Sinn,
> denn der eine muß marschieren,
> und der andre sagt wohin.
>
> Doch wer soll das schon verstehen,
> besser hält man seinen Mund.
> Gestern war die Welt noch eckig,
> heute ist sie kugelrund.

Wecker's affinity for Brecht is certainly no coincidence.[39] In fact it is an affinity to a tradition that reaches back beyond Brecht, to the socially critical *Moritaten* of Frank Wedekind, the political satire of Kurt Tucholsky, and the political cabaret of the Weimar Republic. This line of tradition can be regarded as the origin of the early German singer-songwriter movement,[40] and Wecker's obvious bond with this tradition also brings him closer to the political singer-songwriters of the 1960s and 1970s.

In his song "Im Namen des Wahnsinns" (1983), Wecker adopts a similarly critical approach toward the state as in "Ballade vom Puff." In a sharp and satirical tone he rebukes the abuse of power by the state, which rules "im Namen des Wahnsinns." A state representative threatens the citizens and wants them to conform to official standards; any attempt at self-determination, he warns, will be punished:

> Im Namen des Wahnsinns:
> Sie sind überführt,
> Sie haben sich ab und zu selber gespürt!
>
> Im Namen des Wahnsinns:
> Sie haben gelacht, und
> das hat Ihnen auch noch Spaß gemacht!
>
> Im Namen des Wahnsinns
> wird jeder vernichtet,
> der sich von innen etwas belichtet.

Wecker's criticism remains rather abstract here; he avoids any direct allusion to contemporary political reality in Germany. This vagueness is typical of many of Wecker's political songs. One reason may be that, especially after the release of "Willy," Wecker was wary about getting openly involved in German politics for fear of being instrumentalized by any political organization. At the same time, as Rothschild argues, Wecker's ambiguity exactly matched the mood of the young generation of the 1980s and was therefore a key factor in his success:

> In seinen Liedern ist wiederholt von Bedrohung die Rede. Ängste werden angesprochen. Jeder darf sich als Objekt dieser Bedrohung fühlen. Doch wer ihr Subjekt ist, bleibt geheim. Dies entspricht freilich einer weit verbreiteten Empfindung [. . .]. Die klassischen Erklärungsmodelle, etwa das marxistische des Klassenkampfes, überzeugen eine Generation nicht mehr, die sich der Analyse und der Theorie verweigert [. . .]. Wecker hat den Ton dieser Generation getroffen. (1984, 90)

A closer look at Wecker's song "Im Namen des Wahnsinns" reveals, however, that the lyrics do reflect certain aspects of the political situation in Germany. During the 1980s the term "Wahnsinn" was commonly used in the protest movement to denounce the policies of the Cold War, of nuclear rearmament and the so-called peaceful use of nuclear power. This was most conspicuous in the protests against the reprocessing plant (Wiederaufbereitungsanlage, or WAA) in Wackersdorf, Bavaria, in the first half of the 1980s. In this context the word "WAAhnsinn" was coined. The term indicated the irresponsibility and madness of a state that was willing to risk the dangers of nuclear power. Because one of the capital letter A's was often circled, thus indicating the popular symbol for anarchy, the word also stressed the readiness of the protesters to destroy the state. Seen from this perspective, Wecker's song describes and reflects the political worries of those opposing the government's nuclear policies and offers support and encouragement.

Few of Wecker's political songs refer explicitly to contemporary German politics of the time of their writing. But two of his early songs, released at the beginning of his career, prior to his deliberate change of image into that of an "innerlicher Sänger," do. Wecker's song "Frieden im Land" (1977) sketches a scenario in which, after an obvious period of unrest, law and order have been restored; each of the three verses finishes with the line: "Es herrscht wieder Frieden im Land." However, the peace is false. All resistance has been extinguished ("Endlich geschafft: ein Volk von Phagozyten") and at last any motivation for protest is gone:

> Die Schüler schleimen wieder um die Wette.
> Die Denker lassen Drachen steigen.
> Utopia onaniert im Seidenbette,
> die Zeiten stinken, und die Dichter schweigen.

In the last verse, the lyrical "I" seems to be infected by this paralyzing atmosphere and finally accepts the false peace. Full of bitter satire, the song depicts the total domination of the individual through the power of the state:

> Ich will mich jetzt mit einem runden Weib begnügen,
> drei Kinder zeugen, Eigenheime pflanzen und
> die Menschheit einfach mal um mich betrügen.
> Wohin denn leiden — schließ mir, Herr, den Mund.
> Wirf mir die Augenbinden runter und den Stirnverband:
> Es herrscht wieder Frieden im Land.

With this song, Wecker unerringly describes the atmosphere of resignation characteristic of the mid-1970s, yet again the theme is expressed somewhat generally. His 1978 song "Deutscher Herbst,"[41] on the other hand, deals more specifically with the political situation of the Federal Republic. As the title suggests, the lyrics react to the events of the autumn of 1977, when several prominent figures from politics and big business were assassinated in terrorist attacks. However, Wecker does not describe the violence of the terrorists but instead the subsequent "atmosphere of suspicion and hysteria."[42] He paints a picture of this by introducing each verse with a variation of the line "Da liegt was in der Luft," thus in an ironic way employing a line from a famous hit song of 1954, "Es liegt was in der Luft." In the earlier song, as Christian Pfarr points out, the phrase refers to the many positive effects of the economic miracle. It describes the optimistic and exciting expectations of that time, and the state of security guaranteed by the political class.[43] In Wecker's song, on the other hand, the phrase denotes a situation of socially "deviant" behavior amidst an atmosphere of impending danger:

Die Liebenden treibts noch einmal in die Parks,
und die Gärtner schlafen mit einem Lächeln auf den Lippen ein.
Selbst die eisernen Lungen pulsieren beherzter,
und meine Mutter spielt wieder mit dem Gedanken,
endlich ein Transvestit zu werden.

The auspiciously confused world depicted in these first verses forms the backdrop for Wecker to address the theme of the autumn of 1977, where likewise, Wecker believes, moral standards are being turned on their head, this time by the government:

In den schwarzen Kammern der Gefängnisse stapeln sich die Tränen.
Die Strafverteidiger träumen vom freien Leben der Konditoren,
und die Eliteeinheiten sind seit neuem päpstlicherseits autorisiert,
im Bedarfsfall die letzte Ölung vorzunehmen.

This was at the time the hard core of the Baader-Meinhof Group committed suicide after special forces (GSG 9) foiled the hijacking of an airplane by Palestinian terrorists that had the aim of freeing the imprisoned German terrorists. Wecker condemns the fact that the Federal Government obviously had no qualms about the casualties and was applying a moral double standard. He insinuates a pact between the state and the church, as he does in various other songs, for example "Waidmanns Heil" (1978), "Omoi von vorn ofanga" (1978), and the aforementioned "Habemus Papam" (1979).[44]

Only the last two lines of the song "Deutscher Herbst" finally reveal where the threat that people feel comes from: "am Horizont zeichnen sich braun die Umrisse / einer großen, starken und tödlichen Hand ab." As in "Frieden im Land" Wecker succeeds in capturing both the signs of paralysis among people and the imminent danger of a "perversion of democratic society into a surveillance state."[45] Wecker's reference to the color brown, signifying fascism, is sufficient to show where he sees the peril. Many intellectuals considered the hysteria against terrorism in the 1970s a danger for democracy and compared it with the dictatorship of the Nazis.[46] Obviously Wecker shared this view.

Although Wecker unmistakably refers to real events here, his statements are still somewhat enigmatic. On the one hand this is due to the pretentious style that is typical especially of Wecker's early poetic writings and has frequently been criticized (Eser, 46–54). In an interview as early as 1980, Wecker distanced himself from his ostentatious early verses, which he described as "übertriebene Bildhaftigkeit," "Schwelgereien," and "Poetismen," admitting that, "ich habe da auch viele Fehler gemacht" (21). On the other hand, Wecker deliberately uses a poetically enriched language for his protest lyrics. In an interview in November 2003, Wecker declared that he does not consider his protest songs to merely fulfill a particular political function. Beyond this, they are intended to be read as poetry:

> Der Protestsong an sich hat mich nie richtig beeindruckt. Mich hat aber die Art und Weise, wie Degenhardt textete, sehr beeindruckt, also das sozialkritische Lied, immer sehr stark mit Poesie verwoben. [. . .] Und eigentlich waren auch meine frühen politischen Lieder wie "Frieden im Land" keine klassischen Protestlieder, sondern eher eine Analyse der Gesellschaft auf poetische Weise. (Wecker 2003b, 20)

The continuity of the Federal Republic with the Nazi regime is also the key issue of Wecker's song "Ach, du mein schauriges Vaterland" (1982). Here, he criticizes the lack of open debate within German society about the Nazi past and the fact that, as a result, the old thinking still persists in the present. The chorus makes this continuity apparent:

> Ach, du mein schauriges Vaterland,
> du Land der Richter und Lenker!
> Gestern noch hast du Europa verbrannt,
> und jetzt spielst du schon wieder den Henker.

> Ach, du mein schauriges Vaterland,
> mit deinen geschmeidigen Mannen.
> Wir sind wieder mal vor uns davongerannt,
> aber ewig grünen die Tannen.

With the last line Wecker may well be alluding to Trygve Gulbranssen's novel *Og bakom synger skogene* of 1933, which was first published in Germany in 1935 under the title *Und ewig singen die Wälder* and was extremely popular. The novel echoed the anti-civilizational sentiments of the nationalistically oriented *Blut und Boden* literature that was favored by the National Socialists. If Wecker is indeed deliberately alluding to this book, his objective must be to highlight the extent to which National Socialist thinking still persisted within West German society.

But the lyrics offer more literary references. The motif of a singer or poet thinking of his sick homeland recalls the scenery of Heine's "Nachtgedanken," written in 1844. Wecker's reference to Germany as the "Land der Richter und Lenker" is a play on the longtime epithet of "Volk der Dichter und Denker" for the German nation, attributed originally to Madame de Staël in 1814;[47] in 1909, Karl Kraus had coined his own variation: "Die Deutschen — das Volk der Richter und Henker,"[48] from which Wecker derived the words in his song. By referring to Karl Kraus, Wecker once more positions himself clearly in the tradition of political satire that goes back to Heine and Tucholsky and leads, via the political cabaret of the Weimar Republic, to the postwar singer-songwriter movement.[49]

Following the release of "Ach, du mein schauriges Vaterland" in 1982, Wecker went through a period where he did not engage in German politics through his lyrics. His criticism of the power of the state became rather generalized. Only at the beginning of the 1990s, when an acute wave of xenophobia swept over the newly united Germany, did Wecker react directly to political events within German society in his songs "Prost Deutschland" (1991) and "Die Ballade von Antonio Amadeu Kiowa" (1993).

As demonstrated above, Wecker criticizes institutions that oppress the individual and thus hinder her self-determination. But he also shows that an autonomous and full life is — at least to some extent — the individual's own responsibility, and he blames the individual for being too conformist. On the one hand Wecker condemns a state whose authorities are still entwined with the totalitarian thinking of Nazi ideology. On the other hand, he argues that both *Vergangenheitsbewältigung* and the development of freedom and democracy are the responsibility of the younger generation too:

> Soll das auch noch die Schuld unserer Väter sein?
> Hier geht's nur noch um unser Versagen.
> Wir haben blind und ganz allein
> unsere Freiheit begraben.
>
> Und jetzt würgt uns eine Demokratie,
> deren Recht so verdächtig gerecht ist,
> deren Ordnung hysterisch wie noch nie
> alles prügelt, was offen und echt ist.

Other songs demonstrate Wecker's critique of conformism. In "Triviale Litanei" (1983), for instance, he calls attention to the total standardization of life. Each of the nine verses reiterates images of this standardization and thus drums these negative pictures into the listener's or reader's mind ("Genormtes Leben, / geregeltes Wort"; "Genormte Männer, / geregelte

Welt"; Gemännerte Norm, / geregelte Form, / gewertete Welt"). Wecker criticizes people's habituation to the superficial and standardized life ("Was uns noch passieren kann, / ist schon passiert, / es wird wieder pariert"), which according to him is partly the result of people's conformism and lack of resistance. This is communicated repeatedly throughout the song with lines such as "wir haben das alles uns selbst zu verdanken," "es lag an uns allen," "wir haben das alles selber gewählt," and "wir haben das alles selbst bestellt."

But Wecker includes himself in this criticism. In his song "Fast ein Held" (1984) he introduces a lyrical "I" who undoubtedly represents himself. Displaying a striking level of self-irony, Wecker explains:

> Klar bin ich tapfer, fast ein Held,
> und mach mein Maul auf, wo ich kann,
> kassiere dafür Ruhm und Geld,
> und klage an.

However, he is wondering whether under more difficult conditions, such as existed under the dictatorship of the Nazi regime, he would have been equally ready to articulate his opposition, and he ponders: "Manchmal beschleicht mich das Gefühl, / ich wär sehr stumm geblieben." Similar doubts about his own political *cum* moral steadfastness surface in his song "Was passierte in den Jahren," also from 1984. Having addressed another person whose resignation and conformism he condemns, he states:

> Und ich frag mich, ob ich wirklich
> so viel anders bin als du.
> Zwar, ich kleide meine Zweifel
> in Gedichte ab und zu,
> das verschafft paar ruhige Stunden,
> eigentlich ist nichts geschehn.
> Ach, es gibt so viele Schliche,
> um sich selbst zu hintergehn.

Wecker's self-criticism brings him close to the Burg Waldeck veteran Walter Mossmann, who in the course of his career withdrew more and more from the culture industry and resisted any commercial exploitation of his songs (Rothschild 1980, 126). Wecker has never gone that far, and his open self-criticism may, of course, be no more than a marketing strategy meant to increase his credibility and authenticity as a singer-songwriter. But surely for his audience it makes his criticism of others more convincing.

The same self-critical stance applies to Wecker's observation that in West Germany — and particularly in his homeland, Bavaria — a narrow-minded and conservative attitude is latent and sometimes develops into openly expressed right-wing beliefs and blunt xenophobia. In this context

Wecker often employs the word "fascism," applying it with a rather broad definition. While in his 1977 song "Willy," for instance, Wecker unmistakably employed it in order to describe a Nazi, he has sometimes expressed a much broader understanding of the concept. To the question, "Woher kommt deine Hellhörigkeit auf den Faschismus?" Wecker replied in 1998:

> Mein ganzes Schreiben war immer davon bestimmt, ganz tief in meine Seele zu schauen [. . .]. Und da entdeckt man [. . .] den Faschisten in sich. Wenn der Hanns Dieter Hüsch schreibt: "Der Faschismus beginnt in der Wohnküche," dann könnte ich genauso sagen, er beginnt in einem selbst. Und wenn man ganz deutlich in sich reinschaut, dann merkt man, wo die Gefahren sitzen, wo sie lauern. Nicht beim andern, beim bösen andern, sondern in sich. Und da wird man dann besonders hellhörig. Und dann finde ich, hat man auch ein Recht, eher anzuklagen, wenn man's von sich aus betrachtet, und nicht einfach sich ausklammert und nur nach außen tritt. (*3 SAT* "Porträt" 1998)

This statement illustrates, first, that Wecker aims to include himself in his critique. Secondly, it highlights once more that he considers all his songs, including his political songs, as "Lyrik, von mir Erfahrenes," and finally, it confirms Wecker's self-assessment as "innerlicher Sänger."

Wecker describes the most often latent but sometimes openly expressed fascism in various songs. "Willy," which tells of the murder of a young man by a neo-Nazi, belongs to this group. Both the Bavarian dialect Wecker employs here, and some other details in the lyrics (they mention, for instance, pubs "am Viktualienmarkt") indicate that the song is set in Munich. As stated, Wecker considers his Bavarian homeland particularly traditionalist and conformist.[50] Steadfastness and persistence, which are typically viewed as virtues in conservative and right-wing thinking[51] are contradictory to Wecker's own beliefs and philosophy. He has always called for the individual's changeability and further development, and describes himself as "ein Flußmensch, der sich dauernd verändert" (1998c, 34). Many of his songs and poems confirm this kind of thinking, for example "Man muss den Flüssen trauen" (1980),[52] "So bleibt vieles ungeschrieben," and "Ketzerbriefe eines Süchtigen, Vierter Brief" (1981).[53]

Wecker describes and criticizes Bavarian ultra-conservatism in his song "Haberfeldtreiben" (1979). This term applies to a tradition from Upper Bavaria that goes back to the early eighteenth century but was still practiced in the years after the Second World War: a group of "Haberer" led by a "Habermeister" punished alleged immoral behavior by bringing the accused wrongdoer before a kind of trial, usually in front of the accused person's house and during the night. Wecker performs such a "Haberfeldtreiben" in his song, thus employing the technique of role-play and linking the popular form of the protest song with an old Bavarian tradition. In one of his concerts Wecker introduced the song with the following words, "Das Fehmegericht der Haberer, so eine Art oberbayerischer Ku Klux Klan, sah sich genötigt, nach langen Jahren des Schweigens, wieder zu einem Haberfeldtreiben zusammenzutreten."[54] Here the delinquent is a young man whose political convictions the "Habermeister" describes as "bolschewistischen Schmarrn." With this kind of thinking the young man differs from the conservative majority in his community, and this is enough to start a "Haberfeldtreiben," that is, a hate campaign against him. The norms of behavior are arbitrarily set by the community, and everyone must conform. The "Habermeister" makes this clear:

> Mia schaugn ja lang zua
> bei solchene wia bei dia,
> und koana soll uns nachsagn,
> daß ma ungeduldig warn.
> Aber ungmüatlich kemma werdn.
> Was zweit geht, geht zweit.
> Und wenns Schluß is, is Schluß.
> Mit dera Revoluzzerei
> is jetzt aus und vorbei.

The lyrics demonstrate that the brutal intolerance of the "Haberer" originates from fear of change, which rejects anything new and unknown as dangerous:

> Unsan Himme laß ma uns von dia
> ned vaschiabn.
> Der bleibt, wo a is.
> Da gibts nix zu dischkrian.
> [. . .]
> Und jetzt dema nimma lang rum:
> Du bist überführt.
> Des was immer war, is wahr!

The last part of the song leaves no doubt that the young man will be persecuted, if not murdered, by the "Haberer," who shout at him:

> Jetzt schaug wosd bleibst.
> Jetzt frißt die da Ratz.
> Jetzt kumma mia.
> Jetzt ghörst da Katz.

Regardless of their obvious intolerance and aggression the pursuers regard themselves as "friedliche Leid / bal ma uns in Ruah laßt." Similarly, in his song "D'Zigeiner san kumma" (1982), also written in the Bavarian dialect and also describing a hunt, here against gypsies, Wecker refers to the pursuers as "kreizguate Kerl," thus alluding to their Christian beliefs. Their understanding of Christianity does not seem to interfere with, but rather excuses their violent behavior toward the gypsies. This attitude corresponds with the situation in Bavaria, where right-wing ideas are justified by a brand of Christianity exemplified by the conservative party CSU. In reality, however, the allegedly good character of the respectable "Bürger" is based on narrow-minded, conservative thinking that repudiates everything unfamiliar as detrimental. Wecker's use of the Bavarian dialect, which implies traditional thinking, emphasizes this position even more clearly. In both songs, he denounces the hostility described, as a result of which the victims become fair game without having done anything wrong. He shows that it is not only the power of institutions that hinder the individual's self-determination but the lack of understanding of human beings for each other, and especially the lack of tolerance of the majority for minorities.

The songs just discussed illustrate latent right-wing thinking. But Wecker also describes open right-wing extremism in his songs. In his 1979 song "Vaterland," also in the Bavarian dialect, he reverses the situation typical of the so-called *Väter-Literatur*, that is, the class of literary texts that arose from the late 1970s onwards dealing with the relationships between fathers and sons, fathers and daughters, especially in regard to the involvement of the elder generation in the Third Reich. Using the dramatic monologue or *Rollengedicht*, Wecker introduces a father who during the Third Reich was a Socialist trying to resist the *Gleichschaltung* of the Nazi regime, and who is now faced with the reproaches of his radical right-wing son. The protagonist blames the political climate of the Federal Republik for the development of his son into a right-wing extremist, arguing that the hysteria about communism fosters right-wing thinking:

> Und der Vata woaß ned aus no ein,
> so weit is kumma mit der Duckerei,
> mit Kommunistenhatz und Berufsverbot
> und Wirtschaftswunder und Arbeitsnot.
> Da wehrst di dei Lebn lang gegen all den Schutt,
> und dann machas dafür deinen Sohn kaputt.

Ten years later, in 1989, in a political landscape in which right-wing parties were able to win votes across West Germany and violent acts against foreigners and Jews were on the rise,[55] Wecker responded by writing the song "Sturmbannführer Meier." Like "Vaterland," it is a *Rollengedicht*, and again, Wecker presents an individual perspective, namely that of a former Nazi who now sees a chance for a revival of national-socialist ideas. The song focuses on the significance that Nazi ideology can acquire for the individual by fostering feelings of solidarity and stability, power and pride. Yet the lyrics stop short of describing the social consequences and political implications of neo-Nazism.

Wecker's approach in the song has therefore been criticized by Inke Pinkert-Saeltzer. According to her, Wecker's "Faschismuskritik" lacks a sufficient portrayal of the relationship between economics and fascist ideology (140) and favors individual and socio-psychological explanations at the expense of economic and political ones (146). This is certainly true, however, it misses the point that Wecker is primarily concerned with fascism as an inner disposition of certain individuals rather than as the ideology of particular political movements or parties. Once again, his focus is on the individual. He seeks to understand the reasons why neo-Nazism and other forms of right-wing thinking are attractive for some people, and he is looking for the sources of narrow-mindedness, intolerance, and prejudice.

Wecker's criticism, whether of societal and governmental institutions or of the individual, rarely leads to a direct call for action. Wecker has never believed he can change the political system with his songs. Instead, his main aim has always been to address the emotions, feelings, and thoughts of his audience and perhaps trigger processes of inner reflection rather than concrete political action. He explains that for him, "das Schönste, was man mitbekommen kann [ist,] dass Leute mir sagen, dass ich mit meinen Texten und Liedern geholfen habe, ihr Leben zu verändern" (2002, 36).[56] Wecker considers art that has the potential to change the political status quo dangerous, and has described it as "eine Scheißkunst" (2005, 14). Once more it becomes apparent that the focus of Wecker's thinking is not the political system but the individual and her or his inner disposition. In an interview in 2002 he makes this clear:

> Es geht gar nicht ums Aufrütteln, denn es geht meiner Meinung nach zuerst einmal um einen selbst. Ein politisches Engagement, das keinen dauernden Bezug zum eigenen Selbst hat, ist für die Katz' und führt zweifellos in starre ideologische Haltungen. Dann wird es sogar gefährlich. Wenn man sich politisch engagiert oder wenn man politisch agitieren will, dann muss man also immer wieder die Rückfrage stellen, was in einem selbst in diesem Moment geschieht.[57]

This skepticism toward political agitation explains why Wecker is sparing with direct protest and calls for action.

Wecker's most determined articulation of protest is the song "Sage Nein!," released in 1993. Here he alludes to a theme already prominent in German popular music and literature. In 1986, the rock musician Udo Lindenberg released his song "Say No," in which he combined parts of a speech given by Brecht in 1952 at the Vienna Peace Congress (Brecht, vol. 23, 216) with his own words.[58] In 1947, only a few days before his death, Wolfgang Borchert wrote a short prose piece, "Dann gibt es nur eins!" which shows the same pattern as Wecker's song; it presents situations in which protest and resistance are needed, and every time concludes with the phrase: "Dann gibt es nur eins: Sag nein!"[59] Wecker's "Sage Nein!" was first released shortly after Germany's unification and the subsequent social and political turbulence. An unspecified speaker addresses an unspecified individual who stands for all people, and calls upon her or him to resist xenophobia, neo-Nazism, and discrimination against marginalized groups, namely Jews, women, homosexuals, and foreigners. The examples Wecker mentions here are quite explicit, which, as we have seen, is rather exceptional in his work. He describes this song as "ein programmatisches Lied" (2005, 13). In summer 2000 the *Freundeskreis der Weckerkunst* voted "Sage Nein!" Wecker's best political song (*Wa* 6, 52).

Wecker's appeal for resistance in the song becomes especially intense as each verse and refrain concludes with the slogan "Sage Nein!" The four verses depict situations in which protest and resistance is necessary, and the refrain calls upon the audience to make this resistance happen. Wecker aims to show that protest is possible for everyone, regardless of social status, education, or age. Concern and dismay are not sufficient; direct action is what is needed:

> Ob als Penner oder Sänger,
> Bänker oder Müßiggänger,
> ob als Priester oder Lehrer,
> Hausfrau oder Straßenkehrer,
> ob du sechs bist oder hundert,
> sei nicht nur erschreckt, verwundert,
> tobe, zürne, bring dich ein:
> Sage nein!

Through the various situations he presents in this song Wecker shows that it is not only authorities and institutions that require protest and resistance, but — sometimes to an even greater degree — the intolerance and unjust behavior of individuals. The protest Wecker aims to encourage here is not meant primarily to enable the individual's self-determination but rather to protect minorities from violence and intolerance. This certainly does not mean that the idea of self-determination has lost its significance for Wecker. However, there is a growing awareness that the individual's autonomy can succeed only as a common project that ensures the inner and outer freedom of all.

Since 1993, Wecker has re-released "Sage Nein!" several times, and has also updated the lyrics, which demonstrates the significance he attributes to it. On his album *Gamsig* (1996) and the more recent albums that he released together with his colleagues Hannes Wader and Reinhard Mey,[60] Wecker presents the original version of the song. However, Wecker's 2003 book *Tobe, zürne, misch dich ein! Widerreden und Fürsprachen*, whose title quotes a line from "Sage Nein!," gives a completely new version of the lyrics (210–11), which Wecker has also performed in his concerts and at protest rallies since the beginning of 2003. The basic structure, that is the interplay of verses and refrain, and the refrain itself are still the same, but the contents of the verses are new and topical. Wecker deals with the American war in Iraq and calls upon the audience to defy the machinery of war. Once again his suggestions are very direct:

> Wenn sie dich jetzt rekrutieren
> Hab den Mut zu desertieren
> Laß sie stehn, die Generäle
> Und verweigre die Befehle
> Menschen werden zu Maschinen
> In den Militäranstalten
> Niemand soll mehr denen dienen
> Die die Welt so schlecht verwalten
> Nie mehr solln uns jene lenken
> Die nicht mit dem Herzen denken
> Laß dich nie mehr auf sie ein
> Sage Nein
>
> Doch es tut sich was, ihr Freunde
> Auf den Straßen, auf den Plätzen
> Finden sich die Freunde ein
> Sich dem Wahn zu widersetzen
> Jetzt muss Schluß sein mit dem Schweigen
> Dem Gehorsam, dem Verstecken
> Wenn für unser Wohlbefinden
> Hunderttausende verrecken
> Dann ist's Zeit zu widerstehen
> Wenn, dann aufrecht untergehn
> Gegen alle Schweinerein:
> Sage Nein

This directness, perhaps even boldness, is rather unusual for Wecker and follows from his intense political commitment since about 2001. Wecker has acknowledged that his songs must be more simplistic in order to encourage his audience, and given the times of political tumult he accepts that. With regard to the latest version of "Sage Nein!" he declares: "In Zeiten wie diesen werden die Lieder vielleicht etwas deutlicher, etwas plakativer, warum nicht. Ich verzichte in meinen Konzerten trotzdem nicht auf Liebeslieder" (2003c, 18). But although Wecker makes such concessions, he still estimates the importance of poetry in his life higher than any political commitment. Songs like "Sage Nein!" therefore remain the exception. Engaging with politics, Wecker argues, holds the danger,

> dass einem dadurch das Künstlerische etwas verloren geht, d.h. die Kreativität [. . .] braucht Muse, sie braucht Ruhe, sie braucht Abstand vom Politischen. Das Politische ist ein Schwarz-Weiß Denken, es ist ein rein rationales Denken, wenn man sich zu viel mit Politik beschäftigt, ist das sehr gefährlich für die Poesie. Da muss man aufpassen.[61]

Wecker's constant attempt to link poetry with politics becomes obvious in the reading tour he gave in autumn 2004 under the title "Ich gestatte mir Revolte." Accompanied by two pianists, he presented literary texts of critical thinkers and writers from François Villon, the vagabond poet of fifteenth-century France, to Erich Mühsam, and from Bertolt Brecht to the American documentary filmmaker Michael Moore.

Wecker's Own Vision

Wecker's skepticism toward state control, standardization, and ideological doctrine leads him to believe that anarchy is the best form of social and political (dis-)organization. In his song "Anna" (1984) he highlights the positive aspects of anarchy, using the means of personification in order to make his vision more lively and persuading. Anarchy appears as a woman, called Anna, who guarantees personal freedom and self-determination for her partner, the lyrical "I" of the song. In her generosity she allows other people to be in love with her, too, and the lyrical "I" encourages the audience to engage in relationship with her, "warts ned, warts ned — / gehts as o." This amounts to an open appeal for anarchy.

As highlighted by Pinkert-Saeltzer (295–96) Wecker has repeatedly described himself as an anarchist. In an interview in 1983, for instance, he replied to the interviewer's question: "Du bist ein Anarchist? Aber doch nicht in dem wahrsten Sinne des Wortes, daß du also die Staatsgewalt nicht anerkennst?":

> Im wahrsten Sinne des Wortes eigentlich schon, da ich der Meinung bin, daß wir eine herrschaftslose Lebensform bräuchten. Der Anarchist ist eigentlich einer, der die Menschen sehr liebt und der den Menschen zutraut, daß er mit seiner eigenen Moral, nach seiner eigenen Moral leben kann. Ich bin nach wie vor Anarchist. Und das will ich auch bleiben.[62]

Twenty years later he confirmed this self-assessment. Arguing that his belief in anarchy has been the starting point of all his thinking, he declares, "dass der Künstler eigentlich ein Anarchist sein muss, das ist das Wesen der Kunst eigentlich immer gewesen" (2003d, 22). What makes Wecker stand out in comparison to the singer-songwriters of the student movement such as Degenhardt, Mossmann, and Süverkrüp, who openly fought for socialist ideas, is not only the fact that he does not fight for certain ideological concepts or a particular political system. What also sets him apart is that he regards himself chiefly as an artist, not as a political singer-songwriter.

Given that Wecker favors anarchy, what consequences does this have for his idea of the individual? Wecker's ideal is human beings who are free from restrictive societal norms and state control. Often the protagonists of his songs and poems could on the grounds of bourgeois morals be judged as failures. He presents, for instance, addicts in "Endlich wieder unten" (1981), "Liebesflug" (1981), "Wieder eine Nacht allein" (1982), and "Zigeuner ohne Sippe" (1988); dropouts in "Stur die Straße lang" (1977) and in "Warum sie geht" (1981); prostitutes in "Die Huren werden müde" (1977) and "Ich liebe diese Hure" (1978); and suicides in "Und ging davon" (1981). This empathy with social outsiders is another parallel between Wecker and Brecht. Like Brecht, Wecker regards social outsiders as symbols of liberty because they free themselves from the banality and obligations of everyday life in order to have more profound experiences. For Wecker, the socially excluded have more revolutionary potential and also display more genuine humanity than ordinary people. Wecker's 1981 song "Schafft Huren, Diebe, Ketzer her" makes this apparent. The lyrics describe a totally corrupt and immoral society; the refrain pleads:

> Schafft Huren, Diebe, Ketzer her
> und macht das Land chaotisch,
> dann wird es wieder menschlicher
> und nicht mehr so despotisch.

Wecker considers prostitutes, thieves, and heretics positive counterweights to state control since they live their lives in an anarchic way uneffected by bourgeois standards. Their alleged social failure is in fact a liberation from societal norms, and leads to self-determination. By acting so independently, the socially marginalized appear not only as pioneers of individual freedom. They also represent a new dimension of humanity; a humanity that goes beyond what the state seeks to enforce as "law and order," but which in reality is despotism. Against this background Wecker's recent appeal for a "Kunst des Scheiterns" — by which he means the abolishment of all social constraints — becomes more reasonable:

Es lebt sich gut als "Gescheiterter"! Man muss sich nicht ständig
aufplustern, nicht vordrängen. Man reiht sich auch mal in die zweite
Reihe ein. Man ist den Absonderlichen und Ausgestoßenen nahe,
den sogenannten, Narren und Spinnern. All denen eben, bei denen
es sich lohnt zuzuhören. Weil man ihnen lieber nahe ist, als Ange-
bern und Selbstdarstellern, den heute "Gesellschaftstauglichen."[63]

Wecker's 1983 poem "Zwischenspiel,"[64] written twenty years before
the above statement, further explicates the characteristics of the two op-
posing sides. It also shows that he has long empathized with the "Narren
und Spinner." His portrait of their counterparts, here labeled as "Drüber-
steher," is a caricature. Wecker exaggerates their most prominent features:
their rationality (they discredit "Unvernunft" as "lächerlich"), their arrogance
("denn ihrer ist das Menschenreich"), their education (they "flüstern [. . .]
bestürzt: / Dialektik, mein Freund"; they meet "in Hegel-Seminaren, /
Free-Jazz-Konzerten oder / anderen Geheimclubs, / deren Credo die
Unverständlichkeit ist"), and conformism (they "bückeln vor politischen
Begriffen, moralischen Normen"). Very clearly Wecker supports the other
side, the social outsiders, whom he refers to as follows:

> Da hör ich schon viel lieber denen zu,
> die munter drauflosplappern
> sich versteigen ins Uferlose
> auch wenn sie nicht mehr zurückfinden
> solche
> die rotbäckig werden nach einer Stunde,
> denen irgendwann zwangsläufig
> der Bierkonsum aus der Kontrolle gerät
> Schwärmer,
> die mit dem Körper reden,
> Verzückte,
> Besessene,
> Leidenschaftliche,
> die man immer wieder aufbrechen kann,
> weil sie so zerbrechlich sind,
> und die dann eben auch,
> wenns gar nicht mehr anders geht,
> auf die Straße rennen
> und den Kopf hinhalten.

Obviously, Wecker is exaggerating. He describes neither group of
people realistically. However, he tries to elucidate the opposition between
the insiders, who on the basis of societal norms and guidelines live a stan-

dardized life and therefore enjoy social status and security, and the outsiders, who resist standardization at the price of social exclusion:

> Ich schreib für die, die zwischen allen Stühlen
> Und ohne Trost ihr Leben packen.
> Die Greifer, die in allen Tiefen wühlen
> Und ab und zu genießerisch in sich versacken.
>
> Ich schreib, verdammt noch mal, nicht um zu heilen.
> Propheten hats schon viel zuviel gegeben.
> Ich möchte tauchen, taumeln und verweilen.
> Nicht glücklich werden: sondern leben.
>
> ("Weckerleuchten," 1976)

Conclusion

The political song has, as Thomas Rothschild (1972, 61) argues, three
main functions. It is a means of political struggle, a means of enlightenment, and can serve to establish a better understanding of history. Rolf
Schwendter, as cited by Rothschild (1972, 65), describes the tasks of the
protest song as agitation, information, and propaganda, referring to the
concepts of the agitprop movement, which since its emergence in the aftermath of the Russian October Revolution has been linked with left-
wing ideas. Schwendter also argues that the protest song is most effective
when directly related to political action. Given Wecker's skepticism regarding agitation, propaganda, and political struggle, only very few of his
songs, if measured by these criteria, qualify as as political or as protest
songs. They hardly ever campaign openly, they do not spread political
propaganda, they rarely give clear information about a specific political issue, and they are not normally connected to specific political events, let
alone protest actions. The above criteria, however, presuppose a political
ambition that Wecker does not have.

Much broader is the definition of Matthias Thiel, who describes the
political song as a "literarisch-musikalische Form zur Herstellung von
politischer Öffentlichkeit."[65] To the extent that the concept of the political is understood as referring to societal conditions and relations more
generally rather than just to the acquisition and exercise of power,
Wecker's songs can indeed be described as political songs. Despite the
fact that they are usually not linked to specific political issues and often
lack a clear political stance, they always deal with the individual and her or
his position within society.

However, Wecker's political songs are embedded in his own philosophy. His political thinking goes beyond political ideologies, theories, and

doctrines and is based on humanity and a holistic perception of the world. Both the starting point and the aim of his political songs is the self-determination of the individual, which implies autonomy from the control of any official authority. For long periods, especially during the 1980s, Wecker deliberately adopted an unpolitical attitude in order to keep his independence. However, according to Thomas Rothschild this position was "in erstaunlicher Übereinstimmung mit zeitgenössischen Stimmungen und Moden" and hence reveals Wecker's own conformism:

> Selbst da [. . .], wo er niemandem als sich selbst treu sein wollte, wo er sich weigerte, sich von irgendeiner Gruppe vereinnahmen [. . .] zu lassen, verhielt es sich gerade darin konform mit einer Verweigerungshaltung, die politisch ist, indem sie unpolitisch scheinen will, indem sie nämlich die Politik den Politikern überläßt. (1984, 91–92)

Although this approach differentiates Wecker from the political singer-songwriters of the 1960 and 1970s, he nonetheless positions himself in the same tradition as his immediate predecessors, namely the tradition of Wedekind and Brecht who showed empathy with social outsiders, and of Kästner and Tucholsky, who developed political satire as a means of criticism. With Tucholsky Wecker also shares the use of dialect, pacifism, and the wish not to be instrumentalized by any political organization. It is certainly no accident that in 1995 Wecker was the first artist to be awarded the Kurt Tucholsky Prize.[66]

Notes

[1] Arno Frank Eser, *Konstantin Wecker — Der Himmel brennt* (Berlin: Ch. Links, 1996), 68.

[2] See Thomas Rothschild, "'Das hat sehr gut geklungen.' Liedermacher und Studentenbewegung," in Martin W. Lüdke, ed., *Nach dem Protest: Literatur im Umbruch* (Frankfurt am Main: Suhrkamp, 1979), 156.

[3] "Porträt Konstantin Wecker," TV program, *3 SAT,* 7 September 1998. In the following this program is referred to as *3 SAT* "Porträt" 1998.

[4] See Merle Hilbk, "Das Ende vom Lied," in *Die Zeit* 20, 2000, 13–15 and Peter Kempert, "Wo geht's lank? Peter Pank, Schönen Dank!" in Peter Kemper, Thomas Langhoff, and Ulrich Sonnenschein, eds., *"but I like it": Jugendkultur und Popmusik* (Stuttgart: Reclam, 1998), 299–308.

[5] Konstantin Wecker, *Ich will noch eine ganze Menge leben: Songs, Gedichte, Prosa* (Munich: Ehrenwirth, 1978), 89.

[6] For a comprehensive investigation of these songs see Annette Blühdorn, *Pop and Poetry — Pleasure and Protest: Udo Lindenberg, Konstantin Wecker and the Tradition of German Cabaret* (Oxford, Bern, Berlin, Bruxelles, Frankfurt am Main, New York, Vienna: Peter Lang, 2003), 278–313, and Inke Pinkert-Saeltzer, *Die*

literarische Verarbeitung der bundes-republikanischen Wirklichkeit nach 1968 in den Texten des Liedermachers Konstantin Wecker — Eine literatursoziologische Untersuchung (Ann Arbor, MI: University Microfilms International, 1990).

[7] Konstantin Wecker, *Liebesflug: Ein Liederzyklus* (LP) (Polydor/Deutsche Grammophon, 1981).

[8] *Der Spiegel* 5, 1981, 184.

[9] "Porträt Konstantin Wecker" (TV program) *3 SAT*, 7 September 1998.

[10] Hans Magnus Enzensberger, *Einzelheiten II. Poesie und Politik* (Frankfurt am Main: Suhrkamp, 1976), 127 and 131.

[11] Konstantin Wecker, "Ganz ehrlich sein Selbst herauskehren. Gespräch mit Konstantin Wecker," in *Neue Zeitschrift für Musik* 1 (1980): 21.

[12] Konstantin Wecker, "Ich bin nicht der Willy," in Frank Quilitzsch, ed., *Wie im Westen so auf Erden: Gespräche mit Schriftstellern und Liedermachern, Dichtern und Theaterleuten, Rocksängern und Pastoren 1991–97* (Munich: Kirchheim, 1998), 29.

[13] Wecker's song lyrics are published in the anthology *Schon Schweigen ist Betrug: Die kompletten Liedtexte* (Heidelberg: Palmyra, 2005). References to Wecker's lyrics, unless indicated otherwise, are to this edition and are copyright © of and used by permission of Konstantin Wecker and Management Konstantin Wecker.

[14] This is very much in line with the aims of the *Lebensreformbewegung*. See Thomas Rohrkrämer, *Eine andere Moderne? Zivilisationskritik, Natur und Technik in Deutschland 1880–1933* (Paderborn, Munich, Vienna, Zurich: Schöningh, 1999), 123.

[15] Arnd Schirmer, in *Der Spiegel* 5, 1981, 184.

[16] Bernhard Lassahn, *Dorn im Ohr: Das lästige Liedermacher-Buch* (Zurich: Diogenes, 1982), 237.

[17] Konstantin Wecker, "'Ich möchte weiterhin verwundbar sein.' Interview August 1984," in Kathrin Brigl and Siegfried Schmidt-Joos, eds., *Selbstredend. . . . Neue Interview-proträts* (Reinbek: Rowohlt, 1986), 248–49. Subsequent references to this interview are referred to as Wecker 1984.

[18] Konstantin Wecker, *Brecht* (CD) (BMG, 1998).

[19] Konstantin Wecker, *Es lebte ein Kind auf den Bäumen* (CD) (BMG, 1998).

[20] Konstantin Wecker, "Minna," premiere in Heilbronn in December 2000; script by Michael Wildenhain and Nicolas Kemmer.

[21] Konstantin Wecker, "Schwejk it easy," premiere in Berlin in May 2001; script by Michael Korth and Peter Blaikner.

[22] Konstantin Wecker, *Vaterland* (CD) (BMG, 2001).

[23] See Eser, *Konstantin Wecker*, 55–58; and Wecker, "Ich möchte weiterhin verwundbar sein," 267.

[24] In Konstantin Wecker, *Lieder und Gedichte* (Munich: Ehrenwirth, 1981), 271–74.

[25] Konstantin Wecker, "Konstantin Wecker zu Gast bei Monika Langthaler" (*Redaktion Brainbows*, 2001), reprinted in *Wecker art* 9, 26–28; here: 26. *Wecker art* is a journal published twice a year by the *Freundeskreis der Wecker-Kunst*, which was founded in 1996 and presently has about 160 members. *Wecker art* (in the

following quoted as *Wa*) is committed to circulating information about Wecker among *Freundeskreis* members.

[26] Konstantin Wecker, "Sinnenfreude, Höllenwelten und die Eigenverantwortlichkeit für die Seele," in Bernd Neubauer, ed., *Eigenverantwortung: Positionen und Perspektiven* (Waake: Licet, 1998). Reprinted in *Wa* 2, 13.

[27] Quoted in Thomas Rothschild, *Liedermacher: 23 Porträts* (Frankfurt am Main: Fischer, 1980), 190.

[28] Hermann Glaser, *Deutsche Kultur 1945–2000* (Bonn: Bundeszentrale für politische Bildung (Lizenzausgabe), 2003), 370.

[29] Konstantin Wecker, "Ich muß mich einfach einmischen," in *Tageszeitung Südtirol,* 27–28 July 2002. Reprinted in *Wa* 11, 34.

[30] Thomas Rothschild, "'Das hat sehr gut geklungen,'" in Lüdke, ed., *Nach dem Protest,* 156.

[31] Pinkert-Saelzer, *Die literarische Verarbeitung,* 4 and 12.

[32] Wecker's open commitment to the anti-globalization network *Attac* is a relatively new phenomenon and part of his politicization since the year 2001. After having become a member himself, Wecker soon aimed to encourage other people to get involved in *Attac* via his online-diary, which he initiated in early June 2001 (accessible at: http://www.wecker.de; see entry of 23 July 2001).

[33] See Günter Bauch, ed., *Politisch nicht correct — Konstantin Wecker im Gespräch* (Bassum: Döll Verlag, 2001), 37; Konstantin Wecker, *Diese Welt ist mir fremd,* PHOENIX TV interview, 9 November 2001 (Bassum: Doell Verlag, 2001), 25.

[34] Quoted in Konstantin Wecker, *Tobe, zürne, misch dich ein! Widerreden und Fürsprachen,* ed. Hans-Dieter Schütt (Berlin: Eulenspiegel, 2003), 50.

[35] In Wecker, *Lieder und Gedichte,* 217–21.

[36] In Konstantin Wecker, *Jetzt eine Insel finden: Vorläufige Gedichte und Lieder* (Reinbek: Rowohlt, 1986), 81–85.

[37] See also Wecker's "Interview mit Pfarrer Wahl," in Bauch, ed., *Politisch nicht correct,* 128–42.

[38] The last verse runs: "Denn die einen sind im Dunkeln / und die andern sind im Licht. / Und man siehet die im Lichte / die im Dunkeln sieht man nicht." Bertolt Brecht, *Werke. Große kommentierte Berliner und Frankfurter Ausgabe,* vol. 14 (Berlin and Weimar: Aufbau; Frankfurt am Main: Suhrkamp), 101.

[39] Konstantin Wecker, "Ich denke, wir sind Flußmenschen," in *Dreigroschenheft: Informationen zu Bert Brecht* 2 (1998): 33–36.

[40] Karl Riha, "'Mal singen, Leute.' Couplet, Chanson, Balladensong und Protestsong als literarische Formen politische Öffentlichkeit," in Karl Riha, ed., *Moritat, Bänkelsong, Protestballade: Kabarett-Lyrik und engagiertes Lied in Deutschland* (Königstein/Taunus: Athenäum, 1979), 120–77.

[41] In Wecker, *Ich will noch eine ganze Menge leben,* 32.

[42] Rob Burns and Wilfried van der Will, "The Federal Republic 1968 to 1990: From the Industrial Society to the Cultural Society," in Rob Burns, ed., *German Cultural Studies — An Introduction* (Oxford and New York: OUP, 1996), 280.

[43] Christian Pfarr, *Ein Festival im Kornfeld: Kleine deutsche Schlagergeschichte* (Leipzig: Reclam, 1997), 62.

[44] His criticism becomes most direct in the poem "Über die Moral": "Sie verstehen. / Sie müssen nur im Großen stehlen und rauben und morden, / dann schickt man Ihnen vielleicht auch noch einen katholischen Priester / der Ihre Waffen segnet." In Konstantin Wecker, *Im Namen des Wahnsinns: Ein Spiel von Frieden und Menschlichkeit* (Munich: Ehrenwirth, 1983), 91.

[45] Burns and van der Will, "The Federal Republic 1968 to 1990," 277.

[46] See Alfred Andersch, "Article 3 (3)," and Bernt Engelmann, "Noch ist dies auch unsere Republik," in Klaus Wagenbach et al., eds., *Vaterland, Muttersprache: Deutsche Schriftsteller und ihr Staat von 1945 bis heute* (Berlin: Verlag Klaus Wagenbach, 1979), 297–99 and 309–10.

[47] Inge Stephan, "Kunstepoche," in Wolfgang Beutin et al., eds., *Deutsche Literaturgeschichte* (Stuttgart: Metzler, 2001), 231–32.

[48] Karl Kraus, *Aphorismen.* Edited by Christian Wagenknecht (Frankfurt am Main: Suhrkamp, 1986), 159.

[49] Hans-Peter Bayerdörfer, "Vormärz," in Walter Hinderer, ed., *Geschichte der deutschen Lyrik: Vom Mittelalter bis zur Gegenwart* (Stuttgart: Reclam, 1983), 335

[50] This evaluation is reflected and confirmed by the unbroken period in office of Bavaria's conservative governing party, the Christlich Soziale Union, or CSU.

[51] See Jürgen R. Winkler, "Rechtsextremismus. Gegenstand — Erklärungsansätze — Grund-probleme," in Wilfried Schubarth and Richard Stöss, eds., *Rechtsextremismus in der Bundesrepublik Deutschland: Eine Bilanz* (Bonn: Bundeszentrale für politische Bildung, 2000), 38–68.

[52] In Wecker, *Lieder und Gedichte,* 242.

[53] In Konstantin Wecker, *Und die Seele nach außen kehren: Ketzerbriefe eines Süchtigen — Uns ist kein Einzelnes bestimmt. Neun Elegien* (Cologne: Kiepenheuer & Witsch, 1993), 27.

[54] Konstantin Wecker, *Live,* LP (Polydor, 1979).

[55] See Angelika Königseder, "Zur Chronologie des Rechtsextremismus. Daten und Zahlen 1946–1993," in Wolfgang Benz, ed., *Rechtsextremismus in Deutschland* (Frankfurt am Main: Fischer, 1994).

[56] By attaching importance to the use-value of his lyrics Wecker corroborates his affiliation to the Weimar cabaret and its main representatives, Bertolt Brecht, Erich Kästner, Walter Mehring, and Kurt Tucholsky, who developed the concept of *Gebrauchslyrik* (see Blühdorn, *Pop and Poetry — Pleasure and Protest,* 2003).

[57] "Konstantin Wecker im Gespräch mit Wolf Loeckle," TV-program, α-*Forum,* 30 September 2002.

[58] Udo Lindenberg, *Hinterm Horizont geht's weiter: Alle Texte von 1946 bis heute* (Düsseldorf: Econ, 1996), 275–76.

[59] Wolfgang Borchert, *Das Gesamtwerk.* Edited by Bernhard Meyer-Marwitz (Reinbek: Rowohlt, 1977), 318–21.

[60] Wader and Wecker, *Was für eine Nacht* (Sony BMG, 2001); Wader, Wecker, and Mey, *Das Konzert* (Sony BMG, 2003)

[61] "Doppelkopf," Radio program, *Hessischer Rundfunk,* 16 December 2003.

[62] Interview with Alfred Biolek on the German TV talk show "Bei Bio," *ARD,* 7 April 1983; written version of the interview in *Allgemeine Sonntagszeitung,* Würzburg, 15 April 1983; quoted in Pinkert-Saeltzer, *Die literarische Verarbeitung,* 296.

[63] Online diary of 22 January 2003, accessible at http://www.wecker.de.

[64] In Wecker, *Im Namen des Wahnsinns,* 57–58.

[65] "Politisches Lied," in Ralf Schnell, ed., *Metzler Lexikon Kultur der Gegenwart* (Stuttgart: Metzler, 2000), 417.

[66] Michael Hepp, *Verleihung des Kurt Tucholsky-Preises für literarische Publizistik 1995 an Konstantin Wecker.* Edited on behalf of the Kurt Tucholsky-Gesellschaft (Berlin: Kurt Tucholsky-Gesellschaft, 1996).

7: Wolf Biermann: Die Heimat ist weit

Peter Thompson

WOLF BIERMANN REMAINS PERHAPS the best-known and most influential political song-maker in German history: a central figure against
whom all other political songwriters must be measured, both lyrically and
musically.[1] Peter Graves has commented that "his poetry has a compelling
verve and an infectious candor, a power to sting and to challenge, as well
as to amuse."[2] As Sabine Brandt has also said, his "Gedichte mobilisieren
das Hirn, seine Lieder auch das Herz. Sie ergreifen den Menschen total
[. . .]."[3] For many he was the best example of what David Bathrick has
called the almost libidinal attraction of communism and the GDR in all its
contradictions.[4] From the time when he first arrived in the GDR from West
Germany in 1953 — just as millions were moving in the opposite direction — to the present day, his songs and thoughts have undergone radical
change but have also demonstrated quite clear and definable continuities.

This chapter will attempt to trace Biermann's geographical, personal,
and political journey, demonstrating how, for him, all three aspects of his
life are intimately entwined and represented in his songs and poems. It will
also investigate a further intertwining: Biermann's is, after all, a German
life expressed in German song, but it is, or was, also a communist life expressed in communist song. And the songs carry within them both the
horizontal community of his fellow Germans, communists and Jews as
well as the vertical community of the history and genealogy of his family,
his class, his nation, and his people. As he himself so often maintains, the
political and the personal can never be disentangled.

However, the one thing that unites all of these aspects of his life and
his oeuvre is the Blochian search for a *Heimat* — a homeland — a place
that is impossible to find but must always be sought. He first explicitly alludes to this in his "Deutsches Miserere (Das Bloch-Lied)" of 1977, in
which he asks whether he is now a "heimatloser Gesell."[5] In his 2006
collection of poems, *Heimat: Neue Gedichte*, he returns to this theme in a
much more extensive form, documenting his search for a home in Germany, Israel, Banyuls sur Mer, and, finally, death, of which he says: "das
ist der Tod, da will ich hin / Ankommen doch nie und nimmer."[6] In a
quotation from the dust jacket of that book he states that "Das Zentrum

meiner poetischen Versuche wird aber immer hier an der Elbe sein, wo ich als gebranntes Kind durch das große Feuer der Bombennächte raus in die Welt rannte, immer dorthin, wo keiner je ankommt: in der Heimat." This is a direct reference to the famous final paragraph of Ernst Bloch's work *Das Prinzip Hoffnung,* which contends that

> Die Wurzel der Geschichte aber ist der arbeitende, schaffende, die Gegebenheiten umbildende und überholende Mensch. Hat er sich erfaßt und das Seine ohne Entäußerung und Entfremdung in realer Demokratie begründet, so entsteht in der Welt etwas, das allen in die Kindheit scheint und worin noch niemand war: Heimat.[7]

In Bloch this principle of hope was a socialized one, part of a movement toward the liberation of humanity from the realm of necessity into the realm of freedom. In Biermann the direction taken from Hamburg via the GDR and other places back to Hamburg has also been the journey of an individual trying to find himself as well as a future for humanity. In that sense, for Biermann the geographical also represents the political journey. This intertwining of the literal and the metaphorical in Biermann's biography is also characteristic of his approach to songwriting.

When considering the nature of the *Ich* in any writer's output it is necessary to consider the distance between the real and the implied author and the difference between those authors and the narrator. In Biermann this distance can be very short, despite any irony or self-mythologizing. In the "Ballade vom preußischen Ikarus" of 1976 for example, Biermann clearly identifies himself as Ikarus and the GDR becomes a tower from which, for him at least, escape is impossible: "Und wenn du weg willst, mußt du gehen / Ich hab schon viele abhaun sehn / aus unserem halben Land / Ich halt mich fest hier, bis mich kalt / Dieser verhaßte Vogel krallt und zerrt mich übern Rand (285). The "verhaßte Vogel" here is the cast iron Prussian eagle on the Weidendammer bridge, which carries the Friedrichstraße over the Spree. This bridge was also the closest to West Berlin and the crossing at Friedrichstraße station and became a departure point for many East Germans. The Prussian nature of the eagle is also significant in that it represents the GDR state and the SED itself — especially under Honecker — as Prussian rather than communist entities, the militaristic Prussian "Kasernensozialismus" of the GDR functioning as another means of imprisonment, not only of Biermann as an individual but also of history. The cast-iron nature of this eagle and the fact that it cannot move and yet stands above a river that flows from east to west is also a comment on the process of reification and monumentalization of socialism that Biermann sees as having taken place in the GDR under the SED.

Another representation of the GDR as an imprisoned *Heimat* can be found in the "Hölderlin Lied" of 1967, in which Biermann sees himself as held — voluntarily or not — in an impregnable tower. However it is this very imprisonment that gives him the impetus to write against the "kältre Kälten" of both the GDR's social quietude and alienation as well as the Cold War, which "Über uns hereingebrochen [ist]"; "hereinbrechen" being used normally in association with storms or wars and not, as in this song, with social or international peace: "solcher Friede! / solcher Friede!" (199).

And this 1967 song is in many ways a good starting point for a consideration of Biermann's work, containing as it does the main themes of tradition, alienation, and disillusionment as well as the essential difficulty of living in the GDR and in Germany. The song is based on Hölderlin's book *Hyperion,* the opening line of which is "Der liebe Vaterlandsboden gibt mir wieder Freude und Leid,"[8] expressing very accurately many East German intellectuals' disappointment with their own state.[9] In the "Hölderlin Lied" Biermann sings: "[I]n diesem Lande leben wir wie die Fremdlinge" (199), and it is this sense of alienation and distantiation, of both *Entfremdung* and *Verfremdung,* that gives his songs such presence and urgency. The idea of *Zerrissenheit,* an archetypically romantic notion, has always been the impetus for great writing and Biermann's life and work are characterized by many layers of *Zerrissenheit.*

His family was torn apart by fascism and war, as was his nation, and he was never at home in either of the two Germanys that emerged from that war. For him the torn halves of Germany did not, however, add up to an integral whole and the Germany that has emerged since 1989 is somewhat less than the sum of its parts. And yet he is drawn back constantly to the place of his childhood, Hamburg, to try to seek that *Heimat.* Musically too, his songs are characterized by a sense of *Zerrissenheit,* with the lyrical passages in the texts often working against a raging and atonal musical accompaniment and indeed vice versa. Songs with the most beautiful lyrics are shouted and screamed and the guitar and harmonium parts often strain rhythmically and harmonically against the text.

What an overview of his songs and poetry over the past fifty years demonstrates quite clearly is that the radically subjective search for self, family, and *Heimat* has become at least as important for Biermann as a search for objective historical truth or social change. But it is precisely in this that Biermann is important to us, because his journey is one that stands for the post-1945 world in general and because he lived through and embodied the rise and fall of both the GDR and a system of belief which for many had long provided a sense of *Heimat.* Biermann always described the GDR as his *Vaterland,* and its disappearance, as well as that of the Soviet Union, has left him and many others feeling free but still not at home or at rest. As he says in his song "Um Deutschland is mir gar nicht bang" from 1999: "Deutschland Deutschland ist wieder eins / nur ich bin noch zerrissen."[10]

Biermann and the Dialectic

Change and the dialectic have always been the watchwords of Biermann's work and of his thought, as is a healthy skepticism toward all dogma and a dialectical approach to problems that attempts to identify and exploit their inner *Zerrissenheit*. As Hubert Witt points out, what Biermann learned from Ernst Bloch was to live by the slogan on the latter's gravestone: *Denken heißt überschreiten*.[11] For Biermann that means to overstep one's own dogmas as well. Like both Bloch and Brecht, his dissatisfaction with the leaders of the GDR — the state in which they had all three chosen to live and that they initially wished to defend — was based in the fact that the SED had abandoned the dialectic, had established a "bürgerliche Diktatur" (as Luxemburg had so presciently warned[12]), rather than a proletarian one, and worshipped the dogmatic pursuit of unchanging and privileged access to power over historical progress and change.[13] The Party was unable to change as history changed, because to accept change was to accept the possibility of the loss of power and indeed of the very state itself. Biermann castigated the Stalinists for being Stalinists even though he was aware that the policies they implemented were integral to the maintenance of power within the Soviet bloc. And when he did so, many joined in the chorus, trusting that his defense of hope over the banality of real existing socialism would indeed bring the wall(s) down and lead to a *true* socialism in and for Germany.

The question for the Left was always to what extent it was possible to reform the GDR without bringing about its collapse. How many quantative changes could be made without bringing about qualitative change and what would that new quality be: a reformed GDR or a reunited nation? If the latter, then what kind of nation would it be: capitalist or socialist? As usual, praxis determined the outcome of that theoretical debate, and Biermann embraced its logic by maintaining that the revolutionary change that came about in 1989/90 was an inevitability and was therefore to be welcomed, though not unconditionally. What he had formerly seen as a negative qualitative change he now saw as positive, albeit with negative dimensions. This acceptance of the victory of the West over socialism was, for many of his former admirers, a turn they were not prepared to follow.

But of course Biermann himself, being a constant thorn in the side of his own admirers, sees things somewhat differently. At the famous Cologne concert of 1976 there was the following short dialogue between performer and audience:

BIERMANN: "Tja, und was jetzt?"
SPECTATOR: "etwas Kämpferisches!"

BIERMANN: "brauchst du ein bißchen Kraft in die Knochen?"
SPECTATOR: "Ja!"
BIERMANN: "Dann hilft dir auch kein Lied."[14]

Biermann realizes that his songs engage people's hearts and sees that as their main danger as well as their strength, for once people's hearts are captured, their heads can stop working, as can their ability to take action. Biermann's "Für einen faulen Fan" was written as a response to this exchange in Cologne: "Tief bewegt sein ist was Schönes / Besser ist: sich selbst bewegen! / Also laß dich hier von mir nicht / an den Liederschnuller legen!" (314). On the other hand, his poems do not simply appeal to the *ratio* but also clearly seek, when combined with the driving rythmns of the music, to mobilize emotions.

The whole of Biermann's attitude to his work, his supporters, and his detractors is summed up in that one single retort and the song that issued from it. Whether his songs are about the nature and historical role of the GDR, the German national question and reunification, Israel and the USA, or any number of other issues, his positions are bound to infuriate and to challenge those who grew up loving him, or at least his work, without fully understanding him. As someone said to the author of this chapter recently, "wann ist eigentlich Biermann so unerträglich geworden?" Well, take your pick:

For the SED leadership in 1964 it was when he started to write and perform songs and poems that were too critical and pointed toward the essential betrayal of both socialism and German unity by the SED. In his five songs from *Deutschland. Ein Wintermärchen* written between 1962 and 1965 we see clearly the lines of development. The dialectical relationship between the two Germanys (a theme that emerges time and again in his work) in 1962, less than a year after the building of the Berlin Wall, is shown in his song "Mein Vaterland, Mein Vaterland" from that collection, in which he expresses the simultaneous necessity and impossibility of the two Germanys finding their way back to each other:

> Mein Vaterland, Mein Vaterland
> Hat eine Hand aus Feuer
> Hat eine Hand aus Schnee
> Und wenn wir uns umarmen
> Dann tut das Herz mir weh
>
> Ich hab gesehn, zwei Menschen stehn
> Die hielten sich umfangen
> Am Brandenburger Tor
> Es waren zwei Königskinder
> — das Lied geht durch mein Ohr. (73)

The song referred to in the second verse is that of the two "Königs-kinder" in the traditional German rhyme who, separated by a river in life, are only united in death:

> Es waren zwei Königskinder
> die hatten einander so lieb;
> sie konnten zusammen nicht kommen,
> das Wasser war viel zu tief.[15]

Here we have Biermann's recurrent use of water and specifically the river as a referent and motif of the dialectic of division. It flows on as does history, and yet history itself not only brings people to a destination but also separates and divides those who stand on either bank. In his 1981 song "Bei Flut" he writes

> Bei Flut
> drückt die See
> den Fluß in das Land
> in Altona saß ich am Elbestrand
> und sah, wie die Boje nach Osten hin zeigt
> das Wasser läuft auf und steigt
>
> Verdrehte Welt!
> das seh ich gerne
> der Fluß, er fließt
> zurück!
>
> Die Wassermassen
> der Elbe wollen
> wieder nach Dresden
> zurück
>
> Das sah ich gern aber gelassen
> und bleibe (358–59)

In an interview in *Die Zeit* in November 2006 he still uses the river as metaphor for historical change:

> Wenn das auflaufende Wasser den Elbstrom ins Land drückt, fließt der Fluss zurück. Dieses philosophische Naturschauspiel zeigt uns, dass Heraklit eben doch nicht Recht hat, wenn er sagt, man kann nicht zweimal in denselben Fluss steigen. Man kann dreimal in denselben Fluss steigen: wenn er vorbeikommt, wenn er zurückkehrt und wenn er wieder an derselben Stelle vorbeifließt.[16]

But if we go back to 1963 and his song "Warte nicht auf bess're Zeiten" we find Biermann arguing precisely that one should not simply stand and idly watch the river flow: "Gleich dem Tor, der Tag für Tag / An des Flusses Ufer wartet / bis die Wasser abgeflossen / Die doch ewig fliessen" (98). This is a call for activism and engagement and not mere reflection. In both the *Die Zeit* interview above and "Bei Flut," in contrast, we see that the intervening years have allowed him to recognize that the river does not flow in only one predetermined direction but has ebbs and flows and unexpected consequences. This expresses perfectly Biermann's shift away from a monological certainty of his years of — albeit critical — communist commitment to the increasing uncertainty and complexity of his views since 1976.

In Biermann's 1965 "Gesang für meine Genossen," his commitment to that communist cause led him to make a direct political attack on the Politbüro and its betrayal of socialism using a clear reference to Trotsky's analysis of the Soviet Union, *The Revolution Betrayed:* "Jetzt singe ich für meine Genossen alle / Das Lied von der verratenen Revolution / für meine verratenen Genossen singe ich / und ich singe für meine Genossen Verräter" (77). In this verse we see quite clearly that he had not yet lost hope that the SED leaders whom he felt had betrayed both him and his father's memory might still be open to his pleas for a renewal of socialism. For Biermann, despite his criticism of the "helmsmen" of the revolution, the river continued to flow on its ineluctable course. Despite his continuing commitment to the communist cause, the result of these and other verses was that he was banned from performing and publishing his work in the GDR, even before the 11th Plenum of the SED in 1965, at which Erich Honecker explicitly attacked him for spreading dissent.

In 1968 he again upset the Party with his support for the reform communists around Dubček and for his opposition to the Soviet intervention that crushed the Prague Spring. In "Noch" he sings of the official silence in the GDR about the events in Prague and the way in which the country slept through them: "Das Land ist still / Der Krieg genießt seinen Frieden / Still. Das Land ist still. Noch" (212). The verses here tell of a journey by train through the GDR as Soviet and GDR troops were invading Czechoslovakia. The title "Noch" and the way in which that word is shouted out against the implied quietness of the "still" — though in his performance of this song at the Cologne concert in 1976 this word too is screamed out in one verse — indicates his hope that the GDR too would someday rise against its leaders and fight for a "socialism with a human face." This is particularly clear when we consider the dual meaning of "Noch" in German. It can mean both still, a continuing condition, but it can also be anticipatory, as in "noch nicht." "Das Land ist Still. Noch" as Biermann sings it, carries within it this anticipatory mood.

It was also in 1965 that Biermann became *unerträglich* for the West Berlin state prosecutor because of his song "Drei Kugeln auf Rudi

Dutschke," which apparently insulted the West German chancellor: "Der Edel-Nazi-Kanzler / Schoß Kugel Nummer Drei / Er legte gleich der Witwe / den Beileidsbrief mit bei" (210). The song is a straightforward cry against the assassination attempt by an extreme right-wing activist against Dutschke, the leader of the West German radical and student movement. Dutschke was important for Biermann because he too, almost alone on the Left at this time, was in favor of the reunification of Germany under socialism. Dutschke had grown up in the GDR and fled to the west just one day before the Wall was built. He too followed a Blochian perspective and held on to the dialectical view that a concrete and yet utopian *Heimat* could only be reached through the process of social change, rather than social change being forced in order to attain some pre-existing or teleological goal as determined by the Party.

The "Edel-Nazi-Kanzler" was Kurt Georg Kiesinger, who had been a member of the Nazi party beginning in 1933 and worked in Goebbels's propaganda ministry from 1940 on. This fact seemed to confirm the view widely held on the Left, and certainly by Biermann in 1968, that the Federal Republic was simply a continuation of fascism by other means and that the state and the media had effectively conspired to have Dutschke killed by creating an atmosphere of hatred. In the song "Jetzt klagen sie gross" from 1977 — the time of the so-called *Deutscher Herbst* — Biermann wrote "Ach, das, was gestern noch Jud war / — das wird hier der Sympathisant" (291), comparing the fate of those under surveillance and *Berufsverbot*[17] in the 1970s with that of the Jews under Hitler. In the "Nachwort" to his collected songs he apologizes for that line, but it is a clear indication of the ultra-Leftist mood of the period (462).

Biermann, however, also became *unerträglich* for the Maoist-dominated Left in the Federal Republic in the 1970s because he defended what they called the "social imperialism" of the GDR. Theirs are the critical voices from the audience that can be heard in the background on the recording of the Cologne concert in 1976. For the DKP and those close to the SED view of history, conversely, the turning point in their view of Biermann was when he criticized the GDR — or rather the SED's method of rule in that state — in uncompromisingly radical terms. For the anti-nationalist Left in both east and west Germany in the 1970s and 80s it was when he raised the question of German reunification long before Gorbachev had begun to tear down the columns that supported the post-1945 order of things. All three of these elements are contained in Biermann's 1977 song "Deutsches Miserere (Das Bloch-Lied)":

> Und die Linken hassen einander
> Mehr als den Klassenfeind!
> Eh wir uns selber nicht einen

> Wird Deutschland auch nicht geeint
> Und ein Linker nennt den anderen
> Verräter! und recht! und schlecht!
> Sie schlagen sich in die Fressen
> Mit MAO und MARX und BRECHT (289)

For the Left after 1989, Biermann's abandonment of the utopian socialist project after the collapse of communism led them to talk of betrayal. Then in the 1990s his uncompromising attacks on the PDS and Gregor Gysi in particular for their "collaboration" with the SED regime reached a high point. When he attacked the Prenzlauer Berg poet Sascha Anderson for his work for the Stasi, many understood why he did so but felt he went too far and was — like many other ex-dissidents in the GDR — becoming obsessed with the Stasi and its machinations. This obsession seemed to be driving him further and further to the right. With his support for the state of Israel during the First Gulf War and his criticism of those who opposed US action against Saddam Hussein in Operation Desert Storm he seemed to many on the Left to be crossing class lines into the "imperialist camp," thereby finally putting himself beyond the pale for virtually everyone who had ever supported him.

Biermann and the Politics of the Personal

All of these aspects of Biermann's politics and his work can be understood, however, if one sees them as essentially intertwined. His position on all things derives from a Brechtian desire to search for contradictions and provocation, to find the dialectic at work in the world and to provoke thought and reaction rather than simplistic monological thinking. Even his current and controversial support for Israel is tempered by the feeling that although its Kibbutzim offer an example of a successful socialism, they do so only on a very small scale and in no way offer the world a workable model for larger-scale socialism.

On the other hand, Biermann views the workings of the world in entirely personal terms. If we take his 1991 "Nur wer sich ändert, bleibt sich treu," perhaps the most autobiographical song he has written, we can see that the metaphor of history as a flowing river that has to be forded continues:

> Ich schwamm durch Blut in das große Licht
> Neugierig kam ich aus dem Bauch
> Ich war ein Tier. Und ich war ein Mensch
> Vom Anfang an und lernte auch
> Bei der Gestapo im Verhör

Soff ich am Busen ohne Scheu
Die Wahrheit mit der Muttermilch:
Nur wer sich ändert, bleibt sich treu

Von Hamburg bin ich dann abgehauen
Mit Sechzehn ins gelobte Land
Da sind Millionen den gleichen Weg
Wie ich, bloß umgekehrt gerannt
Ich wollte von zuhause weg
Nach Haus! Die Reise ist nicht neu:
Wer jung ist, sucht ein Vaterland
Nur wer sich ändert, bleibt sich treu

So kam ich drüben an: ohne Arg
Und blindbegeistert wie ein Kind
Bald sah ich, daß rote Götter auch
Nur MenschenSchweineHunde sind
Mein Vater hat mich nicht gemacht
Damit ich Lügen wiederkäu
Drum schrie ich meine Wahrheit aus:
Nur wer sich ändert, bleibt sich treu

Heiß oder kalt, immer war da Krieg
Ich ging von West nach Ost nach West
Und hielt mich an meinen Waffen, die
Gitarre und am Bleistift fest
Ich bleibe was ich immer war
Halb Judenbalg und halb ein Goj
Eins aber weiss ich klipp und klar:
Nur wer sich ändert, bleibt sich treu

Mit Weibern habe ich nichts! Als Glück
Gehabt. Ich war so grün und blind
Und wußt nur vorne im Hinterkopf
Daß auch die Weiber Menschen sind
Nun weiß ich bis ins kleinste Teil
Mit dem ich meine Frau erfreu:
Die Männerherrschaft stinkt mich an
Nur wer sich ändert, bleibt ein Mann

Ich war verzweifelt von Anfang an
Und immer habe ich neu gehofft
— so kann man leben. Bald kommt der Tod
Ich kenn Freund Hein, ich traf ihn oft
Er bleibt mein Feind, dem ich auch nicht

Zum Schluß gereimte Rosen streu
Mit letzter Puste krächze ich:
Nur wer sich ändert, bleibt sich treu (439)

The first verse has a reference to his mother and the fact that he im-
bibed the truth (of communism) at her breast. In the second verse we see
him leave for the promised land of his father; "von zuhause weg / Nach
Haus!" In the third we see that the communist truth is now merged with
his own against those communists who have betrayed his father. Even the
rather artificial-seeming fifth verse with its almost schematic commitment
to feminism and critique of patriarchy is couched again in terms of his
own personal experience. In the final verse he stares death in the face and
repeats again that he will stay committed to constant change. The paradox is that precisely in the autobiographical approach he takes to demonstrate how he has constantly changed as the world around him has
changed, we actually see someone whose motivation has always been the
same, namely to be able to hold his head up alongside his parents and
other heroes of opposition and resistance. As John Shreve has pointed
out, "Seine Toten," above all his father, will not let him go: "Meine Mutter hat mich im Bezug auf meinen Vaterso beeinflußt [. . .] daß ich [. . .]
meinen Vater rächen sollte."[18]

Today, however, Biermann no longer emphasizes the fact that his father died in Auschwitz as a communist political prisoner and saboteur. Instead, he tends to put weight on the fact that he died as a Jew along with
all the rest of his family. This shift in emphasis has also paralleled Biermann's political shift away from communism and its promise of heaven on
earth — which he sees as the root of its dictatorial tendencies — to what
one might term a left-liberal pragmatism. For that reason he is now prouder
of his father for having worn a yellow star than for having worn a red one.
As he says in his 1991 essay "Nur wer sich ändert bleibt sich treu": "Ich
hatte nun mal das schwarze Glück, daß mein Vater in Auschwitz starb
und nicht in Stalingrad. Meine Kindheitsmuster sind eben anders, ich
hatte nichts gutzumachen."[19]

Biermann, the GDR, and the Opposition

For all Biermann's attacks on communist promises of paradise on earth,
however, he wishes to stay on the side of the angels, and for him the angels are always in opposition to established power. Due to the generally
leftist nature of the opposition in the GDR and its love-hate relationship
with the SED, however, it is not at all strange that a convinced democratic communist like Biermann should have played a central role.

The opposition in the GDR has been variously categorized by writers from different parts of the political spectrum; but in general we can say that its history can be divided into three basic periods and three coterminous sociological and political categories. The first period is from 1945 to 1961, that is, from the end of the Second World War to the building of the Berlin Wall. During this period the opposition came primarily from within the social democratic and communist workers' movement as well as from Marxist, social democratic, and communist intellectuals. It fought battles over questions of German unification — of which it was largely in favor — as well as over those of social policy and the class nature of the state and the role of the Party in creating — or in the opposition's eyes preventing — a socialist Germany. Thus the Berlin uprising of June 17, 1953 was neither a CIA-supported fascist coup attempt as the SED tried to claim, nor was it a pro-capitalist, pro-western uprising with the goal of the extension of West Germany to the east. Rather what started out as a demonstration against the increased working hours and wage reductions and other consequences of the New Course issued into general demands for free elections and the unification of Germany. After the uprising it was mainly traditional social-democratic and communist workers who bore the brunt of the SED's disciplinary response to the crisis.[20]

The uprising took place exactly one month after Biermann's arrival in the GDR, though he did not experience it at first hand. However, for many years he maintained, at least partly, the Party line that it was a dangerous and quasi-fascist uprising. At the Cologne concert in 1976 — when he was still trying not to antagonize the SED, knowing that there was a danger of not being allowed back into the GDR if he were to do so — he said of this experience that he, like his "verehrter Meister Brecht," would have dropped to his knees and, with tears in eyes, welcomed the Soviet intervention. He further described the 17th of June as a Janus-headed monster; half revolutionary uprising and half fascist putsch.[21]

The second period is from 1961 to 1976, the highpoint of Biermann's presence and influence in the GDR. During this period the opposition remained essentially left wing and committed to the building of socialism and the ultimate attainment of communism, but the workers were increasingly absent from the struggle for change. Instead, opposition was largely restricted to Marxist intellectuals who were still committed to the ideals of communism but who had relatively little contact with a working class made quiescent by the building of the Wall and the relative stability and prosperity it had brought.

A characteristic Biermann song from this period is "Die habe ich satt!" from 1966, in which he savages teachers, bureaucrats, professors, and ordinary people for their quiescence. In verse six he sings:

Der legendäre Kleine Mann
Der immer litt und nie gewann
Der sich gewöhnt mit jedem Dreck
Kriegt er nur seinen Schweinespeck
Und träumt im Bett vom Attentat
— den habe ich satt! (184)

It was the combination of the New Economic System of the early 1960s and the recentralization and extended subsidization of the "Einheit der Wirtschafts- und Sozialpolitik" under Honecker in the 1970s that demobilized and depoliticized the working class. It was during this period from the mid-1960s on that the bases were laid for what Günter Gaus has described as a *Nischengesellschaft* and what Konrad Jarausch has called a *Wohlfahrtsdiktatur,* in which, in return for public loyalty, the state allowed people to withdraw into their own private niches and also guaranteed the financial subsidization of every aspect of their daily lives.[22] Biermann's songs during this period reflect his frustration with conditions in the GDR: not that people were suffering economically but that they were being bought off with relative prosperity.

Equally, the ordinary person staying passively at home in his niche is criticized in his song "Lied vom donnernden Leben" from 1975, in which he complains:

Das kann doch nicht alles gewesen sein
Das bißchen Sonntag und Kinderschrein
   das muß doch noch irgendwo hin gehn
     hin gehn
. . .
Das soll nun doch alles gewesen sein
Das bißchen Fußball und Führerschein
   das war nun das donnernde Leebn
     Leebn (184)

The third period was from 1976 to 1989, Biermann's years of exile. During this period the welfare dictatorship in the GDR became extensive and all-embracing and the proletarian revolutionary optimism of the first period as well as the Marxist intellectual debate of the second were replaced by increased general skepticism about the veracity of the grand narrative of revolution and socialism. A general shift toward post-social individualism in political and intellectual life as well as global concerns for peace, the environment, and human and women's rights took place. It was during this period that songs such as "Soldat, Soldat" from 1963 and "Ermutigung" from 1966, two decades after they were published, became popular with the post-materialist left in West Germany, with the growth of ecology and peace, the twin motors of the emerging Green movement and party. Within this movement what had previously been thought of as movements subordinate to the struggle for socialism now supplanted that struggle and existential questions took over from class conflict. The opposition in the GDR remained left wing, even socialist to some extent, but also was more concerned with individual human rights than collective social liberation. The opposition groups that emerged in the 1980s saw themselves more closely allied to the West German green movement than to any all-German socialist tradition.

During this period Biermann was fighting both his new and his old dragons in both east and west. The last few songs he wrote in the GDR are already full of the desire and the need to both stay and leave. In his 1976 "Und als wir ans Ufer kamen," perhaps his most beautiful song, he writes of the difference between appearance and reality, of the way the sky looks most beautiful when reflected in water. In the second verse he sings of the death of the dream of socialism and of the fact that it is impossible to live with or to live without that dream, which is inextricably tied up with the question of German division and how to overcome it:

> Was wird bloß aus unseren Träumen
> In diesem zerrissnen Land
> Die Wunden wollen nicht zugehen
> Unter dem Dreckverband
> Und was wird aus unseren Freunden
> Und was noch aus dir, aus mir —
> Ich möchte am liebsten weg sein
> Und bleibe am liebsten hier
> — am liebsten hier (280)

In the same year he also wrote the equally rueful "Ballade vom preußischen Ikarus," which speaks with mythological pathos of leaving and yet having wings too heavy to carry him away. The second verse speaks of the way in which the internal and external isolation of the GDR was also eating into ways of thinking about the world:

> Der Stacheldraht wächst langsam ein
> Tief in die Haut, in Brust und Bein
>   ins Hirn, in graue Zellen
> Umgürtet mit dem Drahtverband
> Ist unser Land ein Inselland
>   umbrandet von bleiernen Wellen (284)

However, 1976 was the year in which he was not only exiled from his *Vaterland* but in which he also began the long process of abandoning the politics of his father. In the years which followed, paradise began to lose its appeal and utopian thought was recognized by Biermann as well as other oppositionists as a danger rather than a blessing.

One overarching factor, though, is that throughout all of these periods the opposition was — apart from the limited opposition that emanated from within the CDU in the early period — fundamentally a socialist or democratic communist one and not nationalist, religious, or right-wing as was the case in many of the other east European states. The reason for this is that the opposition was as constrained by the German question as the SED. It increasingly recognized that the loss of the GDR into a re-united Germany would in all likelihood mean a return to capitalism. The initial hope in the late 1940s and 1950s for a socialist united Germany was replaced in the 1970s and 1980s with an acceptance that the capitalist west was by far the economically and politically stronger of the two world "camps." There was universal, though largely unspoken, recognition that the end of SED rule could only come about if the Soviet Union allowed it and that this could only happen if the balance of power between East and West also shifted in the West's favor.

If that were to come about, not only would the SED lose its political hegemony but the very state itself would cease to exist. This would mean the victory of western capitalism over Soviet communism, and, for all its many faults, most leftists believed that the Soviet Union and its bloc did represent an alternative social model. As Helga Königsdorf put it, again using very Blochian concepts of utopia and hope:

> Wir akzeptierten es nicht, das System das uns umgab, aber wir liebten die Utopie, die es einst auf die Fahnen geschrieben hatte. Und wir hatten eine Hoffnung, wir konnten irgendwie dahin gelangen [. . .]. Wir wollten das System erschüttern, um es zu verändern, aber nicht das Land preisgeben, mit dem sich unsere Utopie verbunden hatte.[23]

1989 showed the logical impossibility of unifying this contradiction in the GDR. Unlike in the rest of Eastern Europe and the Soviet Union, destroying the "leading role" of the ruling Communist Party led ineluctably to the dissolution of the country. Biermann always recognized this contradiction, and, lover of dialectical contradictions that he was, it became central to much of his work. The idea that the GDR was the better of the two Germanys and the chance that the GDR might someday play the role of the magnet toward which West Germany would be drawn were set against the rigid reality of the GDR as a state subordinate to both the SED and the Soviet Union. As Biermann says in "Es senkt das deutsche Dunkel": "Das kommt weil ich mein Deutschland / So tief zerrissen seh / Ich lieg in der besseren Hälfte / Und habe doppelt weh."[24] His painful dilemma was that he did indeed consider the GDR to be the better of the two states and his *Vaterland* — in the sense of being the land of his communist father — but that it was also the worse of the two Germanies due to the way in which it was run by the SED. The key political characteristic of the GDR was, of course, that its unswerving loyalty and subordination to the strategic interests of the Soviet Union could only act as a repellent force to those workers in the west to whom Biermann hoped communism would one day appeal.

Biermann, Utopia, and Real-Existing Socialism

As pointed out in chapter 1, political song in Germany has long been affected by the dichotomy of utopian revolutionary developments and the reaction and conservatism that followed them. Wolf Biermann also deals centrally with this dichotomy but also with its reverse in the form of reaction and conservatism within the SED leading to revolutionary failure.

Biermann moved to the GDR both willingly and at the behest of his mother in order to take part in building what they both felt was the embodiment of the revolutionary tradition in German history. The GDR officially saw itself in precisely those terms, the preamble to the 1974 constitution talking of the state as the "Fortsetzung der revolutionären Tradition der deutschen Arbeiterklasse,"[25] and the fact that many writers, poets, and intellectuals chose to return to the Soviet Zone of Occupation and the GDR rather than to West Germany in the early years after the war showed that they too shared the hope that this new state would be the continuation of the *Dichter und Denker* tradition. Within a short period, however, it became clear to Biermann that this half-revolution in half a country did not open the way to the promised land and that it in fact represented a dichotomous mixture of utopia and reaction, of revolutionary rhetoric covering up conservative reality led by an authoritarian party in thrall to an external power.

The process of coming to terms with the fact that his and his family's utopia had been deformed and corrupted in the GDR was a long struggle. From the start his songs and poems wrestle with the question as to what extent the deformities were the product of contemporary pressures or were systemic and inherent in the very desire to create a utopian paradise on earth. In 1963 Biermann quite clearly still saw true socialism as something almost platonically transcendent and certainly as something different than the form socialism was taking in the GDR. His 1963 song "Warte nicht auf bess're Zeiten," for example, begins "Manchen hör ich bitter sagen / "Sozialismus — schön und gut / Aber was man uns hier aufsetzt / Das ist der falsche Hut!" (96).

But this was complemented in the same song by the revolutionary optimism of the following verse:

> Viele werden dafür sorgen
> daß der Sozialismus siegt
> Heute! Heute, nicht erst morgen!
> Freiheit kommt nie verfrüht
> Und das beste Mittel gegen
> Sozialismus (sag ich laut)
> Ist, daß ihr den Sozialismus
> AUFBAUT!!! Aufbaut! (aufbaut) (97)

And yet in this verse too, despite its optimism, the way in which the final line is written and sung, with his voice growing quieter with each re-iteration of the word *aufbaut,* a note of caution is creeping in, a sense that the *Aufbau* itself is not what it should be and will not bring the results he hopes for. But still, despite these reservations, the imperative tone of the "AUFBAUT!" and the fact that it is addressed collectively to the workers, imploring them to do the work for socialism despite and even against the Party demonstrates his continued support for communism and the desirability and possibility of achieving it. For Biermann the faults lay not with socialism but with socialists. By 1967 — two years after the 11th Plenum of the SED and now two years into his performance ban — the "Hölderlin-Lied" already sounded a more pessimistic tone: "Ausgebrannt sind die Öfen der Revolution / früherer Feuer Asche liegt uns auf den Lippen / kälter, immer kältre Kälten sinken in uns" (199). In this song it is not only the "Kalte Kippen auf den Lippen" of day to day events mentioned in "Warte nicht auf bess're Zeiten" (96) which have fallen into people's hearts but now it is the very power house of socialism as an ideal, the ovens of the revolution, that have grown cold.

However, since the fall of the Wall, Biermann has begun to see the pursuit of paradise and utopia itself as ineluctably totalitarian and bound to lead to dictatorship. In his book *Paradies uff Erden,* he opens the poem "Paradieschen" with the lines "Ganz bin ich Jude und, nebbich, ganz Goj / Süsses Leben, saures Leben / Paradieschen wird's nie geben / Höllen gibts schon eh'r / Manchmal bin ich menschenmüde" (Biermann 1999, 134). To him it is no longer relevant whether there is a dictatorship of the proletariat or of the bourgeoisie; the emphasis has shifted from the class character of a dictatorship to its abstract essence as dictatorship per se and he is exasperated by those who cling to the idea that heaven can be brought to earth and that there can be, as Heine put it, "Zuckererbsen für jedermann!" As he pointed out in an interview in *Focus:*

Weil ich mit der marxistisch-leninistischen Erziehung, die meine El-
tern mir eingepflanzt hatten, wie ein Kind gesagt habe: Wenn die
Kapitalisten entmachtet werden, dann kann das doch nur gut sein für
alle ehrlichen, fleißigen, lustigen Menschen. Aber schon die Hoffnung des Kommunismus auf eine Gesellschaft, in der die Menschen
alle Brüder sind, hat sich nicht nur als schwer durchführbar erwiesen,
sondern auch als falsch und gefährlich. Deshalb kann ich mich heute
auch nicht mehr Kommunist nennen. Ich bin der Meinung, daß
niemand gefährlicher war in der Geschichte der Menschheit als die,
die das Paradies auf Erden erzwingen wollten. Die haben uns in
Höllen geführt, die schlimmer sind als alles, was wir bisher kannten.
Wir müssen lernen, uns für eine bessere Gesellschaft einzusetzen
ohne diesen Kindertraum vom Paradies.[26]

Biermann's recognition of the problems of utopianism is also reflected in his understanding of Heinrich Heine (one of his greatest heroes
and influences alongside Hölderlin, Brecht, and Villon), who, after the
February revolution of 1848 in France, took to his bed (or *Matratzengruft*, as he called it), turned to God, and despaired about the future of
socialist revolution in which he had once so fervently believed. He comments that Heine "wohl [das Proletariat] ehren wollte, aber nicht riechen
konnte."[27] Similarly, since 1989, it could be said that Biermann has taken
to his own ideological *Matratzengruft* and rejected the revolution in
which he just as fervently once believed.[28] For Biermann, the ruling clique
who held on to power in the name of the proletariat in the Soviet bloc
besmirched the very name of communism in a way that could never be
undone.[29]

Where Heine had been frightened by the violence and uncultured nature of the revolutionary workers, Biermann was equally disgusted by the
political ignorance, brutal cynicism, and uncultured nature of the Stalinist
bureaucracy. The real Heine-like irony for Biermann in 1989, however,
was that it was the intervention of the East German working class that
helped to turn the potential of a leftist political revolution against the bureaucracy into a socioeconomic revolution against the state. The paradox
of a working class using its social weight to bring about the reintroduc-
tion of capitalism was not lost on him, and yet he saw it as something
inevitable. Thus, after 1989, Biermann became critical not only of the nature of unification but of the inability of East and West Germans to live
with and deal with its consequences. In 1991, as the resignation and despair about real existing unification had begun to set in, Biermann wrote
the song "Dideldumm," which talks of the "Mauer im Kopf" as a "Riss
durch die Erde":

Nun endlich ist mein Land wieder eins
Und blieb doch elend zerrissen
Aus Geiz und Neid. Kein Aas will im Grund
Vom andern da drüben was wissen
Der Todesstreifen, man sieht kaum noch
Wo gestern die Wachtürme standen
Wir Deutschen haben uns wieder verloren
Noch eh wir einander fanden (435)
[. . .]
Der Schwejk im Goldenen Prag, er vergleicht
Sein Heute vergnügt mit dem Gestern
In Halle Herr Schulze ist verzweifelt, der Mann
Vergleicht immer nur mit den Schwestern
Und Brüdern im goldenen Wessiland
Die einzigen die fröhlich klotzen
Sind Stasischweine im Manager-Rausch
— ach ich finde den Osten zum Küssen (437)

Thus Biermann criticizes West Germans for their complacency and ignorance of East Germany as well as the way in which they made money from unification and he criticizes the East Germans for being surprised that that is what capitalism is like. The once eternally subversive Schwejk is rendered complacent. In this song he also draws attention to the difference between Stalinist rule in the GDR compared to the rest of Eastern Europe and the way in which the omnipresence of West Germany continues to be a central concern. The Czech Schwejk compares his situation with that under communism, whereas the East German compares himself with West Germans, just as he always did. In the same song he describes westerners as crooks and swindlers trawling through the East looking for a quick killing:

Provinzganoven, Graf Rotze im Benz
Die letzte verbrannte Asche
Sie fingern dem nackten Mann in Schwerin
Das druckfrische Geld aus der Tasche
Die Glücksritter, die von der schnellen Mark
Beschubsen mit Recht und Gesetze
Die Dummenfänger, sie schleppen durchs Land
Wie Hochseefischer die Netze (437)

Paradoxically, though, when Biermann berates *Ossies* for taking fright at these developments and being romantic about the GDR and the security it offered, for wishing it back and for seeing it as *das bessere Deutschland,* he is merely repeating a critique that was leveled against him during his exile from the GDR. After all, there are great similarities between his situation in 1976 and that of East Germans after 1989. Both were suddenly forced to accept West German control of their lives and both were forced to swap the dubious security of the welfare dictatorship of the SED for the equally dubious freedom of the market. As he himself said at the time, in the GDR he had always worried whether his songs would be banned; in West Germany his fear was that they would not sell. East Germans today are as much in exile in their own country as was Biermann between 1976 and 1989, and the nostalgia they have for the old country is no different from the one he had for his *Vaterland*. At least he has the comfort that his records did indeed sell, whereas East Germans are still finding it hard to find a market for their labor power.

However, once Biermann's period of anger at the way in which unification was taking shape had passed, he left his own past behind with increasing velocity. He condemned anyone concerned about the redistribution of wealth as a utopian and therefore — by necessity — a totalitarian demagogue. He sees plans for or even narratives about the path of history as inherently dictatorial: a planned utopia can apparently only bring about an unplanned dystopia. His trajectory has been from revolutionary and critical communist to liberal pragmatist, accepting the world as it is rather than how it might be; accepting power relationships at face value and giving up his former Marxist concern with structures of power. Biermann's interventions in the political arena are no longer rooted in the overarching grand narrative of dialectical Marxism, but concern themselves predominantly with the micronarrative of his own family's story and how it stands in relation to historical events.

The Return of Oma Meume

From his 1966 song "Moritat auf Biermann seine Oma Meume in Hamburg" (180) we know that Wolf Biermann was brought up steeped in a communist tradition. His father's death as a political prisoner and a Jew in Auschwitz and his mother's communist convictions meant that he remained a romantic revolutionary committed to wresting the idea of socialism back from the bureaucrats who were administrating it to death. His current support for Israel and the US — which has dismayed his fans and supporters perhaps more than anything else he has ever done — is no different in that regard. That an emotional defense of Israel as a homeland for the Jews has pushed him into an ideological camp to which he never thought he could have belonged is yet another of those ironies of history that he himself is so fond of exposing. To paraphrase Marx, Biermann has made his own history but not in conditions of his own making. But now the Marx Biermann once understood is lumped in with Heine, Cabet, and

St. Simon as a utopian communist, even though he, Marx, was as much against their utopianism as Biermann is now. In an article in *Der Spiegel* Biermann quotes the following verse from Heine's 1844 poem "Deutschland. Ein Wintermärchen":

> Ein neues Lied, ein besseres Lied
> Oh Freunde, will ich Euch dichten!
> Wir wollen hier auf Erden schon
> Das Himmelreich errichten

He then goes on to say of it: "Die letzten beiden Zeilen formulieren die Substanz des ganzen Kommunistischen Manifests in lapidarer Kurzfassung: das Himmelreich auf Erden. Genau dieses falsche Hoffen beflügelte vor 150 Jahren die besten Köpfe."[30]

Essentially, Biermann's oeuvre is a forty-year exposition and development of his *Bewältigung* of communism, punctuated and driven by seismic events such as the workers' uprising of 1953, Hungary in 1956, Czechoslovakia in 1968, his expulsion from the GDR in 1976 and the reaction to it, and finally and most fundamentally the revolution of 1989. For Biermann, this latter event further complicates the traditional historical tensions of revolution in Germany from Heine to the present day in that at last there occurred a successful revolution on German soil but it was also Janus-headed, both a success and a failure. As Biermann put it in 1991:

> Ja, der aufgeklärte Kapitalismus hat sogar doppelt gesiegt: über unsere stalinistischen Feinde und zugleich über unseren Traum von einer gerechteren Gesellschaft. Deswegen bin ich auch heilfroh und niedergeschlagen zugleich. Der Abschied von der Leiche des Kommunismus dauert schon mein halbes Leben.[31]

The successful and bloodless transformation of 1989 represented a powerful revolution from outside and above in the form of Gorbachev, and from below in the form of a mass popular response to his reforms. But the immediate dynamic of the revolution brought an end to the idea of a progressive development toward socialism in any form. Indeed, history seemed to be moving in the opposite direction, bringing — in Heine's words — freedom but also bankruptcy.[32] For many it has also brought new forms of power operating from above and outside, this time West German power from above and US power from outside. This is also expressed in Biermann's song "Um Deutschland ist mir gar nicht bang":

> Um Deutschland ist mir gar nicht bang
> Die Einheit geht schon ihren Gang
>   unter Milliardenregen
> Wir werden schön verschieden naß

> Weh tut die Freiheit und macht Spaß
>   ein Fluch ist sie, ein Segen
>
> Heimweh nach früher habe ich keins
> nach alten Kümmernissen
> Deutschland Deutschland ist wieder eins
> nur ich bin noch zerrissen[33]

The verses here contain perhaps an attempt to reconsider the very nature of *Zerrissenheit;* that it may well be a part of the natural order of things. The billions unleashed by the recapitalization of East Germany and reunification is shown as rain that falls on everyone and yet falls unequally. This is of course negative for some but positive for others, liberating their energies. In the first line of the refrain we have, in contrast to the Blochian idea of the creation of or a return to *Heimat* as a source of social change, the acceptance of the lack of a sense of belonging. Biermann is leaving his old concerns behind and sees them as belonging to the past, as unreachable as his own childhood. Germany is then reiterated so that there are two of them in a line which says that they have become one. In the second verse we are told that the country, though united, is not yet healed:

> Die deutsche Wunde ist noch lang
>   nicht ausgeheilt, es rinnen
> Schmerzbäche, wo die Narbe klafft
> Nur blutet jetzt der schwarze Saft
> Statt raus tief tief nach innen

And yet the pain and the blood no longer runs in rivers but only in "Bäche," and they run only back into Germany itself. The national question is solved, yet the question of social inequality remains. The final line of the refrain has only him, Biermann, divided, and yet we know that this internal division and dialectical tension is the motor that will drive his creativity on. If the dialectic of a divided Germany used to be the source of his creative drive, then in a united Germany the division has to be found within. Far better, he seems to be saying, to accept pain, tension, and division as a part of life that cannot and should not be wished away.

Biermann's take on political song in Germany combines all the aspects of tradition discussed in this volume but it also tries to undermine and to change those traditions. He pokes fun at his own supporters, challenges those who assume all share their political convictions, those who are not prepared to see that the world is changing. And yet he understands the difference between objective trends and the subjective effect that one can have in shaping that change, and in that context he has always steered a healthily ironic course between determinism and activism. As a *Fischkop* from Hamburg his attachment to water and his nautical references have given him the air of the "Klabautermann," the guardian angel of all mariners, able to steer them home in times of trouble. In "Seestück, Hochpolitisch," written in 1990, we see him referring ironically to himself as the savior of the GDR:

> Nur einer zittert nicht im Sturm
> das ischa der Klabautermann
> mit der Gitarre, das Filou
> der Poltergeist, der Tatzelwurm
> er kam zurück vom Westen her
> Wolf Biermann rettet die De-de-er
> im Kuddelmuddel mit starkem Arm
> er lenkt das Wrack dem Hafen zu
>   hält fröhlich Kurs auf die Kommune
>   und zieht die Freiheitsflagge auf

But he knows that it is a hopeless task, that the wreck is too far gone and that he can do nothing to save it. It can only be beached at best but certainly not salvaged: "Du rettest uns vorm Höllenschlund / du machst den toten Mann gesund / die DDR geht nie zugrund / so singen die Kinder im Dunkeln" (423–25). It is the voices of those children of the revolution singing in the dark to which Biermann addresses himself, asking them to finally see that the Soviet dream is over and that the GDR was nothing without the Soviet Union. And as those brief hopes for an independent socialist GDR, democratized but not privatized, cleansed of bureaucrats but not of socialism, a GDR in which a political but not a social revolution would take place and to which the masses would flee faded, Biermann set a new yet unknown course in the face of the next winds of change: "Durch allen Wandel bin und bleib ich auch mit weißem Bart / Gebranntes Kind, das neugierselig nach dem Feuer sucht."[34] Biermann would probably reluctantly agree with *Neues Deutschland*'s statement in an article published thirty years after his expulsion from the GDR: "Längst kein Kommunist mehr, ist er sich auch im Westen in einem treu geblieben: jeden auf eine andere Art zu enttäuschen."[35]

Since the early 1990s, Biermann has moved politically in ways that are common to many former Marxists who were at one point part of the Stalinist cause. In abandoning Stalinism, they have abandoned the idea of socialism in its entirety: they have thrown Marx's baby out with the Stalinist bathwater. As Richard Rorty has put it in another context, the best one can do now is to recognize the reality of "North Atlantic postmodern bourgeois-liberal neo-pragmatis(m)"[36] as the only way forward for humanity, and if this is the case then an unconditional defense of those liberal pragmatic values must also logically involve military action. And once again Biermann explains this not only in terms of political developments but also in terms of the way in which his family, "seine Toten," would react to the new world order.

In *Heimat: Neue Gedichte*, Biermann has a detached, almost elegaic poem called "Blutiges Morgenrot" in which he observes a blood-red sunrise over the Mediterranean and yet is not tempted, as he would have been in his youth, into seeing it as a metaphor for the imminence of communist revolution: "Ich habe es genossen und fiel nicht drauf rein."[37] He hears the seagulls screeching — like a "Marx-Engels-Chor" of angels — the refrain from his 1967 song "Großes Gebet der alten Kommunistin Oma Meume in Hamburg": "O GOTT LASS DU DEN KOMMUNISMUS SIEGEN! / Ein welt-re-volu-tio-närer Rabatz" (196). This time, however, it is a scarcely comprehensible din rather than the clarion call to arms it used to be. The poem then continues as a dialogue between Biermann and his grandmother, who has returned as a foreboding black raven.[38]

> Und plötzlich flog Oma Meume allein
> Zu mir durch das Fenster, verzaubert als Rabe
> Und krachzte auf sächsisch: Fall ploß nicht druff rein
> Mei Junge! Dis Rot gommt vom Osten her
> Da pluten und pluten die Völker aus
> Weit hintn, noch hinter dem Mittlmeer!

She is warning of the continuing struggles of the poor in the world, of how history continues to move forward and that the east beyond Europe is still red, as though she were still clinging to the Soviet dream. But Biermann's response is one of calm reassurance and of detachment from her struggles. There is nothing portentous in the sky; there are no omens and no warnings of impending revolution. The bloody struggles going on beyond the Mediterranean are reduced to a natural phenomenon, like the "milliardenregen" in "Um Deutschland ist mir gar nicht bang," to which human beings can have no response other than acceptance.

> Ich tröstete sie: Mein Raabanaas
> Mein schwarzes gefiedertes Großmütterlein
> Das Rot hier am Himmel ist doch nur Spaß
> Kein Blut und kein Klassenkampfgeschrei
> Es ist nur'n Spektakel der Geophysik

And then the final line of the poem makes another reference; namely to the first line of the foreword to the *Communist Manifesto*, written in 1848 by Marx and Engels, which states: "Ein Gespenst geht um in Europa. Das Gespent des Kommunismus."[39] Perhaps Biermann's answer to Marx and Engels comes in the final line of "Blutiges Morgenrot":

> Und gleich ist der ganze Spuk vorbei!

Notes

[1] "Die Heimat ist Weit" is the title of a Spanish Civil War Song included on Biermann's 1975 album *Es gibt ein Leben vor dem Tod* (Altona: Wolf Biermann Liederproduktion, 1996)

[2] Peter Graves, *Three Contemporary German Poets: Wolf Biermann, Sarah Kirsch, Reiner Kunze* (Leicester: Leicester UP, 1985), 17.

[3] Sabine Brandt, as quoted in Jay Rosellini, *Wolf Biermann* (Munich: Beck Verlag, 1992), 59.

[4] David Bathrick "The End of the Wall Before the End of the Wall" in *German Studies Review* 14,2 (1991): 299.

[5] Wolf Biermann, *Alle Lieder* (Cologne: Kiepenhauer & Witsch, 1991), 290. Unless otherwise specified, all references to Biermann's lyrics are to this volume by page number. All quotations from Biermann's lyrics are copyright © and used by permission of Wolf Biermann.

[6] Wolf Biermann, *Heimat: Neue Gedichte* (Hamburg: Hoffmann und Campe Verlag, 2006), 11.

[7] Ernst Bloch, *Das Prinzip Hoffnung* (Frankfurt: Suhrkamp, 1959), 1628.

[8] Friedrich Hölderlin, *Hyperion* (Stuttgart: Reclam, 1983), 7.

[9] For a comprehensive discussion of Hölderlin's influence in the GDR see Karen Leeder, "Towards a Profane Hölderlin: Representations and Revisions of Hölderlin in Some GDR Poetry" in *Neue Ansichten: The Reception of Romanticism in the GDR,* ed. Howard Gaskill, Karin McPherson, and Andrew Barker, German Monitor, No 6 (Amsterdam: Rodopi, 1990), 212–31.

[10] Wolf Biermann, *Paradies uff Erden: Ein Berliner Bilderbogen* (Cologne: Verlag Kiepenhauer & Witsch, 1999), 11.

[11] Hubert Witt, "Nachwort" in Wolf Biermann, *Liebespaare in politischer Landschaft: Gedichte und Lieder* (Stuttgart: Reclam, 2000), 161.

[12] Rosa Luxemburg, *Gesammelte Werke,* vol. 4. *August 1914—January 1918* (Berlin: Dietz Verlag, 1979), 363.

[13] Brecht considered emigration to China shortly before he died, partly because of the anti-dialectical positions of the SED. See Klaus Völker, *Bertolt Brecht: Eine Biographie* (Munich: dtv, 1978), 414.

[14] Cologne Concert 1976, *Das geht sein' sozialistischen Gang* (Altona: Wolf Biermann Liederproduktion, 1996).

[15] Arbeitskreis für Haus- und Jugendmusik, *Bruder Singer Lieder unseres Volkes* (Kassel, Bärenreiter 1960).

[16] *Die Zeit,* 2 November 2006, 51. http://nurtext.zeit.de/2006/45/L-Interview-Biermann.

[17] *Berufsverbot* was the name given to the system of removing radical leftwingers from jobs in the public service in West Germany. This law was introduced by the prime ministers of the federal states in 1972.

[18] John Shreve, *Nur wer sich ändert, bleibt sich treu: Wolf Biermann im Westen* (Frankfurt, Bern: Peter Lang Verlag, 1989), 2.

[19] Wolf Biermann, "Nur wer sich ändert bleibt sich treu," in *Über das Geld und andere Herzensdinge* (Cologne: Kiepenhauer and Witsch, 1991), 63.

[20] See Peter Thompson, *The Crisis of the German Left* (New York and Oxford: Berghahn, 2005), 53.

[21] This was how he described it at the Cologne concert of 1976. For further information on Biermann's views on the uprising today see "Vorher war ein Unrummel. Wolf Biermann über den fehlenden Aufstand der Intellektuellen," in *aspekte* http://www.zdf.de/ZDFde/inhalt/7/0,1872,2050087,00.html.

[22] See Thompson, *The Crisis of the German Left*, 30.

[23] In "Die Literatur in der DDR von der Biermann-Ausbürgerung bis zu Beginn der 80er Jahre," http://www.petersell.de/ddr/2_ueberblick.htm.

[24] Biermann, *Alle Lieder*, 1991, 198.

[25] Gesetzesblatt der DDR Teil I Nr. 47, 27 September 1974.

[26] *Focus* No. 36, 1999. Interview with Jobst-Ulrich Brand.

[27] Wolf Biermann, "Bertolt Brecht — wichtige Nichtigkeiten," in Wolf Biermann, *Über Deutschland unter Deutschen* (Cologne: Kiepenhauer und Witsch, 2002), 139.

[28] Wolf Biermann, "Heine und die Zuckererbsen," *Berliner Zeitung*, 31 May 1997, M1.

[29] And yet even in some of his bitterest songs from 1989, a degree of respect is still paid to Honecker for having, like his father, been imprisoned by the Nazis. In "Ballade von den verdorbenen Greisen" he sings: "Ich habe dich verachtet und hab dich gefürchtet / Und trotzdem bleibt da ein Rest von Respekt / Es haben dich die verfluchten Faschisten / Elf Jahre in Brandenburg eingesteckt" (413).

[30] Wolf Biermann, "Heine und Le Communisme" in *Der Spiegel* 13 February 2006, 118.

[31] Wolf Biermann, *Über das Geld und andere Herzensdinge* (Cologne, Verlag Kiepenhauer & Witsch 1991), 42.

[32] Heinrich Heine, in a letter dated 30 March 1848 to his mother, in *Briefe 1843–1849*, vol. 22 of *Werke. Briefwechsel. Lebenszeugnisse*, Säkularausgabe, ed. Nationale Forschungs- und Gedenkstaetten der klassischen deutschen Literatur in Weimar und das Centre National de la Recherche Scientifique in Paris (Berlin: Akademie-Verlag, 1972), 270.

[33] Wolf Biermann, *Paradies uff Erden*, II.

[34] Biermann, *Paradies uff Erden*, 148.

[35] Gunnar Decke, "Der preußische Ikarus" in *Neues Deutschland* 15 November 2006, http://www.nd-online.de/artikel.asp?AID=100449&IDC=4&DB=O2P

[36] Richard Rorty, "Moral Identity and Private Autonomy: The Case of Foucault," in *Essays on Heidegger and Others* (Cambridge: Cambridge UP, 1991), 194.

[37] Wolf Biermann, 2006, 160.

[38] Indeed, in the last verse he even calls her Raabanaas (Rabenaas), an extremely pejorative name for someone whom he once worshipped. In "Großes Gebet der alten Kommunistin Oma Meume in Hamburg" it is only Stalin who is referred to as an Aas.

[39] Karl Marx and Friedrich Engels *Werke,* vol. 4 (Berlin: Dietz Verlag, 1972), 461.

8: Political Song in the GDR: The Cat-and-Mouse Game with Censorship and Institutions

David Robb

MEDIA ASSESSMENTS HAVE OFTEN projected an erroneous, undialec-tical image of the GDR political song scene in which art and crea-tivity were simply sacrificed to censorship. On the one hand there are Wolf Biermann, Bettina Wegner, Gerulf Pannach, and Stephan Krawczyk who were banned and — albeit under varying circumstances — forced to leave the GDR for the West. On the other hand there is the Oktoberklub, showpiece of the FDJ-Singebewegung, which performed for years in the ideological service of the state. But just as in the GDR literature scene, the reality of the *Liedermacher* was more contradictory. Between the dis-sidents and the loyal *Singeklubs* there existed a substantial middle ground of critical *Liedermacher* in the GDR who cannot be slotted into these op-posing categories of rebels and conformists. These include Hans-Eckardt Wenzel and his group Karls Enkel, Duo Sonnenschirm, Udo Magister, Pension Volkmann, Gerhard Gundermann, Gerhard Schöne, Barbara Thalheim, and many more.

From the 1960s right up until the *Wende* of 1989 political song was a popular and important cultural force in the GDR. The attraction for many fans lay in the singers' exploitation of a basic contradiction within GDR cultural policy. On one hand political song was nurtured at an official level as a proudly coveted *Erbe* of revolutionary tradition. On the other hand it was constantly viewed with suspicion due to its potential as a means of subversion. Faced with this contradiction, GDR singers trod a precarious tightrope between prohibition and tolerance. In the absence of an open media, they enjoyed elevated status as the bearers of unofficial tidings. Concert halls, student clubs, and informal gatherings were in-variably packed. Editions of the records released on the state record label *Amiga* were snapped up immediately. Some of the most critical song productions such as Karls Enkel, Wacholder, and Beckert & Schulz's *Hammer-Rehwü* were only published after the *Wende*. Others such as Wolff and Beckert's *Die Booten des Todes,* banned at the Leipzig Folk Fes-tival of 1982, have never been published at all.

This chapter deals with a generation of singers who were born and grew up in the GDR.[1] Loyal teenagers of the FDJ-Singeklubs in the 1960s and 70s, their metamorphosis into the critically-minded *Liedermacher* of the 1980s will be examined with regard to boundary-breaking experimentation in performance technique and textual strategies. This was often conducted within a climate of censorship and, as we shall see in the case of the group Karls Enkel, involved balancing subversion with intermittent conformity.

The GDR viewed the whole democratic and revolutionary song tradition as its own cultural inheritance. The *Kampflieder* of Brecht and Eisler and songs from the Spanish Civil War were learned in schools and in the army.[2] In the late 1940s and throughout the 1950s these appeared in song books of the Free German Youth (FDJ) and the Young Pioneers alongside German folk songs and new, so-called *Aufbaulieder* written specially for the GDR youth. Songs such as "Fleißig, nur fleißig" and Johannes R. Becher's "Nationalhymne der DDR" encouraged diligence and a joyful common purpose in the building of the new socialist state.[3] In general, however, the political song genre did not prosper in the 1950s. It was a serious, sacred tradition, not to be tampered with, and the writing of new songs critical of the GDR was unthinkable. On the other hand, as Kirchenwitz notes, for the young poets of the 1950s, who were inspired by the creation of a socialist state on German soil, the political crises caused by the uprising of 17 June 1953 and the Soviet invasion of Hungary in 1956 created an atmosphere of disillusionment that was detrimental for the writing of new political poetry and song (1993, 14).

By the early 1960s, however, a completely new kind of protest song culture was being encountered. The American civil rights song was filtering over the air waves via West Germany through to East Berlin. The building of the Berlin Wall in August 1961 had given the GDR government a sufficient sense of security to relax the severity of censorship in the arts. During this political thaw, which lasted roughly up until the infamous 11 Plenum of the SED in December 1965, an independent folk music scene emerged in East Berlin, based on the informal Hootenanny model made famous by American folk singers such as Pete Seeger. The Berlin Hootenannies were guided by the resident banjo-playing Canadian Perry Friedman. With his uninhibited performance style, Friedman made German folk songs attractive for the youth and freed the workers' songs of their sacred aura (Böning 2004, 201). In general during the cultural thaw there was easier access to western pop music and jazz. In this respect the formation of the Hootenanny-Klub in 1966 was the culmination of four years of musical eclecticism in a vibrant scene in East Berlin that also included Wolf Biermann, Eva-Maria Hagen, Manfred Krug, and Bettina Wegner. It was during the political thaw that Biermann made his name with his uniquely critical political songs. His credentials as son of a communist Jew who was murdered in Auschwitz gave him a certain invulnerability that other songwriters did not possess. Moreover, he came from Hamburg in West Germany, where he had been brought up by his communist mother, and had chosen GDR citizenship at the age of seventeen of his own free will. This, as well as the fact that he was a decade older than many of the other emerging singers, who only had experience of the GDR, gave him a distance and objectivity that the others, again, did not have. Two of Biermann's songs about the military, one before the building of the Wall and the other after, document his political transformation toward the stance of state critic during this period. The first one, "Soldaten-Lied" from 1960, was already a controversial soldier's song by GDR standards in that it was by no means propagandistic in a promilitary sense. As Holger Böning states, the very presentation of the theme of war in the form of a discussion met with resistance from the authorities: "Zu so heiklen Problemen wie diesem war Agitation erwünscht, nicht aber ernsthafte Diskussion [. . .]" (2004, 194). In the final verse, however, Biermann concludes that war is justifiable if it is necessary to defend the socialist states: "Mein Junge, es gibt Herrn, / die rüsten für den Krieg / gegen die Arbeiterstaaten / drum kann ich dir nur raten: / Geh zu unseren Soldaten."[4] In "Soldat, Soldat" from 1963, on the other hand, there is a marked shift. Here he says there can never be any sense to war: "Soldat soldat, wo geht das hin / Soldat Soldat, wo ist der Sinn / Soldat Soldat, im nächsten Krieg / Soldat Soldat, gibt es kein Sieg." The song is reminiscent of Brecht's "Legende des toten Soldaten" in referring to the facelessness of soldiers in life and in death: "Soldaten sehn sich alle gleich / lebendig und als Leich."[5] In the same year, 1963, Biermann incurred his first performance ban. He was also controversially thrown out of the Party. The performance ban was lifted, however, and in 1964 he played at the famous *Die Distel* cabaret and also did a tour of West Germany, where he performed with the famous cabarettist Wolfgang Neuss. His subsequent celebrity in the West meant that after his performance and publication ban in the GDR he continued to support himself from his sales of books and records in the West.

The political thaw came to an abrupt end with the 11th Plenum of the Zentralkomitee of the SED in December 1965. Biermann had already been banned by the FDJ one month previously. Pop groups were also banned for their alleged corrupting Western influence. But as Jürgen Trinkus writes, this created a space for folk and singing groups to emerge.[6] In late 1966 it was decided at the highest of levels that the Hootenanny-Klub was to be taken over by the FDJ. With the agreement of several leading members, the group's name was changed to the Oktoberklub. The writer Gisela Steineckert was installed as a supervisor. This appropriation of the

singing youth movement by the FDJ was ideologically motivated. With
effective control over all popular performance events, the FDJ had the
means to bring it to the masses, and by 1968 thousands of singing clubs
had formed all over the GDR. Leaders of the singing clubs were frequently
reminded that they had to remain "politische Instrumente des Jugend-
verbandes."[7] In this way the movement became increasingly instrumentalized as an agent of state propaganda. From 1968 onwards, under the
slogan *DDR-Konkret,* the FDJ encouraged young students and workers
to write new songs dealing with their everyday lives and with issues of importance to them. This gave a new twist to the concept of revolutionary
Gebrauchslyrik pioneered by Erich Mühsam in his early-twentieth-century
Kampflieder. The official role of the political song in the GDR was defined by Inge Lammel as follows:

> Die neuen Lieder werden für die Politik von Partei und Regierung
> geschaffen. Sie sind nicht mehr Kampfmittel einer unterdrückten
> Klasse gegen eine Klasse von Ausbeutern, sondern Ausdruck der ge-
> meinsamen Interessen aller Werktätigen.[8]

The songs of *DDR-Konkret* aimed to create a strong GDR identity
amongst the youth and instill a sense of pride in its achievements. The most
famous example is the song that became the unofficial anthem of the
GDR *Singebewegung.* It has been claimed that Hartmut König's "Sag mir
wo du stehst!" was originally non-ideological, representing the Hootenanny-Klub's solidarity with the American civil-rights movement and its
song "Which Side Are You On?"[9] There is, however, no mistaking the
SED rhetoric, the slightly threatening tone, and the either with us or
against us argumentation:

> [Chorus] Sag mir, wo du stehst, sag mir, wo du stehst,
> 　　　sag mir, wo du stehst und welchen Weg du gehst!
>
> Zurück oder vorwärts, du mußt dich entschließen!
> Wir bringen die Zeit nach vorn Stück um Stück.
> Du kannst nicht bei uns und bei ihnen genießen,
> denn wenn du im Kreis gehst, dann bleibst du zurück.
> [. . .]
> Wir haben ein Recht darauf, dich zu erkennen,
> auch nickende Masken nützen uns nicht.
> Ich will beim richtigen Namen dich nennen.
> Und darum zeig mir dein wahres Gesicht.[10]

As a public declaration of their support for the Warsaw Pact's invasion
of Czechoslovakia, the Oktoberklub was coaxed into singing "Sag mir,
wo du stehst" at an FDJ concert in Lenz on 26 August 1968. Group

member Lutz Kirchenwitz is captured on film explaining the current significance of the song to the audience:

> Wir glauben in dieser Situation, wo darum geht's die Konterrevolution in einem sozialistischen Land zurückzudrängen, wo unser Klassengegner versucht, die gesamte kommunistische Weltbewegung zu diskreditieren, erhält dieses Lied eine ganz neue Bedeutung.[11]

Interviewed in 1993, Kirchenwitz judged that he had been blinded by propaganda. Another example of political manipulation can be seen in the song "Ich bin wie alle blind geboren." Commissioned by the FDJ, it was written by the eighteen-year-old Regina Scheer as a response to the situation of August 1968. The song is practically an endorsement of the GDR leadership's political paranoia:

> Ich bin wie alle blind geboren.
> Sehen lernt' ich in diesem Land.
> [. . .]
> Und ich lernte, die uns hassen,
> Sind nicht plötzlich unser Freund.
> Auch, wenn wir sie loben lassen, was uns trennt,
> Sind sie uns Feind,
> Und ich lernte aufzupassen.[12]

At this point Bettina Wegner, co-founder of the Hootenanny-Klub and later a leading dissident *Liedermacher* in the 1970s, had already left the group as a result of the FDJ takeover in 1967. In 1993 she still talked with bitterness about this, claiming that the group members had allowed themselves to be manipulated:

> Sie haben sich kaufen lassen und verkauft. Und hätte keiner mitgemacht und sich nicht erst die Wurst und die Butter und dann die Rinde und dann das Brot nehmen lassen, und am Ende ist kein Substanz mehr da. Und so standen sie auf der Bühne! Eeeeeh![13]

Despite these differences it appears clear that all these young singers — like Biermann, who always claimed to be living "in der bessren Hälfte" — saw themselves as living on the right side of the ideologically divided world. This was reflected in their songs. In the early years of the *Singebewegung* two of the main songwriters were Reinhold Andert and Bernd Rump. The group Pasaremos sang a pathos-laden Rump song encouraging loyalty to the state: "Das ist meine Fahne / Das ist deine Fahne / Freunde macht mit / Wer will sich uns entgegenstellen / Vorwärts im Schritt."[14] But as Rump later assessed, the singers made the mistake of confusing the utopian spirit generated within the *Singeklub* culture with the broader political reality of the GDR itself. The songs were produced in a scene that mit einer fantastischen Bewegung die Realität negierte, indem sie den Horizont — vermeintlich und unvermeidlich — zum eigenen Bezugspunkt setzte. Hier waren die neue Gesellschaft und der neue Mensch da, sobald man den Mund aufmachte.[15]

Another example was Andert's utopian "Lied vom Vaterland" in which he proclaimed: "Kennst Du das Land, wo die Fabriken uns gehören, / wo der Prometheus schon um fünf aufsteht. / [. . .] wo sich die Leute alles selber reparieren, weil sie das Werkzeug haben, Wissen und die Macht."[16] Here Andert was latching onto an established tradition since the *Vormärz* of parodying Goethe's "Kennst Du das Land, wo die Zitronen blühn." Examples of these include Erich Kästner's war satire "Kennst du das Land, wo die Kanonen blühn" which was well-known in the 1920s Berlin cabarets. The difference with the Andert text lies in the complete lack of irony. It has often been claimed, however, that Andert has been misunderstood as a songwriter. He himself, who once trained to become a priest, explains that "Lied vom Vaterland" can best be understood as a religious song. The claims he made about the GDR may not always have been accurate, but were rather an expression of faith in how he wanted his country to be:

> Und das ist das Magische, das Religiöse: Man gibt ein Bild vor und sagt nicht, so *soll* es sein oder so möchte ich es, sondern es *ist* so. Und viele sagen, da sollten wir uns Mühe geben, daß es so wird, wenn der schon davon singt, daß es so ist.[17]

Whether this had the intended effect on the listener is highly questionable. Moreover, the singers must have realized the limitations of their freedom to change anything. As Böning writes in general about the *Singebewegung:* "Vielleicht muß man sogar von Heuchelei sprechen, denn natürlich wußten die Sänger darüber Bescheid, welchen Einschränkungen der Meinungsfreiheit die DDR-Bevölkerung und auch sie selbst unterlagen" (2004, 222).

From 1970 to 1990 the main focal point of the GDR political song movement was the annual Festival des politischen Liedes.[18] This became the biggest festival of its kind in the world. With enormous FDJ funding it was able to invite top international acts: prominent guests over the years included Mikis Theodorakis, Hermann van Veen, Franz Josef Degenhardt, Dick Gaughan, and Billy Bragg among many others. The West German folk acts Zupfgeigenhansel, Liederjahn, and Hannes Wader were regular visitors, as were the agitprop rock group Floh de Cologne. The Festival des politischen Liedes was in essence the first "world music"[19] festival, long before the term was even coined. The festival maintained its popularity right up until 1990, a showcase event for socialism that simultaneously permitted a forum for considerable artistic interchange. It was here that the newly emerging GDR folk scene in the late 1970s and early 1980s came across the Irish and Scottish sounds of artists such as the Sands Family and Dick Gaughan, and *Liedertheater* groups were inspired by the Italian clowns troupe Columbioni or the Scottish 7:84 theater company.

The encounter with music groups from countries with strong socialist movements also had a politically reaffirming function, as Böning writes. The young singers and their audience could personally meet people from countries where the international struggle was real as opposed to something one only learned about at school (2003, 213). By the mid 1970s, however, the *Singebewegung* was already falling into disrepute. Kirchenwitz recalls how the enormous popularity in the late 1960s had sunk drastically (1993, 46). By 1979 only two percent of teenage youth admitted to liking the singing clubs (64). Reinhold Andert, Kirchenwitz's colleague in the Oktoberklub, later discovered that secret questionnaires had found that ninety-five percent of GDR youth had not liked the Oktoberklub, contrary to what was declared in the media. Andert recalled: "Wir aber dachten, es sei umgekehrt, denn so erfuhren wir es in vollen Sälen, lasen es in den Zeitungen, hörten es im Radio und sahen es im Fernsehen."[20] The movement reached its climax at the Weltfestspiele in 1973, when the FDJ invested lavishly in inviting *Singegruppen* from all over the republic to propagate the Party message before international guests. The latter were witness to the political misuse of these teenage singers, many of whom displayed little musical talent. From this point on, the singing-club culture, faced with increasing public indifference, found itself in an irretrievable decline.[21] Biermann famously nicknamed the *Singeklubs* as the "Kaiser-Geburtstags-Sänger,"[22] an accurate description given that Jahrgang 49 (the first professional song-group in the GDR, which in 1973 emerged from the Oktoberklub) actually performed at Erich Honecker's birthday celebrations.[23] An official advisory group from inside the *Singebewegung* remarked on this development in 1978:

> Waren die Klubs in den Anfangsjahren der FDJ-Singebewegung noch kleine Freizeitkollektive, die hauptsächlich aus Spaß an einer gemeinsamen Sache zusammenkamen [. . .] so sind heute sehr viel junge Gruppen eigentlich nur noch "Auftrittsgruppen." Sie werden von Institutionen zu beinahe jeder Gelegenheit vermittelt, sei es zur Umrahmung einer Festrede oder zur Unterhaltung eines Essens [. . .] Das bestimmt ihr Repertoire, denn es werden ja nur noch "Anlaß Lieder" gebraucht [. . .] Damit verkümmert [. . .] ihre Spontanität, ihre Lockerheit und die Heiterkeit der Singeveranstaltungen.[24]

Even as late as 1976 the *Singebewegung* could be cajoled into voicing its support for state policy. This was evident in its response to Wolf Biermann's expatriation from the GDR after his concert in Cologne on 13

November 1976. On one hand this step was publicly opposed by *Lieder-macher* including Kurt Demmler, Bettina Wegner, and Gerulf Pannach, lyricist of the rock group Renft. On the other hand the members of Jahrgang 49 were among those who signed a declaration in support of the measure that read:

> Wir als Interpreten und Schöpfer politischer Lieder [bekennen uns] zu dem in unserer Republik real existierenden Sozialismus. Wir meinen, Wolf Biermann hat [. . .] unserer Sache geschadet. Deshalb stehen wir zu den Entscheidungen von Partei und Regierung.[25]

Despite such unfavorable responses to Biermann within the *Singebewegung,* many of its protagonists were becoming politically disillusioned. This coincided with a trend toward a greater subjectivity. The collective "wir" of *DDR-Konkret* increasingly became "ich," as *Singebewegung* stalwarts such as Bernd Rump, Reinhold Andert, and Gerd Eggers from Jahrgang 49 began addressing the limitations of the individual within the collective. While still affirming allegiance to the GDR and its socialist aims, these singers were growing increasingly aware of the gulf between ideal and reality. Bernd Rump's "In meinem Namen" from 1976 tackles the lack of accountability of the press and questions the absence of his own opinion in its publications: "Die Zeitung bei uns drucken sie täglich in meinem Namen / [. . .] Mein guter Name ist mir teuer, drum will ich wissen, was ich unterschreib' / [. . .] Denn so wie meine Arbeit zählt, zähle auch meine Stimme."[26] Andert's "Der vorletzte Gang des Thomas Münzer" of 1980 implies that the revolutionary hero of the peasant wars of the early sixteenth century (whose face appeared on GDR banknotes) would have been considered an anarchist had he lived in the GDR: "Was mußtest du auch deiner Zeit vorgreifen / anstatt zu warten auf die rechte Frist / bis deine Fürsten selbst zu Bauern reifen / du wärst auch heute noch ein Anarchist."[27] At this time Andert was in the process of being expelled from the SED, and was to endure periods of performance bans throughout the 1980s.[28] Several other otherwise loyal *Liedermacher* also were expelled from the Party, for example, Barbara Thalheim in 1980 and Gerhard Gundermann in 1982. None of these, however, had to endure the treatment of former Hootenanny-Klub member Bettina Wegner, who had a long-standing confrontation with the authorities. In 1968 she had been briefly imprisoned for distributing leaflets protesting the Warsaw Pact invasion of Czechoslovakia. Throughout the 1970s and early 1980s she was the leading dissident female singer/singwriter in the GDR and enjoyed a hit single in West Germany with "Sind so kleine Hände." Affiliated with Biermann's circle of friends, she moderated the *Eintopp* (1973–75) and *Kramladen* (1975–76) series of evenings in Berlin, both of which featured *Liedermacher* and rock performances as well as poetry and literary readings, and both of which were eventually banned. In 1983 she was finally forced out to West Berlin by the Stasi.[29]

Despite its tarnished reputation the *Singebewegung* spawned a wealth of talent, which became clear as these once-teenagers matured and found their critical voices and their own artistic niches. From the late-1970s singers and songwriters such as Barbara Thalheim, Udo Magister, Gerhard Schöne, Werner Karma, Gerhard Gundermann, and Hans-Eckardt Wenzel emerged. Some of these were solo performers, others linked to groups with new aesthetic visions that were emerging out of the *Singeklubs*. Schicht developed out of Songgruppe der TU Dresden and the Singeklub der EOS Hoyerswerda, which also produced Gerhard Gundermann's Brigade Feuerstein. Hans-Eckardt Wenzel's Karls Enkel was formed at the Humboldt University in Berlin in 1976. Schicht, Brigade Feuerstein, and Karls Enkel all embarked on new theatrical-based approaches to political song. This new development, known as *Liedertheater* was supported and supervised by the Liedzentrum of the Akademie der Künste. Its leader, Karin Wolf, organized frequent workshops and discussions and documented performances on video.

Despite its official status, the Liedzentrum was generally not viewed as a censor. It even intervened to support performers who received performance bans, as it did when the *Hammer-Revue* of Karls Enkel, Wacholder, and Beckert & Schulz was banned in Cottbus in March 1983. But in general *Liedertheater* was viewed by the authorities as a suspicious development. The popular annual *Lieder & Theater* workshops in Dresden organized by Schicht from 1980 to 1983 were discontinued after FDJ funding was withdrawn.[30] The workshops had gained a reputation for their critical level of discussion and had become a magnet for academics, journalists, and artists in general including leading rock groups such as Pankow.[31] None of Schicht's, Karls Enkel's, or Brigade Feuerstein's productions were ever published in the GDR.[32]

A New Generation Tests the Boundaries

These new *Liedertheater* groups and critical singer/songwriters were of the same generation as the young poets of the so-called Prenzlauer Berg scene. While these were two separate scenes inhabiting different sociopolitical areas of GDR public life, there were significant overlappings in terms of aesthetic-cultural concerns. As Karen Leeder writes, the work of the young Prenzlauer Berg poets was governed by the tension between being born into GDR structures ("Hineingeboren") and attempting to break out of them ("Entgrenzung").[33] This generation born in the 1950s, which had not experienced the catastrophe of war followed by the *Aufbau* years, and whose life experience had been totally restricted to the

GDR, did not share their elders' unconditional belief in the concept of historical progress. As Leeder writes: "the narrative of history [had] degenerated into almost terminal stagnation" (109).[34] This stance clashes drastically with the historical certainty reflected in lyrics of the early *Singebewegung* such as "Wir bringen die Zeit nach vorn Stück um Stück" from "Sag mir, wo du stehst." But by the mid to late 1970s this was changing. Already in Wenzel's early songs one encounters the acknowledgment of a break with history. In his songs and those of other *Liedermacher* of his generation the theme of "living life in the now" emerges; of a basic existential longing. The consolation of a utopian commune in the distant future is no longer acceptable, as expressed in "Heute oder Niemals" from Karls Enkel's 1977 song program "Vorfahrt":

> Ich lasse mich nun nicht länger
> verarschen, jetzt oder nirgendwann
> werd' ich leben, Atmen, Essen, Lieben [. . .]
> Ich warte länger nicht mehr,
> länger laß ich mich nicht vertrösten auf später [. . .]
> Es geht darum das Leben
> zu genießen [. . .] Den besten
> Wein, die feinsten Speisen heute oder niemals.[35]

In the aforementioned collaborative project *Die Hammer-Rehwü* of 1982 the same basic demand for a "life in the now" can be seen in the parodic recasting of motifs from Brecht and Weill's *Mahagonny*. For example, as quoted in chapter 2, the lines from the *Mahagonny* song "Laßt euch nicht verführen" are transformed into a parody of the shattered communist ideal in the GDR. The Brecht lines "Laßt euch nicht verführen / Zu Fron und Ausgezehr. / Was kann euch Angst noch rühren / Ihr sterbt mit allen Tieren / Und es kommt nichts nachher"[36] now appear as: "Du, laß dich nicht einwickeln / Von Liebe, Fron und Her / Wir sind Verbrauchsartikel / Und sterben wie Karnickel. / Und es kommt nichts nachher." In the conclusion of the *Hammer-Rehwü* this lust for life amidst stagnation is expressed via a verse from Erich Mühsam: "Ich möchte vom Glücke gesunden. / Die Seele sehnt sich nach harten Streichen, / Die Seele sehnt sich nach frischen Wunden, / Nach Kämpfen und Bängnissen, ohnegleichen."[37]

Historical stagnation results in an image of "waiting." Throughout the 1980s Hans-Eckardt Wenzel was only one of several writers to exploit the "waiting" motif, a controversial symbol of the GDR's failure to fulfill its self-proclaimed historical destiny. Leeder writes: "What had been [. . .] the sheer enthusiasm of *Aufbau* ('*er*warten'), becomes in the texts of the 1980s, a passive and alienated waiting ('Warten')" (53). This was true in other literary spheres as well: the playwright Heiner Müller, for instance, equates contemporary life with "ein großer Wartesaal."[38] In the 1988 song "Lancelot" Gerhard Gundermann sings: "Ich weiß nicht, ob ich noch warten kann / Bis die Welt mich zählt."[39] Wenzel's "Die Wartung eines Landes," from 1989, presents the GDR as a country in waiting: "Das Mädchen wartet auf den Brief / Der Redner wartet auf die Rede / Der Junge im Park wartet auf das Nichts / Das Land wartet auf goldene Zeiten."[40]

The attempts to break out of pre-ordained structures and discourses could also be seen in terms of performance techniques and form. Karls Enkel's specific intention in the late 1970s was to escape from what Wenzel described as the "Ghetto der Singebewegung."[41] *Liedertheater* pioneered a new multi-media approach using text, drama, costumes, masks and electronic music. This enabled a form of indirect criticism of the state. Through the 1980s there emerged numerous amateur and professional *Liedertheater* groups throughout the GDR, which formed a scene distinct from cabaret. Gundermann sang in a clown's mask to rock music accompaniment in Brigade Feuerstein's marketplace spectaculars in 1980.[42] Karls Enkel began its *Liedertheater* experiment in 1979 with the song program *Zieharmonie*. According to Wenzel the advantage of the genre lay in the possibility of freeing oneself from the role of the political singer/songwriter and its personality cult: "Vom Kostüm und von der Schminke her schaffen wir Abgehobenheit, Spielerei, Spielraum und relativieren damit für die Leute im Zuschauerraum, was oben gesungen wird."[43] With masks and role-play it was possible for a Brechtian dialogic interplay to emerge between person and role. Standpoints expressed did not have to be attributed to the singer or "personality" concerned. As elucidated in chapter 2, Biermann's performances — which incorporated irony, mimicry, and gestures — and the musical compositions underpinning his texts had also reflected this dialogic aesthetic. But there was a difference: Biermann's criticism was simply too direct to be tolerated in the GDR; in the eyes of the authorities his personality cult was so firmly associated with opposition that it overshadowed the philosophical ambivalence of his art. Biermann, as a performer and person, marked the clear boundary line between what was acceptable and what not. The question now for the younger *Liedermacher* was how far they could push this boundary line out.

Karls Enkel's testing of this boundary was the most artistically and politically adventurous. As well as recognizing the potential of masks, costumes, ironic gestures and facial expressions to impart a subtle critical message, they also gave music a theatrical function, like Biermann before them. They were strongly influenced by the montage aesthetic of Weill and Eisler, whereby diverse musical styles with their respective associations were used to relativize the text in a dialectic and often parodic way. In Karls Enkel's 1980 production " 's geht los! Aber nicht mit Chassepots"[44] they sang forbidden SPD songs from the period of the *Sozial-*

istengesetze. The melodies, however, were interrupted in order to point ironically to parallels between censorship in the Bismarck period and the political restrictions in the GDR. Out of this formal approach emerged a montage aesthetic that relativized verbal expression and contributed to a philosophical ambivalence hitherto unseen in the *Singebewegung.*

The historical treatment of "'s geht los!" pointed to another highly creative aspect of Karls Enkel's work. They were appropriating the sacred, untouchable revolutionary *Erbe* of the GDR for their own purposes; approaching it with respect, but ultimately inverting it in such a way as to criticize the GDR. This was apparent, as dealt with in chapters 1 and 2, in their Erich Mühsam program with its poetry from the Spartakus movement, in their treatment of the International Brigade in "Spanier aller Länder," and in their controversial use of Marx texts concerning the 1848 revolution in Paris in "Die komische Tragödie des 18. Brumaire."[45]

The case of Karls Enkel shows how Leeder's aforementioned observation on the tension between being born into boundaries and the desire to break out of them in the work of the Prenzlauer Berg poets also applied to *Liedertheater.* It was undoubtedly the expression of artists learning to use the constraints that bound them to their own advantage.

A related development was the new trend in folk groups, which enjoyed their high point of popularity between 1976 and 1983. The most famous groups were Folkländer from Leipzig, Wacholder from Cottbus, and Liedehrlich from Gera. As stated, their appropriation of the German democratic folksong tradition of the *Vormärz* and 1848 was particularly creative. Jürgen Wolff of the group Folkländer summed up how this contradiction worked in favor of the musicians with regard to their reviving of German folk songs that had been oppositional in their particular period of history:

> Besonderer Wert wird dabei neben den beliebten Gesellen- und Trinklieder auf Gesellschaftskritisches gelegt: oppositionelle Soldatenlieder, Auswandererlieder, 1848er Texte. Kann man doch damit Parallel zu Miss-Ständen in der DDR andeuten, die vom Publikum sehr wohl verstanden werden, obwohl diese Lieder offiziell als fortschrittliches Kulturerbe gelten.[46]

This practice was apparent on several songs from the first Folkländer LP in 1981. For example, with its taboo associations of *Republikflucht,* the song "Auswanderer-Lied," as mentioned in chapter 1, was transformed into a metaphor for the longing of the East German people for travel. The ostensibly harmless "Auf, du junger Wandersmann" acquired similar subversive associations.[47] "Ich bin Soldat, doch bin ich es nicht gerne," sung by numerous folk groups at informal sessions, became a secret anthem of the unwilling GDR conscripts to military service. Audience and performers alike participated enthusiastically in the game of hidden meanings.

The presence of censorship, however, had an obvious effect on artistic approaches developed within critical songwriting. Taking the example of Wenzel and Mensching and their group Karls Enkel, the next section will look at the tension between these artistic developments and the political structures of "supervision."

The Various Literary Publics in the GDR[48]

As stated, the political contradictions of being a *Liedermacher* in the GDR make it difficult to place these singers into rigid political camps of dissidents and loyalists. David Bathrick's model of three literary public audiences in the GDR helps us to locate these *Liedermacher* politically. These are firstly an official "Parteiöffentlichkeit," secondly a public audience created by the West German media, and thirdly an unofficial, semi-autonomous public. The latter included the Prenzlauer Berg poets' scene, which was "historisch die jüngste und am schwersten zu definierende" and consisted of "gegenoffiziellen Stimmen, die entweder den Dialog mit der herrschenden Stimme oder mit dessen Unterminierern suchten" (2000, 244). Bathrick notices at the same time an interaction between the three categories, which contributes to a blurring of the "Linien zwischen offiziell und inoffiziell, zwischen Dissidenz und Repräsentanz, zwischen außerhalb und innerhalb" (244). Such overlapping illustrates the often ambivalent position of the *Liedermacher* mentioned above, who did not in every case belong to the autonomous scene, but could not always be classified as supporters of the official line either. This contradictoriness is particularly illustrated in the case of Karls Enkel: their dialogue with the official ideology was provocative, but took place within boundaries sanctioned by the state; they accepted the GDR's basic utopian principles, but radically deconstructed the state-controlled public discourse, revealing it as falling far short of those principles. However, the mere fact that they had embraced the ideology as well as their reliance on tried and trusted forms of social engagement[49] resulted in the discounting of the poetry of Hans-Eckardt Wenzel and Steffen Mensching by literary critics immediately after the *Wende*. The post-1989 trend preferred the experimentalism of the Prenzlauer Berg poets (such as Uwe Kolbe, Stefan Döring, Jan Faktor, and Bert Papenfuß-Gorek). More explicitly than Wenzel and Mensching, these poets had rejected the ideology, language, traditions, and social structures inherited from the parents' generation. Leeder took issue with Emmerich on this subject in her book *Breaking Boundaries* (1996, 41). She argued for a new understanding of the literature of the young generation in the GDR, one that dissolves the division between a (simplistically homogeneous) understanding of "Prenzlauer Berg" on the one hand and the other more established "political" or "conventional" poetry on the other (42).

Here Leeder finds a basic commonality between both groupings in the aforementioned dialectic of being "born into" structures and the attempt to break out of them. She mentions this with regard to Wenzel and Mensching's treatment of the GDR literary *Erbe* and their interpretations of flashpoints of proletarian history. It is significant, however, that this dialectic also applies to Karls Enkel's and other *Liedertheater* groups' appropriation of forms of revolutionary theater such as agitprop revue.[50] For example, the *Hammer-Rehwü* of 1982 in essence used the formal trappings of Piscator's red revues of the 1920s in order to parody the shortcomings of socialism in the present — again using the coveted socialist heritage to criticize the GDR itself. Furthermore, on a practical production level this dialectic was also apparent in the attempts of *Liedermacher* to push the boundaries of what was possible from within the official institutions that sponsored them. Taking Karls Enkel as an example, the following section examines the juggling act singers and groups had to perform to survive within the bureaucratic world of GDR political song.

Karls Enkel: A Balancing Act over the Cultural Landscape of the GDR

Karls Enkel was founded in autumn 1976 amidst the controversy of the Biermann affair. The group's first song program "Komm rücken wir näher zusammen" (1977) was criticized by a Stasi informer for political and ideological mistakes. The texts were ambiguous and could be interpreted positively or negatively according to one's particular standpoint. The informer advised that this song program was not appropriate for future performances.[51] The group was only allowed to continue performing after the intervention by a friend in the FDJ-Bezirksleitung.[52] But after the success of its next program, "Vorfahrt," Karls Enkel was promoted to the highly privileged status of FDJ-Reisekader and was allowed to travel to perform in West Berlin on 14 and 15 July 1979. After the renewal of controversy over texts in their new program, "Zieharmonie," in the autumn of 1979, contact to the FDJ was finally broken off, which ruled out further travel to the West. The song "Liebste laß die Lampe an," for example, addressed the increasing distance between the government and the people:

> Genosse, der du über mir stehst,
> Ich will, was du vorhast, verstehn.
> Weil ich doch nur lieben kann,

Eben alles geben kann
In allerbesten Nähen.
Ich will, was du durchsetzt mit unserer Macht,
Ich will, was wir machen wolln, eben auch verstehn.

The meaning of these songs did not escape the Ministerium für Staatssicherheit, or Stasi. According to the files they kept on Karls Enkel, what annoyed the Stasi most was the group's reluctance to accept guidance and to change their songs after discussions with comrades who — the Stasi claimed — knew more about the issues than the group itself.[53]

Breaking with the supervision and sponsorship of the FDJ left Karls Enkel in a vulnerable situation. Performers needed to be sponsored by an institution (usually the FDJ) in order to gain a permit to play in public. In the GDR the world of *Liedermacher*, cabaret, and rock music was controlled by three institutions. Festivals, workshops, and concerts were monopolized by the FDJ.[54] Tours were organized by the Konzert- und Gastspieldirektion (KGD), and a further body, the Komitee für Unterhaltungskunst, with its various departments including Sektion Liedermacher/Chansonier and Sektion Rockmusiker, functioned as a state music agency that simultaneously supervised the careers of its artists. The Sektion even ran a two-year training course to teach the trade of *Liedermacher/Chansonier*,[55] this an indication of the extent to which the political song was nurtured in the GDR as cultural heritage. To be recognized by the appropriate department guaranteed performers a respectable living from music.[56] At the same time, these institutions were closely connected with one another and had the power at any time to withdraw an artist's license to perform. But there were many inconsistencies and idiosyncracies in the cultural landscape of the GDR that could not always be explained by official cultural policy. There was, for example, no unified policy on culture. This gave the cultural functionaries, those in the various organizations who had powers of decision in the area of the promotion of arts and culture, a certain amount of freedom to implement their own form of artistic control. As Andert wrote after the expulsion of Stephan Krawczyk in 1988: "Jeders andersdenkende Kulturfunktionär hat das Recht, die Flinte aus dem Schrank zu holen und mit dem Geschoß 'Staatsfeind' dem Liedermacher die Beine weg zu schießen."[57]

The story of Karls Enkel on the other hand illustrates how it was sometimes possible to exploit such inconsistencies. It also shows how there were indeed *Kulturfunktionäre* who were prepared to intervene on behalf of critical artists or at least to turn a blind eye to their criticism. After Karls Enkel's break with the FDJ, the group began operating as a "freie Theatergruppe," a status that did not officially exist in the GDR. As Kirchenwitz observed, the ambiguity of their artistic form enabled them to play institutions off against each other: Wenzel and Mensching "arbeit[et]en auf mehereren Ebenen (Musik, Literatur, Theater usw.) und ha[tt]en dadurch Möglichkeiten auszuweichen, Institutionen gegeneinander auszuspielen und Projekte, die an einer Stelle auf Schwierigkeiten stoßen, an einer anderen zu realisieren."[58] They had good connections in the cultural establishment, particularly the Kulturbund, which sponsored two Karls Enkel's productions, despite it not being in its cultural remit to do so. A further ally was the Berlin Volksbühne, where the group began rehearsal for the *Liedertheater* production "Von meiner Hoffnung laß ich nicht — oder der Pilger Mühsam" with dramaturg Heiner Maaß in autumn 1979. The conflicting reactions of key institutions to this production illustrates the aforementioned lack of unity, which Karls Enkel could exploit. The Mühsam program was supposed to be the Volksbühne's contribution to the Festival des politischen Liedes in February 1980, but was vetoed by the FDJ.[59] According to a Stasi file, "[man könnte] bei diesem Programm, wenn man nicht beachtet in welcher Zeit Mühsam die Texte geschrieben hat, zu falscher politischer Aussage kommen."[60] The Volksbühne, however, remained loyal to the group and continued to provide a stage for the production to be performed.

The Stasi was now even more determined to eliminate Karls Enkel's critical potential by establishing an informer within the group. A report stated: "Der Kandidat muß den negativen Inhalt der Programme erkennen und von der Schädlichkeit der Wirkung dieser Programme überzeugt sein."[61] The person they aimed to recruit was Wenzel. Nothing came of this, as Wenzel persistently failed to attend arranged meetings. Due to his "ablehnender Haltung" the recruitment attempt was called off.[62] After this the group was largely left in peace to pursue its artistic aims, although reports by casual informers reveal continuous observation right up until autumn 1989.

Censorship or Support:
The Conflicting Role of the Cultural Functionary

Due to their friends in high places, Wenzel and Mensching were envied by other *Liedermacher* colleagues who, despite being less critical of the regime, came into greater conflict with the authorities.[63] For example, the folk opera "Die Boten des Todes"[64] was banned at the Leipzig Folk Festival of 1982 after the dress rehearsal. A critical highlight of the folk movement, this was based on the Grimm brothers' fairy tale, but was intended as a parable of what Jürgen Wolff of Folkländer called "den gesteuerten Niedergang der Folkszene."[65] Written by Wolff, Dieter Beckert, and Erik Kross, and directed by Wenzel, it was banned before its premiere for lines such as:

Wenn die Folkloristen tanzen
Schimpfen Ordner und Emanzen.
Sie beweisen in den Schenken
Sehr bewußtes Umsatzdenken.
Sie sorgen für Kultur auf Erden
Was nicht ist, kann ja noch werden.[66]

Six months later the *Hammer-Rehwü,* performed by another collective of
musicians including Karls Enkel, Wacholder, and Beckert & Schulz, and
featuring texts just as critical as "Die Boten Des Todes," was paradoxically
allowed to tour. But it is precisely this inconsistency that shows the frequently ambivalent role of the *Kulturfunktionären* in the GDR. For all
the nervous or dogmatic functionaries who would punish the slightest de-
viation from the Party line, there were also those who were ready to take
risks to support certain projects. The *Hammer-Rehwü,* for example, es-
caped a ban that Stasi officials threatened to impose in spring 1983 in
Cottbus due to good references from cultural officials in Berlin.[67] According to Kulturbund member Karin Hirdina, the tour may well have met
bureaucratic resistance at its outset had it not been for the fact that many
of the cultural officials, some of whom were friends of the group, were
conveniently on holiday at the time of the dress rehearsal.[68]

A look at some of the issues dealt with in the *Hammer-Rehwü* illustrates its potential for controversy: the revue reflected the general dis-
content among young artists at the suppression of the unofficial peace
movement (known under the slogan "Schwerter zu Pflugscharen"), which
had arisen in the early 1980s as a response to the intensification of the
nuclear arms race. In the *Hammer-Rehwü* the taboo subject of pacifism
was dealt with via the parody of the army general played by Dieter Beckert.
In his performance of Peter Rühmkorf's song "Bleib erschütterbar —
doch widersteh," already referred to in chapter 3 of this volume, he takes
off his officer's jacket and drops it symbolically on the ground (see video
1982).[69] This gesture reflects the young GDR generation's rejection of
militarism and the logic of the Cold War. The song was interpreted by the
Cottbuss District Council as a call to organized resistance against the
GDR.[70] In a further caricature of militarism, the text of the well-known
GDR peace song "Kleine weiße Friedenstaube" was transformed into
"Kleine weiße Bürgermeise." The Cottbus Stasi's report of this song
shows that the informer understood Karls Enkel's technique of parody
and association. The agent also noticed the disrespectful lines "Wir tragen
unser Schicksal mit Geduld / An der ganzen Scheiße sind wir selber
schuld," which formed a recurring motif through the entire second part
of the program, and further songs and scenes whose negative connotations were intensified by the theatricalities on stage.[71] Even the Berlin

Wall was mocked. In "Das Berlin-Lied" the eternal Spree is portrayed flowing past the Palast der Republik. The image of carefree anglers on the river is thus contrasted with intimidating structures of power. This conflict of worlds is expressed in the chorus, which refers to the Wall: "Nicht aus Stahl und Pappmasché / nein aus Wasser ist die Spree" (1982). This veiled criticism did not escape the Stasi officer, who commented on

> das Große Berlin [. . .] welches nicht durch Stahl und Pappmasché, sondern durch die Spree getrennt wird. Hierin wurde nach uns vorliegenden Hinweisen die Staatsführung der DDR und die internationalen Beziehungen verspottet."[72]

The production was banned and the local group Wacholder received a general *Auftrittsverbot* for the area. This ban was, however, soon lifted after friends in the Komitee für Unterhaltungskunst and in the Akademie der Künste in Berlin vouched for the musicians.[73]

With Karls Enkels' next production, 1983's "Die komische Tragödie des 18. Brumaire nach Karl Marx," this dependence on the good will of the cultural officials led to an almost irreconcilable contradiction. Wenzel, Mensching, and dramaturg Heiner Maaß were concerned to show — in a highly compelling subtext — that it was the basic corruptibility of people that hindered the achievement of a real socialism. It was an audacious move to use Marx's sacred Brumaire analysis to illustrate this point. Marx's account of Louis Bonaparte's appeasing of the Parisian proletariat with petit-bourgeois comforts was staged using montage technique in such a way as to make clear to the audience that the subject matter also related to the GDR.[74] The subject of corruption is set side by side with the famous lines from Marx's *Brumaire* about the farcical repetition of history:

> Es lernten von Napoleon, Bismarck und andre Fürsten
> Wie er gekauft das Lumpenpack mit Schnäpsen und Würsten
> Das ist ein clevres Stück mein Kind
> Der Stoff ist bekannt, aber neu sind die Stars.
> So endet manche Hungersnot
> Das eine Mal als Tragödie, das andre Mal als Farce

Setting up Marx quotations to imply that the GDR's historical self-image was a farce presented problems. The production was commisioned by the Kulturbund for the celebration of the centenary of Karl Marx's death in 1983. A Kulturbund report from 29 March 1983 illustrates clearly that Karls Enkel was not operating without external pressure. It stipulates that after every concert there should be a discussion with members of the young intelligentsia about the current significance of Marxist theory for the continuing class struggle.[75] Furthermore the content of the production was to be supervised by the Zentrale Kommission Literatur.

Despite this monitoring the group did not tone down its criticism in the program. The dress rehearsal at the Kulturbund conference "Karl Marx und die Künste" on 12 March 1983 in Gera provoked an embarrassed response from the Kulturbund members, as Wenzel remembered:

> Der Kulturbund als Institution war zu feige auszusteigen und zu feige, sich zu bekennen. Die regionalen Veranstalter [wollten das Programm haben] haben sich aber nicht getraut, offiziell gegen die ganze Organisation vorzugehen.[76]

The program was not allowed to be performed during the official Marx centenary celebrations. Thereafter, however, Karls Enkel toured the production without any interference from censors. Within the group, however, tension had been caused because of the presence of the Kulturbund as sponsor. Director Heiner Maaß had complained to the group that this was politically and artistically restricting, although he was delighted in the end with the artistic success of the project.[77] However, in their production of the following year, "Spanier aller Länder," sponsored by Das Festival des politischen Liedes, the effects of self-censorship became obvious, as the group struggled to depict the implications for the GDR of the Stalinist purges in the Republican forces and International Brigade in the Spanish Civil War.[78]

The secret to the survival of "Die komische Tragödie" lay in the use of a text by Marx to show the inadequacies of socialism in the GDR, but without questioning Marx's ideology itself. This approach illustrates Bathrick's assessment of GDR literature in general: that such challenges to the hegemony of the official discourse — despite being basically socialist in intention — were able to create a linguistic sub-public that endangered the dominant discourse.[79] The Stasi's reports on audiences' reactions to Karls Enkel performances show that it was well aware of this danger.[80] However, it was limited to relatively narrow intellectual circles and therefore kept under control. In essence "Die komische Tragödie" was an example of the contradictory relationship of GDR dissidents to the ruling powers. As Bathrick observes, it was precisely their inability and reluctance to question the system as a whole that enabled them to do what they did. If they had taken their criticism further they would have been silenced (246).

The case of Stephan Krawczyk, formerly of the group Liedehrlich, illustrated the alternative. In 1985 he rejected compromise and embarked on a path of direct confrontation with the authorities. He was aware of the consequences of doing this, as shown in the lyrics of "Das geht solange gut": "Das geht solange gut, solang das gutgeht / solange du dich an den Regeln hältst / doch wenn du fällig bist, dann bist du fällig / weil du dann meistens auf die Schnauze fällst" (1988). Krawczyk quit the

Party in 1985, was banned from performing and subsequently confined to playing in churches — the church being an institution free from Party control. In January 1988 Krawczyk and his partner, the artist Freya Klier, were arrested and given the alternatives of jail or exit to the West. They chose the latter, a decision which was strongly disapproved of by other critical musicians. While a statement from the Sektion für Liedermacher made clear that it held the government responsible for the fiasco[81] (this in itself a criticism which the organization would not have dared to make a few years earlier and an indication of a changed political atmosphere since the coming to power of Gorbachev in the Soviet Union in 1985), the established singers did not show active solidarity with Krawczyk. The debate on this issue raged well into the 1990s. It was, however, symptomatic of a wider conflict on the contentious issue of the advantages of internal versus external opposition.

In general, however, with the dawning of the Gorbachev era in 1985 a new directness emerged in GDR political songwriting. The *Liedermacher* were no longer content to couch their message in complex literary metaphors. Frustrated with the government's refusal to entertain Gorbachov's new policies of *glasnost* and *perestroika,* they began to take more risks in their criticism. This change was documented in the *Aktiva* pamphlet series produced by the Akademie der Künste. The first edition includes K. P. Schwarz's satirical adaptation of Brecht and Eisler's "Einheitsfrontlied": "Damit der Mensch ein Mensch wird / Mauer' er sich nicht zu Haus ein / Es muß sein Blick und soll sein Glück, / Ohn' alle Grenzen sein" (1985, 18). When Politbüro member Kurt Hager criticized Gorbachev's *perestroika* in public as a mere change of wallpaper, former Karls Enkel member Stefan Körbel reacted at the Frankfurt/Oder Song Festival of 1987 with the following lines: "Sie sagen: wir sind aus ganz anderem Holz / Sie meinen: wir hätten doch Grund zum Stolz / Sie sagen: wir bräuchten nicht zu tapezieren / Seitdem träum ich nur vom Renoviern."[82] As an answer to the official covering-up of a disastrous collision of an intercity train with a Soviet tank in 1988, the Duo Sonnenschirm wrote and performed the macabre "Zugroulette."[83] In conclusion the song sarcastically links the criminal negligence of the rail authorities with the government's neglect of the people's concerns: "So hat man auch mit unserm Leben / Schon Hasard gespielt / Doch das Gute ist daran — wir wissen's nicht / Wie bei der Eisenbahn." In 1987, during a visit to Nicaragua, Gerhard Schöne wrote "Mit dem Gesicht zum Volke"[84] implicitly contrasting the accountability of the Sandinista government at public meetings with the lack of openness in the GDR.

The summer and autumn of 1989 saw the mass exodus of GDR refugees over the Hungarian and Czech borders. An example of a song from this period is Dieter Kalka's "Holde Ost-Germania." This song is explicitly coarse, very much in the style of Villon or the satirical *Fliegende Blätter* of the 1848 revolution. Using sexual imagery for contrasting effect, it depicts a prudish state which, the song suggests, would not lose so many people if it would only show a more relaxed, human side:

> O holde Ost-Germania
> Du zeigst kein bißchen Brust
> Das wär was gegen Frust
> Du wiegst nicht mit den Hüften
> Darum gehen die Leute stiften
> Denen verging die Lust.

Indeed, the final verse reflects the willingness of many intellectuals to give the GDR the chance to survive:

> O holde Ost-Germania
> Mich läßt du nicht kalt
> Noch bist du nicht so alt
> Mach was gegen den Speck
> Durch Bewegung geht er weg
> [. . .]
> Lach mit offenem Mieder
> Dann kommen die Leute schon wieder.[85]

Faced with the draining away of its population, the *Liedermacher* could no longer postpone direct confrontation with the government. For Wenzel it felt like sitting

> in einem Nichts [. . .], einem Land, zu dem man sich überhaupt nicht mehr bekennen konnte. Selbst bei den Funktionären gab es nur noch einen halbherzigen Dogmatismus ohne einen Funken Identität.[86]

In September 1989, GDR *Liedermacher* and rock musicians came out in support of the newly formed civil rights organization Neues Forum. A resolution with a list of demands was drafted, and performers all over the country read it out before concerts.[87] This — against the background of increasingly large demonstrations in Leipzig and other towns — was for many a daring act. No one knew how the police and military would respond. On 7 October, the fortieth anniversary of the GDR, police reacted heavy-handedly to the counter-demonstrations in Berlin. The same evening Wenzel and Mensching's performance of "Altes aus der Da Da eR"[88] in Hoyerswerda was suddenly cancelled and the duo was arrested by the Stasi. The MfS report reveals that this was not necessarily due to the critical nature of their songs, but rather because of the Neues-Forum resolution, which they had been reading out before their concerts.[89] They spent

ten hours under arrest before being set free. This event caused a great up-
roar at a meeting of the Präsidium des Schriftstellerverbandes der DDR
on 11 October when the arrest of the duo became known. The Stasi report reads as follows:

> Einige Präsidiumsmitglieder [sprangen] erregt auf. Es wurde durch-
> einandergeschrien, so daß zeitweise keine Versammlungsführung
> möglich war. Mit den Worten, daß er sich um die Umstände, welche
> dazu geführt haben, kümmern wird, beendete Genosse Kant diese
> Diskussion.[90]

Such intimidation, however, was fruitless against the avalanche of
grassroots democracy that began taking hold in the GDR. The euphoria
of this period is evident from a video recording of a concert at the
Akademie der Künste on 24 October 1989 during a week of *Kleinkunst*
events called the "Roter Rummel" (after Piscator's famous 1924 revue),
in which Gina Pietsch, Gerhard Gundermann, and Wenzel and Mensching
performed. One notices how the audience spurs on the performers,
practically forcing them into roles as the bearers of a new truth.[91] On 4
November *Liedermacher* including Gerhard Schöne, Kurt Demmler,
Jürgen Eger, and Wenzel and Mensching performed before a demonstration of half a million people on the Alexanderplatz in Berlin. Five nights
later the Wall fell.

During the *Wende* these *Liedermacher* of the GDR were in the right
place at the right time, providing satirical commentary on the daily un-
winding fate of the beleaguered government. But as it turned out, the results of autumn 1989, that is, the fall from power of the Politbüro and
the Stasi, meant that *Liedermacher* quickly had to look around for new
themes to write about. Suddenly stripped of their function as the bearers
of truth for a public deprived of credible news reporting, many of the
singer/songwriters were to endure difficult times in the 1990s.

In conclusion, the above examples serve to illustrate the inadequacy
of the customary division of GDR *Liedermacher* into either subversives or
opportunists. Their story shows how it was possible to challenge the
boundaries of censorship. The presence of censorship did not inevitably
suppress creativity, but rather created a climate in which taboos could be
subverted by creative use of irony. On the other hand the necessity of
having an official sponsor often entailed a readiness to compromise, which
led to the phenomenon of self-censorship. It is important to remember,
however, that many of these artists were not against the GDR state as
such. The artistic success of a production such as *Die komische Tragöde des
18. Brumaire* proved that an acceptance of the basic ideology of the GDR
did not exclude a subversive criticism of GDR reality. Dieter Beckert of
Karls Enkel and later of Duo Sonnenschirm has spoken of the "sozial-

romantische Utopie" that characterized the approach of many: "Es ging um konstruktive Anarchie. Wir waren eben Träumer."[92] David Bathrick describes how such ambiguity among the GDR writers and intellectuals reshaped the binary for-or-against mentality of the official discourse, posing the question: "Sind diese Autoren und ihre Texte letzten Endes innerhalb oder außerhalb des diskursiven Systems zu verorten? Auf der einen oder der anderen Seite der Macht?" (248). This question, which is relevant to many of the GDR *Liedermacher* as well as authors and playwrights has been much debated since 1989. Heiner Müller's remark "Ich war immer auf beiden Seiten"[93] is indicative of the attitude of many and is echoed in this assessment by Wenzel: "Es ist ja so, daß heute die Geschichte so betrachtet wird, als ob es eine klare Trennung in Dissidenten und Doktrinäre gegeben hätte. Und so war es nicht. Der Riß ging durch die Leute durch."[94]

But as the arguments about artists' political behavior in the former GDR died down in the course of the 1990s the question remained as to the current relevance of the genre of political song. For many former GDR citizens in the new Germany the *gestus* of the *Liedermacher* was firmly associated with the utopian visions of what appeared to be an increasingly distant past.

Notes

[1] An earlier stage of this research on the GDR Singebewegung was published in David Robb, "The GDR Singebewegung: Metamorphosis and Legacy," *Monatshefte* 92, 2 (2000): 199–216.

[2] For a summary of the beginnings of the *Singebewegung* see Lutz Kirchenwitz, *Folk, Chanson und Liedermacher in der DDR* (Berlin: Dietz Verlag, 1993), 16–33.

[3] See Holger Böning, *Der Traum von einer Sache: Aufstieg und Fall der Utopien im politischen Lied der Bundesrepublik und der DDR* (Bremen: Lumière, 2003), 185–91.

[4] Wolf Biermann, "Soldaten-Lied" in *Alle Lieder* (Cologne: Kiepenheuer & Witsch, 1991), 36–37. All quotations from Biermann's lyrics are copyright and used by permission of Wolf Biermann.

[5] Wolf Biermann, "Soldat Soldat," in *Alle Lieder,* 103. The subject of military songs in the GDR is discussed at length by Peter Fauser in "Friedensthematik und soldatische Prägung," in *Die Entdeckung des sozialkritischen Liedes,* Volksliedstudien vol. 7, ed. Eckhard John (Münster, New York, Munich and Berlin: Waxmann, 2006), 97–120.

[6] Jürgen Trinkus, "Vom Hootenanny zum Oktoberklub und wieder weg!" in *Lieder Leute gestern — heute,* Reader zu den 1. Boltenhagener Liedertagen (2–6 December 1998) http://www.klangkontext.de/boltenhagen/liedertage/oktoberklub.html, 3.

[7] Günther Jahn, "6. Tagung des ZK der SED" (1972, 55). Quoted in Kirchenwitz (1993, 50). As David Bathrick states, the public arena tended to be viewed as "ein Forum für Bewußtseinsbildung und nicht für die öffentliche Auseinandersetzung" (Bathrick, "Kultur und Öffentlichkeit in der DDR," in *Literatur der DDR in den siebziger Jahren*, ed. P. U. Hohendahl and P. Herminghouse [Frankfurt am Main: Suhrkamp, 1983], 57).

[8] Inge Lammel, *Das Arbeiterlied* (Leipzig: Reclam 1970, 82). Quoted in Kirchenwitz, *Folk, Chanson und Liedermacher*, 86.

[9] Kirchenwitz interviewed on Axel Grote and Christian Steinke, *Sag mir wo du Stehst: Die Geschichte vom Oktoberklub* (TV documentary ORB, 1993).

[10] Oktoberklub, *Unterm Arm die Gitarre* (VEB Deutsche Schallplatten, 1968).

[11] See Grote and Steinke, *Sag mir wo du Stehst*.

[12] Oktoberklub, "Ich bin wie alle blind geboren," on Grote and Steinke, *Sag mir wo du Stehst*.

[13] Bettina Wegner, interviewed on Grote and Steinke, *Sag mir wo du Stehst*.

[14] DDR-Singegruppen, *Junge Leute, Junge Lieder* (VEB Deutsche Schallplatten, 1969).

[15] Bernd Rump, "Die Singe. Eine Replik" in Jürgen Maerz, ed., *Singe in der DDR. Variante Frankfurt: Ein Bewegungsbuch* (Frankfurt an der Oder: Kapiske, 2002), 102. Quoted in Böning, *Der Traum von einer Sache*, 205.

[16] Oktoberklub, *Das Beste*. CD. (Edition Barbarossa, 1995).

[17] Reinhold Andert, "Lieder eines Konvertiten," in *Lieder aus einem verschwundenen Land* (1998, 17). Quoted in Böning, *Der Traum von einer Sache*, 219–20.

[18] See Kirchenwitz, *Folk, Chanson und Liedermacher*, 67–81.

[19] "World music" was a term coined in the mid-1980s to describe the current boom in groups, predominantly from Africa, South America, and eastern Europe, who often, but not always, combined folk tradition with elements of rock music and new musical technologies.

[20] Reinhold Andert, on the inside cover of the CD *Oktoberklub: Das Beste*.

[21] Kirchenwitz, *Folk, Chanson und Liedermacher*, 64.

[22] *Ran* 4 (1975): 32. Quoted in Kirchenwitz, *Folk, Chanson und Liedermacher*, 51.

[23] Grote and Steinke, *Sag mir wo du Stehst*.

[24] See Kirchenwitz, ed., *Lieder und Leute: Die Singebewegung der FDJ* (Berlin: Neues Leben, 1982), 53–54.

[25] Declaration of Jahrgang 49 in *Neues Deutschland* (22 November 1976). Quoted in Kirchenwitz, *Folk, Chanson und Liedermacher*, 119.

[26] Bernd Rump, "In meinem Namen" in Fred Krüger, ed., *DDR — konkret. Lieder der Singebewegung*. Volume 1 (1976, 78–79). Quoted in Böning, *Der Traum von einer Sache*, 226.

[27] Quoted in Petra Schwarz and Wilfried Bergholz, *Liederleute* (Berlin: Lied der Zeit, 1989), 22.

[28] Kirchenwitz, *Folk, Chanson und Liedermacher*, 100.

[29] Kirchenwitz, *Folk, Chanson und Liedermacher*, 188.

[30] Kirchenwitz, *Folk, Chanson und Liedermacher*, 87.

[31] See "Werkstaat Lieder & Theater. Dresden 1981/1982. Diskussionsprotokolle" (Berlin: Liedzentrum der Akademie der Künste der DDR, 1982).

[32] Many were, however, recorded on amateur video and collected by Karin Wolf in the Lied-Zentrum of the Akademie der Künste der DDR.

[33] Karen Leeder, *Breaking Boundaries: A New Generation of Poets in the GDR* (Oxford: Clarendon Press, 1996), 4.

[34] See also the section on montage in chapter 2 of this book.

[35] Karls Enkel, "Vorfahrt," unpublished manuscript and tape recording from 1977, collected by Karin Wolf, archive of the Akademie der Künste der DDR, Berlin, Liedertheater-Dokumentation, Forschungsabteilung Musik/Liedzentrum.

[36] Bertolt Brecht, *Aufstieg und Fall der Stadt Mahagonny,* in *Die Stücke von Bertolt Brecht in einem Band* (Frankfurt am Main: Suhrkamp, 1987), 214.

[37] Karls Enkel, Wacholder, and Beckert & Schulz, "Die Hammer-Rehwü," unpublished video from 1982, collected by Karin Wolf, archive of the Akademie der Künste der DDR, Berlin, Liedertheater-Dokumentation, Forschungsabteilung Musik/Liedzentrum. CD *Die Hammer-Rehwü von 1982* (Nebelhorn, 1994).

[38] Heiner Müller, *Rotwelsch* (West Berlin: Merve Verlag, 1982), 51. Quoted in Leeder, *Breaking Boundaries,* 53.

[39] Gerhard Gundermann, "Lancelot," on LP *Männer, Frauen und Maschinen* (Amiga, 1988; CD Buschfunk, 1995).

[40] Hans-Eckardt Wenzel, "Die Wartung eines Landes," on LP *Reise-Bilder* (Amiga, 1988; CD Buschfunk, 1995).

[41] Wenzel, radio program *Sag mir wo du stehst,* Rockradio B (20 October 1992).

[42] *Gundermann,* documentary (DDR-Fernsehen 1983). This was drastically censored and was only shown once in the GDR.

[43] Karin Hirdina, "Präzision ohne Pingelichkeit. Wenzel und Mensching im Gespräch mit Karin Hirdina," *Temperamente* 4 (1984): 38.

[44] Karls Enkel, "'s geht los! Aber nicht mit Chassepots," unpublished manuscript and tape recording from 1980, collected by Karin Wolf, archive of the Akademie der Künste der DDR, Berlin, Liedertheater-Dokumentation, Forschungsabteilung Musik/Liedzentrum.

[45] See David Robb, *Zwei Clowns im Lande des verlorenen Lachens: Das Liedertheater Wenzel & Mensching* (Berlin: Ch. Links, 1998).

[46] Jürgen B. Wolff, "Von Folkländer über das Duo Sonnenschirm zur Leipziger Folk Session Band," *Folker!* 3/2001, http://www.folker.de/200103/wolff.htm.

[47] Folkländer's version of this song, on the LP *Wenn man fragt, wer hat's getan . . .* (Amiga, 1982), borrowed an instrumental passage from the well-known song "Wandersmann" by the banned rock group Renft. The passage was disguised by being played on fiddles, mandolins, and whistles rather than electric instruments. This is a further example of how subversive associations could be made.

[48] The following section contains translated excerpts from David Robb, "Zwischen Zensur und Forderung: Das Liedertheater Karls Enkel in der DDR, in *Zensur im modernen deutschen Kulturraum,* ed. Beate Müller, 215–33 (Tübingen: Niemeyer, 2003).

[49] See Wolfgang Emmerich, *Kleine Literaturgeschichte der DDR. Erweiterte Neuausgabe* (Leipzig: Kiepenheuer, 1996), 415.

[50] See the section on agitprop revue in chapter 2 of this book.

[51] BStU MfS X5/2522/78, report from 9 May 1977, 103. This and subsequent similar abbreviations refer to files of the Ministerium für Staatssicherheit.

[52] Personal interview with Karls Enkel member Stefan Körbel (29 September 1993).

[53] BStU MfS XV/2522/78, report from 2 March 1980, 170.

[54] Kirchenwitz, *Folk, Chanson und Liedermacher,* 43.

[55] Petra Schwarz and Wilfried Bergholz, *Liederleute* (Berlin: Lied der Zeit, 1989), 28.

[56] Kirchenwitz, *Folk, Chanson und Liedermacher,* 103.

[57] Reinhold Andert, in Sektionsbrief (20 June 1988). Quoted in Kirchenwitz, *Folk, Chanson und Liedermacher,* 95).

[58] Kirchenwitz, *Folk, Chanson und Liedermacher,* 98)

[59] BStU MfS XV/2522/78, report from 4 February 1980, 207.

[60] BStU MfS XV/2522/78, report from 4 February 1980, 207.

[61] BStU MfS XV/2522/78, report from 31 May 1978, 40.

[62] BStU MfS XV/2522/78, report from 11 March 1981, 281.

[63] Reinhard Ständer writes: "'Die Hoffnarren der Nation' (wie sie selbst sangen), dürften sich alles erlauben. Später stellte sich heraus, daß diese Gerüchte von der Stasi inszeniert waren. Beide konnten auf reichlich Verbote verweisen." See Ständer, "Wenzel und Mensching. Die Kult-Clowns aus der Da Da eR," *Folk Michel* 4 (1997): 25.

[64] Jürgen Wolff, Dieter Beckert, Erik Kross, and others, "Die Boten des Todes. Nach dem Märchen der Gebrüder Grimm," unpublished, performed in Leipzig, 1982.

[65] Jürgen Wolff, interview by Reinhard Ständer, "Folk-Urgestein und Brachialromantiker Jürgen Wolff," *Folker* 3 (2001): 16. http://www.folker.de/200103/wolff.htm.

[66] Quoted in Kirchenwitz, *Folk, Chanson und Liedermacher,* 91–92.

[67] See Matthias Kießling, "Kurze Geschichte eines Auftrittsverbots" in *Hammer-Revue 82. Dokumentation* (Potsdam: Brandenburgische Landeszentrale für politische Bildung, 1993), unpaginated.

[68] Personal interview with Karin Hirdina (9 June 1992).

[69] Karls Enkel, *Hammer-Rehwü,* unpublished manuscript and video recording (Berlin: Liedzentrum der Akademie der Künste der DDR, 1982).

[70] Kießling, "Kurze Geschichte eines Auftrittsverbots."

[71] BVfS Cottbus AKG178, report from 5 April 1983, 13. For an analysis of the carnivalesque significance of the body language and slapstick of the *Hammer-Rehwü* see Robb, *Zwei Clowns*, 51–70).

[72] BVfS Cottbus, 14.

[73] Kießling, "Kurze Geschichte eines Auftrittsverbots."

[74] See Robb, *Zwei Clowns*, 72–76.

[75] Sekretariatssitzung of the Kulturbund (29 March 1983). Beschluß Nr. III/44–50. Bundesarchiv Berlin, SAPMO-BArch DY27/2109, 4–5; here: 4.

[76] Personal interview with Wenzel (9 March 1994). Nothing about this conflict appeared in the Kulturbund report.

[77] See Robb, *Zwei Clowns*, 88–90.

[78] See Robb, *Zwei Clowns*, 103–6.

[79] Bathrick, "Die Intellektuellen und die Macht. Die Repräsentanz des Schriftstellers in der DDR," in *Schriftsteller als Intellektuelle: Politik und Literatur im Kalten Krieg* (Studien und Texte zur Sozialgeschichte der Literatur, Band 73), ed. Sven Hanuschek, Therese Hörnigk, Christine Malende, 246.

[80] See, for example, the remarks: "Das Programm (Komm rücken wir näher zusammen) wurde von einigen, wenigen, begeistert aufgenommen." BStU MfS XV/2522/78, 105. "Solche Textzeile (in der Hammer=Rehwü) wie 'Wir wissen nur aus den Zeitungen, wie gut es uns geht' begrüßte das Publikum mit großem Beifall." BVfS Cottbus AKG178, BStU, 13.

[81] Kirchenwitz, *Folk, Chanson und Liedermacher*, 50)

[82] Quoted in Kirchenwitz, *Folk, Chanson und Liedermacher*, 125.

[83] Duo Sonnenschirm, *Flucht nach vorne*, CD (Löwenzahl, 1990).

[84] Gerhard Schöne, "Mit dem Gesicht zum Volk," on LP *Du hast es nur noch nicht probiert* (Amiga, VEB Deutsche Schallplatten, 1989).

[85] Dieter Kalka, "Holde Ost-Germania," from *Musikalischer Protest* (radio documentary), Deutsche Welle (2 September 1990).

[86] Wenzel, *Junge Welt* (6 October 1990). Quoted in Kirchenwitz, *Folk, Chanson und Liedermacher*, 135.

[87] Kirchenwitz, *Folk, Chanson und Liedermacher*, 35–36.

[88] Wenzel & Mensching, "Altes aus der Da Da eR," unpublished manuscript and video recording from 1989, collected by Karin Wolf, archive of the Akademie der Künste der DDR, Berlin, Liedertheater-Dokumentation, Forschungsabteilung Musik/Liedzentrum.

[89] BStU MfS HAXX/AKG, Nr. 1493, report from 8 October 1989, 356.

[90] BStU MfS HAXX/AKG, Nr. 1493, report from 12 October 1989, 366.

[91] Wenzel and Mensching, Gina Pietsch, Gerhard Gundermann, *Roter Rummel*, video tape, unpublished video recording from 1989, collected by Karin Wolf, archive of the Akademie der Künste der DDR, Berlin, Liedertheater-Dokumentation, Forschungsabteilung Musik/Liedzentrum.

[92] Personal interview with Dieter Beckert (23 August 2004).

[93] Heiner Müller, "Jetzt ist da eine Einheitssoße. Der Dramtiker Heiner Müller über die Intellektuellen und den Untergang der DDR," in *Der Spiegel*, 44, 31 (30 July 1990), 141. Quoted in Bathrick, "Die Intellektuellen und die Macht," 240.

[94] Hans-Eckardt Wenzel in interview with Jens Rosbach, Deutschland-Radio (15 April 1998).

9: The Demise of Political Song and the New Discourse of Techno in the Berlin Republic

David Robb

H OLGER BÖNING, IN HIS 2004 BOOK *Der Traum von einer Sache: Aufstieg und Fall der Utopien im politischen Lied der Bundesrepublik und der DDR*, writes that the respective conditions in the two German states gave rise to a particular counterculture ("Gegenöffentlichkeit") in which the political song prospered — in the 1960s in West Germany and from the 1960s up until 1989 in the GDR.[1] It resulted from a situation in which mainstream political and cultural discourse was thoroughly at odds with unofficial discourse, that is, the opinions and debates of the people. One could argue that by the mid to late 1970s in West Germany this crisis was already considerably mitigated by a political system that was flexible enough to integrate many countercultural initiatives into mainstream public policy. In the GDR on the other hand the crisis persisted up until 1989. By the onset of 1990 and unification, however, it was clear that the conditions for a broad, popular political song movement no longer existed in any part of Germany. Songs of Wenzel and Mensching and Gundermann, who are among the few key *Liedermacher* who survived the fall of communism, will be analysed in this chapter. In view of the crisis, however, which the political song has entered in the past years, this chapter will culminate in an investigation into new possibilities for political expression in music by taking developments in techno into consideration.

With the demise of the GDR, the Festival des politischen Liedes ceased to exist in its known form. A mixture of former officials, helpers, and friends of the festival continued to put on an event with a new name, the Zwischen-Welt-Festival, up until 1994. But with insufficient public funding due to its reputation as having been a political propaganda showcase for the GDR, it could no longer attract reputable international acts, and became a gathering for the loose remnants of the GDR political song scene that had survived unification. Another significant loss was the closure of the Liedzentrum of the Akademie der Künste der DDR in 1993. Run by Karin Wolf, this had archived the many unpublished songs and programs of the political song and *Liedertheater* movement and provided a focal point through its workshops and conferences up until 1992.

Thereafter Das Lied und Sozialbewegung e V., led by former Oktober-klub member Lutz Kirchenwitz, attempted to fill the vacuum. Through-out the 1990s it organized sporadic events, workshops, and discussions. These were mostly aimed at the reassessment of the history of the GDR song movement, often showing videos from the former Liedzentrum's ar-chive. The atmosphere in several of these early gatherings up to 1993, however, was tense, with *Liedermacher* still reproaching one another for their behavior regarding past events such as the FDJ takeover of the Ok-toberklub in 1967 and the treatment of Bettina Wegner in its aftermath, the Biermann affair of 1976, and the Krawczyk affair of 1988.[2]

In essence, however, the pre-1990 infrastructure of the political song scene had completely collapsed. This was paralleled by a drastic waning of public interest in the genre itself. The days when it had been fashionable and subversive to hold an acoustic guitar and communicate a message were firmly in the past. The Festival des politischen Liedes now had the status of one of the many marginalized fringe cultural events in Berlin. On one hand the new festival organizers asserted (similarly to claims made by the successor party to the SED, the Partei des Demokratischen Sozialismus, of itself) that true believers now held the reins, the careerists and opportunists in the FDJ and SED who had previously run the festival long since having departed the scene. On the other hand, it was clear that few of those remaining on the festival committee had the experience to run an international festival. Many of them consisted of disaffected uto-pian idealists who were still having difficulties coming to terms with the collapse of the GDR and its assimilation into the Federal Republic. Many had lost their employment and status in society and were now involved in temporary ABM (*Arbeitsbeschaffungsmaßnahmen*) projects.

It is significant that the demise of the political song festival was paral-leled by the rise of the annual Tanz- und Folkfestival in Rudolstadt, Thur-ingia. Organized by a circle of friends attached to the folk scenes of Saxony and Thuringia, including Ulli Doberenz and Jürgen Wolff, for-merly of the Leipzig group Folkländer, this was able in the early 1990s to link up the East and West German folk (as opposed to political song) scenes and, with strong public sponsorship and media support, create a successful folk and world music festival of international standing. In GDR times it had primarily been a folk dance festival and, although it had been politicized to the extent that all art and culture in the GDR was, Rudol-stadt did not have the same ideological and didactic associations that stamped the Festival des politischen Liedes. By the same token, the Rudolstadt Tanz- und Folkfestival, with its new organizational and man-agement structure, had no political agenda at all, whereas the new Zwischen-Welt-Festival in Berlin was clearly still a meeting point for left-

wing intellectuals and artists, which contributed to it being given the cold
shoulder by the media.

The political song festival from 1990 up until its final demise in 1994
was a forum for the expression of cultural humiliation, and directionless-
ness perceived by those who had lost out in the wake of unification. The
frustration among the *Liedermacher* themselves, who had enjoyed the
status of a cultural elite in the GDR, would be evident for years to come.
At a book launch in the Kulturbrauerei in Prenzlauer Berg in March 1998
Hans-Eckardt Wenzel spoke of the personal setback the *Wende* represented; the rupture in their careers, broken off "in der Blüte unserer
Jugend" by the collapse of the GDR.[3] Although the critical acclaim
Wenzel has received since then in both east and west has presumably gone
some way to alleviating this disappointment (several prizes of the
Deutschen Schallplatten Kritiker, the 2002 Deutscher Kleinkunstpreis,
the RUTH prize at the 2003 Rudolstadt Festival among others) the same
cannot be said for most of the others.

One *Liedermacher*, Gerhard Gundermann, however, formed, alongside Wenzel, a further exception to the above trend. He emerged as the
musical and poetic mouthpiece for left-leaning East Germans who had
lost their position in society or were simply grappling with the pain of the
final shattering of their socialist ideal. Assisted in the studio by musicians
from the celebrated rock band Silly, Gundermann was one of the few
Liedermacher who continued performing at a high professional level after
unification, his popularity in the East even soaring (in inverse relationship
to the fate of most others) up until his premature death in 1998. Named
the "Springsteen des Ostens" (due to the sound of his live backing band
Seilschaft), or "Dylan de Tagebaus" (he worked as a full-time excavator
operator until 1995), Gundermann released a series of acclaimed albums
throughout the 1990s. At times patronized by certain elements of the
west German press,[4] he undoubtedly hit the nerve of the times in the east.
This was acknowledged by *Der Spiegel:* "Kaum ein anderer Künstler hat
die Entäuschung vieler Ostdeutschen nach der Vereinigung in so präg-
nante Verse gefaßt wie er."[5] The lines "mein herzblatt was bist du so
traurig / nur weil dieser tag / wieder nicht gehalten hat / was er ver-
sprach" from the song "herzblatt" on the 1993 album *Der 7te Sumarai*[6]
sum up the singer's upbeat resilience in the face of disappointment. On
the other hand, the painful experience of the empty promises of socialism
is constantly at hand, as evident in "pferd aus holz," a parable of the
dashed expectations of past and present. In the song he relates the story
of the boy who wanted a real horse for Christmas only to receive a wooden
one: "mama hör her / ich wünsche mir sehr / so ein pferdchen / mama
was solls / das hier ist nur ein pferd aus holz." In the conclusion the lyrical "ich" appears haunted by his unfulfilled dreams:

> für drei jahre und noch heute im traum
> ist es mir treu hinterhergerollt
> ich habs nie geliebt als es zu mir kam
> seit es fort ist kenn ich keine märchen mehr
> ich krieg jedes jahr hundert grosse pakete
> aber sie sind alle leer[7]

Gundermann conveys the negative experience of capitalism in the song "ruhetag" from the same album, in which he sings: "sag dem bettler vor der tür / mein herz hat grade heut ruhetag."[8] And in the song "kann dich nicht mehr leiden" he sums up the antipathy felt toward supposed western benefactors: "du hast mich auf dein traumschiff mitgezottelt / doch ich kann dich nicht mehr leiden / du drückst mich an dein herz aus stein / und ich sollte dankbar sein."[9]

In 1994 Gundermann (similarly to Barbara Thalheim one year later) controversially admitted to having been a Stasi informer. Expelled from the Army Officer's School and later from the Party itself, he had been ultimately relieved of his Stasi duties in 1984, after which point he became the object of Stasi observation himself.[10] Gundermann hints at the complexities surrounding the theme of informers and reflects East German skepticism at the media's handling of revelations from Stasi files in the 1993 song "sieglinde." In this the singer ironically bemoans the loss of a friend who he discovers had been informing on him:

> sie sagen du hast mich belauscht
> doch ausser dir hat mir nie einer zugehört
> und schneller als das wasser rauscht
> hab ich dir meine geheimnisse diktiert
>
> sie sagen du hast mich beschattet
> für deinen schatten danke ich
> bei zuviel sonne auf die platte
> krieg ich doch nurn sonnenstich
>
> sie sagen du hast mich verraten
> doch fehlt mir ja bis heute kein bein
> der teufel wollte braten
> und die pfanne sollte deine sein
> [. . .][11]

Despite beginning a new apprenticeship as a carpenter after being made redundant in 1995, he continued to perform tirelessly with Seilschaft, releasing a further CD *Frühstück für immer*[12] followed by *Engel über dem Revier*[13] in 1997. Songs such as "leine los" ominously hint at Gundermann's depression: "alle filme die ich drehen wollte sind schon gedreht /[. . .]/ alle lieder, die ich machen wollte singt schon der boss / ich bin nurn armer hund aber wer / wer liess mich von der leine los."[14] Having lost his culture, his country, and now his job, Gundermann expresses in the title track "engel über dem revier" that his guardian angel is no longer watching over him: "er war mein seil über den schwarzen fluss der fluss war so breit ich fuhr mehr als zwanzig jahr / jetzt da ich frei an das andere ufer springen muss merke ich wie gut sein feuerschutz war."[15] Gundermann's death from heart failure in 1998 at the age of forty-three was greeted with shock throughout the whole *Liedermacher* fraternity in East Germany.

Throughout the 1990s Wenzel and Mensching were still playing to their loyal following in the Maxim-Gorki-Theater in Unter den Linden in Berlin. In 1992, over two years after the fall of the Wall, they performed a production inspired by Rimbaud's *Une Saison en Enfer* entitled "Aufenthalt in der Hölle."[16] The production displayed thematic parallels to Brecht and Weill's *Aufstieg und Fall der Stadt Mahagonny* — which concluded that Mahagonny was effectively a hell on earth — in terms of its analysis of the "hell" that Wenzel and Mensching felt constituted capitalist society in the 1990s. Here a world is portrayed in which everyone acts like a winner, but all are in fact prisoners of a hellish existence. Lost in what Walter Benjamin called the "höllische Ewigkeit der Geschichte,"[17] the clown figures Weh and Meh search in vain for the poetic values of Rimbaud, which have no place in the market-oriented world.[18]

In general, however, Wenzel and Mensching had been departing even before the *Wende* from a fixation on East German issues and the discourse of the communist/capitalist conflict. The Third World had increasingly become an issue, its misery portrayed as the result of the developed world's political actions. The theme of "Sieger und Verlierer" becomes prominent in their work. The ambiguity of their texts and clownesque performance techniques in "Aufenthalt in der Hölle" allowed this theme to be interpreted in both a local and a universal, globalized context: the theme of the losers in German unification on one level side by side with the far greater losers of the Third World, both the victims of a rampant capitalism that views itself as the historical victor.

On the local level it was clear, in the immediate aftermath of unification that the "losers" had no voice. They had been banished to the fringes. This was reflected in the lack of discourse on opposition culture in the media (and the lack of interest in the Zwischen-Welt-Festival of 1992, which had just ended). Faced with this climate Wenzel and Mensching had been inspired by Rimbaud. For them he was both poetically and socially the expression of a man on the fringes. Surrounded on all sides by what Wenzel termed a "Siegerkultur,"[19] the clowns Weh and Meh sing: "Nur der ist ein verlorener Mann / Der in der Haut des Siegers tanzen kann."[20] But the search for the "other" values that Rimbaud represented was doomed to failure because, as the duo declare, these values are only to be found on the margins of society: "im Reich der Schatten [. . .] dort, / Wo niemand ist." At the end they conclude: "Diese Poesie des Lebens ist einfach nicht MEHRHEITSFÄHIG!"[21] This recalls Volker Braun's provocative comment in his 1985 essay "Rimbaud: Ein Psalm der Aktualität," in which he had claimed the avant-garde poet for the literary *Erbe* of the GDR: "Poesie [. . .] ist nicht zu brauchen, wo man die *vortrefflichen Verhältnisse* nicht ändern will."[22] But after the demise of the GDR, the restorative, conservative climate of postunification Germany that Wenzel and Mensching perceived was also no home for those who sought to challenge dominant discourses. Now bereft of the (albeit illusive) utopian perspective that the GDR offered, not even their clowns' masks offered them a sanctuary for their "otherness" in the 1990s. This was illustrated by a comment in the concert program: "Am Ende ihrer ODYSSEE, auf Straßen aus Beton mit unbelebter Landschaft erstarrt das Lächeln der Clowns zur Fratze: ZWEI ARBEITSLOSE APOKALYPTISCHE REITER, die sich ins Dunkel der Geschichte trommeln."[23]

In *Der Abschied der Matrosen,* first performed in January 1993, Wenzel and Mensching again address the issue of the absence of the utopian ideals in which one could formerly seek sanctuary. They sang: "Jetzt gibt es ja nicht mal mehr die Flucht, / Du bleibst der Ewige Doofe. / Na dann, bis gleich. Mit voller Wucht / Hinein in die Katastrophe."[24] Behind the irony there is socialist resentment, on a local level, at the GDR's assimilation into the Federal Republic, but also anger, on a global level, at the devastating repercussions of the *Sieger* mentality on the developing world. The production finishes with a parody of "Die Internationale," emphasizing the artists' view of people in general — not just East Germans — as refugees in an alien world: "Völker hört die Matrosen! / Ob an Bord, ob auf Grund / Die ewig Heimatlosen, / Die beißt zuletzt der Hund."[25]

Wenzel and Mensching continued performing as a duo throughout the 1990s, but by the late 1990s were increasingly concentrating on solo projects. Wenzel's creative dialogue with the Brecht, Weill, and Eisler tradition continued with his Eisler program *Hanswurst und andere arme Würste,* which had its premiere in June 1998 for the Berliner Ensemble's celebration of Eisler's 100th anniversary. The production consists of a collage of Eisler texts and music set alongside texts by Hölderlin, Brecht, and others. The montage emphasizes the uncomfortable, critical figure that Eisler had been both in his exile abroad and in the GDR. This image is enhanced by Wenzel's appearance as a Hanswurst clown that sings or recites the collage of texts. In the prologue Wenzel (donning the clown's mask and costume as he spoke) explained the reluctance of the Berlin authorities to sponsor a tribute to Eisler, a "Mann mit linken Idealen und

Konsequenz," substantially enough so that a proper orchestra could be included. Wenzel therefore had to confine himself to piano, tuba, clarinet, and his own Hanswurst character: "Für so was gibt uns keine Muse mehr den Götterstempel / So bleibt Hanswurst uns nur als störrisches Exempel."[26] Hanswurst, famously banned in Leipzig in 1737 for being too provocative for bourgeois morals, can thus be viewed as an appropriate medium for Wenzel to convey the essence of Eisler at the end of the twentieth century.

The collages deal with Eisler's exile from the Nazis as well as his ostracism in the GDR when he was accused of being a formalist. Fragments of poems by Hölderlin are set alongside melancholy music to express the theme of asylum and exile. This echoes Wenzel's poetic and musical appropriation of Hölderlin in the GDR,[27] but also reflects his feelings of alienation in the Berlin Republic. In this way a dialogue takes place between the music of Eisler, the poetry of Hölderlin, and the overall vision of Wenzel — all mediated through his clown figure of Hanswurst. Other scenes deal with the music business and above all with Eisler's attitude toward the opera. The scene "Der Musikbetrieb," a montage of written notes from Eisler, is reminiscent of Kurt Weill's determined attempt in *Mahagonny* to renew the outdated form of the opera and shake audiences out of their passive consumption of art. In the scene, the Wenzel clown, alternating between roles, performs Eisler's funny anecdote about the head waiter who criticizes the exaggerated behavior of the orchestra conductor. Waiter and conductor are dressed alike, both have "scheinbar etwas zu servieren," but the waiter is altogether more tasteful and refined. The waiter says: "Wenn ich mit einem solchen Aufwand von Grimassen, Gesichtsverzerrungen und bombastischen oder süßlichen Gebärden meine Speise servieren würde, könnte ich mich kaum acht Tage halten." In the final scene, "Nachwurf und Zeitschleife," Wenzel, once again playing the part of Eisler, laments that, at this late time in his life, nothing much has changed:

> Was momentan notwending ist, weiß ich nicht. Da ich die Oper für schwachsinnig halte, schon wegen der Sänger, die ja unerträglich sind, und die Sinfonien, wie Sie sehen, auch für schwachsinnig halte, gibt es nur etwas, was notwending wäre: das Schweigen. In meinem Alter wäre das Schweigen vielleicht viel gemäßer als das Reden. Deshalb höre ich jetzt auf zu reden, und lasse Sie darüber nachdenken, was ich jetzt zu schweigen habe.

All that remains for Eisler is to be silent. With the montage effect caused by the ambiguous role-play it is clear that this is as much the artist Wenzel speaking as Eisler. Wenzel, too, can now only be silent. As in the conclusion to his and Mensching's 1982 clown program *Neues aus der Da*

Da eR, there is no moral apart from silence. Just as there seemed to be no way out of the stagnation in the GDR in 1982, the capitalism of the 1990s is too powerful for anyone to believe that society could be changed by music or literature. Perhaps only through laughter at a successful parody is it possible for artists like Wenzel or Mensching to inspire their audience to think critically about themselves or promote an alternative consciousness among like-minded people.[28]

Despite the isolated successes of Gundermann and Wenzel, the East German scene, now without a strong festival in Berlin, struggled to rediscover a focal point that could channel the remaining interest in political song. As with the Rudolstadt Folk Festival, however, the key seemed to lie in linking up with activists in the West. By the mid to late 1990s Das Lied und Sozialbewegung had become more active. With support from the Friedrich Ebert Stiftung it put on one-day conferences in Rostock and Griefswald in 1997 and 1998 respectively. The latter celebrated the 1848 political song tradition to coincide with the 150th anniversary of the revolution; a delegation from Burg Waldeck attended and formed a discussion panel. This was indicative of the resumed contacts with the folk and political song scene in West Germany and its infrastructure, for example, the musicians' association PROFOLK e.V. and the media, in particular Michael Kleff, editor of the magazine *Folker.* In 2000 the Festival des politischen Liedes was revived in Berlin for the thirtieth anniversary of the original festival, not only conveying a new unified vision of east and west with the figures of Hans-Eckardt Wenzel, Stephan Krawczyk, Liederjahn, and Franz Josef Degenhardt, but also including a modest international dimension in the figures of Billy Bragg and Nora Guthrie. The festival continued on this much reduced scale, centering around the venues Die Wabe, Die Volksbühne, and Club Voltaire. 2001 and 2002 saw appearances from Bettina Wegner, Barbara Thalheim, Leon Gieco, Dick Gaughan, Tom Sands, and Fermin Muguraza. Although the majority of the performers and organizers were from this "old guard," younger influences and musical directions were seeping in at the sides. The festival was renamed Festival Musik und Politik from 2001 onwards to encompass the greater variety of musical styles (other than purely *Lied*) that had been witnessed at the previous year's festival: "vom klassischen Liedermacher über Agitfolk und avancierte E-Musik bis zum Diskursrock und zum HipHop."[29] The presence at the festival of artists drawing on hiphop styles since 2001 such as Mellow Mark in 2004 and Rainer von Vielen in 2007 has indeed been a significant development. Both these performers are linked to the organization Attac, which sees itself as an international, extraparliamentary, anti-globalization movement and network, boasting 90,000 members in fifty countries, and which regularly demonstrates at G8 summits. Von Vielen, who began his young career in 1998, prefers to describe his act as

"Elektropunkhop," because he rejects the platitudes of hiphop, but acknowledges the comparison to hiphop due to his rapping. But his music is more complex than mainstream rap, combining musical styles ranging from rock to punk and even folk (he plays the accordion). The ever-changing rhythms, generated by samples or by his backing band of guitar, bass and drums, form a counterpoint to his thoughtful and mostly political lyrics. His voice is unique, inspired by the religious chants of Tibetan monks and resembling at times the low, prolonged pulses of a didgeridoo. But he also has the ability to switch vocal registers from his uncannily deep *Kehlkopfgesang* to a normal pitch, which enables him to play with perspectives in his songs.

"Sandbürger" from 2005 deals with rampant consumerism, observing that "the truth" of those who subscribe to it is built on sand:

> Ihre Wahrheit ist auf Sand gebaut,
> daß man mit knirschenden Zähnen an den Folgen kaut
> und wer die ganze Zeit nur auf den Fortschritt schaut:
> Kann sich nicht umdrehen, kann sich nicht umsehen
> und vor allem nicht mit seiner Erde umgehen.[30]

In the same song Rainer von Vielen calls on people to "Use the Media, confuse the media, / Nutz die Medien, verschmutz die Medien." He calls on the ego of individualism promoted by the consumerist, standardizing media to be countered by the "wir" of an emerging network:

> Obwohl ich zwischen tausend Sendern wählen kann,
> seh ich immer nur das selbe Programm.
> Es ist mein Ego, das sich durch die Medien formt.
> Nimm dich in Acht Baby, der Gedanke ist genormt.
> Da muss ein Netzwerk her, ein Wir, ein Wir ein Wir ein
>
> Wir und die Unseren haben uns gefunden,
> Du und die Meinen, Ich und die Deinen.

The song "Die Wahrheit ist ein Virus" predicts how the alternative truth that is emerging from this network will gradually take hold. Not all von Vielen's songs, however, are overtly political. "Leben den Lebenden" attacks the taboos associated with death in our western cultures, and advocates embracing the reality of death and living life to the full:

> Leben den Lebenden,
> Liebe den Liebenden
> und ein "Yeah" auf die innerlich lebendig gebliebenen.
> Auf die Soulrider, die ihre Zeit bewusst leben
> Jederzeit bereit sind, von sich aus alles zu geben.[31]

Rainer von Vielen appeared at the 2007 Festival Musik und Politik alongside Duo Sonnenschirm and Stellmäcke as a prize winner of the *Liederbestenliste* of the Verein deutschsprachige Lieder e.V. It is clear that the youthfulness of performers at the festival such as von Vielen and Mellow Mark stands in sharp contrast to the majority of political song acts, spectators, and participants in discussion rounds, who range in age from the mid-forties to mid-seventies. It is clear that this elder generation, while enjoying the annual social reunion atmosphere which the festival brings with it, is also aware of the dire need to revitalize the German political song. For example, at the 2004 festival the headliners Konstantin Wecker and Hans-Eckardt Wenzel felt it incumbent on themselves to introduce talent from a younger generation, who due to lack of media attention would otherwise have had little hope of exposure to such a large audience. On Saturday 28 February, therefore, Wecker and Wenzel shared top billing in the BKA-Luftschloß with Mellow Mark, the chanson singer Klaus-Andre Eickhof, and the klezmer group Der singende Tresen.

The afternoon before, the same performers formed part of a podium discussion with the president of the German Bundestag Wolfgang Thierse on the subject "'Tobe, zürne, misch dich ein!' Engagiertes Lied ohne Loby." Here the current role of the political song was debated along with the question why the media and general public showed no interest in it. While portions of the audience took the opportunity to attack Thierse for the SPD's squeezing of welfare state subsidies and demanded that political song should address the issue, Wenzel doubted the effectiveness of such knee-jerk political reaction in songs. The threat to Germany's welfare state paled in significance compared to the catastrophe of the Third World. For the public to recover an interest in political song, there would have to be a new and greater vision, expressed not only in the texts, but also in the music.

This debate continued the next day in the podium discussion on the 1960s Burg Waldeck festivals and their legacy. Michael Kleff and Lutz Kirchenwitz chaired a panel that included Oss and Hein Kröher. As the brothers remembered, Nazism had caused such a rupture in the workers' historical and cultural tradition in Germany that the rediscovered folk and political song had seemed to galvanize a whole generation of alternatively minded youth. At the same time, the panel agreed that the popularity of protest song in the 1960s was also a reflection of the cultural revolution of the time. It was argued that the political reductionism and simplification evident in the songs of the 1960s was no longer possible in the face of the "Unübersichtlichkeit" of current society. It remains to be seen whether in such times of cultural disorientation and social fragmentation the traditional political song can present a clear enough vision to unite a sizeable majority of people and thus have renewed social relevance.

In the 1960s and 1970s the *Liedermacher* had voiced the concerns of youth — including generational resentments and anti-militarism — in songs such as Degenhardt's "vatis argumente" and "Befragung eines Kreigsdienstverweigerers." But when the older stalwarts of the Burg Waldeck and the *Singegruppe* movements of west and east Germany complain of the lack of interest in political song today, they appear to overlook the fact that the folk music genre was actually fashionable at the time it was pioneered three or four decades ago. It was new, daring, and associated with subversion. This is clear from the video recordings of the later Waldeck festivals, which have images reminiscent of Woodstock (albeit on a smaller scale) with hippies smoking hashish and anti-nuclear emblems conspicuous. For the youth of the 1990s on the other hand the image of long haired protest singers accompanying themselves on guitars was no longer fashionable. It was associated with their parents' generation and no longer with rebellion.

Techno and the Politics of Youth Culture

Where were the youth going in the 1990s? Certainly not to *Liedermacher* concerts. What was the discourse of the intellectual youth? Was there a political or ideological aspect to it, and how did this express itself in music? The singer-songwriter (even in the rock context of a Herbert Gronemeyer) was no longer at the cutting edge of fashion. What was fashionable, and indeed emerged in the early 1990s in Germany as the most popular mass musical attraction, was the new digitalized electronic music known as techno. While mainstream techno, such as the music associated with the phenomenally popular annual Berlin Love Parade — and its various offshoots throughout the 1990s — can by no means be considered as representing political protest, various "underground" strands within this movement have endeavored to represent and promote countercultural stances. Because techno is for the most part devoid of lyrics, the protest has articulated itself by means of distinctive sounds and rhythms. In particular the avantgarde Frankfurt label Mille Plateaux, inspired by the philosophy of Deleuze and Guattari, has endeavored to promote "soundscapes" that challenge the listener and disrupt a uniformity in music that encourages passivity and conformity. In this respect their approach has certain echoes of Hanns Eisler's attempts in the 1930s to create a music to counter fascism. But it is significant, as we will see, that the philosophy of Mille Plateaux had little in common with the Marxist-based discourses that had characterized the *Liedermacher*.

These avant-garde strands have existed on the fringes of the techo scene. The majority of techno adherents do not subscribe to political protest. Indeed, what characterizes their attitude is an unwillingness in general to search for answers to the world's problems in political ideology. In mainstream techno, the seriousness of the 1968 parents' generation is thus rejected in favor of an apolitical hedonism and the banal mottos of the annual Love Parade such as "Friede, Freude, Eierkuchen."[32]

But in turn, with the growing mass popularity of techno in Germany in the 1990s this very rejection of traditional politics has been intellectualized and investigated as a social phenomenon. The new discourse of techno, discussed in the media and in university Kulturwissenschaft departments, reflected new perceptions, identities and political consciousness in the new globalized and digital world of the 1990s. Themes such as the dancers' relationship to technology and fashion, the shaman-like DJ figure, and the significance of the spatial coordinates of the dance floor were addressed. Techno's supporters in the academic world hailed the emancipatory aspect of "sampling" whereby a creative appropriation of culture takes place — both in the musical collages of the DJ and in the dressing up of the ravers. Not dissimilar in essence to the montage technique of the dadaists in the Weimar Republic, this do-it-yourself, "cut 'n' mix" sampling approach to music and fashion was seen by some as a force against the uniformity promoted by the pop and fashion industry. But differing discourses emerged. The underground techno scene rejected the false harmony and the symmetrical aesthetic structures of the mass rave, which it saw as fascistic. For example, to counter the happy unified image portrayed by the Love Parade and the mass conformity promoted by its metronomic beats, the techno-punk of Atari Teenage Riot used aggressive cross-rhythms to create "a sound-picture of social disintegration and instability."[33]

Germany has had a particularly close relationship to purely electronic music since the 1970s. Techno originated in the mid-1980s in Detroit and Chicago, where avant-garde disco DJs made no secret of their admiration for the Düsseldorf group Kraftwerk. In particular their albums *Autobahn* (1975), *Transeuropa Express* (1977), and *Die Mensch-Maschine* (1978) contributed to their reputation as the "Godfathers of Techno."[34] From the stable of "Krautrock," which had included Can, Faust, and Neu!, Kraftwerk were the first to create sounds and rhythms purely electronically — from analogue synthesizer, vocoder, and beat box. Simultaneously, Kraftwerk's zany science laboratory worker's uniforms and gags such as sending puppets of themselves to press conferences betrayed an ironical attitude toward technology which would be mirrored in the playful sampling culture of 1990s techno.

The Berlin Underground

The new "techno" music was first heard in Germany in West Berlin in the late 1980s. DJ Westbam and Dr. Motte put on raves in the club UFO and co-founded the Love Parade in 1989 as a small insider party. After the fall of the Wall, this scene moved to Berlin's east side, where a growing network of illegal rave parties was publicized largely through the distribution of flyers. It was also promoted by "D-Jane" Marusha on the cult youth radio station DT64 which had survived the collapse of the GDR. In the period from 1990 to 1991 techno experienced an underground explosion in Berlin that was in no small part due to the reunification of the old capital city. In a transitory period of legal uncertainty in the aftermath of the collapse of the GDR it was possible to stage illegal parties. The GDR's legacy of derelict bunkers, ex-army warehouses, unused factories, and closed-down supermarkets offered ideal locations for a burgeoning dance scene. Indeed, for youth from both sides of the former Wall, techno offered "die neue kulturelle Identität in der Wendezeit."[35] The scene emerged amidst a maze of international musical guests including Underground Resistance DJs from Detroit, and influences such as Dutch "gabba," and Belgium and Canadian "hardcore." The Berlin sound fused these with the local avant-garde, which included DJ Westbam and DJ Tanith.[36]

As a counterpart to the increasingly popular hardcore and trance, more subtle and avant-garde trends in techno emerged in techno centers throughout Germany. It was at this more experimental edge of "intelligent techno," where artists have attempted to make political statements via music, or at least to express through music new perspectives on life and society. The ultimate expression of German "intelligent" electronic music can be found in the deconstructionist "art-tekno/post rock" of the Cologne school (e.g. the group Mouse on Mars) and in the catalogue of the Frankfurt label Mille Plateaux, a subsidiary of Force Inc.[37] Mille Plateaux began in the early 1990s, and as early as 1993 it was being lauded by the magazine *Spex* as a post-structuralist label; one of its groups, Spacecube, was described as hovering on the point of dissolution with no beat the same as another.[38] This development, which will be examined in more detail below, had particular significance in view of the increasing commercialization of German rave and its standardizing effect on the music.

Commercialization and Institutionalization

Hand in hand with sponsorship from tobacco giants such as Camel, West, and Marlboro the German rave establishment began to consolidate itself by 1994. It consisted of The Friends of Mayday and Planetcom organizations behind the Love Parade, the affiliated label Low Spirit, the mass-circulation techno magazine *Frontpage,* and the music channel *viva TV.* The commercialization was further apparent in that tuneful melodies and even lyrics began to appear over the techno beats such as in Marusha's version of "Somewhere over the Rainbow." This commercialization, indeed institutionalization, was also evident in the Chromapark techno art exhibition,[39] which the Goethe-Institut exported abroad as a standard-bearer of German culture.[40] Meanwhile the Love Parade had grown from 150 participants in 1989 to 200,000 in 1994. It had outgrown its traditional route on the Kürfürstendamm and moved to the Straße des 17. Juni and the Tiergarten area. By the late 1990s it was attracting over one million people.

The institutionalization of techno in Germany had no precedent elsewhere. Dimitri Hegemann from Tresor stated: "Techno ist ein deutsches Thema, deshalb wird es weiter gepflegt werden."[41] Such nationalistic utterances were greeted with contempt by the marginalized underground. The acclaimed young German DJ Alec Empire perceived the emergence of a new nationalism within the techno scene and cited examples of foreigners being turned away from raves.[42] His agit-techno-punk group Atari Teenage Riot rallied against neo-Nazism with titles in English such as "Hunt Down the Nazis." Another target of the group's rage was the commercialization of rave. The dictates of sponsorship ensured that all music on the Love Parade floats was reduced to the level of mass marketability, and this had resulted in a group of people being refused access to the parade because they played underground gabba, a particularly hard, abrasive style of techno.[43] The underground response to this was the announcement in 1997 of the Fuck Parade as a counter-demonstration to the Love Parade. This returned successfully in subsequent years, following a route from Reinhardtstraße in Mitte via Hackescher Markt and ending up at Rotes Rathaus. In 1999 it received the support of several big Berlin nightclubs.[44] In 2001 it took the form of a demonstration in Friedrichshain for the right to demonstrate, simultaneously adding its voice to the loud chorus of criticism of the Love Parade for causing environmental damage in the Berlin Tiergarten.[45] Musically, the rebellion of the Fuck Parade took the form of hard gabba and the syncopated breakbeat rhythms of "jungle," sometimes known as "drum & bass." The breakbeat is a feature of hip hop, a soul drum-break sampled and "looped" into an extended sequence. In the late 1990s it served as "an antidote to Germanic techno's Aryan funklessness."[46] It was also used by Empire's Atari Teenage Riot. The overlapping cross-rhythms reflected the jungle principle of destabilizing the beat and clashed with the rhythmic rigidity of the Love Parade's 4/4 time.

Cultural Theory

As has already been mentioned, the cultural importance of techno in Germany in the 1990s was registered in academic writings by university cultural studies scholars. These academics generally identify with trends in pop theory since the late 1970s as pioneered by British cultural studies theorists. These tend to be at odds with Adorno and Horkheimer's 1943 theory of the hegemony of the capitalist culture industry over the needs and consciousness of the masses. They stress instead the dialectic relationship between dominant and popular culture. It is no longer merely a question of dominant culture imposing its will on the masses, but of a dialectic relationship whereby the consumer also has an active, creative role in his or her "appropriation of culture." Techno has been singled out as illustrating this sampling process, both in terms of music and fashion: the DJ digitally records sounds from other records and stores them up for use in new combinations. Similarly, in clothing, this cut n'mix ethos, reflecting the paractice generally known as "bricolage"[47] in cultural studies, is evident in the forming of new styles.[48] Demonstrating a symbolic creativity, the raver, like punk rockers before, appropriates items of clothing, accessories, and advertising motifs and transforms them by subsuming them within his or her own aesthetic.[49]

In her book *Electronic Vibration,* Gabriele Klein takes the concept of appropriation further, developing a theory of rebelliousness that articulates itself via the body and dance. She rejects the traditional split between the mind and the body, arguing that the body, too, constructs and conveys meaning. In doing so she makes use of Pierre Bourdieu's concept of the *habitus.*[50] The *habitus* is made up of body gestures that express one's distinctive relationship to his or her surrounding culture. On one hand the *habitus* is determined by external social factors including class. On the other hand, the individual creates his or her own *habitus* by an act of simulation that Klein sees as a process akin to traditional mimesis.[51] This mimesis is not just a copy of reality, but also constructs a new world (264). Klein's arguments thus attempt to counter the common view in the press that ravers are a mass of "Image-Äffchen" und "Konsumflitt-chen."[52] What seems overgeneralized about Klein's theory, however, is that it seems to suggest that all ravers are involved in an act of creativity that challenges the hegemony of the cultural industry. This relates to the "democratic" possibility of art in the modern age that she and other cultural studies scholars want to emphasize. She refers back to Benjamin's observations on the reproducibility of art in the age of technology,[53] whereby art is no longer seen as an object for contemplation by the privileged few. It can be used for purposes that take it far beyond its traditional borders and influence everyday life itself. This has led to a democratization of art. Techno lends itself as an example of this, according to its supporters: it is a do-it-yourself culture in which everyone can take part.

Klein makes further claims about the democratizing principle of rave with regard to body in space. Arguing that civilizing trends since the Renaissance resulted in people's loss of connection to their bodies, she suggests that the body has now been regained as a tool of public communication, as evident in the physical abandon and exhibitionism of the ravers (205). No longer required for industrial labor, the body acquires a new creative significance in the new dance locations of leisure time. In this respect Klein suggests that the Love Parade should be seen not only as an instrument for manipulating and depoliticizing the masses, but also as a medium through which urban space is revived, communal experiences are created, and a public, festive culture is rediscovered (108).

Love Parade: Carnival Minus the Grotesque

It is here, in the idea of public, festive culture, that comparisons with the medieval and Renaissance carnival as defined by Mikhail Bakhtin may be tempting. For Bakhtin, carnival, like rave, had an "Ersatzfunktion" in terms of being a time-out from reality.[54] The grotesque disguises and the temporary state of wild abandon emphasized the corporeality of the people. The carnival encouraged role and gender swapping, and was also a ritualized form of mass enjoyment.[55] In carnival and rave, the political significance lies in their symbolizing of an "otherness," in their enactment of roles and social models unattainable in everyday reality. In medieval carnival, according to Bakthin, the role-play was an escape from the rigidity of social hierarchies; the fun, laughter, and celebration of the grotesque body a reaction against the piousness of the church. In the rave, on the other hand, as the academic Jankowski has pointed out, the spirit of togetherness can be seen as a reaction to the increased isolation of the individual in society, the show of body sensuality an ironic enactment of unrealizable community experiences.[56] In both carnival and rave, "otherness" is expressed via dressing up. In carnival the mask was a parody of the official mask of seriousness and authority. The mask of rave, according to Jankowski, reflects the artificiality of society itself — it is an empty surface onto which self-made dreams are projected.[57] Both masks symbolize transformation. The carnival swapping of roles reflects the utopian longing for change, while the dressing up at raves denotes that the raver can be anyone he or she wants to be — everyone can be a star. Everyone can be together.

Where the comparison falters, however, is in the image of carnivalesque grotesque, which is absent in rave. Rave's "mask of dreams" is a mixture of ironical but harmless and familiar images associated with style and fashion. The celebration of beautiful, youthful bodies, which is a central feature of the rave, reflects rave's social conformity: the image projected can be marketed without contradiction in today's event society where youthfulness has become the defining metaphor.[58]

But if the carnivalesque grotesque (with its associations of death) is missing from the image mainstream rave projects of itself, an intrinsically darker side lurks not far beneath the surface. According to the journalist Simon Reynolds, a nihilistic dystopianism forms an inseparable duality with rave's utopianism, reflected in the vitalizing powers and negative aftereffects of the drug Ecstasy.[59] The German techno scene of the early 90s — after the initial euphoria — plummeted into darkness as the effects of drug abuse took hold.[60] For Reynolds, the utopian/dystopian duality embodied the struggle between Apollonian and Dionysian tendencies within techno. Hardcore was essentially Dionysian as opposed to the Apollonian genres of ambient and trance.[61] This reflected, for Reynolds, the perennial class conflict within pop music culture (185). Where the Dionysian "smidgeon of underclass rage" and "druggy hedonism" forms a recipe for musical innovation, the heady Apollonianism of "intelligent" techno hinted at self-importance and stagnation (xvii).

Indeed, the neglect of this darker, dystopian side and the rejection of the class divide is typical of much academic writing on techno in Germany, which tends to highlight the harmonious unity, the democracy and tolerance of the Love Parade. The theme of intoxication is merely subsumed within the totality of the rave event. Nobody loses out. For writer and journalist Rainald Goetz, the ego of every raver, far from disintegrating into drug-fueled nihilism, constitutes a perfect universe: the individual remains intact while simultaneously becoming one with the voluntary "unity of commonality."[62] Jankowski addresses this with a hint of irony:

> Die Geburt einer *raving nation* aus dem Geist der Maschinen: Bachanalen der Künstlichkeit [. . .], Stammesritual der Atome, demokratische Ästhetik aus dem Computer — angesiedelt im toten Raum der zerfallenden Industriegesellschaft, mit genau geregelter Anfangs- und Schlußzeit, Merchandising- *und* Müllkonzept [. . .]. Eine gelunge Revolte — ohne Opfer (1999, 33).

This image of harmony is a convenient one on which to hang all-embracing theories that unite mainstream and subculture and accommodate the multifarious "tribes" of postmodern society. The idea of top and bottom in a vertical power hierarchy is gone, because, as Klein assumes, pop culture is not the educational privilege of the few but rather everyday practice. The cultural industry and its consumers therefore share power in a dynamic democratic relationship. Categories such as educated/uneducated class and subculture/mainstream, according to Klein, no longer form oppositions but rather an inseparable dynamic. The various cultural fields are no longer closed-off cultures or classes but numerous socially differentiated part-cultures, tribes, or "Lebenswelten." Continually in flux, these are no longer defined in terms of what divides them but what joins them (292).

Such theories are, however, so abstract and general that the tensions between social and aesthetic groups within rave itself, with their differences in style and philosophy, become obscured. Sarah Thornton's useful idea of subcultural capital[63] is often invoked without its full implications being explored. Following on from Bourdieu's concept of cultural capital,[64] subcultural capital is possessed by people with an instinct for style who are at the cutting edge of innovation. But this is no different from previous pop movements in the crucial respect that it is only ever a few innovators — in the short period of time before an underground cultural trend becomes appropriated by the mainstream — for whom the acquisition of culture is a genuinely original act. The defenders of the creativity and democracy of techno culture seem to ignore this. The emphasis on rave's democratic, do-it-yourself aspect often leaves the impression that subcultural capital is as easily accessible as the Internet.

Outside the Harmonious Vision

The nihilistic hedonism of Spiral Tribe, a traveling British "free party" cooperative, presented an example of a dystopianism that sat uneasily with the party spirit of the beautifully groomed teenagers of German mainstream techno. Back in 1993, as Reynolds writes, this group briefly formed an integral part of Berlin's illegal party scene. Spiral Tribe's loud and hard "terra-technic" music, stripped down to harmony and rhythm, took a stance against formal notions of music in civilized Western society that demand melody. It set out to combine the voodoo pulses of primitive African tribal music with technology,[65] the aim being to unlock "the primal energy of Mother Earth" (138). Spiral Tribe's anarchic philosophy was influenced by the writings of avant-garde poet-philosopher Hakim Bey, for example, *The Temporary Autonomous Zone* (1990).[66] The title of the book refers to a

> "microcosm" of that "anarchist dream" of a free culture [whose] success depends on its very impermanence. The "nomadic war machine" conquers without being noticed, filling "cracks and vacancies" left by the State, then scattering in order to regroup and attack elsewhere. (143)

Such a nomadic existence in search of "cracks and vacancies" was very much the story of Spiral Tribe in the early 1990s. Arrested at the Castlemorton festival in 1992 for "causing a public nuisance contrary to common law" (144), they subsequently fled to Europe and in October 1993 were to be found camped out in their lorries on the derelict no-man's-land of Potsdamer Platz in Berlin. They were attracted by the exciting period of transition in Berlin after the reunification of the city, where cultural scenes had not yet solidified. The cooperative put on illegal raves and after only three weeks in Berlin had their PA system confiscated by the police.[67] Later they moved to the grounds of *Tacheles,* the legendary venue run by autonomous punks and artists, before leaving Berlin in May 1994 complaining that the city was settling down into a commercial rut again; the creative in-between period was over.[68]

It is precisely this creative "Zwischenstand" and the exploitation of society's "cracks and vacancies" that forms the basis of the philosophy behind Achim Szepanski's Frankfurt based "art-techno" label Mille Plateaux, named after Gilles Deleuze and Felix Guattari's *A Thousand Plateaus,* whose theory it is guided by. According to Deleuze and Guattari, society is no longer governed by a basic class conflict but is subdivided in a more complex way. They see a social field (a "plateau") riven with lines and cracks, one that constitutes a multitude of constantly mutating relationships and conflicts between mainstream and subcultures.[69] In a process termed "deterritorialization," subcultures continually create new space outside the bounds of the mainstream. This space is, however, eventually "reterritorialized" by the mainstream. Mille Plateaux represents the search for this new space in music. Szepanski's philosophy is: "nach Strategien und Fluchtlinien zu suchen: [. . .] die Schnittstellen finden, an denen man sich an die maschinellen Gefüge ankoppelt [. . .] und danach wieder an einem anderen Ort sein, an dem man uns nicht vermutet."[70] Translated into music on the *Gas* project of the techno artist Mike Inc, this comes across like an amorphous sound of strings — similar to a plane ("plateau") — that mutates gradually as a result of subtle ever-new rhythmic pulses or sonic effects creeping in from the periphery.[71]

Mille Plateaux's political stance also expresses itself in regard to the process of sound creation. Szepanski relates how recorded music restricts the sound current by filtering out noise and crackles: "Perfekte Melodien und perfekte Akkorde bieten uns Volks- und Popmusik täglich, das Zirkulieren eines gesäuberten Klangstroms, gesäubert von all den Geräuschen und Klängen, die den Wohlstand stören könnten."[72] This has a numbing effect on the listener. For Szepanski the challenge for new electronic music is to reveal the full intensity of the mechanical process of sound creation: "Man muß das Tor für das Geräusch selbst öffnen, den Kanal für den Klangstrom selbst zum Beben bringen" (190). Alec Empire from Atari Teenage Riot, who also released solo work with Mille Plateaux has spoken of the need for an "Aufsplitterung von Hörgewohnheiten" in order to expose the media's manipulation of ways of perception, "weil wir uns auf eine Gesellschaft zubewegen, die schlimmer ist als das Dritte Reich."[73] The less overtly politicized group Oval has a likewise deconstructionist approach, as in its use of samples of noises a CD makes when written on with a felt pen (2000). Similarly, the fifth (unnamed) track on the *Gas* album of 1996 forms a diffusely cloudy sound with an endlessly looped unresolving dominant seventh chord. A base kick-drum gives a muffled pulse, but this rhythm is continually undermined by the sound of a record scratch.

Mille Plateaux exploits the potential of technology to create a deterritorializing effect whereby perceptions of time and space are destabilized. It uses, for example, unexpected, jarring rattles and creaks and sound perceptions reminiscent of madness, such as hissing or screaming. Another example is the stereo effect where the sound dances from one side of the spectrum to the other. Such techniques necessitate, according to Szepanski, a new schizoid, deterritorialized form of hearing: "denn der Schizophrene selbst ist deterritorialisiert, er folgt den Klangströmen, er spielt mit der Wirkung und der Kraft der Droge, ohne auf Droge zu sein" (193). In contrast to this, Szepanski, referring to Deleuze's comment on music's fascist potential, relates how mainstream techno feeds the masses a diet of what they already know: "Man mobilisert die Massen mit Images und Wiedererkennungswerten und stellt sie zugleich still" (194).

Like Klein, Szepanski notes the creative potential of the club's space of simulation, not defined by four walls, but by the virtuality of the lighting, music, and the dancing-body motion that alters perceptions of space and time. But the locations of mass raves do not encourage this. Rather than corresponding to the concept of the decentralized dance floor, they in fact produce areas where lines of escape are cut off; where "durch visuelle und nichtvisuelle Säule tradierte geometrische Anordnungen der Räume neu aktualisiert [werden]." For Szepanski, this type of space defines the contours within which the masses can move. It is reflected in the music, which is reduced to "Erkennungsmelodie und stupide Metrik" where only the bass drum predominates (196).

In this criticism of a conformist, even fascistic aesthetic in music we appear to go full circle back to Eisler's political song theory of the late 1920s. There is a parallel, for example, between Oval's defamiliarization of sounds in their sampling techniques and Eisler's use of montage: the cutting up and recasting of familiar musical styles in order to jar the listener into alertness. There are also similarities in the use of rhythm: the cross-rhythmic beats of Atari Teenage Riot are a counterpart to the mind-numbing rhythms of popular *Schlager,* which Eisler considered to be fascistic. But where Eisler and Brecht envisaged a mass movement as the recipients and practitioners of their political songs and believed that their songs could change the world, the oppositional music of the German alternative techno DJs has more modest ambitions: it is subcultural resistance of an aesthetic nature. It remains to be seen whether the multitude of "tribes" and "Lebenswelten" of postmodern society's "big mix" can ever be united sufficiently by any one political cause to give rise to a music or song movement with aspirations to change society such as was experienced in the *Vormärz,* in the revolutionary 1920s, in the 1960s and 1970s in West Germany, and from the 1960s until 1990 in the GDR.

Notes

[1] Holger Böning, *Der Traum von einer Sache: Aufstieg und Fall der Utopien im politischen Lied der Bundesrepublik und der DDR* (Bremen: edition Lumière, 2004), 5–6.

[2] For example, the one-day conference "Zwischen Liebe und Zorn" in Kulturhaus-Mitte, Berlin, October, 1993, attended by this author. Bettina Wegner accused her former colleagues in the Hootenanny-Klub of crossing the street to avoid her in the years after her arrest in 1968. Jürgen Eger and others were involved in a heated discussion regarding whether or not the *Liedermacher* had done enough to help Stephan Krawczyk in 1988.

[3] Wenzel speaking in the *Kulturbrauerei,* Berlin, 3 March 1998.

[4] See Wiglaf Droste, "It's a Zoni. Fußnote zu Gundermann" in *TAZ,* 17 July 1998, 16.

[5] "Sänger ohne Schützengel" in *Der Speigel,* 2 July 1998, 179.

[6] Gerhard Gundermann, *Der 7te Sumarai* (Buschfunk, 1993).

[7] Gerhard Gundermann, "pferd aus holz," on CD *Der 7te Sumarai.*

[8] Gerhard Gundermann, "ruhetag," on CD *Der 7te Sumarai*

[9] Gerhard Gundermann, "kann dich nicht mehr leiden," on CD *Der 7te Sumarai.*

[10] "Gundermann, Kein Leben ohne Engel," in *Berliner Zeitung,* 23 June 1998, 9.

[11] Gerhard Gundermann, "sieglinde," on CD *Der 7te Sumurai.*

[12] Gerhard Gundermann, *Frühstück für immer* (Buschfunk, 1995).

[13] Gerhard Gundermann, *Engel über dem Revier* (Buschfunk, 1997).

[14] Gerhard Gundermann, "leine los," on CD *Engel über dem Revier.*

[15] Gerhard Gundermann, "engel über dem revier," on CD *Engel über dem Revier.*

[16] Wenzel & Mensching, "Aufenthalt in der Hölle," unpublished manuscript and video recording in Wenzel's archive, 1992.

[17] See Rolf Tiedemann's comments on "die Ewigkeit der Hölle" in his introduction to Walter Benjamin, *Das Passagenwerk, Erster Teil* (Frankfurt am Main: Suhrkamp, 1983), 21.

[18] The following section on *Aufenthalt in der Hölle* and *Hanswurst und andere arme Würste* contains extracts from David Robb, "Epic Operette and Anti-Culinary

Clowning: Exposing the Illusion in the Liedertheater of Wenzel & Mensching," *The Brecht Yearbook* 30 (2005): 335–52.

[19] Personal interview with Wenzel, 9 March 1994.

[20] Wenzel and Mensching, "Aufenthalt in der Hölle," act 5, page 6). Published in Steffen Mensching, *Berliner Elegien: Gedichte* (Leipzig: Faber & Faber, 1995), 49.

[21] Wenzel and Mensching, "Aufenthalt in der Hölle," act 5, page 4.

[22] Volker Braun, *Rimbaud: Ein Psalm der Aktualität*, in *SuF* 5 (1985) 986, quoted in Leeder, 151.

[23] Concert program for *Aufenthalt in der Hölle* (May 1992).

[24] Wenzel and Mensching, "Linksoptimist," on CD *Der Abschied der Matrosen vom Kommunismus* (Nebelhorn, 1993). This song does not appear in the published text *Der Abschied der Matrosen vom Kommunismus* (Berlin: Eulenspiegel Verlag 1999).

[25] Wenzel and Mensching, *Der Abschied der Matrosen*, 181.

[26] CD booklet of Hans-Eckardt Wenzel, *Hanswurst und andere arme Würste* (Conträr, 2001).

[27] See Wenzel, "Grenzen (sechs Gedichte für Hölderlin)," in *Lied vom wilden Mohn: Gedichte* (Halle and Leipzig: Mitteldeutscher Verlag, 1984), 53–58. See also Karls Enkel, "Die komische Tragödie des 18. Brumaire," unpublished manuscript and video recording from 1983, collected by Karin Wolf, archive of the Akademie der Künste der DDR, Berlin, Liedertheater-Dokumentation, Forschungsabteilung Musik/Liedzentrum.

[28] See Mensching's solo program "Amok," 2001.

[29] Lutz Kirchenwitz, "Nachwort zu einem Festival" in *Festival Musik und Politik 2001: Vorträge und Protokolle* (Berlin: Lied und soziale Bewegungen e.V., 2001), 4.

[30] Rainer von Vielen, "Sandbürger," on *Rainer von Vielen* CD (Ebenso-Musik, 2005).

[31] Rainer von Vielen, "Leben den Lebenden," on *Rainer von Vielen*.

[32] Sections of this analysis of German techno have already appeared in David Robb, "Techno in Germany: Musical Origins and Cultural Relevance," *German as a Foreign Language* 8, 2 (2002): 130–49 (Special issue: Youth Literature and Culture, ed. Susan Tebbut).

[33] Simon Reynolds, *Energy Flash: A Journey through Rave Music and Dance Culture* (London: Picador, 1998), 239.

[34] Philip Anz and Patrick Walder, eds., *Techno* (Reinbek: Rowohlt, 1999), 14–15.

[35] Olivia Henkel and Karsten Wolff, *Berlin Underground: Techno and Hiphop; Zwischen Mythos und Ausverkauf* (Berlin: FAB Verlag, 1996), 64.

[36] See Reynolds, *Energy Flash*, 108–12. See also Henkel and Wolff, *Berlin Underground*, 84.

[37] See Reynolds, *Energy Flash*, 221–23.

[38] Harald Fricke, "Von der Motorik weit entfernt" in *TAZ*, 19 February 1993, 16. The Deleuze/Guattari theoretical influence behind Mille Plateaux and its relationship to the German techno scene will be analyzed in the final section of this chapter.

[39] See Markus Klemm, "Tanzen bis zum Umfallen" in *TAZ,* 2 April 1994, 48.

[40] Henkel and Wolff, *Berlin Underground,* 167.

[41] Quoted in Henkel and Wolff, *Berlin Underground,* 163.

[42] Reynolds, *Energy Flash,* 392–93.

[43] Wolle Neugebauer, interview with *Tip* "Aus lauter Liebe" in *Tip* 15 (1999): 19.

[44] Events, *Minitip,* July 1999, 11.

[45] For information on the Fuck Parade see http://www.bembelterror.de/fuckparade/2001/fp2001_about.html.

[46] Reynolds, *Energy Flash,* 392.

[47] See Christof Meuler, "Auf Montage im Techno-Land" in SpoKK (Arbeitsgruppe für symbolische Politik, Kultur und Kommunikation), ed., *Kursbuch Jugendkultur* (Mannheim, Bollmann, 1997), 243–50. The term "bricolage" was introduced by Claude Lévi-Strauss in an anthropological context in *Das wilde Denken* (Frankfurt am Main: Suhrkamp, 1968).

[48] See Dick Hebdige: *Subculture: The Meaning of Style* (London: Routledge, 1979).

[49] Paul Willis and others, ed: *Jugend-Stile. Zur Ästhetik der gemeinsamen Kultur* (1991, 24). Described in Gabriel Klein, *Electronic Vibration: Pop Kultur Theorie* (Hamburg: Rogner & Bernhard bei Zweitausendeins, 1999), 235.

[50] Klein, *Electronic Vibration,* 249. See Pierre Bourdieu, "Zur Genese der Begriffe Habitus und Feld," in *Der Tote packt den Lebenden: Schriften zu Politik und Kultur 2,* ed. Margareta Steinrücke (Hamburg: VSA-Verlag, 1997), 59–72.

[51] Klein, *Electronic Vibration,* 262–63.

[52] "Weltstadt Berlin!" in *Die Zeit,* 14 July 1995, 5. Quoted in Klein, *Electronic Vibration,* 18.

[53] See Walter Benjamin, *Das Kunstwerk im Zeitalter seiner technischen Reproduzierbarkeit* (Frankfurt am Main: edition suhrkamp 28, 1966).

[54] Falko Blask and Michael Fuchs-Gamböck, *Techno. Eine Generation in Ekstase* (Bergisch Glabach: Bastei-Lübbe, 1995), 77–136.

[55] At the Love Parade a bricolage of fancy dress and accessories greets the eye: jokers firing giant water pistols into the crowd, red cat suits, gas masks, rubbish-collector jackets and space-age Mr Spock outfits; men in drag, sexily, scantily dressed women (and men) with dyed, waxed hair and tinsel covered bodies.

[56] Martin Jankowski, "Tanz nach zwölf. Techno als Erscheinungsform Democratischer Decadence Reality," *Deutsche Vierteljahrsschrift für Literaturwissenschaft und Geisteswissenschaft,* LXXIII, 1 (1999): 32

[57] Jankowski, "Tanz nach zwölf," 33.

[58] Klein, *Electronic Vibration,* 65

[59] Reynolds, *Energy Flash,* xxxi

[60] Reynolds, *Energy Flash,* 392.

[61] For Nietzsche, Dionysus was the god of wine and decadence, while Apollo presided over logic, light, and clarity.

[62] Mark Terkessidis, "Life after History: How Pop and Politics are Changing Places in the Berlin Republic," *Debatte: Review of Contemporary German Affairs* 6, 2 (1998): 181.

[63] Sarah Thornton, *Club Cultures: Music, Media and Subcultural Capital* (Cambridge: Polity Press, 1995), 11–14.

[64] Pierre Bourdieu, *Distinction: A Social Critique of the Judgement of Taste*, trans. R. Nice (Cambridge, MA: Harvard UP, 1984).

[65] Reynolds, *Energy Flash*, 143.

[66] Hakim Bey, *The Temporary Autonomous Zone* (Brooklyn: Autonomedia, 2004).

[67] Anita Kugler, "Leben im Niemandsland" in *TAZ*, 29 October 1993, 11.

[68] Wolfgang Borrs, "Mutoid Waste Company" in *TAZ*, 17 May 1994, 20.

[69] See Christian Höller, "Widerstandsrituale und Pop-Plateaus. Birmingham School, Deleuze/Guattari und Popkultur heute," in Tom Holert and Mark Terkessidis, eds., *Mainstream der Minderheiten: Pop in der Kontrollgesellschaft* (Berlin: Edition ID-Archiv, 1996), 64.

[70] Achim Szepanski, in interview with Katja Diefenbach, "Den Klangstrom zum Beben bringen," in Anz and Walder, *Techno*, 191.

[71] Gas, *Gas* (Mille Plateaux, 1998).

[72] Szepanski, interview with Diefenbach, "Den Klangstrom zum Beben bringen," in Anz and Walder, *Techno*, 191.

[73] Alec Empire, quoted in Gerrit Bartels, "Der Schaum der Tage" in *TAZ*, 25 November 1995, 36.

Works Cited

Primary Works

Books, Collections of Lyrics, Articles, Manuscripts

Aktiva 1–7: Forschungs- und Gedenkstätten: Lieder, Texte, Dokumente. Berlin: Liedzentrum der Akademie der Künste der DDR, 1985–89.

Biermann, Wolf. *Alle Lieder.* Cologne: Kiepenheuer & Witsch, 1991.

———. *Deutschland. Ein Wintermärchen.* Berlin: Verlag Klaus Wagenbach, 1972.

———. *Die Drahtharfe.* Berlin: Klaus Wagenbach, 1965.

———. *Heimat: Neue Gedichte.* Hamburg: Hoffmann and Campe Verlag, 2006.

———. *Liebespaare in politischer Landschaft: Gedichte und Lieder.* Stuttgart: Reclam, 2000.

———. *Mit Marx- und Engelszungen.* Berlin: Klaus Wagenbach, 1965.

———. *Nachlaß 1.* Cologne: Kiepenheuer & Witsch, 1977.

———. *Paradies uff Erden: Ein Berliner Bilderbogen.* Cologne: Kiepenheuer & Witsch, 1999.

———. *Der Sturz des Dädalus.* Cologne: Kiepenheuer & Witsch, 1992.

———. *Über das Geld und andere Herzensdinge.* Cologne: Kiepenheuer & Witsch, 1991.

———. *Über Deutschland unter Deutschen.* Cologne: Kiepenheuer & Witsch, 2002.

———. *Verdrehte Welt — das seh' ich gerne.* Cologne: Kiepenheuer & Witsch, 1982.

Borchert, Wolfgang. *Das Gesamtwerk.* Ed. Bernhard Meyer-Marwitz. Reinbek bei Hamburg: Rowohlt, 1977.

Brecht, Bertolt. *Arbeitsjournal.* Berlin and Weimar: Aufbau Verlag, 1977.

———. *Gedichte.* Leipzig: Reclam 1976.

———. *Gesammelte Werke.* Vol. 8. Frankfurt am Main: Suhrkamp, 1967.

———. *Die Stücke von Bertolt Brecht in einem Band*. Frankfurt am Main: Suhrkamp, 1978.

———. *Werke: Große kommentierte Berliner und Frankfurter Ausgabe*. Ed. Wolfgang Hecht, Jan Knopf, Werner Mittenzwei, and Klaus-Detlef Müller. 30 vols. Berlin and Weimar: Aufbau; Frankfurt am Main: Suhrkamp, 1988–93.

Busch, Ernst, ed. *Canciones de las Brigadas Internacionales*. Madrid: Im Auftrag der 11. Internationalen Brigade, 1937.

Degenhardt, Franz Josef. *Im Jahr der Schweine: 27 Neue Lieder mit Noten*. Hamburg: Hoffmann und Kampe, 1970.

———. *Laß nicht die roten Hähne flattern: Lieder mit Noten*. Munich: Bertelsmann, 1974.

———. *Spiel nicht mit den Schmuddelkindern: Balladen, Chansons, Grotesken, Lieder*. Reinbek bei Hamburg: Rowohlt, 1969.

Eisler, Hanns. *Musik und Politik. Schriften 1924–1948*. Leipzig: VEB Deutscher Verlag für Musik, 1973.

———. *Musik und Politik: Textkritische Ausgabe*. Leipzig: Deutscher Verlag für Musik, 1982.

Enzensberger, Hans Magnus. *Einzelheiten II: Poesie und Politik*. Frankfurt am Main: Suhrkamp, 1976.

Heine, Heinrich. *Atta Troll; Deutschland, ein Wintermärchen*. Ed. Barker Fairley. London: Oxford UP, 1966.

———. *Briefe 1843–1849*. Vol. 22 of *Werke: Briefwechsel. Lebenszeugnisse*. Säkularausgabe. Ed. Nationale Forschungs- und Gedenkstaetten der klassischen deutschen Literatur in Weimar and the Centre National de la Recherche Scientifique in Paris. Berlin: Akademie-Verlag, 1972.

———. *Deutschland. Ein Wintermärchen*. Heine, *Werke*, vol. 2. Berlin and Weimar: Aufbau Verlag, 1974.

———. *Reisebilder*. Munich: Goldmann, 1982.

Herwegh, Georg. *Herweghs Werke: Erster Teil. Gedichte eines Lebendigen*. Berlin: Deutscher Verlagshaus Bong & Co., 1909.

Hölderlin, Friedrich. *Hyperion*. Munich: Goldman, 1981.

———. *Hyperion*. Stuttgart: Reclam, 1983.

Karls Enkel. "Dahin! Dahin! Ein Göte-Abend." Unpublished manuscript and tape recording from 1982, collected by Karin Wolf, archive of the Akademie der Künste der DDR, Berlin, Liedertheater-Dokumentation, Forschungsabteilung Musik/Liedzentrum.

———. "Deutschland meine Trauer — neun Arten einen Becher zu beschreiben. Ein Johannes-R.-Becher-Abend." Unpublished manuscript and tape recording from 1981, collected by Karin Wolf, archive of the Akademie der Künste der DDR, Berlin, Liedertheater-Dokumentation, Forschungsabteilung Musik/Liedzentrum.

———. "Komm rücken wir näher zusammen." Unpublished manuscript in Wenzel's archive, 1977.

———. "s'geht los! aber nicht mit Chassepots: Eine Collage über die Zeit des Sozialistengesetzes." Unpublished manuscript and tape recording from 1980, collected by Karin Wolf, archive of the Akademie der Künste der DDR, Berlin, Liedertheater-Dokumentation, Forschungsabteilung Musik/Liedzentrum.

———. "Spanier aller Länder." Unpublished manuscript and tape recording from 1985, collected by Karin Wolf, archive of the Akademie der Künste der DDR, Berlin, Liedertheater-Dokumentation, Forschungsabteilung Musik/Liedzentrum.

———. "Vorfahrt." Unpublished manuscript and tape recording from 1977, collected by Karin Wolf, archive of the Akademie der Künste der DDR, Berlin, Liedertheater-Dokumentation, Forschungsabteilung Musik/Liedzentrum.

———. "Zieharmonie." Unpublished manuscript and tape recording from 1978, collected by Karin Wolf, archive of the Akademie der Künste der DDR, Berlin, Liedertheater-Dokumentation, Forschungsabteilung Musik/Liedzentrum.

Kolbe, Uwe. *Hineingeborenen: Gedichte 1975–1979*. Berlin and Weimar: Aufbau, 1980.

Kraus, Karl. *Aphorismen*, ed. Christian Wagenknecht. Frankfurt am Main: Suhrkamp, 1986.

Lammel, Inge., ed. *Das Lied im Kampf geboren: Heft 1: Lieder der Revolution von 1848*. Leipzig: VEB Friedrich Hofmeister, 1957.

Lindenberg, Udo. *Hinterm Horizont geht's weiter: Alle Texte von 1946 bis heute*. Düsseldorf: Econ, 1996.

Luxemburg, Rosa. *Gesammelte Werke*. Vol. 4. August 1914–January 1918. Berlin: Dietz Verlag, 1979.

Marx, Karl. *Der 18. Brumaire des Louis Bonaparte*. Berlin: Dietz Verlag, 1974.

Marx, Karl, and Friedrich Engels. *Werke*. Berlin: Dietz Verlag, 1972.

Mehring, Walter. *Chronik der Lustbarkeiten: Die Lieder, Gedichte und Chansons 1918–1933*. Düsseldorf: Classen Verlag, 1981.

Mensching, Steffen. *Erinnerung an eine Milchglasscheibe: Gedichte*. Halle and Leipzig: Mitteldeutscher Verlag, 1984.

———. *Tuchfühlung: Gedichte.* Halle and Leipzig: Mitteldeutscher Verlag, 1987.

Mossmann, Walter, and Peter Schleuning. *Alte und neue politische Lieder: Entstehung und Gebrauch. Texte und Noten.* Reinbek bei Hamburg: Rowohlt Taschenbuch, 1978.

Mühsam, Erich. *Brennende Erde: Verse eines Kämpfers.* Munich: Kurt Wolff Verlag, 1920.

———. "Generalstreik!" *Kain* 5 (1912): 65.

———. "Generalstreikmarsch." *Freiheit* 28, 34 (1906): 1.

———. *Der Krater: Gedichte.* Berlin: Morgen Verlag, 1909.

———. *Sammlung 1898–1928: Auswahl aus dem dichterischen Werk.* Berlin: J. M. Spaeth, 1928.

Rimbaud, Arthur. *Une Saison en Enfer.* Reclam: Stuttgart, 1992.

Ringelnatz, Joachim. *Kuttel-Daddeldu.* Zurich: Diogenes, 2006.

———. *Kuttel-Daddeldu: Mit Zeichnungen von Karl Arnold.* Munich: Kurt Wolff Verlag, 1923.

Schwendter, Rolf. *Ich bin noch immer unbefriedigt: Lieder zum freien Gebrauch.* Berlin: Rotbuch Verlag, 1980.

Stern, Annemarie. *Lieder gegen den Tritt: Politische Lieder aus fünf Jahrhunderten.* Oberhausen: Asso, 1972.

Stipriaan, Ulrich von. *55 Volkstänze — niederdeutsche Kreistänze und Quadrillen, Polkas, Walzer, Rundtänze.* Nottuln: Folkshop-Edition, 1978.

Tucholsky, Kurt. *Das Kurt Tucholsky Chanson Buch: Texte und Noten.* Reinbek bei Hamburg: Rowohlt, 1983.

Wacholder. "Trotz Alledem: 1848 Revolutionslieder." Unpublished manuscript and video from 1984, collected by Karin Wolf, archive of the Akademie der Künste der DDR, Berlin, Liedertheater-Dokumentation, Forschungsabteilung Musik/Liedzentrum.

Wecker, Konstantin. *Ich will noch eine ganze Menge leben: Songs, Gedichte, Prosa.* Munich: Ehrenwirth, 1978.

———. *Im Namen des Wahnsinns: Ein Spiel von Frieden und Menschlichkeit.* Munich: Ehrenwirth, 1983.

———. *Jetzt eine Insel finden: Vorläufige Gedichte und Lieder.* Reinbek bei Hamburg: Rowohlt, 1986.

———. *Lieder und Gedichte.* Munich: Ehrenwirth, 1981.

———. *Schon Schweigen ist Betrug: Die kompletten Liedtexte.* Heidelberg: Palmyra, 2005.

————. *Tobe, zürne, misch dich ein!: Widerreden und Fürsprachen,* ed. Hans-Dieter Schütt. Berlin: Eulenspiegel, 2003. (= Wecker 2003a).

————. *Und die Seele nach außen kehren: Ketzerbriefe eines Süchtigen — Uns ist kein Einzelnes bestimmt. Neun Elegien.* Cologne: Kiepenheuer & Witsch, 1993.

Wedekind, Frank. *Gesammelte Werke.* Vol. 1. Munich: Georg Müller Verlag, 1920.

Wegner, Bettina. *Wenn meine Lieder nicht mehr stimmen.* Reinbek bei Hamburg: Rowohlt Taschenbuch, 1979.

Wenzel, Hans-Eckardt. *Lied vom wilden Mohn: Gedichte.* Halle and Leipzig: Mitteldeutscher Verlag, 1984.

Wenzel, Hans-Eckardt, and Steffen Mensching. *Der Abschied der Matrosen vom Kommunismus.* Berlin: Eulenspiegel Verlag 1999.

————. *Allerletzes aus der Da Da eR / Hundekomödie.* Ed. Andrea Doberenz. Halle and Leipzig: Mitteldeutscher Verlag, 1991.

————. "Aufenthalt in der Hölle." Unpublished manuscript from 1992 in Wenzel's personal archive and unpublished video recording from 1992 in Mensching's personal archive.

————. "Neues aus der Da Da eR." Unpublished manuscript and video recording from 1983, collected by Karin Wolf, archive of the Akademie der Künste der DDR, Berlin, Liedertheater-Dokumentation, Forschungsabteilung Musik/Liedzentrum.

Zupfgeigenhansel. *Es wollt ein Bauer früh aufstehn. 222 Volkslieder.* Verlag pläne, 1978.

————. *Kein schöner Land in dieser Zeit.* Verlag pläne, 1984.

Audio Recordings

Ape, Beck & Brinkmann. *Regenbogenland.* LP: FolkFriends, 1981.

Atari Teenage Riot. *Atari Teenage Riot: 1995.* CD: DHR, 1995.

Baier, Frank. *Auf der schwarzen Liste.* LP: Pläne 1981.

Biermann, Wolf. *aah-ja!* LP: CBS, 1974; CD: zweitausendeins, 1996.

————. *Chausseestraße* 131. LP: Verlag Klaus Wagenbach, 1968; CD: Zweitausendeins, 1996.

————. *Es geht sein' sozialistischen Gang.* LP: CBS, 1977; CD: Zweitausendeins, 1996.

————. *Es gibt ein Leben vor dem Tod.* LP: CBS, 1975; CD: Zweitausendeins, 1996.

————. *Heimat: Neue Gedichte.* CD: Hoffmann und Campe, 2006.

———. *Nur wer sich ändert.* CD: Anzahl Discs, 1991.

———. *Paradies uff Erden: Ein Berliner Bilderbogen.* CD: Anzahl Discs, 1999.

———. *Trotzalledem.* LP: CBS, 1977; CD: Zweitausendeins, 1996.

———. *Warte nicht auf bess're Zeiten.* LP: CBS, 1973; CD: Zweitausendeins, 1996.

Busch, Ernst. *Lieder der Arbeiterklasse & Lieder aus dem Spanischen Bürgerkrieg.* CD: Pläne, 1989.

———. *Merkt ihr nischt: Ernst Busch singt Tucholsky/Eisler.* CD: Barbarossa, 1997.

———. *Der rote Orpheus.* CD: Barbarossa, 1996.

Cochise. *Wir wollen leben.* LP: FolkFreaks, 1981.

DDR-Singegruppen. *Junge Leute, Junge Lieder.* LP: VEB Deutsche Schallplatten, 1969.

Degenhardt, Franz Josef. *Degenhardt live.* LP: Polydor, 1968; CD: Polydor, 1992.

———. *Mutter Mathilde.* LP: Polydor, 1972; CD: Polydor, 1992.

———. "Sacco and Vanzetti" and "Befragung eines Kriegsdienstverweigerers." Single: Polydor, 1972.

———. *Spiel nicht mit den Schmuddelkindern: Chansons.* LP: Polydor, 1966; CD: Polydor, 1987.

———. *Von Damals und von dieser Zeit.* CD: Polydor, 1988.

———. *Die Wallfahrt zum Big Zeppelin.* LP: Polydor, 1971; CD: Polydor, 1992.

———. *Zwischen Null Uhr Null und Mitternacht.* LP: Polydor, 1963.

Duo Sonnenschirm. *Flucht nach vorne.* CD: Löwenzahl, 1990.

Fiedel Michel. *Deutsche Folklore.* LP: Autogramm, 1974.

Floh de Cologne. *Profitgeier.* LP: Ohr, 1971; CD: ZYX Music, 1999.

Floh de Cologne & Dieter Süverkrüp. *Vietnam — für fünf Sprech- und Singstimmen Streicher, Bläser, Orgel, Baß, Schlagwerk, Klavier und Gitarren.* LP: Pläne, 1968.

Folkländer. *Wenn man fragt, wer hat's getan . . .* LP: Amiga, 1982; CD: Buschfunk, 1996.

Gas. *Gas.* CD: Mille Plateaux, 1996.

———. *Der Zauberberg.* CD: Mille Plateaux, 1998.

Gundermann, Gerhard. *Der 7te Samurai.* CD: Buschfunk, 1993.

———. *Engel über dem Revier.* CD: Buschfunk, 1997.

———. *Frühstück für immer*. CD: Buschfunk, 1995.

———. *Männer, Frauen und Maschinen*. LP: Amiga, 1988; CD: Amiga Masters, 1993.

Hersterberg, Trude. "Die kleine Stadt." On Various Artists, *Ramona Zundloch: Musikalisches Kabarett in klassischen Interpretationen von 1921–1933*. CD: Edition Berliner Musenkinder, 1999.

Hüsch, Hanns Dieter. *Carmina Urana: Vier Gesänge gegen die Bombe*. EP: Pläne, 1963.

Jam & Spoon. *Tales from a Danceographic Ocean*. EP: R&S, 1992.

Kannmacher, Tom. *Wackawacka Boing & Boom Boom Bang und andere deutsche Lieder*. LP: Songbird, 1974.

Karls Enkel, Wacholder, and Beckert & Schulz. *Die Hammer-Rehwü*. CD: Nebelhorn, 1994.

Kattong. "Rotes Liebeslied" and "Wenn einer Macht besitzt." Single: Eigenverlag/ Juso NRW, 1973.

———. *Stiehl dem Volk die Geduld*. LP: Schwann, 1972.

Krawczyk, Stephan. *Wieder-Stehen*. LP: Self-published, 1988.

Marusha. *Wir*. CD: Low Spirit, 1995.

Mey, Reinhard. *Ich wollte wie Orpheus singen*. LP: Chanson-Edition Reinhard Mey, 1967.

Mossmann, Walter. *Chansons, Balladen, Flugblattlieder* (Box Set). CD: Trikont, 2004.

Mouse on Mars. *Vulvaland*. CD: Rough Trade, 1994.

Oktoberklub. *Das Beste*. CD: Barbarossa, 1995.

———. *Unterm Arm die Gitarre*. LP: VEB Deutsche Schallplatten, 1968.

Oval. *Ovalprocess*. CD: Zomba Records, 2000.

Rohland, Peter. *Lieder deutscher Demokraten*. LP: Teldec, 1967; CD: Thorofon, 1998.

———. *Lieder von anderswo*. LP: Thorofon, 1977.

———. *Seh ich Schwäne nordwärts fliegen*. CD: Thorofon, 2001.

Schöne, Gerhard. *Du hast es nur noch nicht probiert*. LP: Amiga, 1989.

Schwendter, Rolf. *Lieder zur Kindertrommel*. LP: 1970.

Süverkrüpp, Dieter. *Die widerborstigen Gesänge des Dieter Süverkrüp*. LP. Pläne, 1967.

———. *1848: Lieder der deutschen Revolution*. LP: Pläne, 1974; CD: Conträr, 1998.

Süverkrüp, Dieter, and Fasia and the Conrads et al. *Ça ira: Ostersongs 62/63 gegen die Bombe.* LP: Columbia, 1962.

Süverkrüp, Dieter, and Walter Andreas Schwarz. *Ich lade euch zum Requiem.* CD: Conträr, 1995.

Various artists. *1848 . . . weil jetzt die Freiheit blüht: Lieder aus der Revolution von 1848/49.* CD: Südwest Records/Deutsches Volksliedarchiv, 1998.

Various artists. *Bauer Maas — Lieder gegen Atomenergie,* LP: pass op, 1978.

Various artists. *Burg Waldeck Festival 1967.* CD: Wedemark, 2004.

Various artists. *Lieder des europäischen Widerstands gegen den Faschismus.* LP: Pläne, 1965.

Various artists. *Schöner wohnen — Abber fix!* LP-Sampler: pass op, 1981.

Väth, Sven. *Accident in Paradise.* CD: Eye Q, 1993.

von Vielen, Rainer. *Rainer von Vielen.* CD: Ebenso-Musik, 2005.

Wader, Hannes, and Konstantin Wecker. *Was für eine Nacht.* CD: Sony BMG, 2001.

Wader, Hannes, Konstantin Wecker, and Reinhard Mey. *Wader, Wecker, Mey: Das Konzert.* CD: Sony BMG, 2003.

Wecker, Konstantin. *Brecht.* CD: Sony BMG, 1998.

———. *Es lebte ein Kind auf den Bäumen.* CD: Sony BMG, 1998.

———. *Gamsig.* Sony BMG, 1996.

———. *Konstantin Wecker.* CD: Polydor/Zweitausendeins, 1997.

———. *Live.* Double LP: Polydor 1979.

———. *Vaterland.* CD: Sony BMG, 2001.

Wegner, Bettina. *Die Lieder 1978–81.* Vol. 1. CD: Buschfunk, 1997.

Wenzel, Hans-Eckardt. *Hanswurst und andere arme Würste: Hanns-Eisler-Collage.* CD: Conträr Musik, 2001.

———. *Himmelfahrt.* CD: Conträr Musik, 2005.

———. *Reisebilder.* LP: Amiga, 1989; CD: Buschfunk, 1995.

———. *Schöner Lügen.* CD: Conträr Musik, 2000.

———. *Stirb mit mir ein Stück: Liebeslieder.* LP: Amiga, 1987; CD: Buschfunk, 1995.

———. *Ticky Tock: Wenzel singt Woody Guthrie.* CD: Conträr, 2003.

Wenzel, Hans-Eckardt, and Steffen Mensching. *Der Abschied der Matrosen vom Kommunismus.* CD: Nebelhorn, 1993.

Westbam. *Bam Bam Bam.* CD: Low Spirit, 1994.

Video Recordings

Karls Enkel. "Die komische Tragödie des 18. Brumaire des Louis Bonaparte: Nach Karl Marx. Oder Ohrfeigen sind schlimmer als Dolchstöße." Unpublished manuscript and video from 1983, collected by Karin Wolf, archive of the Akademie der Künste der DDR, Berlin, Liedertheater-Dokumentation, Forschungsabteilung Musik/Liedzentrum.

——. "Von meiner Hoffnung laß ich nicht: Der Pilger Mühsam." Unpublished video and manuscript from 1980, collected by Karin Wolf, archive of the Akademie der Künste der DDR, Berlin, Liedertheater-Dokumentation, Forschungsabteilung Musik/Liedzentrum.

Karls Enkel, Wacholder, and Beckert & Schulz. "Die Hammer-Rehwü." Unpublished video from 1982, collected by Karin Wolf, archive of the Akademie der Künste der DDR, Berlin, Liedertheater-Dokumentation, Forschungsabteilung Musik/Liedzentrum.

Radio and Television Broadcasts

"Doppelkopf." Radio program. *Hessischer Rundfunk*. 16 December 2003.

Engel, Richard. *Gundi Gundermann*. TV documentary film. Fernsehen der DDR, 1982.

Grote, Axel, and Christian Steinke. *Sag mir wo du Stehst: Die Geschichte vom Oktoberklub*. TV documentary. ORB, 1993.

"Konstantin Wecker im Gespräch mit Wolf Loeckle." TV program. α-*Forum*. 30 September 2002.

"Porträt Konstantin Wecker." TV program. *3 SAT*. 7 September 1998.

Films

Dudow, Slatan, dir. *Kuhle Wampe*. Germany, 1931/32.

Foth, Jörg, dir. *Letztes aus der Da Da eR*. DEFA, 1990.

Secondary Works

Adorno, Theodor, and Max Horkheimer. *Die Dialektik der Aufklärung: Philosophische Fragmente*. Frankfurt am Main: Fischer, 1988.

Altenhofer, Norbert. *Dichter über ihre Dichtungen: Heinrich Heine*. Vol. 2. Munich: Heimeran Verlag, 1964.

Andert, Reinhold. "Lieder eines Konvertiten." In *Lieder aus einem verschwundenen Land,* ed. Lied und soziale Bewegung e.V., 14–25. Schwerin: Friedrich-Ebert-Stiftung, 1998.

Anz, Philip, and Patrick Walder, eds. *Techno.* Reinbek bei Hamburg: Rowohlt, 1999.

Arbeitskreis für Haus- und Jugendmusik. *Bruder Singer Lieder unseres Volkes.* Kassel, Bärenreiter 1960.

Arnold, Heinz Ludwig, ed. *Franz Josef Degenhardt: Politische Lieder 1964–1972.* Munich: Edition Text + Kritik, 1972.

―――, ed. *Väterchen Franz: Franz Josef Degenhardt und seine politischen Lieder.* Reinbek bei Hamburg: Rowohlt Taschenbuch, 1975.

―――, ed. *Wolf Biermann Text und Kritik.* Munich: Edition Text + Kritik, 1980.

Badisch-Elsässische Bürgerinitiativen, ed. Text pamphlet for the double LP *Dreyeckland — Neue Lieder und Gedichte aus Wyhl, Marckolsheim, Kaiseraugst und Fessenheim.* Munich: Trikont-Verlag, 1977.

Baier, Frank. "Ruhrgebiet — Leben, Kämpfen, Solidarisieren." In Robert von Zahn, *Folk & Liedermacher an Rhein und Ruhr* (Musikland Nordrhein-Westfalen Band 3), ed. Robert von Zahn, 129–93. Münster: Agenda Verlag, 2002.

Bakhtin, Mikhail. *The Dialogic Imagination.* Austin: U of Texas P, 1981.

―――. *Rabelais and his World.* Bloomington: Indiana UP, 1984.

Ball, Hugo. *Flight out of Time: A Dada Diary.* New York: Viking, 1974.

Bathrick, David. "Die Intellektuellen und die Macht: Die Repräsentanz des Schriftstellers in der DDR." In *Schriftsteller als Intellektuelle: Politik und Literatur im Kalten Krieg,* ed. Sven Hanuschek, Therese Hörnigk, Christine Malende, 235–48. Studien und Texte zur Sozialgeschichte der Literatur, vol. 73. Tübingen: Niemeyer 2000.

―――. "Kultur und Öffentlichkeit in der DDR." In *Literatur der DDR in den siebziger Jahren,* ed. P. U. Hohendahl and P. Herminghouse, 51–82. Frankfurt am Main: Suhrkamp, 1983.

Bauch, Günter, ed. *Politisch nicht correct: Konstantin Wecker im Gespräch.* Bassum: Döll Verlag, 2001.

Bausinger, Hermann et al. *Grundzüge der Volkskunde,* vol. 34. 2nd ed. Darmstadt: Wissenschaftliche Buchgesellschaft, 1989.

Bayerdörfer, Hans-Peter. "Vormärz." In *Geschichte der deutschen Lyrik: Vom Mittelalter bis zur Gegenwart,* ed. Walter Hinderer, 308–39. Stuttgart: Reclam, 1983.

Benjamin, Walter. *Das Kunstwerk im Zeitalter seiner technischen Reproduzierbarkeit.* Edition Suhrkamp 28. Frankfurt am Main: Suhrkamp, 1966.

―――. *Lesezeichen, Schriften zur deutschsprachigen Literatur.* Leipzig: Reclam, 1970.

———. *Das Passagenwerk*. Frankfurt am Main: Suhrkamp, 1983.

Betz, Albert. *Hanns Eisler: Political Musician*. Trans. Bill Hopkins. Cambridge: Cambridge UP, 1982.

Bey, Hakim. *The Temporary Autonomous Zone*. Brooklyn: Autonomedia, 2004.

Blask, Falco, and Michael Fuchs-Gamböck. *Techno: Eine Generation in Ekstase*. Bergisch Glabach: Bastei-Lübbe, 1995.

Bloch, Ernst. *Naturrecht und menschliche Würde*. Frankfurt am Main: Suhrkamp, 1961.

———. *Das Prinzip Hoffnung*. 2 vols. Frankfurt am Main: Suhrkamp, 1959.

Blühdorn, Annette. *Pop and Poetry: Pleasure and Protest. Udo Lindenberg, Konstantin Wecker and the Tradition of German Cabaret*. Oxford, Bern, Berlin, Bruxelles, Frankfurt am Main, New York, Vienna: Peter Lang, 2003.

Böning, Holger. *Der Traum von einer Sache: Aufstieg und Fall der Utopien im politischen Lied der Bundesrepublik und der DDR*. Bremen: Edition Lumière, 2004.

Böpple, Friedrich, and Ralf Knüfer. *Generation XTC: Techno & Ekstase*. Munich: Deutscher Taschenbuch Verlag, 1998.

Bourdieu, Pierrre. *Distinction: A Social Critique of the Judgement of Taste*. Trans. Richard Nice. London: Routledge; Cambridge, MA: Harvard UP, 1984.

———. "Zur Genese der Begriffe Habitus und Feld." In *Der Tote packt den Lebenden: Schriften zu Politik und Kultur 2,* ed. Margareta Steinrücke, 59–72. Hamburg: VSA-Verlag, 1997.

Brand, Karl-Werner, Detlef Büsser, and Dieter Rucht. *Aufbruch in eine andere Gesellschaft: Neue soziale Bewegungen in der Bundesrepublik*. Frankfurt am Main and New York: Campus Verlag, 1983.

Braun, Volker. "Rimbaud: Ein Psalm der Aktualität." *Sinn und Form* 5 (1985): 978.

Brocken, Michael. *The British Folk Revival: 1944–2002*. Aldershot: Ashgate, 2003.

Budzinski, Klaus. *Die öffentlichen Spaßmacher*. Munich: List-Verlag, 1966.

Bullivant, Keith, and C. Jane Rice. "Reconstruction and Integration: The Culture of West German Stabilization 1945 to 1968." In *German Cultural Studies,* ed. Rob Burns, 209–25. Oxford: Oxford UP, 1995.

Bundesministerium für Bildung und Wissenschaft, ed. "Soziokultur — Innovation für Kultur, Bildung und Gesellschaft. Dokumentation des Symposiums am 9.–10.10.1987 in Tübingen." Typescript. Bonn: Bundesministerium für Bildung und Wissenschaft 1988.

———, ed. "Vielfalt als Konzeption, Zu der Arbeit soziokultureller Zentren und den Anforderungen an ihre Mitarbeiter." Typescript. Bonn: Bundesministerium für Bildung und Wissenschaft, 1990.

Burns, Rob, and Wilfried van der Will. "The Federal Republic 1968 to 1990: From the Industrial Society to the Cultural Society." In *German Cultural Studies: An Introduction*, ed. Rob Burns, 257–323. Oxford and New York: Oxford UP, 1996.

Club Voltaire, ed. *Pressedokumentationen des Tübinger Festivals*. Tübingen: Eigenverlag, 1976–86.

———, ed. *Programmbücher des Tübinger Festivals*. Tübingen: Eigenverlag, 1975–87.

Contraste: Zeitung für Selbstverwaltung. 1984–.

Cook, Susan C. *The Opera for a New Republic: The Zeitopern of Krenek, Weill, and Hindemith*. Ann Arbor, MI: UMI Research Press, 1988.

Dehm, Diether (Lerryn). *Politik live gemacht, Kulturarbeit und* politische *Praxis*. Wuppertal: Peter Hammer Verlag, 1984.

Deutscher Städtetag, ed. *Wege zur menschlichen Stadt*. Stuttgart: Kohlhammer Verlag, 1973.

Diefenbach, Katja. "Den Klangstrom zum Beben bringen" (Interview with Achim Szepanski). In *Techno*, ed. Philip Anz and Patrick Walder, 188–96. Reinbek bei Hamburg: Rowohlt, 1999.

Dümling, Albrecht. *Laßt Euch nicht verführen: Brecht und die Musik*. Munich: Kindler, 1985.

Emmerich, Wolfgang. *Kleine Literaturgeschichte der DDR*. Expanded edition. Leipzig: Kiepenheuer, 1996.

Eser, Arno Frank. *Konstantin Wecker: Der Himmel brennt*. Berlin: Ch. Links, 1996.

Flender, Christine, Ansgar Jerrentrupp, and Uwe Husslein. *Tief im Westen, Rock und Pop in NRW*. Musikland Nordrhein-Westfalen, vol. 2. Cologne: Emons-Verlag, 1999.

Folker!: Das Magazin für Folk, Lied und Weltmusik. 1998–.

Foster, Stephen C. *Dada/Dimensions*. Ann Arbor, MI: UMI Research Press, 1985.

Frey, Jürgen, and Kaarel Siniveer. *Eine Geschichte der Folkmusik*. Reinbek bei Hamburg: Rowohlt Taschenbuch, 1987.

Frith, Simon. *Performing Rites: Evaluating Popular Music*. Oxford and New York: Oxford UP, 1998.

Gaskill, Howard, Karin McPherson, and Andrew Barker, eds. *Neue Ansichten: Reception of Romanticism in the Literature of the GDR. German Monitor* 6 (1990).

Glaser, Hermann. *Deutsche Kultur 1945–2000.* Bonn: Bundeszentrale für politische Bildung (Lizenzausgabe), 2003.

Graves, Peter. *Three Contemporary German Poets: Wolf Biermann, Sarah Kirsch, Reiner Kunze.* Leicester: Leicester UP, 1985.

Habermas, Jürgen. *Die neue Unübersichtlichkeit.* Frankfurt am Main: Suhrkamp, 1985.

Hanneken, Bernhard. "Folk in Nordrhein-Westfalen." In *Folk & Liedermacher an Rhein und Ruhr,* ed. Robert von Zahn, 11–75. Musikland Nordrhein-Westfalen, vol. 3. Münster: Agenda-Verlag, 2002.

Hasche, Christa. "Bürgerliche Revue und 'Roter Rummel.' Studien zur Entwicklung massenwirksamen Theaters in den Formen der Revue in Berlin 1903–1925." Diss. Berlin: Humboldt University, 1980.

Hebdige, Dick. *Subculture: The Meaning of Style.* London: Routledge, 1979.

Henke, Matthias. *Die großen Chansonniers und Liedermacher: Verflechtungen, Berührungspünkte, Anregungen.* Düsseldorf: ECON, 1987.

Henkel, Olivia, and Karsten Wolff. *Berlin Underground: Techno and Hiphop: Zwischen Mythos und Ausverkauf.* Berlin: FAB Verlag, 1996.

Hepp, Michael. *Verleihung des Kurt Tucholsky-Preises für literarische Publizistik 1995 an Konstantin Wecker.* Ed. on behalf of the Kurt Tucholsky-Gesellschaft. Berlin: Kurt Tucholsky-Gesellschaft, 1996.

Hermand, Jost. *Grüne Utopien in Deutschland: Zur Geschichte des ökologischen Bewußtseins.* Frankfurt am Main: Fischer, 1991.

Hilbk, Merle. "Das Ende vom Lied." *Die Zeit* 20 (2000): 13–15.

Hirdina, Karin. "Präzision ohne Pingelichkeit: Wenzel und Mensching im Gespräch mit Karin Hirdina." *Temperamente* 4 (1984): 35–43.

Höller, Christian. "Widerstandsrituale und Pop-Plateaus. Birmingham School, Deleuze/Guattari und Popkultur heute." In *Mainstream der Minderheiten: Pop in der Kontrollgesellschaft,* ed. Tom Holert and Mark Terkessidis, 55–71. Berlin: Edition ID-Archiv, 1996.

Holler, Eckard. "Ästhetik des Widerstands und politisches Engagement in der bündischen Jugend." In *Künstliche Paradiese der Jugend,* ed. Peter Ulrich Hein, 74–99. Cologne: Lit-Verlag, 1984.

———. "Grüne Kulturpolitik und kulturelle Bewegung 'von unten.'" In *Öko-Kunst? Zur Ästhetik der Grünen,* ed. Jost Hermand and Hubert Müller, 55–70. Argument-Sonderband AS 183. Hamburg: Argument-Verlag, 1989.

———. "Peter Rohland — Volksliedsänger zwischen bündischer Jugend und deutschem Folk-Revival." *puls. Dokumentationschrift der Jugendbewegung* 24 (2005): 4–63.

Huber, Joseph. *Wer soll das alles ändern: Die Alternativen der Alternativbewegung.* Berlin: Rotbuch Verlag, 1980.

Hübner, Irene. *Kulturelle Opposition.* Munich: Damnitz-Verlag, 1983.

Hug, Markus. *Kultur- und Freizeitpolitik in der Mittelstadt. Zum Beispiel: Universitätsstadt Tübingen.* Untersuchungen des Ludwig-Uhland-Instituts der Universität Tübingen im Auftrag der Tübinger Vereinigung für Volkskunde, vol. 68. Tübingen: Tübinger Vereinigung für Volkskunde, 1986.

Hüsch, Hanns Dieter. *Du kommst auch drin vor: Gedankengänge eines fahrenden Poeten.* Munich: Kindler-Verlag, 1990.

James, Barbara, and Walter Mossmann. *1848. Flugblätterlieder und Dokumente einer zerbrochenen Revolution.* Darmstadt: Luchterhand, 1983.

Jankowski, Martin. "Tanz nach zwölf: Techno als Erscheinungsform Democratischer Decadence Reality." *Deutsche Vierteljahrsschrift für Literaturwissenschaft und Geisteswissenschaft* 73, no. 1 (1999): 28–42.

Jelavich, Peter. *Berlin Cabaret.* Cambridge, Mass. and London: Harvard UP, 1996.

John, Eckhard, ed. *Die Entdeckung des sozialkritischen Liedes: Zum 100. Geburtstag von Wolfgang Steinitz.* Volksliedstudien, vol. 7. Münster, New York, Munich, and Berlin: Waxmann, 2006.

Jungheinrich, Hans-Klaus. "Protest-Noten." In *Franz Josef Degenhardt: Politische Lieder 1964–1972,* ed. Heinz Ludwig Arnold, 45–54. Munich: Edition Text + Kritik, 1972.

Kauffeldt, Rolf. *Erich Mühsam: Literatur und Anarchie.* Munich: Fink Verlag, 1983.

Kempert, Peter. "Wo geht's lank? Peter Pank, Schönen Dank!" In *"but I like it": Jugendkultur und Popmusik,* ed. Peter Kemper, Thomas Langhoff, and Ulrich Sonnenschein, 299–308. Stuttgart: Reclam, 1998.

Kerbs, Diethart. "Zur Geschichte und Gestalt der deutschen Jungenschaften." In *Neue Sammlung,* ed. Hellmut Becker et al., 146–70. Göttingen: Vandenhoeck & Ruprecht, 1966.

Kießling, Matthias. "Kurze Geschichte eines Auftrittsverbots." In "Hammer-Rehwü 1982: Dokumentation," ed. Die Brandenburgische Landeszentrale für politische Bildung, unpaginated. Potsdam: Die Brandenburgische Landeszentrale für politische Bildung, 1993.

Kindlers Literatur Lexikon im dtv in 14 Bänden. Vol. 9. Munich: Deutscher Taschenbuch Verlag, 1986.

Kirchenwitz, Lutz, ed. *Lieder und Leute: Die Singebewegung der FDJ.* Berlin: Neues Leben, 1982.

———. "Nachwort zu einem Festival." In *Festival Musik und Politik 2001: Vorträge und Protokolle,* ed. Lied und soziale Bewegung e.V. 4–4. Berlin: Lied und soziale Bewegung e.V., 2001.

———. *Folk, Chanson und Liedermacher in der DDR: Chronisten, Kritiker, Kaisergeburtstagssänger.* Berlin: Dietz, 1993.

Klein, Gabriele. *Electronic Vibration: Pop Kultur Theorie.* Hamburg: Rogner and Bernhard bei Zweitausendeins, 1999.

Koenen, Gerd. *Das rote Jahrzehnt: Unsere kleine deutsche Kulturrevolution 1967–1977.* Frankfurt am Main: Fischer Taschenbuch Verlag, 2002.

Köhnen, Diana. *Das Literarische Werk Erich Mühsams.* Würzburg: Königshausen und Neumann, 1988.

Königseder, Angelika. "Zur Chronologie des Rechtsextremismus: Daten und Zahlen 1946–1993." In *Rechtsextremismus in Deutschland,* ed. Wolfgang Benz, 246–315. Frankfurt am Main: Fischer, 1994.

Kröher, Oss, and Hein Kröher. *Rotgraue Raben: Vom Volkslied zum Folksong.* Heidenheim: Südmark, 1969.

Kühn, Georg-Friedrich. "Kutsche und Kutscher. Die Musik des Wolf Biermanns." In *Wolf Biermann,* ed. Heinz Ludwig Arnold, 106–31. Munich: Edition Text + Kritik, 1980.

LAKS Baden-Württemberg, ed. *Soziokulturelle Initiativen und Zentren in Baden-Württemberg: Situation und Perspektiven.* LAKS-Schriftenreihe, 4. Pforzheim: Penn-Verlag, 1998.

Lammel, Inge. *Das Arbeiterlied.* Leipzig: Reclam, 1970.

Laqueur, Walter Z. *Die deutsche Jugendbewegung: Eine historische Studie.* Cologne: Verlag Wissenschaft und Politik, 1962 (Originally published in English as *Young Germany: A History of the German Youth Movement.* New York: Basic Books, 1962.)

Lassahn, Bernhard. *Dorn im Ohr: Das lästige Liedermacher-Buch.* Zurich: Diogenes, 1982.

Lau, Ellinor, and Barbara Brassel. *Frauenliederbuch.* Munich: Weismann Verlag/ Frauenbuch Verlag, 1979.

Leeder, Karen. *Breaking Boundaries: A New Generation of Poets in the GDR.* Oxford: Clarendon, 1996.

Lévi-Strauss, Claude. *Das wilde Denken.* Frankfurt am Main: Suhrkamp, 1968.

Liedzentrum der Akademie der Künste der DDR, ed. "Werkstaat Lieder & Theater 80. 19. bis 23. November 1980 in Dresden: Diskussionsprotokolle." Berlin: Liedzentrum der Akademie der Künste der DDR, 1980.

———, ed. "Werkstaat Lieder & Theater. Dresden 1981/1982: Diskussionsprotokolle." Berlin: Liedzentrum der Akademie der Künste der DDR, 1982.

Linklater, Beth. "'Und unverständlich wird mein ganzer Text.' GDR Studies in Britain Post-1989." *Debatte: Review of Contemporary German Affairs* 7 (1999): 200–226.

McNally, Joanne. "Shifting Boundaries: An Eastern Meeting of East and West German 'Kabarett.'" *German Life and Letters* 54, 2 (2001): 173–90.

———. *Neues Ketzerbrevie: Balladen und Songs.* Cologne and Berlin: Kiepenheuer & Witsch, 1962.

Meier-Lenz, D. P. *Heinrich Heine. Wolf Biermann: Deutschland. Zwei Wintermärchen.* Bonn: Bouvier, 1977.

Meuler, Christoph. "Auf Montage im Techno-Land." In *Kursbuch Jugendkultur,* ed. SpoKK (Arbeitsgruppe für symbolische Politik, Kultur und Kommunikation), 243–50. Mannheim: Bollmann, 1997.

Mey, Reinhard. *Von Anfang an.* Bonn: Voggenreiter, 1977.

Müller, Beate, ed. *Zensur im modernen deutschen Kulturraum.* Tübingen: Niemeyer, 2003.

Müller, Heiner. *Jenseits der Nation.* Berlin: Rotbuch Verlag 1991.

Münz, Rudolf. *Das "andere" Theater:. Studien über ein deutschsprachiges teatro'dell arte der Lessingzeit.* Berlin: Henschel Verlag, 1979.

Nerohm [Pseud. Fritz M. Schulz]. *Die letzten Wandervögel.* Baunach: Spurbuch, 1995.

Niess, Wolfgang. *Volkshäuser, Freizeitheime, Kommunikationszentren: Zum Wandel kultureller Infrastruktur sozialer Bewegungen. Beispiele aus deutschen Städten 1848–1984.* Hagen: Kulturpolitische Gesellschaft e.V., 1984.

Nyffeler, Max. *Liedermacher in der Bundesrepublik Deutschland.* Bonn: Internationes, 1983.

Ottens, Rita. "Der Klezmer als ideologischer Arbeiter: Jiddische Musik in Deutschland." *Neue Zeitschrift für Musik* 3 (1998): 26–29.

Paulin, Don. *Das Folk-Music-Lexikon.* Frankfurt am Main: Fischer Taschenbuch, 1980.

Pfarr, Christian. *Ein Festival im Kornfeld: Kleine deutsche Schlagergeschichte.* Leipzig: Reclam, 1997.

Pinkert-Saeltzer, Inke. *Die literarische Verarbeitung der bundesrepublikanischen Wirklichkeit nach 1968 in den Texten des Liedermachers Konstantin Wecker: Eine literatursoziologische Untersuchung.* Ann Arbor, MI: University Microfilms International, 1990.

Pläne: Zeitschrift für Politik und Kultur (1957–1966),

Probst-Effah, Gisela, ed. *Lieder gegen "das Dunkel in den Köpfen": Untersuchungen zur Folkbewegung in der Bundesrepublik Deutschland.* Schriftenreihe des Instituts für Musikalische Volkskunde der Universität zu Köln, vol. 12. Essen: Die Blaue Eule, 1995.

Pross, Harry. *Jugend Eros Politik: Die Geschichte der deutschen Jugendverbände.* Bern: Scherz, 1964.

Reynolds, Simon. *Energy Flash: A Journey through Rave Music and Dance Culture.* London: Picador, 1998.

Riewoldt, Otto F. "Wir haben jetzt hier einen Feind mehr." In *Wolf Biermann,* ed. Heinz Ludwig Arnold, 6–39. Munich: Edition Text + Kritik, 1980.

Riha, Karl. "'Mal singen, Leute': Couplet, Chanson, Balladensong und Protestsong als literarische Formen politische Öffentlichkeit." In *Moritat, Bänkelsong, Protestballade: Kabarett-Lyrik und engagiertes Lied in Deutschland,* ed. Karl Riha, 120–77. Königstein/Taunus: Athenäum, 1979.

———. *Moritat, Bänkelsong, Protestballade: Zur Geschichte des engagierten Liedes in Deutschland.* Frankfurt am Main: Fischer, 1975.

Robb, David. "Clowns, Songs and Lost Utopias: Reassessment of the Spanish Civil War in Karls Enkel's 'Spanier aller Länder.'" *Debatte: Review of Contemporary German Affairs* 11, 2 (2001): 156–72.

———. "Epic Operette and Anti-Culinary Clowning: Exposing the Illusion in the Liedertheater of Wenzel & Mensching." *The Brecht Yearbook* 30 (2005): 335–52.

———. "The GDR Singebewegung: Metamorphosis and Legacy." *Monatshefte* 92, 2 (2000): 199–216.

———. "Reviving the Dead: Montage and Temporal Dislocation in Karls Enkel's Liedertheater." In *Politics and Culture in Twentieth-Century Germany,* ed. William Niven and James Jordan, 143–61. Rochester, NY: Camden House, 2003.

———. "Techno in Germany: Musical Origins and Cultural Relevance." *German as a Foreign Language* 8, 2 (2002): 130–49. (Special issue: Youth Literature and Culture, ed. Susan Tebbut.)

———. *Zwei Clowns im Lande des verlorenen Lachens: Das Liedertheater Wenzel & Mensching.* Berlin: Ch. Links Verlag, 1998.

———. "Zwischen Zensur und Förderung: Das Liedertheater Karls Enkel in der DDR." In *Zensur im modernen deutschen Kulturraum,* ed. Beate Muller, 215–34. Tübingen: Niemeyer, 2003.

Rohkrämer, Thomas. *Eine andere Moderne? Zivilisationskritik, Natur und Technik in Deutschland 1880–1933.* Paderborn, Munich, Vienna, Zurich: Schöningh, 1999.

Rohland, Peter. "Gedanken über das Chanson." In pamphlet for EP *Vertäut am Abendstern.* Thorofon, 1963.

Rorty, Richard. "Moral Identity and Private Autonomy: The Case of Foucault." In *Essays on Heidegger and Others,* ed. Richard Rorty, 193–98. Cambridge: Cambridge UP, 1991.

Rosellini, Jay. *Wolf Biermann.* Munich: Beck, 1992.

Rothschild, Thomas. "'Das hat sehr gut geklungen': Liedermacher und Studentenbewegung." In *Nach dem Protest: Literatur im Umbruch,* ed. Martin W. Lüdke, 140–57. Frankfurt am Main: Suhrkamp, 1979.

———. "Das politische Lied: Ansätze zur Kommunikationstheorie einer literarischen Gattung." In *Lechzend nach Tyrannenblut: Ballade, Bänkelsang und Song. Colloquium über das populäre und politische Lied,* ed. Hans-Dieter Zimmermann, 57–63. Berlin: Gebr. Mann Verlag, 1972.

———. "Liedermacher." In *Politische Lyrik,* ed. Heinz Ludwig Arnold, 85–93. Munich: Edition Text + Kritik, 1984 (= *Text + Kritik,* Heft 9/9a).

———. *Liedermacher. 23 Porträts.* Frankfurt am Main: Fischer, 1980.

———. *Wolf Biermann: Liedermacher und Sozialist.* Reinbek bei Hamburg, Rowohlt, 1976.

Rump, Bernd: "Die Singe: Eine Replik." In *Singe in der DDR: Variante Frankfurt: ein Bewegungsbuch,* ed. Jürgen Maerz, 102–7. Frankfurt an der Oder: Kapiske, 2002.

Runge, Brigitte, and Fritz Vilmar. *Handbuch Selbsthilfe.* Frankfurt am Main, Verlag Zweitausendeins, 1988.

Sanders, Ronald. *The Days Grow Short: The Life and Music of Kurt Weill.* London: Weidenfeld and Nicolson, 1980.

Schebera, Jürgen Schebera. "Ernst Busch auf Schellack." In CD leaflet for Ernst Busch, *Der rote Orpheus: In originalaufnahmen aus den dreißiger Jahren.* Edition Barbarossa, 1996.

Schirmer, Arndt. "Zur Großmutter." *Der Spiegel* 5 (1981): 184.

Schmid, Fritz, ed. *tusk — Eberhard Koebel.* Stuttgart: Südmarkverlag — Verlag der Jugendbewegung, 1994.

Schneider, Hotte. *Die Waldeck — Lieder, Fahrten, Abenteuer.* Berlin: Verlag Berlin-Brandenburg, 2005.

Schnell, Ralf. *Geschichte der deutschsprachigen Literatur seit 1945*. Stuttgart: Metzler, 2003.

———, ed. *Metzler Lexikon Kultur der Gegenwart*. Stuttgart: Metzler, 2000.

Schrift 22: Schriften des Bundes Deutscher Jungenschaften (1964).

Schwarz, Petra, and Wilfried Bergholz. *Liederleute*. Berlin: Lied der Zeit, 1989.

Schwendter, Rolf. "Protest im Lied ist Widerstand." In *Lechzend nach Tyrannenblut: Ballade, Bänkelsang und Song. Colloquium über das populäre und politische Lied*, ed. Hans-Dieter Zimmermann, 64–66. Berlin: Gebr. Mann Verlag, 1972.

———. *Theorie der Subkultur*. Cologne: Kiepenheuer & Witsch, 1973.

Semmer, Gerd. *Ça ira*. Berlin: Rütten & Loening, 1958.

Shreve, John. *Nur wer sich ändert, bleibt sich treu: Wolf Biermann im Westen*. Frankfurt, Bern, New York, Paris, London: Peter Lang Verlag, 1989.

Sibley Fries, Marilyn, ed. *Responses to Christa Wolf: Critical Essays*. Detroit: Wayne State UP, 1989.

Siebig, Karl. *"Ich geh mit dem Jahrhundert mit": Ernst Busch. Eine Dokumentation*. Reinbek bei Hamburg: Rohwohlt, 1980.

Siniveer, Kaarel. *Folk Lexikon*. Reinbek bei Hamburg: Rowohlt, 1981.

Song: Zeitschrift für Chanson, Folklore, Bänkelsong 1 (1966)–4 (1970).

———. Special edition *Chanson Folklore International IV* (1967).

———. Special edition *Chanson Folklore International V* (1968).

Sorge, Veit. *Literarische Länderbilder in Liedern Wolf Biermanns und Wladimir Wyssozkis*. Frankfurt am Main: Peter Lang, 1998.

Spiekermann, Gerd. *Soziokulturelle Zentren in Zahlen im Jahr 2002: Ergebnisse der Umfrage der Bundesvereinigung*. Stuttgart: Staatsministerium Baden-Württemberg, 1990. http://soziokultur.de/_seiten/zahlen2002 accessed 31 August 2005.

Ständer, Reinhard. "Folk-Urgestein und Brachialromantiker Jürgen Wolff." Interview with Jürgen Wolff. *Folker* 3 (2001): 16–19.

———. "Wenzel und Mensching: Die Kult-Clowns aus der Da Da eR." In *Folk Michel* 4 (1997): 24–26.

Stein, Peter. "Vormärz." In *Deutsche Literaturgeschichte: Von den Anfängen bis zur Gegenwart*, ed. Wolfgang Beutin, 208–58. Stuttgart: Metzler, 1994.

Steinbiß, Florian. *Deutsch-Folk: Auf der Suche nach der verlorenen Tradition*. Frankfurt am Main: Fischer Taschenbuch, 1984.

Steinitz, Wolfgang. *Deutsche Volkslieder demokratischen Charakters aus sechs Jahrhunderten*. 2 vols. Berlin: Akademie Verlag, 1954 and 1962.

Stephan, Inge: "Kunstepoche." In *Deutsche Literaturgeschichte,* ed. Wolfgang Beutin et al., 182–238. 6th revised edition. Stuttgart: Metzler 2001.

Terkessidis, Mark. "Life after History: How Pop and Politics Are Changing Places in the Berlin Republic. *Debatte: Review of Contemporary German Affairs* 6, 2 (1998): 173–90.

Thompson, Peter. *The Crisis of the German Left.* New York and Oxford: Berghahn, 2005.

Thornton, Sarah. *Club Cultures: Music, Media and Subcultural Capital.* Cambridge: Polity Press, 1995.

Turmgespräche: Blätter für kritisches Gegenwartsverständnis 1–14 (October 1963–April 1968).

Völker, Klaus. *Bertolt Brecht: Eine Biographie.* Munich: dtv, 1978.

Von Bormann, Alexander. "Franz Josef Degenhardt." In *Kritisches Lexikon zur deutschsprachigen Gegenwartsliteratur,* ed. Heinz-Ludwig Arnold, 5. Munich: Edition Text + Kritik, 1978.

Wader, Hannes. *Lieder.* Frankfurt: Zweitausendeins, 1977.

Wagenbach, Klaus et al., ed. *Vaterland, Muttersprache: Deutsche Schriftsteller und ihr Staat von 1945 bis heute.* Berlin: Verlag Klaus Wagenbach, 1979.

Wagenbach, Klaus, ed. *Quartheft Kerbholz.* Berlin: Klaus Wagenbach, 1966.

Walz-Richter, Brigitte, and Rainer Wendling. *68 — Eine Weltrevolution.* Pamphlet for the CD-ROM of same name. Berlin and Zurich: Edition 8–Assoziation A, 2001.

Wapnewski, Peter. "Wolf Biermann ein deutscher Liedermacher." In *Wolf Biermann,* ed. Heinz Ludwig Arnold, 67–105. Munich: Edition Text + Kritik, 1980.

Wecker, Konstantin. "Ich denke, wir sind Flußmenschen" (interview). *Dreigroschenheft. Informationen zu Bert Brecht* 2 (1998): 33–36. (= Wecker 1998c).

———. "Politisch Lied, garstig Lied. Musik ohne Zukunft?" (interview). *Arte TV Magazin* 11/2003. Reprinted in *Wa* 14 (2003): 19–21. (= Wecker 2003b).

———. "'Ich möchte weiterhin verwundbar sein.' Interview August 1984." In *Selbstredend . . .: Neue Interviewproträts,* ed. Kathrin Brigl and Siegfried Schmidt-Joos, 219–67. Reinbek: Rowohlt, 1986. (= Wecker, 1984).

———. "Ganz ehrlich sein Selbst herauskehren. Gespräch mit Konstantin Wecker." *Neue Zeitschrift für Musik* 1 (1980): 19–22.

———. "Ich bin nicht der Willy." In *Wie im Westen so auf Erden: Gespräche mit Schriftstellern und Liedermachern, Dichtern und Theaterleuten, Rocksängern und Pastoren 1991–97,* ed. Quilitzsch, 28–33. Munich: Kirchheim, 1998. (= Wecker 1998a).

————. "Ich muß mich einfach einmischen" (interview). *Tageszeitung Südtirol* 27–28 July 2002. Reprinted in *Wa* 11 (2002): 34–36.

————. "Konstantin Wecker zu Gast bei Monika Langthaler" (interview). *Redaktion Brainbows* 8/2001. Reprinted in *Wa* 9 (2001): 26–28.

————. "Sinnenfreude, Höllenwelten und die Eigenverantwortlichkeit für die Seele." In *Eigenverantwortung: Positionen und Perspektiven,* ed. Bernd Neubauer. Waake: Licet, 1998. Reprinted in *Wa* 2 (1998): 13–14. (= Wecker 1998b).

————. "Vom Mut sich selbst zu begegnen" (interview). *Materialheft der Ökonomischen Friedensdekade,* spring 2003. Reprinted in *Wa* 14 (2003): 18–19. (= Wecker 2003c).

————. "Wenn der Hunger nicht verschwindet, wird die Gewalt nicht verschwinden" (interview). *The Link* 2/2003, 16 April 2003. Reprinted in *Wa* 12 (2003): 19–24. (= Wecker 2003d).

————. *Diese Welt ist mir fremd.* PHOENIX TV-interview of 9 November 2001. Printed version: Bassum: Doell Verlag, 2001.

Willis, Paul, ed. *Jugend-Stile: Zur Ästhetik der gemeinsamen Kultur.* Hamburg and Berlin: Argument-Verlag, 1991.

Winkler, Jürgen R. "Rechtsextremismus. Gegenstand — Erklärungsansätze — Grund-probleme." In *Rechtsextremismus in der Bundesrepublik Deutschland: Eine Bilanz,* ed. Wilfried Schubarth and Richard Stöss, 38–68. Bonn: Bundeszentrale für politische Bildung, 2000.

Der Wohltemperierte Baybachbote. Special edition: *Chanson Folklore International, Bericht über das erste internationale Chanson- und Folklore-Festival zu Pfingsten 1964 auf Burg Waldeck im Hunsrück,* ed. Studentischen Kreis in der Arbeitsgemeinschaft Burg Waldeck, Dorweiler o.J. (1964).

————. Special edition: *Chanson Folklore International, Bericht über das erste internationale Chanson- und Folklore-Festival zu Pfingsten 1964 auf Burg Waldeck im Hunsrück,* ed. Studentischen Kreis in der Arbeitsgemeinschaft Burg Waldeck, Dorweiler o.J. (1965).

Wolff, Jürgen. "Folk-Urgestein und Brachialromantiker Jürgen Wolff." Interview with Jürgen Wolff. By Reinhard Ständer. *Folker* 3 (2001): 16–19. http://www.folker.de/200103/wolff.htm.

Zahn, Robert von. *Folk & Liedermacher an Rhein und Ruhr.* Musikland Nordrhein-Westfalen vol. 3. Münster: Agenda, 2002.

Zentralrat der Freien Deutschen Jugend, ed. *Leben Singen Kämpfen: Liederbuch der FDJ.* Leipzig: Verlag Neus Leben, 1949.

Notes on the Editor and Contributors

DAVID ROBB is Senior Lecturer in German at the Queen's University of Belfast. He is also a musician and songwriter who performed extensively in the GDR while a student of German in the 1980s. His book *Zwei Clowns im Landes des verlorenen Lachens: Das Liedertheater Wenzel & Mensching* (1998) examines Wenzel and Mensching's satirical clown cabaret act in the GDR from the perspective of Bakhtin's carnivalesque theory. His edited volume *Clowns, Fools and Picaros in Theatre, Fiction and Film* is appearing with Rodopi in 2007.

ECKARD HOLLER is a retired school teacher from Tübingen, where he co-managed the Club Voltaire and co-organized the Tübingen Festival from the 1970s up until the 1990s. He has researched widely on the German youth movement, the German folk revival, and the 1968 movement. Published articles include "Hans Scholl und die Ulmer Trabanten" (1999) and "Peter Rohland — Volkssänger" (2005). He has written a biography of the youth leader Eberhard Koebel-tusk and co-edited Koebel-tusk's 12-volume works (2002–2005).

PETER THOMPSON is a Lecturer in German at the University of Sheffield. He has published widely in the History of Ideas as well as on Bertolt Brecht, Marxism, Green Politics, and the PDS-Left Party. His book *The Crisis of the German Left: The PDS, Stalinism and the Global Economy* was published in 2005 by Berghahn. He is currently researching the works and influence of Ernst Bloch and has recently established the Ernst Bloch Centre for Post-Secular Studies at the University of Sheffield.

ANNETTE BLÜHDORN teaches at the University of Bath and has published on Udo Lindenberg and Konstantin Wecker. In her book *Pop and Poetry: Pleasure and Protest. Udo Lindenberg, Konstantin Wecker and the Tradition of German Cabaret* (2003) she applies the concept of *Gebrauchslyrik* to contemporary German popular song.

Index

Präsidium des Schriftstellerverbandes, 248
Prenzlauer Berg poets, 43, 89, 207,
235, 238, 239, 240
Probst-Effah, Gisela, 109, 128 n.
12, 146
PROFOLK e. V., 262

Quinn, Freddy, 103

Rambling Pitchforkers, 150
Rau, Fritz, 166 n. 55
Rebscher, Renno, 144
Red Army Faction (RAF), 51, 81,
133, 165 n. 47
Reinhardt, Max, 43, 64 n. 33, 84
Remidemis, 146
Renft, 234, 251 n. 47
Republikanischer Club Tübingen,
152
Reynolds, Simon, 9, 271, 272
Rheintreue, 146
Rice, C. Jane, 94 n. 10
Riewoldt, Otto F., 59
Riha, Karl, 8, 44, 69, 72, 94 n. 7,
95 n. 29, 196 n. 40
Rilke, Rainer Maria, poem by:
"Schlußstück," 60
Rimbaud, Arthur, works by:
Une Saison en Enfer, 259–60
Ringelnatz, Joachim, poem by:
"Kuttel Daddeldu," 70, 71
Rohland, Peter, 5, 6, 12, 13, 14,
15, 16, 17, 21, 30, 69, 98, 99,
100–104, 108, 109, 112, 126,
127, 149, 161, 162
Rohland, Peter, works by:
chanson programs: "Deutsche
Volkslieder — entstaubt und
unverblümt," 103;
"Landstreicherballaden," 103,
108; "Der Rebbe singt," 102;
"Vertäut am Abendstern,"
100–102

LPs/CDs: 48er Lieder — Lieder
deutscher Demokraten, 13;
"Lieder der Matrosen"
(planned LP), 102; Lieder von
Anderswo, 102
Rollengedicht, 2, 5, 38, 67, 70, 71,
73, 75, 77, 80, 84, 186
Rorty, Richard, 221
Das rote Sprachrohr, 55
Roter Rummel, 53, 65 n. 45, 240
Rothschild, Thomas, 8, 174, 178,
183, 193, 194
Rühmkorf, Peter, poem by: "Bleib
erschütterbar doch widersteh,"
90–91, 243
Rump, Bernd, songs by:
"In meinem Namen," 234;
"Lied der Fahne," 231
Rzewski, Frederic, 156

Sacco, Nicola, 40
Saint Simon, 219
Saitenwind, 141
Salvatore, Gaston, 105
Samandar, Aviva, 112
Sampling, 266, 269, 274
Samson, Russ, 104
Sands Family, 150, 233
Schaeder, Burkhard, 100
Schebera, Jürgen, 59
Scheel, Walter, 6, 149
Scheer, Regina, song by: "Ich bin
wie alle blind geworden," 231
Schelsky, Helmut, 98
Schicht, 19, 27, 53, 83, 235
Schiller, Friedrich, 21, 87
Schillinger, Ernst, 146, 164 n. 25
Schirmer, Arnd, 170
Schlager, 50, 55, 103, 144, 155,
166 n. 55, 169, 274
Schmetterlinge, 138, 141, 156
Schmidt, Eberhard, 60, 61
Schmidt, Markus, song by:
"Jack Miller," 122
Schnappsack, 151